S0-BAF-560

THE ILLUSTRATED ATLAS OF
JERUSALEM

THE ILLUSTRATED

ATLAS OF
JERUSALEM

Dan Bahat
with Chaim T. Rubinstein

Translated by Shlomo Ketko

SIMON & SCHUSTER

New York   London   Toronto   Sydney   Tokyo   Singapore

Wingate College Library

Copyright © 1989, 1990 by Carta,
The Israel Map and Publishing Company, Ltd.
Printed in Israel

Designed and produced by Carta, Jerusalem
Managing Editor: Barbara Ball
Design: Jack Corcos
Maps: Carta, Jerusalem

First English-language edition published in 1990 by
Simon and Schuster

All rights reserved. No part of this book may be
reprinted or reproduced or utilized in any form
or by any electronic, mechanical, or other means,
now known or hereafter invented, including
photocopying and recording, or in any information
storage or retrieval system, without permission
in writing from the publishers.

Academic Reference Division
Simon and Schuster
15 Columbus Circle, New York, NY 10023

Library of Congress Cataloging-in-Publication Data
Bahat, Dan.
   The illustrated atlas of Jerusalem.

   Copyright by Carta, The Israel Map and Publishing
Company.
   Includes bibliography and index.
   English ed., rev. and translation of: Atlas Karta
ha-gadol le-toldot Yerushalayim. 1989.
      1. Jerusalem—Maps. I. Rubinstein, Chaim T.
II. Bahat, Dan. Atlas Karta ha-gadol le-toldot
Yerushalayim. III. Title.
G2239.J4B34   1990   912. 5694'42   90-675114
ISBN 0-13-451642-7

Contents

Picture Sources

Page

12 View of Old City. Courtesy of Z. Radovan.

15 Cross sections of city. After A. Sharon, *Planning Jerusalem*, Tel Aviv, 1973, p. 113.

20 Pottery vessels. From L. H. Vincent, *Underground Jerusalem*, London, 1911.

22 Libation tray and stele. After L. H. Vincent and F. M. Abel, *Jérusalem Nouvelle*, Paris, 1926, pl. LXXIX 8, 12.

22 Clay figurine. After G. Posener, *Princes et pays d'Asie et de Nubie*, Brussels, 1940, frontispiece.

22 Bronze Age gate (reconstruction). Courtesy of L. Ritmeyer.

23 City of David (cross section). Courtesy of L. Ritmeyer.

24 Ophel ostracon. Courtesy of Israel Department of Antiquities and Museums.

26 Window frame (reconstruction). Courtesy of L. Ritmeyer.

26 Warren's Shaft (reconstruction). Courtesy of S. Cohen.

26 Siloam Inscription. Courtesy of Museum of Archaeology, Istanbul.

27 Terraced structure. Courtesy of Z. Radovan.

28 Iron arrowheads. Courtesy of N. Avigad.

28 Entrance to Tell Ta'yinat temple (reconstruction). Courtesy of L. Ritmeyer.

29 Section of First Temple period wall. Courtesy of N. Avigad.

32 Tomb inscriptions. After N. Avigad, *Eretz Israel*, vol. 3, Jerusalem, 1954, pl. 3, 4.

32 Tomb of "Pharaoh's Daughter" (reconstruction). Courtesy of L. Ritmeyer.

32 Burial caves (reconstruction). Courtesy of L. Ritmeyer.

33 Tombs T1 and T2 (reconstruction). Courtesy of S. Cohen.

36 Council Building (reconstruction). Courtesy of L. Ritmeyer.

37 The "First Wall" (reconstruction). Courtesy of L. Ritmeyer.

38 Hasmonean period Citadel (reconstruction). Courtesy of L. Ritmeyer.

40 The "Palatial Mansion" (plan and reconstruction). Courtesy of L. Ritmeyer, after N. Avigad, *Discovering Jerusalem*, Jerusalem, 1983.

42 Temple Mount in Second Temple period (reconstruction). Courtesy of L. Ritmeyer.

44 Entrance ban inscription. After *Quarterly of the Department of Antiquities in Palestine* VI, 1938, p. 2.

44 Stone of the Trumpeting Place (reconstruction). Courtesy of L. Ritmeyer.

44 Southwest corner of Temple Mount (reconstruction). Courtesy of L. Ritmeyer.

45 Theodotus inscription. Courtesy of Israel Department of Antiquities and Museums.

45 Cross section of Barclay's Gate (reconstruction). Courtesy of L. Ritmeyer.

46 Antonia fortress (reconstruction). Courtesy of L. Ritmeyer.

47 Double Gate (reconstruction). Courtesy of L. Ritmeyer.

49 Siloam Pool (reconstruction). Courtesy of L. Ritmeyer.

50 Burial tomb (reconstruction). Courtesy of L. Ritmeyer.

51 Tombs of Zechariah and Hezir's Priestly Family (cross section). Courtesy of L. Ritmeyer.

52 Incised *menorah* design (with reconstruction). After N. Avigad, *Discovering Jerusalem*, Jerusalem, 1983, fig. 154.

52 Judaea Capta coin. Courtesy of Reuben and Edith Hecht Museum, University of Haifa.

54 Map of Jerusalem as center of the world. From H. Bünting, *Itinerarium sacrae scripturae*, 1581, frontispiece.

56 Gethsemane. Courtesy of University Library, Istanbul.

57 Sheep's Pools (reconstruction). Courtesy of L. Ritmeyer.

57 Mounting stone. From C. Warren and C. R. Conder, *The Survey of Western Palestine*. Jerusalem, London, 1889, p. 334.

57 Reconstruction of Jesus' tomb. After L. H. Vincent and F. M. Abel, *Jérusalem Nouvelle*, Paris, 1914, vol. II, fig. 53.

60 Memorial stone to Marcus Junius. Courtesy of Z. Radovan.

62 Roman period Damascus Gate (reconstruction). Courtesy of L. Ritmeyer.

64 Ecce Homo Arch (reconstruction). Courtesy of S. Cohen.

65 Muristan area. Courtesy of Z. Radovan.

66 Temple of Aphrodite (reconstruction). Courtesy of L. Ritmeyer.

Page

66 Roman relief (reconstruction). Courtesy of L. Ritmeyer.

67 Siloam Pool (reconstruction). Courtesy of L. Ritmeyer.

70 Domine Ivimus inscription. Courtesy of Garo Nalbandian.

72 Church of Siloam (reconstruction). Courtesy of L. Ritmeyer.

73 Sheep's Pools (reconstruction). Courtesy of L. Ritmeyer.

75 Inscription on Western Wall. Courtesy of B. Mazar.

75 Nea Church inscription. Courtesy of N. Avigad.

76 Madaba Map. Courtesy of R. Cleave.

76 Cardo (reconstruction). Courtesy of L. Ritmeyer.

77 Gold ring. Courtesy of B. Mazar.

82 Umayyad palace remains. Courtesy of Z. Radovan.

83 Arculf map. Courtesy of Bayerische Staatsbibliothek München, Codex Ratisbon 13002 (civ. 2), fol. 4v.

86 Mosaic from Abbasid period. Courtesy of M. Piccirillo, Studium Biblicum Franciscanum.

88 Stone inscription. Courtesy of Museum of Archaeology, Istanbul.

89 Page from Cairo Genizah. After M. Braslavy, *Eretz Israel*, vol. 7, Jerusalem, 1964, pl. 16.

92 Montpellier map. Courtesy of Bibliothèque Interuniversitaire de Montpellier, Codex Montpellier H152, fol. 67v.

92 Damascus Gate (reconstruction). Courtesy of L. Ritmeyer.

97 Copenhagen map. Courtesy of University of Copenhagen, Det Arnamagnæanske Institut, AM 736, I, 4to, fol. 2r.

98 Brussels map. Courtesy of Bibliothèque royale Albert Ier, Bruxelles, Ms. 9823–24, fol. 157r.

99 St. Anne's Church. Courtesy of Z. Radovan.

99 Crusader oil lamp. Courtesy of Abdallah Kalbunah, curator of Islamic Museum on Temple Mount. Photo: Z. Sagiv.

100 Paris map. Courtesy of Phot. Bibl. nat., Paris, Codex Lat. 8865, fol. 133.

100 Florence map. From Röhricht, *Zeitschrift des Deutschen Palästina-Vereins* 15, 1892, pl. 1.

100 Stuttgart map. Courtesy of Württembergische Landesbibliothek, Cod. bibl. fol. 56, 135r.

101 London map. Courtesy of The British Library, Codex Harley 658, fol. 39v.

101 Saint-Omer map. Courtesy of Bibliothèque Municipale, Saint-Omer, Ms. 776, fol. 50v.

102 Tancred's Tower (reconstruction). Courtesy of L. Ritmeyer.

102 Cambrai map. Courtesy of Centre Culturel de Cambrai, Ms. 466, fol. 1r.

103 The Hague map. Courtesy of Koninklijke Bibliotheek, Den Haag, 76 Fs, L. 1r.

106 Ayyubid tower (reconstruction). Courtesy of L. Ritmeyer.

106 El-Malik el-Adel inscription. Courtesy of Israel Department of Antiquities and Museums.

110 Aqueducts. Courtesy of A. Grozow.

110 Turbat el-Kubakiyya. Courtesy of Z. Radovan.

111 Marino Sanuto map. Courtesy of The British Library, Codex 27376.

112 Turbat Jaliqiyya inscription. Courtesy of S. Ben-Yosef.

112 Streetfront of the Iron Gate. Courtesy of British School of Archaeology in Jerusalem.

115 Glass lamp. Courtesy of Abdallah Kalbunah, curator of Islamic Museum on Temple Mount. Photo: Z. Sagiv.

116 Fourteenth-century map of Jerusalem. Courtesy of Biblioteca Medicae Laurenziana, Firenze, Plut. LXXVI 56, fol. 97.

116 Turbat Turkan Khatun. Courtesy of Z. Radovan.

122 Jaffa Gate. Courtesy of University Library, Istanbul.

127 Jerusalem stonemasons. Courtesy of University Library, Istanbul.

128 British memorial. Courtesy of Israel Government Press Office.

129 General Allenby's address. Courtesy of Imperial War Museum, London.

142 Jaffa Gate area. Courtesy of Z. Radovan.

All other illustrations or photographs are from the picture archives of Carta Ltd. and the authors.

Great care has been taken to establish sources of illustrations. If inadvertently we failed to do so, due credit will be given in the next edition.

Foreword

The Illustrated Atlas of Jerusalem by Dan Bahat is a most informative work, highly illustrated with maps, photographs and diagrams. This study has a special place in the abundant literature dealing with Jerusalem because it covers all aspects of research carried out on Jerusalem throughout its history, from its beginnings up to the present, when it has once more become a united city.

Dan Bahat, one of the leading researchers of Jerusalem, has taken upon himself to present visually the history of Jerusalem in each of its periods, to reconstruct its image during the times when it prospered and flourished, as well as when it was destitute and in decay. He has also set out to trace the processes which determined the character of its fortifications, institutions, and magnificent buildings that have survived or been revealed in archaeological excavations. But above all, his major contribution has been to create a synthesis between the archaeological findings and the written sources in order to present a comprehensive and updated historical picture of the metropolis which constitutes the very basis of the Jewish people's bond with its homeland, and of the city which is holy to Jews, Christians, and Muslims alike. The atlas contains extensive material drawn from research carried out by scholars and archaeologists who have explored Jerusalem during the past one hundred and fifty years, thereby making a major contribution to the knowledge about the city. The author must be commended for this, as well as for inviting Chaim T. Rubinstein to bring the information contained in the atlas up to the present day through the addition of the last two chapters—Divided Jerusalem (1948–1967) and United Jerusalem (since 1967).

Jerusalem, May 1990   *Benjamin Mazar*

Introduction

The publication of the first true atlas of Jerusalem is an occasion for much rejoicing, for Jerusalem has held a firm grip on the hearts and imaginations of men and women since King David made it the capital of ancient Israel some 3,000 years ago. Straddling the Judean desert to the east and south, Jerusalem's mountainous terrain makes the approach to the city difficult for adversaries and tedious for pilgrims. It was the western hill of Jerusalem that the historian Josephus named the City of David. He also called it "the Stronghold," and in Jesus' time it became known as the Upper City (Josephus, *The Jewish War*, 5.4.1). This western spur of the city continues to bear the imprint of David's memory in David's Tower at the western (Jaffa) gate of the Old City and in the Islamic Prayer Niche of David close by. What Josephus understood as another hill in the Lower City, farther to the east and referred to as the "hog's back," is what we know today from archaeology to be the true City of David.

Such is the charm of the Holy City. What one generation took to be a sacred place another understood to be profane. The area known today as the City of David lies well outside the walls of the present Old City. It was the alleged presence of tombs there that so outraged the sensibilities of religious extremists who sought to halt the City of David excavations. In all these sorts of changes of names and adjustments resulting from new historical interpretations one senses the heavy weight of tradition and faith. Hardly a stone can be moved or a street paved without stumbling upon some

important relic of Jerusalem's past. In the summer of 1989, for example, in laying down a new portion of the street outside Jaffa Gate a section of a medieval street was uncovered and traffic in one of Jerusalem's busiest intersections was rerouted so that the archaeologists could uncover a few more pages of the history of the city that has been important to so many traditions.

Although Jerusalem's known history begins before the time King David made the city his capital, it is the story of Jerusalem's rise to preeminence from 1000 BCE to the present that is the main focus of this remarkable book. Muslims dominated the city from 638 CE to 1917, and because Jerusalem is the center of focus in both biblical testaments, the city serves a unique purpose in the history of religions: as the place of God's presence and messianic redemption, as the place where Jesus the Christ died and was resurrected, and as the place where Abraham nearly sacrificed Isaac (this latter spot is enshrined today within the Dome of the Rock and commemorated as the scene of Muhammad's ascent to heaven). The prophet Zechariah proclaimed that in the end of time "Many people and strong nations shall come to seek the Lord of hosts in Jerusalem, and to pray before the Lord" (8:22), thereby unifying peoples of diverse backgrounds, languages, and cultures. That of course is at the core of what is so appealing about this great city; it is everybody's city, everyone's home, for somehow east and west meet in Jerusalem as do Jew, Christian, and Muslim. No one who has ever been there can forget Jerusalem:

"If I forget thee, O Jerusalem, let my right hand forget her cunning … let my tongue cleave to the roof of my mouth" (Psalms, 137:5–6).

Dan Bahat's *Illustrated Atlas of Jerusalem*, a translation from the 1989 Hebrew edition published by Carta, provides an extraordinary opportunity to view Jerusalem as it has evolved through the ages and as it exists today. With tremendous insight into Jerusalem's diverse cultural heritage and a keen eye for detail, Bahat leads the reader on a journey through each cultural era. As a Jerusalemite and district archaeologist for many years with oversight responsibility for Jerusalem, Bahat illuminates many of the important nooks and crannies of Jerusalem's past. What is most unusual about this work is that it is not done only through pictures but also through maps, line drawings, and many isometric reconstructions, featured here for the first time in an English-language publication. Bahat has worked closely with Carta's excellent graphics department, and the result of their collaboration is nothing short of fabulous. Some of the drawings have appeared in similar form in Nahman Avigad's Jerusalem Quarter excavation reports, Yigal Shiloh's City of David excavation reports, and Benjamin Mazar's writings on the Temple Mount excavations, but in every case the drawings have been simplified or improved for this atlas and make the text readily understandable. For the later periods the author has included old maps and drawings mostly from the nineteenth century to fill in where no new archaeological data were available.

The English edition differs in several important ways from the Hebrew edition. First, an entirely new section, "Jerusalem at the Time of Jesus," has been added. Second, a handy bibliography on Jerusalem has been included. This atlas transcends politics and acquaints even the nontraveler with the most important aspects of Jerusalem's development through the ages. For the person who has visited the Holy City or who is contemplating going there, this work is a powerful call to ascend the city's holy mountains as a pilgrim:

I was glad when they said unto me, Let us go into the house of the Lord.
Our feet shall stand within thy gates, O Jerusalem.
Jerusalem is builded as a city that is compact together:
Whither the tribes go up, the tribes of the Lord, unto the testimony of Israel, to give thanks unto the name of the Lord.
For there are set thrones of judgment, the thrones of the house of David.
Pray for the peace of Jerusalem: they shall prosper that love thee.
Peace be within thy walls, and prosperity within thy palaces.
For my brethren and companions' sakes, I will now say, Peace be within thee.
Because of the house of the Lord our God I will seek thy good.

Psalm 122
A Song of Degrees

The author's dedication is worth noting also. The atlas is dedicated to Bahat's teacher, the late Professor Michael Avi-Yonah, who was Israel's most noted historian of the archaeology of the ancient Near Eastern classical world and who supervised for many years the construction of the stone-by-stone scale model of Jerusalem in the Second Temple period at the Holyland Hotel in Jerusalem. The book is also dedicated to Teddy Kollek, long-term mayor of Jerusalem, who has strived so hard to keep the peoples of Jerusalem together after the city was unified in 1967. This work is a fitting tribute to both of them, superior in every scientific way to all existing books of this kind on Jerusalem. It beckons all lovers of the city to protect its archaeological treasures and to safeguard its unique legacy of hope for future generations.

Eric M. Meyers
Duke University
Durham, North Carolina

To my teachers,
Michael Avi-Yonah,
who taught me about Jerusalem of the past,
and Teddy Kollek,
who taught me about Jerusalem of the present —————————————————————

Preface

The comprehensive and highly illustrated atlas before us has grown out of a small modest atlas first published in 1967 when Jerusalem was united during the Six-Day War. It has developed as a result of the tremendous amount of research on Jerusalem carried out since then, and which is still continuing incessantly.

The beginnings of research on Jerusalem is generally attributed to attempts by Josephus Flavius, who lived at the end of the Second Temple period, to identify places mentioned in the Bible. Pilgrims who visited Jerusalem during the Middle Ages as well as in modern times followed in his footsteps, and a long list of locations exists based on their descriptions. The beginning of the scientific examination of the history of Jerusalem can be dated to Edward Robinson's visit to the city in 1838. He was the first in a long line of great explorers who based their identifications on proof which was not prejudiced by religious or traditional beliefs. A major contribution to the research of Jerusalem has been made by the archaeological excavations, the first of which was carried out by Felicien de Saulcy in 1860. Since then, historical sources and archaeological findings have gone hand in hand with scientific research.

At first the explorers concentrated their efforts on the reconstruction of the appearance of Jerusalem in the Second Temple period. In the course of time, a process began, which is still continuing, which has established the study of Jerusalem as a subject in its own right and no longer the exclusive field of scholars of religion or historians. Today, scholars are endeavoring to recreate the appearance of the city in its various periods, to locate various sites and structures referred to in historical documents. Research is no longer solely a means by which to pursue the nationalist propensities of explorers hailing from various countries.

The density of habitation and the unceasing occurrence of historic events, fluctuating between construction and destruction, constituted difficulties for the examination of the city above the surface. Already in the nineteenth century, various explorers attempted to date buildings in the city according to the manner in which their stones were cut, but the secondary usage of building stones have confounded their conclusions. In fact, the nineteenth-century scholars were required to begin from the very beginning. They had to dig down through the various levels of filling to reach bedrock. The first of these explorers was Charles Warren, who in the 1860s began to sink shafts at diverse points and thus was enabled to trace the network of riverbeds which surrounded and crisscrossed the city. His findings, the majority of which have proved accurate and are still of great value to this day, enabled scholars who came after him to draw their conclusions as to the extent of the remains of the densely populated habitation in Jerusalem, according to its various levels and different periods. Jerusalem is not a "tell" in the accepted connotation of the term which can be "peeled" off level by level, thus revealing each of the periods of the city's history. Due to the fact that the hilltops were invariably the point of habitation, the agglomerations of the previous period were always leveled off, and thus excavations have been limited to sites which have not been destroyed in this manner. Thus, for example, the most important discoveries in the City of David area have been made on the slopes of the hill and not on the hilltop. It is for this reason as well that archaeologists are unable to reconstruct the city as it existed during the flourishing periods of David and Solomon, as well as in other periods of prosperity.

Already in the 1860s, it began to be apparent that the hill southeast of the Temple Mount was where the City of David should be located, and it was here that the historical origins of the city were to be found. In 1881, the German scholar, Hermann Guthe, began to excavate at various locations on the hill of the City of David, but the methods he used (shafts and channels) limited the information that could be obtained. In 1894, Frederick Bliss and Archibald Dickie began their excavations which continued up to 1897, during the course of which they even examined sections of the anterior walls. It was only then that the actual structure of the city began to become apparent. In 1904, it was generally accepted that the City of David had been situated on the southeastern hill and Mount Zion had been the site of the city during the Second Temple period. From then on, research on Jerusalem began to move forward on firm ground. The biblical city was explored in the main during the latter period of Ottoman rule in digs carried out by Raymond Weill in the City of David. After World War I, Weill resumed his excavations in the City of David, and thus began the series of archaeological digs that have continued up to the present.

In addition to the above-mentioned explorers, mention must be made of persons who were not explorers in the accepted meaning of the term, but for various reasons carried out research in Jerusalem and witnessed changes that came about in the city at the time. Charles Wilson visited Jerusalem in 1864 with the purpose of preparing a modern map of the city and to examine its water system. His research aroused considerable interest in Jerusalem and pointed up the numerous possibilities for future exploration. His work led to the founding of the British Palestine Exploration Fund and the sending out of Charles Warren to carry out his expeditions in Palestine. During this same period another outstanding scholar of Jerusalem, Ermete Pierotti, was in the city. He had been invited to Jerusalem by the municipality as a consulting engineer, and during the course of his work in this area (1854–1866), he took a profound interest in the city's past and made many discoveries of great significance. Some of his assumptions were not accepted by scholars, but many of his findings to this very day serve as a basis for information about sites which he was the first to describe in detail, and which in the course of time, with the rapid development of Jerusalem have disappeared forever.

William Tipping, who visited Jerusalem in 1841, was one of those courageous tourists who succeeded in entering sites closed to the public and exposing them to the world. One of the many places he penetrated was the "Double Gate," and he was the first to publish a description of it. Prior to that, Frederick Catherwood (1834) wrote a description of the Temple Mount and prepared a map of it during the period when entrance to Europeans was strictly forbidden. Charles Clermont-Ganneau, an official at the French Consulate in Jerusalem during the 1870s, raised the study of Jerusalem to new heights. Apart from his outstanding ability to distinguish between matters of importance and those which were insignificant (he became famous for his exposure of the forgeries of the apostate Jew, Shapira, as well as his discovery of the Mesha Stele) proved that it was possible to examine any discovery against the background of the historical sources. In this manner, he probed many aspects of the city's history, especially those relating to the Middle Ages. Even though he did not carry out any excavations, Marquis Melchior de Vogüé gathered material during his visit to Jerusalem (1853) on the basis of which he wrote three books which are still of profound interest today. His first work, *The Churches of the Holy Land*, contains the first description of the churches in Palestine in general and especially in Jerusalem. His works are a virtual treasure house of historical sources, especially relating to the Crusader period. His work on the Temple Mount, *The Temple of Jerusalem*, contains important material on the construction of the Dome of the Rock and its history.

Another explorer of this type was the Swiss Titus Tobler. His most famous discovery was "Wilson's Arch" (it was he who brought it to Wilson's attention). His scientific study, *Jerusalem and Its Environs* (1853), is still a basic work on many sites in the city.

Mention must also be made of Conrad Schick, who closely followed the development of Jerusalem from when he arrived in 1846 up to his death in 1901. His skills in the areas of surveying and art enabled him to record in illustration the image of many structures existing at the time. His literary ability left vivid descriptions of all he saw. He published numerous articles and wrote a book on the Temple Mount, and anyone researching Jerusalem after the destruction of the Second Temple must refer to his descriptions, even though not all have been published.

The beginning of the twentieth century saw the introduction of modern scientific methods in research on Jerusalem. It was no longer the individual, pioneering explorers who happened upon discoveries, but the work of organized missions using systematic methods sent out by scientific bodies and governments.

Of late there has been a significant change as regards the research of Jerusalem. Until about two decades ago research was devoted mainly to the Second Temple period, and to a lesser extent to the First Temple period. Today, the later periods—the Byzantine, Early Arab, the Crusader, Mamluk, and Ottoman periods—have attracted the attention of many students and scholars.

The recent research being carried out have led to the restoration and reconstruction of many sites in the city, thus maintaining the concept of the past in the minds of the present generation.

The data relating to Jerusalem throughout its various periods are so vast that it is impossible to include it all in a single atlas, no matter how extensive it may be. However, the purpose of an atlas is to present the main situations and events to the extent possible in graphic and cartographic form. And this is what we have endeavored to do in this atlas. We have done our utmost to demonstrate the history of Jerusalem according to its various periods in a perceivable manner, as concise and popular as possible and at the same time, even though we have not used a cumbersome scientific apparatus, ensured that it is scientifically exact.

This undertaking would not have been possible without the assistance of many individuals. I wish to express my appreciation to all of them, first and foremost to Chaim T. Rubinstein, who wrote the final chapters and arranged maps for them, thus bringing the atlas up to the present time. I also wish to thank Shlomo Ketko for his excellent translation of the Hebrew edition. The staff of Carta have been most supportive throughout the production process: Jack Corcos designed the atlas, thoroughly scrutinized the original Hebrew manuscript, and added maps to make the text more readily comprehensive; Barbara Ball undertook the enormous task of preparing the English edition; Joseph Valency and Amnon Shmaya drew most of the maps and illustrations. The reconstructions are the work of Leen Ritmeyer and Shlomo Cohen. Very special thanks are due to the heads of the Carta publishing house, Messrs. Emanuel and Shay Hausman, who were always prepared to accede to my numerous requests. Thanks to them we have succeeded in incorporating in this atlas new material which is published here for the first time in a work which is not specifically academic. The Jerusalem *Waqf* has been most accommodating in assisting us whenever we requested it and our most sincere thanks are due to its officials. Last, but not least, my most sincere appreciation to my revered mentors, Prof. Benjamin Mazar and Prof. Nahman Avigad, who put at my disposal new material from their own excavations. Furthermore, my thanks go to the many persons whom I have not mentioned specifically and who assisted me throughout.

I am most grateful for the opportunity I have been given to prepare this atlas and sincerely hope that those who use it will find it of value. I apologize for any mistakes that may have crept in and would kindly request that they be brought to my attention.

Dan Bahat

The Topography of the City

Jerusalem is situated in the heart of the Judean mountains, on the crest of the ridge that forms the watershed partition line between the Judean foothills to the west and the Judean desert to the east. The topographical features enabled the city's defense, as it is built on a hilltop and its walls rest on natural barriers such as dry riverbeds and ridges that surround the inhabited hill. This is what occurred in Jerusalem from its beginnings, and this fact determined to a large extent the area of the city, its boundaries, and the direction in which it expanded throughout the ages.

The city began on the hill called the "City of David." It later extended to the north, encompassing the Temple Mount, and in the course of time expanded in the direction of Mount Zion and the western and northern hills. All these hills come within the area of the Kidron Valley drainage basin. The course of the Kidron and that of the other streams draining into it have influenced the alignment of the city's boundaries on all sides.

The source of the Kidron is near a broad valley north of the Old City, near the present-day Mea She'arim quarter. At this point it is called Simon the Just Valley (or Wadi el-Joz in Arabic). The valley continues to the east, and a short distance further on, to the south, running between the city and the Mount Scopus–Mount of Olives range. The only

perennial spring—the Gihon—is located in this section of the Kidron Valley. It was near the spring, on the west bank of the valley, that the city was founded on a hill enclosed by riverbeds—to the east (the Kidron), to the west and south (the Tyropoeon), and the spring below. These advantages, probably the reason for the establishment of the city on this site, have constituted the essence of Jerusalem's existence throughout the millennia. The Kidron Valley, therefore, has always formed the city's eastern boundary. At the end of the Second Temple period, the northern extension of the valley served as the city's northern boundary, since the Third Wall stood on the crest above that section, namely, the Valley of Simon the Just, which served as a natural moat. From the south of Jerusalem, the Kidron continues downward until it empties into the Dead Sea.

To the south of the hill on which the City of David was first built, is the Valley of Hinnom, which runs into the Kidron Valley. It originates at the watershed, near the present-day France Square, runs eastward down to the approaches of Jaffa Gate, turns south skirting Mount Zion, and continues eastward to its egress. This valley marked the southern and southwestern boundaries of Jerusalem until 1860, when the Mishkenot Sha'ananim quarter was founded on the western side of the Hinnom Valley.

View from the north of the Old City and its environs.

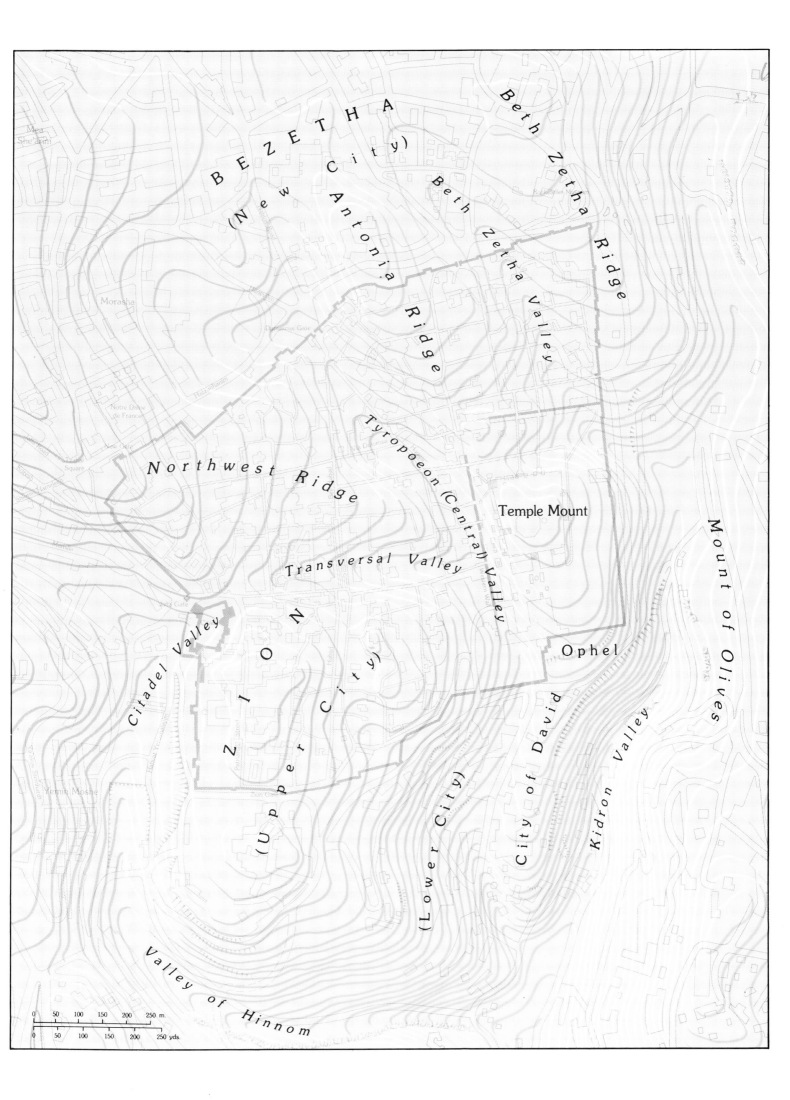

BEZETHA

(New City)

Beth Zetha Ridge

Beth Zetha Valley

Antonia Ridge

Mea She'arim

Morasha

Notre Dame
de France

New Gate

Northwest Ridge

Temple Mount

Mount of Olives

Tyropoeon (Central) Valley

Transversal Valley

Citadel Valley

ZION

(Upper City)

Ophel

City of David

Kidron Valley

Yemin Moshe

(Lower City)

Valley of Hinnom

0   50   100   150   200   250 m.

0   50   100   150   200   250 yds.

The Tyropoeon Valley runs through the center of the Old City. The only reference to the name "Tyropoeon" appears in the writings of Josephus (*Wars* 5, 4, 1) and this is probably a corruption of the original name, which is unknown. Josephus apparently altered the name to make it easier for the non-Jewish readers of his works, because a name such as Tyropoeon (the cheesemakers) would be easier to remember than some transliteration of a word with no meaning whatsoever for his readers. The real name of the valley and its identification with the biblical "valley"—*gai* in Hebrew—(Neh. 2:15) has not yet been clarified. We will, therefore, call the central valley by the name Tyropoeon.

The Tyropoeon Valley divides the city into eastern and western sections. It originates in the present-day Morasha quarter, descends toward the Damascus Gate, passes through it, bisecting the city from north to south along Haggai Street (el-Wad in Arabic), continues to the east through the Dung Gate, and joins the Kidron Valley north of its junction with the Hinnom Valley near the Siloam Pool. This valley formed the western boundary of the City of David, and in the course of time the western wall of the Temple Mount (the "Western [or Wailing] Wall") and the western wing of the Antonia fortress were built to retain the Temple Mount against the valley. During the early history of Jerusalem, the Tyropoeon formed a natural barrier to the city's westward expansion, but when it did begin to expand in this direction, a bridge was built providing a link between both banks. During the course of time further overpasses were constructed, and the last of them which is still in existence, is that known as "Wilson's Arch," the date of whose construction is not clear, but seems to be the eighth century CE.

The Beth Zetha Valley (the St. Anne Valley) is the northernmost of the valleys that run into the Kidron Valley. It originates in the vicinity of the present-day American Colony, from where it runs under the city wall, west of the Rockefeller Museum, cuts through the Muslim Quarter, and enters the Kidron Valley at the foot of the northeastern corner of the Temple Mount. Near this point it is joined from

the west by a small ravine, which runs through the northern corner of the Temple Mount. The course of the Beth Zetha Valley determined the position of the northern boundary of the Temple Mount (and thus also the boundary of the entire city) from the time of King Solomon until the construction of the Third Wall during the reign of King Agrippa. Despite the fact that this is only a short valley, it is filled with abundant quantities of rainwater and its basin contains several of the city's largest pools: the Sheep's (or Bethesda) Pools and the Pool of Israel (in Arabic: Birket Isra'in or Isra'il).

The western section of the Old City is crossed by the Transversal Valley, the only one of the city's valleys running from west to east. It is called the "Transversal Valley" because it traverses the general direction of all Jerusalem's valleys. It originates near the Citadel and runs into the Tyropoeon Valley in the vicinity of the Western Wall plaza. The watershed was the source of the Transversal Valley and the Citadel Valley, a short and deep valley which flows into the Hinnom Valley. These two valleys served as the northern boundary of the Upper City and along them ran the First Wall during the Second Temple period, and possibly the northern city wall as well during the last centuries of the Judean kingdom. Their source, at the watershed, was the weak point of the city's defenses, and it was for this reason that Herod built three well-fortified towers at the corner of the wall: Hippicus, Mariamme, and Phasael. Another valley which may have perhaps limited the city's expansion to the west toward the end of the First Temple period, is that which runs along the Street of the Jews in the Jewish Quarter (from south to north) and joins the Transversal Valley.

Not all the valleys mentioned above are still discernible along their entire course. Certain sections have been filled in or leveled off over the centuries. However, measurement of the height of the rocks at various points that have been carried out, as well as available historical evidence, have made it possible to trace the course of these valleys with a fair degree of accuracy.

The formation of ancient Jerusalem's hills and valleys make

(above) Aerial view of **Jerusalem on November 23, 1917,** less than one month before the British entered the city. This is one of a series of aerial photographs taken by the German Air Force during World War I.

it possible for us to understand some basic facts relating to the city's history. The Temple Mount and the Upper City had a natural system of defense. This was not the case of the hills to the northwest of the city—the northwestern hill, as well as the Antonia and Beth Zetha ridges—where no natural defense from the north existed. Attempts were made to overcome these weak spots artificially in the Middle Ages (the exact date is not known) through the excavation of a system of moats, still partly in existence. These are to be seen along the wall between Tzahal Square and the Rockefeller Museum. Josephus states that the northern section of the city encompassed by the Third Wall was called Bezetha (*Wars* 5, 4, 2). He also stated that the Antonia fortress was separated from the northern extension of the Antonia ridge by a moat. This moat was indeed discovered during recent archaeological excavations in the Muslim Quarter, in the Convent of the Sisters of Zion and west of it. However, it appears that the name Bezetha refers to the entire area north of the present-day Old City wall, including all the mountain ridges. It is for this reason that the valley to the east of the Antonia and the ridge to the east of that valley are called Beth Zetha.

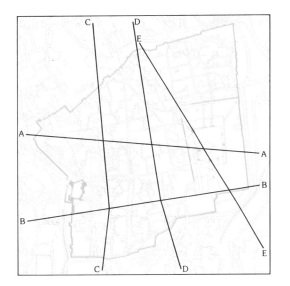

(right and below) **Sections of the city** showing the influence of the topography on its expansion. The system of hills and valleys determined the direction of its expansion.

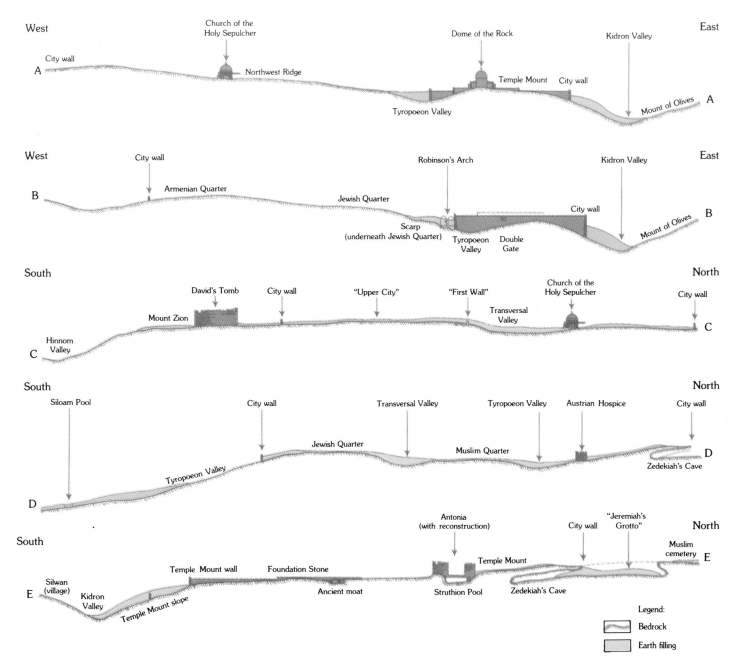

The Archaeological Study of Jerusalem

(right) The **Double Gate** on the Temple Mount as seen during the visit of the explorer **Tipping** in 1846. The Temple Mount was a focal point of archaeological research in Jerusalem during the nineteenth century. European explorers and other visitors succeeded in entering its precincts and to publish detailed accounts of their findings, despite the ban imposed on such visits by the Turkish authorities. Already in 1807, a European visitor succeeded in entering the Temple Mount and published a description of it. Among the later visitors to the site was Frederick Catherwood, the foremost researcher of the Temple Mount in the early nineteenth century. Catherwood first visited the Temple Mount and published a detailed plan of it in 1833, when Jerusalem was under Egyptian rule and foreigners were permitted to enter the site. With the return of the Ottomans to the city, the gates of the mount were closed to foreigners. Regardless, Tipping succeeded in becoming the first European to enter the Double Gate and hastily sketched the site in fear of being caught. Nevertheless, he made an important contribution to the study of this Second Temple period gate.

(opposite) Plate 37 of **Warren's Atlas** published in 1880, containing a graphic account of his work in Jerusalem during the late nineteenth century. In the upper left section of the plate is a sketch of the Struthion Pool, dating to the Second Temple period, and above it the pattern of the modern streets. In the lower section of the plate is a sectional view from the east through the Struthion. The construction of the pool under Herod cut off the course of a Hasmonean water conduit which ran from the north of the city to one of the water cisterns on the Temple Mount (possibly cistern No. 22). After the pool was completed the upper section of the canal (in the sketch to the left of the pool) probably continued to convey water to the pool itself; the pool is still in use today. The continuation of the conduit became superfluous when the pool was built.

Charles Warren, one of the most outstanding explorers of Palestine who worked under the auspices of the Palestine Exploration Fund, traversed this canal on a raft (in October 1867) from the Struthion Pool in the direction of the Temple Mount, until he reached the Temple Mount wall in the vicinity of the Seraya Gate (no longer in existence). Claude Reignier Conder, also an explorer under the auspices of the Palestine Exploration Fund, who visited the site shortly after Warren, discovered two sections of a wall built in typical Herodian style. A sketch of one of them appears in the center right of the plate. Below it, to the left, is a plan of the area under the Seraya Gate, with the "chamber" where Conder discovered the Second Temple period structure and the canal traversed by Warren. At the right is the section of the Temple Mount wall reached by Conder. This is the only section extant, according to which we can see that the Temple Mount wall was embellished with attached pillars (similar to the wall of the Cave of the Patriarchs at Hebron). Since Conder's discovery, any attempt to reconstruct the Temple Mount area is based on this assumption.

On March 16, 1987, the system was rediscovered by Israeli archaeologists in its entirety.

An examination of the data on this plate reveals that since Warren, almost no additional data have become available that could warrant any basic change in Warren's concept of his discoveries in the area.

(below) Illustrations from **Pierotti's*** work in which he attempts to date the remains of ancient buildings in Jerusalem according to the style of construction and stonecutting. Fig. 1 shows the style Pierotti considered to date from King Solomon's time; Fig. 2, reconstruction of the style from the time of the Prophet Nehemiah; Fig. 3, wall from Herodian period; Fig. 5, wall from the period of Suleiman the Magnificent.

Pierotti's definitions have no scientific basis, and there are numerous reservations as to his method. Stonecutting in Jerusalem cannot be dated, except in exceptional cases. The city was under the domination of many conquerors, and in every period stones from the previous period were used for building; thus many errors were made by scholars when stone quarrying and the method of stonecutting were used as a basis to determine the period of construction of the city's buildings.

Fig 1

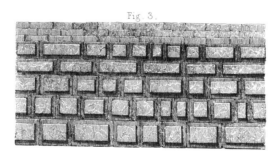

Fig. 3.

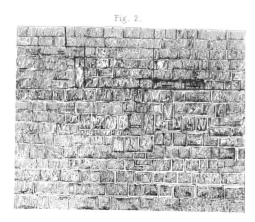

Fig. 2.

Fig. 5.

* **Ermete Pierotti**, an Italian engineer, was brought to Jerusalem by the Jerusalem municipality during the Turkish administration, and lived there from 1854 to 1860. He traveled throughout the country and described the sites he visited in written and illustrated works. Many of these sites are no longer extant. Under examination, Pierotti's descriptions of the "historical topography" of the city have not always appeared to be reliable.

JERUSALEM EXCAVATIONS BY CAPT. CHARLES WARREN. R.E. 1867-70.

PALESTINE EXPLORATION FUND. PL.XXXVII

See Plates IV. & XII.

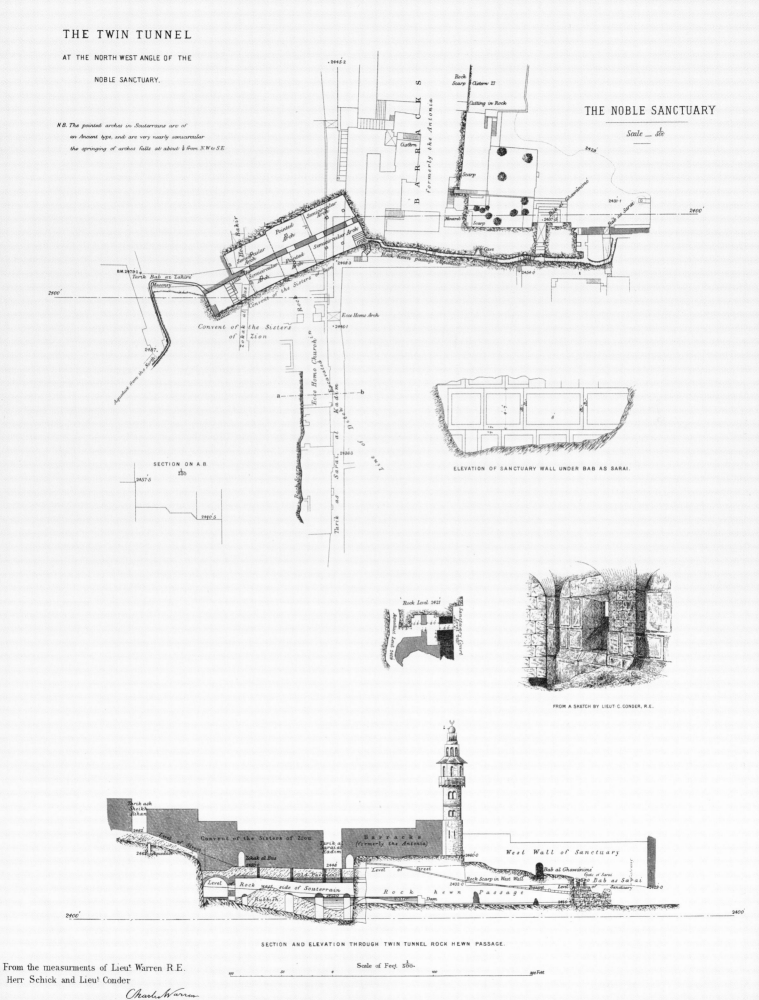

THE TWIN TUNNEL

AT THE NORTH WEST ANGLE OF THE

NOBLE SANCTUARY.

N.B. The pointed arches in Souterrains are of
an Ancient type, and are very nearly semicircular
the springing of arches falls at about ⅓ from N.W to S.E.

THE NOBLE SANCTUARY

Scale — 1/500

SECTION ON A.B.
1/250

ELEVATION OF SANCTUARY WALL UNDER BAB AS SARAI.

FROM A SKETCH BY LIEUT C. CONDER, R.E.

SECTION AND ELEVATION THROUGH TWIN TUNNEL ROCK HEWN PASSAGE.

Scale of Feet 1/500.

From the measurments of Lieut. Warren R.E.
Herr Schick and Lieut Conder

Charles Warren

Vincent Brooks Day & Son Lith

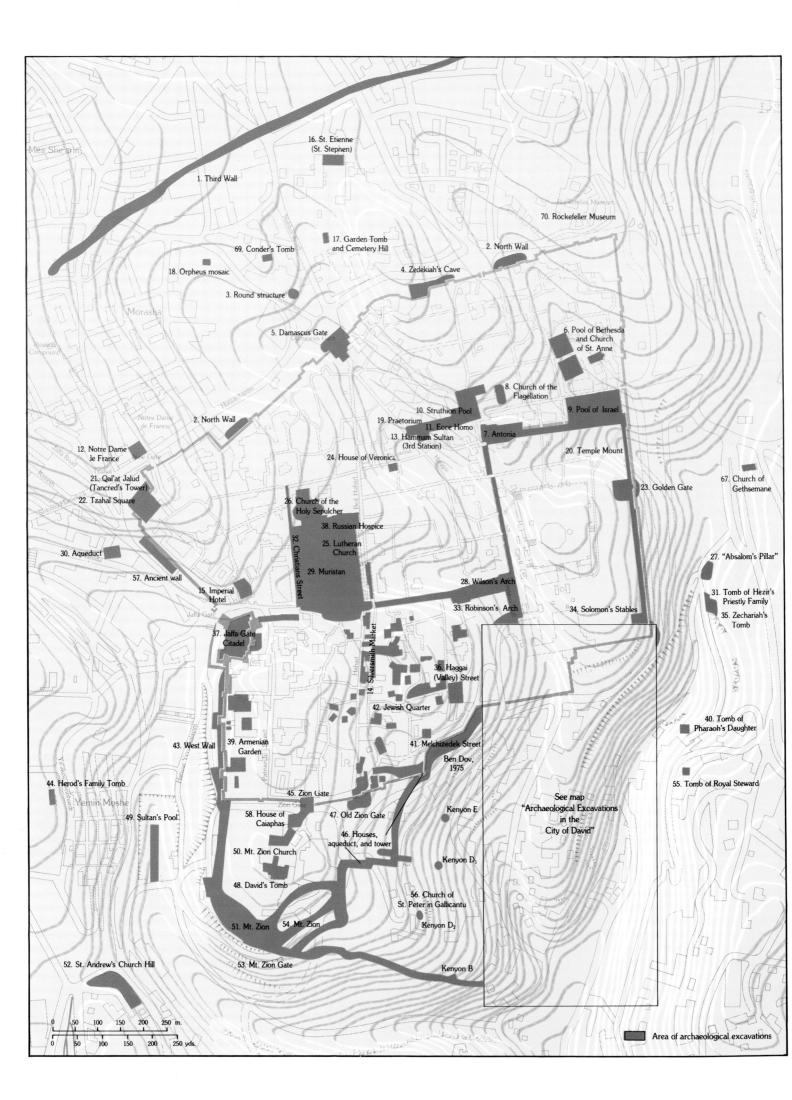

1. Third Wall
16. St. Etienne (St. Stephen)
70. Rockefeller Museum
69. Conder's Tomb
17. Garden Tomb and Cemetery Hill
2. North Wall
18. Orpheus mosaic
4. Zedekiah's Cave
3. Round structure
5. Damascus Gate
6. Pool of Bethesda and Church of St. Anne
8. Church of the Flagellation
10. Struthion Pool
9. Pool of Israel
19. Praetorium
11. Ecce Homo
7. Antonia
2. North Wall
13. Hammam Sultan (3rd Station)
20. Temple Mount
12. Notre Dame Je France
24. House of Veronica
21. Qal'at Jalud (Tancred's Tower)
23. Golden Gate
67. Church of Gethsemane
22. Tzahal Square
26. Church of the Holy Sepulcher
38. Russian Hospice
25. Lutheran Church
27. "Absalom's Pillar"
30. Aqueduct
32 Christians Street
29. Muristan
31. Tomb of Hezir's Priestly Family
57. Ancient wall
35. Zechariah's Tomb
28. Wilson's Arch
15. Imperial Hotel
33. Robinson's Arch
34. Solomon's Stables
37. Jaffa Gate Citadel
36. Haggai (Valley) Street
14. Silversmith Market
42. Jewish Quarter
40. Tomb of Pharaoh's Daughter
43. West Wall
39. Armenian Garden
41. Melchizedek Street
Ben Dov, 1975
44. Herod's Family Tomb
Kenyon E
See map "Archaeological Excavations in the City of David"
55. Tomb of Royal Steward
45. Zion Gate
49. Sultan's Pool
58. House of Caiaphas
47. Old Zion Gate
46. Houses, aqueduct, and tower
Kenyon D₁
50. Mt. Zion Church
48. David's Tomb
56. Church of St. Peter in Gallicantu
Kenyon D₂
51. Mt. Zion
54. Mt. Zion
52. St. Andrew's Church Hill
53. Mt. Zion Gate
Kenyon B

0   50   100   150   200   250 m.
0   50   100   150   200   250 yds.

Area of archaeological excavations

Archaeological excavations in Jerusalem increased rapidly from 1860. At first they took the form of pillaging of antiquities rather than archaeological excavations, but in the course of time experience was gained and scientific data became available. The numerous historical sources and the many excavations have made it possible to devise, even if only in theory, reconstructions of the city's layout in its various periods. The maps of the archaeological sites presented here are evidence that a large part of the city has already been excavated. However, questions about the basic topography of the city, which could have been resolved through excavations, have not yet been determined since the dense settlement of the city makes it possible to carry out extensive excavations in nonbuilt-up areas only.

(opposite) **Map of archaeological excavations in the Old City and its environs.**

Archaeologists and Dates of Excavation:

1. Wilson: 1864
   Sukenik and Mayer: 1925–1927
   Netzer, Ben-Arieh: 1973
   Kenyon, Hamrick: 1961–1967
2. Hamilton: 1937–1938
   De Groot, Terler: 1979
3. Netzer, Ben-Arieh: 1977
   Schick: 1879
4. Mazar: 1983
5. Hamilton: 1937–1938
   Hennessy: 1964–1966
   Magen: 1979–81
6. Mauss: 1863–1876
   White Fathers: 1889
7. Clermont-Ganneau: 1873–1874
   Vincent: 1912
8. Franciscans: 1884, 1889, 1901
9. Warren: 1867–1870
10. Warren: 1867–1870
11. Clermont-Ganneau: 1873–1874
    Benoit: 1972
12. Warren: 1867–1870
    Bahat, Goethert: 1981–1985
    Chambon: 1985
13. Clermont-Ganneau: 1873
14. Schick: 1876
15. Schick: 1887
    Guthe: 1885
    Merrill: 1902
16. Dominicans: 1881–1894
17. Warren, Wilson: 1867
    Schick: 1867, 1873, 1894, 1896
18. Bliss: 1894
19. Clermont-Ganneau: 1874
    Greeks: 1906
20. Warren and Conder: Examination of walls around Temple Mount, 1867–1870
21. Warren: 1867–1870
    Vincent: 1912
22. Bahat, Ben-Ari: 1971
23. Schick: 1872, 1891
24. Greeks: 1895
25. Lux: 1970–1971
26. Wilson: 1863
    Harvey: 1933–1934
    Corbo: 1961–1963
    Broshi: 1975
27. Clermont-Ganneau: 1870
    Slouschz: 1924
    Avigad: 1945–1947

28. Wilson, Warren: 1867
29. Warren: 1867–1870
    Schick: 1872, 1882, 1888, 1894, 1895, 1899, 1900
30. Merrill: 1902
31. Avigad: 1945–1947
32. Margalit and Chen: 1977
33. Warren: 1867–1870
34. de Saulcy: 1863
    Warren: 1867–1870
35. Slouschz: 1924
    Avigad: 1945–1947
    Statchbury: 1960
36. Hamilton: 1931
37. Johns: 1934–1940
    Amiran and Eitan: 1968–1969
    Geva: 1976–1980
    Sivan, Solar: 1980–1984
38. de Vogüé: 1855, 1862
    Pierotti: 1857–1860
    Clermont-Ganneau: 1873–1874
    Hitrowo: 1883
39. Kenyon, Tushingham: 1961–1967
    Bahat, Broshi: 1970
40. Avigad: 1945–1947
    Ussishkin: 1968
41. Edelstein: 1977
42. Avigad: 1969–1982
43. Broshi: 1970
44. Schick: 1891
45. Broshi, Tsafrir: 1971
46. Margovski: 1970
47. Broshi: 1974
48. Pinkerfeld: 1949
49. Kloner: 1974
50. Eisenberg, Hess: 1984
51. Modsley: 1871–1875
52. Barkay: 1975–1983
53. Margalit and Chen: 1979–1981
54. Bliss and Dickie: 1894–1897
    Clermont-Ganneau: 1870
55. Avigad: 1945–1947
    Ussishkin: 1968
56. Germer-Durand: 1882–1912
57. Schick: 1878
58. Broshi: 1971

(right) **Map of archaeological excavations in Jerusalem.**

59. a. Sukenik: 1928–1929
    b. Avigad: 1967
    c. Reich, Geva: 1972
60. de Saulcy: 1863
    Clermont-Ganneau: 1869
61. Tsaferis, Reich, Kloner, Bahat: 1967–1980
62. Palmer: 1898
    Palestine Exploration Fund: 1900
    American School: 1902
    Slouschz, Sukenik, Ben-Zvi: 1924
63. Avi-Yonah: 1949
64. Rahmani: 1954
65. Vincent: 1910–1913
    Corbo: 1959
66. Bagatti and Milik: 1953–1955
    Saller, Lamer: 1954
67. Orfali: 1909
68. Russian Church: 1870, 1881, 1893
69. Schick: 1881
70. Vincent: 1913
    Baramki: 1931
71. Johns: 1938
    Katsimbinis: 1973

(right) **Map of archaeological excavations in the City of David.**

Archaeologists and Dates of Excavation:

1. Warren: 1867–1870
2. Mazar: 1968
3. Kenyon: 1961–1968
4. Kenyon: Areas J, L, 1961–1968
5. Mazar: 1968–1982
6. Kenyon: 1961–1968
7. Warren: 1867–1870
8. Kenyon: 1961–1968
9. Kenyon: 1961–1968
10. Kenyon: 1961–1968
11. Parker: 1909–1911
    Warren: 1867–1870
    Shiloh: 1980
12. Shiloh: 1978–1984
13. Macalister and Duncan: 1923–1925
14. Crowfoot and Fitzgerald: 1927–1928
15. Guthe: 1881
16. Kenyon: 1961–1968
17. Schick: 1886–1900
    Parker: 1909–1911
    Warren: 1867–1870
18. Parker: 1909–1911
19. Shiloh: 1978–1984
20. Shiloh: Area K, 1978–1984
    Shiloh: 1983
    Kenyon: 1961–1968
21. Clermont-Ganneau: 1873
22. Shiloh: 1982–1984
23. Bliss and Dickie: 1894–1897
24. Kenyon: 1961–1968
25. Kenyon: 1961–1968
26. Shiloh: 1982
27. Guthe: 1881
28. Shiloh: 1978
29. Bliss and Dickie: 1894–1897
30. Kenyon: 1961–1968
31. Weill: 1923–1924
32. Kenyon: 1961–1968
33. Kenyon: 1961–1968
34. Bliss and Dickie: 1896–1897
35. Warren: 1867–1870
    Schick: 1880
36. Kenyon: 1961–1968
37. Weill: 1913–1914
    Shiloh: 1978–1984

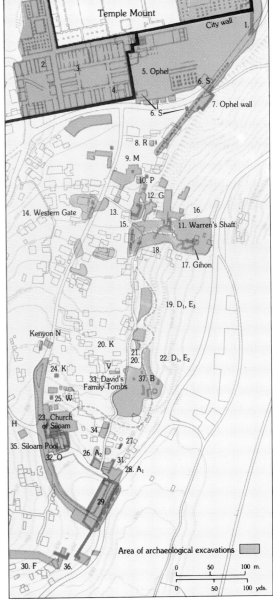

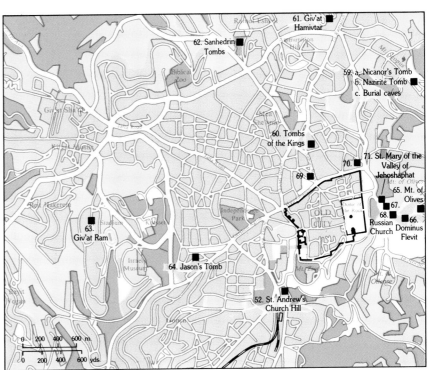

Ancient History
Until circa 1000 BCE

Early settlement of Jerusalem developed on the hill which we call the City of David, despite the fact that graves from this period have been found outside its boundaries, beyond the valleys encompassing it. There are few archaeological finds from this, the Chalcolithic, period (fourth millennium BCE), a fact which makes exact dating of the beginnings of settlement of the site most difficult.

The site was inhabited by new settlers in the Early Bronze Age (circa 3000 BCE). Excavations have revealed remains of square dwellings with a long wall containing an opening. Inside, there are shelves around the walls with one or two columns supporting the ceiling. This settlement was destroyed and was inhabited once again during the first half of the Middle Bronze Age, characterized by temporary settlements, based mainly on tribal organization. Evidence of this was found in graves uncovered in the village of Siloam.

The process of habitation in the form of permanent settlements and their transformation into fully-fledged cities is described in the Egyptian Execration Texts, which list the cities of the land of Israel as well as their rulers. The earlier Execration Texts, dating to the twentieth century BCE, refer to a number of rulers for each city. The later texts, from the nineteenth century BCE, mention only one or two rulers for each city. In the earlier writings, the names of two rulers of Jerusalem appear—Shas'an and Y'qar'am. The later writings refer to only one ruler, of whose name only the first syllable "Ba..." has been preserved. Scholars have interpreted the decrease in the numbers of rulers as evidence of an urbanization process characteristic of the Bronze Age in the land of Israel—the transition from a tribal to a city-state society. These two references are the only source of information about the history of Jerusalem during this period.

The earliest evidence of dense occupation of the hill on which the City of David stood is from the eighteenth century BCE. Remnants of the city's fortifications have been discovered on its eastern slopes, including a section of a wall, and what appears to be a large gate, of which only a part of a tower remains (see reconstruction on page 22). This tower was unearthed near the Gihon Spring, and this may have been part of the Fountain Gate, one of the most important gates of the city (Neh. 2:14–15). This gate together with its tower remained intact until the destruction of Jerusalem by Nebuchadnezzar.

Thus, Jerusalem became a fortified Canaanite city-state situated on a hilltop, as were most of the important cities in the land of Israel. Confirmation of this is also found in the el-Amarna Letters (fourteenth century BCE), a primary

Pottery vessels found mainly in the **Ophel burial tombs** have been dated to the first part of the Early Bronze Age (about 3200 BCE). These tombs were discovered in the vicinity of the Gihon Spring in an excavation carried out by the English archaeologist Montague Parker in 1909. Their discovery is evidence that a settlement existed in the area of the City of David during this ancient period.

The pottery vessels shown here have served as an example of the quality of the decoration of vessels during this period, as well as a point of departure for the dating of other sites in the country.

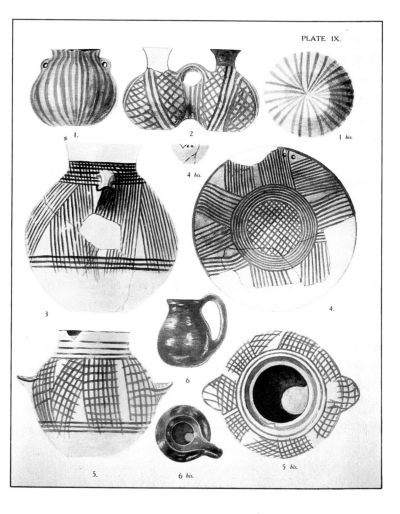

PLATE IX.

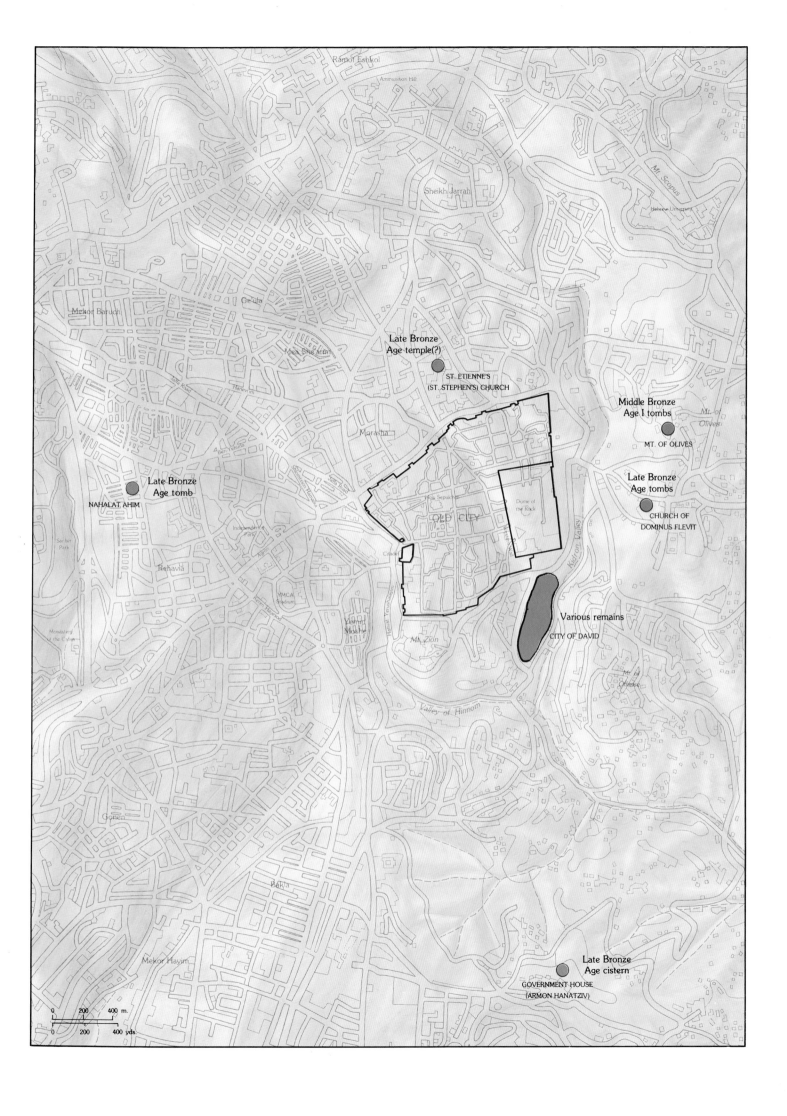

Late Bronze
Age temple(?)
ST. ÉTIENNE'S
(ST. STEPHEN'S) CHURCH

Middle Bronze
Age I tombs
MT. OF OLIVES

Late Bronze
Age tombs
CHURCH OF
DOMINUS FLEVIT

Late Bronze
Age tomb
NAHALAT AHIM

OLD CITY

Various remains
CITY OF DAVID

Late Bronze
Age cistern
GOVERNMENT HOUSE
(ARMON HANATZIV)

0   200   400 m.

0   200   400 yds.

(above right) The Egyptian **Execration Texts** are the first documents to provide data on the geography of the land of Israel during the twentieth and nineteenth centuries BCE. These are texts written on clay vessels, or on clay figurines in the form of slaves with their hands bound. The names and rulers of cities of the country were inscribed on them. Two groups of Execration Texts have been discovered: the earlier writings, dating to the twentieth century BCE, were written on clay bowls, and the later texts, from the nineteenth century BCE, were inscribed on figurines. In the early group mention is made of a number of cities and the names of a number of rulers of each city. In the later inscriptions, the number of rulers is reduced to one or two.

The Execration Texts refer to two cities in the mountain region of the land of Israel—Shechem (Nablus) and Jerusalem. Only Jerusalem is referred to in both groups of inscriptions, but both these cities had important status in the region.

Archaeological excavations have not revealed finds which could stress the importance of the city during the period referred to in the Execration Texts. It would appear that the remains from those periods were destroyed during the building that went on in the Middle Bronze Age IIB.

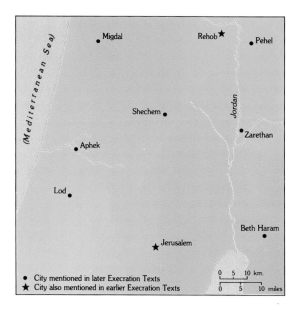

(below) **Clay figurine** from Sakkara, Egypt, from the nineteenth century BCE (the later Execration Texts), with curses inscribed on it. The figurines were used by the Egyptian priests as magic to counter uprisings of the cities. When a revolt against Egyptian rule broke out, the priests would break the figurine on which the name of the rebellious city was engraved, in the belief that the spirit of the revolt would thus be broken.

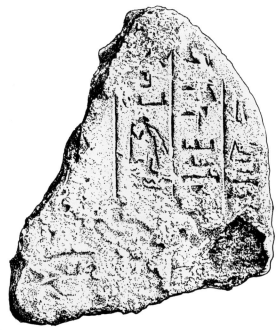

source for the history of that period. From these letters dispatched by Abdi-Hepa, Canaanite king of Jerusalem, we learn that his kingdom stretched over a sizable part of the northern Judean mountains. Ancient Egyptian remains from this period discovered in Jerusalem (in the grounds of the Church of St. Etiénne) provide further evidence. A libation tray and a fragment of an Egyptian stele probably attest to the existence of an Egyptian temple in the city or its environs, attached to the Egyptian garrison.

The most striking building complex from this period was found in the City of David. A system of terraces uncovered here formed a type of tell or artificial plinth, reinforced by retaining walls about 33 feet (10 meters) high. It appears that these walls were built with the purpose of creating a base upon which a palace or citadel were constructed. The most vulnerable point of the city's fortifications, in the northern section, was certainly well defended by this complex. The comparatively large number of vessels from this period discovered on Government House (Armon Hanatziv) hill, south of the City of David, as well as graves on the slopes of the Mount of Olives and the Nahalat Ahim neighborhood, are all evidence of the city's status during a period which was relatively unknown until recently.

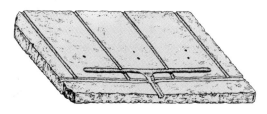

(above) Remains of a **libation tray** discovered during the reconstruction of the **Church of St. Etiénne** in the nineteenth century.

A small Egyptian temple had existed on this site, from which this libation tray has remained. It has grooves along which fluids flowed into a stone-carved basin. The identification of this site as a temple is based on the discovery there of a **stele** (center left) engraved with hieroglyphics. It appears that this was a small temple serving the soldiers of the Egyptian garrison which existed in Jerusalem at the time of one of the pharaohs of the Eighteenth Dynasty.

(below left) Reconstruction of the eighteenth-century BCE **Bronze Age gate** discovered on the eastern slopes of the City of David. The gate led from the city to the Gihon Spring, and was a part of the defense system. This system, which included sections of the wall and the gate, served as the basis of Jerusalem's fortifications until its destruction by Nebuchadnezzar (at the end of the First Temple period).

The only remains of the gate is a section of the tower. Although it is not possible at the moment to excavate a larger area of this site, it would appear that this tower is part of a large gate, referred to in the Bible as the "Fountain Gate." This assumption is based on the fact that the structure lies near the spring and to its right above, and is certain that a gate was required to lead to it. The purpose of the tower (or the two flanking towers) seems to have been for the defense of the gate. These remains were discovered by Kathleen Kenyon, who determined the date of the gate, which has been confirmed by recent Israeli excavations. It was during these latter digs that the section of the wall adjacent to the tower were uncovered. (The illustrations of the crenellations on the wall's embattlements and the towers have been made on the basis of similar structures described in the sources, as well as fortifications found in Syro-Palestinian cities.)

During the twelfth century BCE, Jerusalem's power began to decline. Its king, Adoni-Zedek, led an alliance of kings from the south of the country in battle against Joshua (Josh. 10:1). The allies were defeated in the battle of Gibeon–Aijalon valley, and even though the Bible makes no allusion to the destruction of the city following the military defeat and the death of its king, the Book of Judges (1:8) does state that the tribe of Judah destroyed Jerusalem and set it on fire.

The weak situation of the Canaanite city attracted new inhabitants—the Jebusites. Allusions to the origin of this people, who constituted a new factor in the country, and their link to the Hittites, can be found in various places in the Bible. For example, Ezekiel 16:3: "Thus saith the Lord God unto Jerusalem; Thy birth and thy nativity is of the land of Canaan; thy father was an Amorite, and thy mother an Hittite." Later in that chapter (verse 45) it states: "your mother was an Hittite, and your father an Amorite." Araunah, the ruler of Jerusalem in David's time, is also a Hittite name, and of course so is Uriah the Hittite who was a descendant of Jebusite inhabitants of the city before David conquered it. The Jebusites dominated Jerusalem for a period of approximately two hundred years, and the record of their impact is found mainly in descriptions in the Bible. Excavations in the City of David have uncovered few archaeological finds relating to this period.

(center left) The **El-Amarna Letters** are an important source of information about the land of Canaan in general and of Jerusalem in particular in the fourteenth century BCE. The letters were found in the royal archive at Tell el-Amarna (Akhetaton), the capital of Middle Egypt during the rule of King Akhenaton. The archives contained 350 letters written in Accadian on clay tablets. These letters were sent by the kings of the Canaanite cities to the king of Egypt, who reigned over the region at that time. Most of the letters contained reproaches and requests for assistance from the Egyptian government in the conflicts between the kings of the cities.

From the six letters sent by Abdi-Hepa, Canaanite king of Jerusalem, it appears that settlement in the mountain region was sparse, and Jerusalem, Shechem, and perhaps Bethlehem were the centers of habitation in the area. There was a constant struggle between Abdi-Hepa and Lab'ayu, king of Shechem, for control of the mountain region, and the king of Jerusalem requested assistance from Pharaoh, king of Egypt, in this conflict.

The map presented here shows the **mountain region** as recorded in the el-Amarna Letters, especially letter No. 290 which reads as follows: "To the king, my lord, say: Thus spake Abdi-Hepa, thy servant. At the two feet of the king, my lord, seven times and seven times I fall. Behold the deed which Milkilu [king of Gezer] and Shuwardata [king of Keilah] did to the land of the king, my lord [that is, Jerusalem, which is loyal to the king]. They rushed troops of Gezer, troops of Gath, and troops of Keilah; they took the land of Rubutu [possibly Beth Shemesh]; the land of the king went over to the 'Apiru people. But now even a town of the land of Jerusalem, Bit Ninurta [possibly Beth Horon] by name, a town belonging to the king, has gone over to the side of the people of Keilah. Let my king harken to Abdi-Hepa, thy servant, and let him send archers to recover the royal land for the king. But if there are no archers, the land of the king will pass over to the 'Apiru people. This was done at the command of Milkilu and at the command of Shuwardata... So let my king take care of his land."

El-Amarna Letter.

(below) **Cross section of the City of David,** from the Kidron Valley in the east, up to the eastern slopes of Mount Zion in the west.

In the past, the riverbed (a) was lower than at present (b) since it has filled up with silt. This is the reason that it is difficult to see the Gihon Spring from the riverbed. To do this, one must descend from the riverbed to the valley by way of a stairway (c). The slope descending to the Kidron is the main area which provides information about the City of David.

The depression at the left (d) is the Tyropoeon Valley. The cross section delineates the manner in which the valley was filled up. In the Byzantine period, buildings were constructed on the layers of silt in the valley which concealed the riverbed completely (e). To the east, remains can be seen of the structure (f) built by the Canaanite kings of Jerusalem as an artificial basis for fortifications. Above the ruins of the fortifications, the palaces of the Davidic dynasty were erected (g), but these too have disappeared, probably at the time of the destruction of the First Temple. The illustration shows the Bronze Age (Canaanite) structure within the limits of the excavation, but it was certainly much larger. Parts of the supports of the Canaanite structure were destroyed about the time of King Hezekiah's reign, to make possible the building of a residential quarter on the site (h).

All these remains were covered over with a thick layer of silt during the Hasmonean period, when the area was being prepared for the erection of fortifications (i). To the east, halfway down the slope, the city walls can be seen (j). These walls, built in the eighteenth century BCE, existed until the destruction of the First Temple. This cross section shows the wall that was attached to the Canaanite wall (k), probably during the time of King Manasseh, whose great building works in the city are described in the Bible. It also shows the city's water system—especially Warren's Shaft (l) and Hezekiah's Tunnel (m).

The large First Temple fortification (n), discovered by Crowfoot and Fitzgerald in the 1920s, can be seen on the western side. During the course of the excavations a large gate was unearthed, the dating of which is still a matter of controversy among scholars. Some believe that it was built during the First Temple period (during Solomon's reign), while others consider that it was built in the time of Alexander Jannaeus (o).

Kathleen Kenyon discovered a densely populated Second Temple settlement (p) in the course of her excavations. She concluded that these were public buildings erected during the period of Hellenization in the second century BCE.

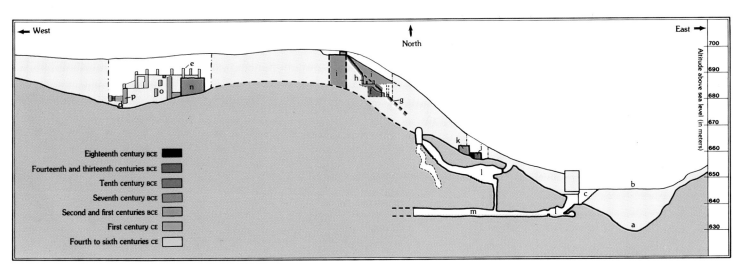

West   North   East

Eighteenth century BCE
Fourteenth and thirteenth centuries BCE
Tenth century BCE
Seventh century BCE
Second and first centuries BCE
First century CE
Fourth to sixth centuries CE

Altitude above sea level (in meters)
700 690 680 670 660 650 640 630

The First Temple Period
1000 BCE – 586 BCE

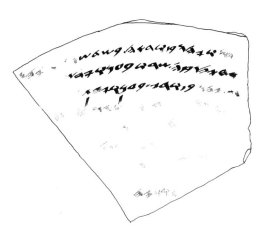

The **Ophel Ostracon (Clay Tablet)**, from the eighth to seventh centuries BCE, with the longest inscription found in Jerusalem in cursive script, was discovered in 1924 by J. G. Duncan in excavations on the hill of the City of David. The inscription was written with a scribe's pen on a whitewashed pottery sherd, but has not been preserved in its entirety and thus its exact interpretation is questionable.

The accepted reading of the inscription is: "Hezekiah son of Karah son of Sharash son of Bakihu, Ahihu son of Hasharak son of Amakihu, Yahu son of Kari son of Amakihu." Many other readings, however, have also been suggested.

The First Temple period begins with the conquest of Jebus (Jerusalem) by David. The description of this conquest appears in the Bible in two versions: in the Second Book of Samuel (5:6–9) and in the First Book of Chronicles (11:4–7). It would appear that these descriptions are contradictory, since in the first, David is described as actually conquering the city, while Chronicles ascribes the conquest to Joab son of Zeruiah. As the biblical text in the Second Book of Samuel is to a certain extent distorted as a result of various traditions that have merged, it is difficult to determine with any amount of accuracy whether this is a contradictory description or a different account.

The biblical account of the manner in which the city was captured is also enigmatic. At first it was believed that David conquered the city by a ruse: by entering by way of a "gutter" (according to 2 Samuel). According to this version, the city was penetrated by way of the city's water system, today called Warren's Shaft, but through recent studies, it became apparent that the shaft was built in a later period, probably at the end of the reign of King Solomon, or of one of the early kings of his dynasty. The Hebrew term *tzinor*, mentioned twice in the Bible, probably has two meanings: in our case (2 Sam. 5:8), a utensil similar to a pitchfork, used as a magic instrument with which to fend off the enemy and prevent him from conquering the city. This definition is based on the fact that the Jebusite king also used magic and placed the blind and lame on the walls, as a warning that anyone attempting to conquer the city would suffer the same fate. The second meaning of *tzinor* is a musical instrument. According to this definition, the conquest of the city was carried out in a manner similar to that of the capture of Jericho. Jericho was taken with the aid of *shofars* and the Jebusite city with trumpets. Support for this theory is to be found in Psalms (42:7) where the term *tzinor* is also mentioned with what would appear to be a reference to a musical instrument which gives forth a blaring sound. Menachem ben Saruk, a tenth-century Jewish sage, also explained this term as meaning a "musical instrument."

After the conquest, the city's name was changed to the City of David. The area of the city remained the same and

its boundaries were its ancient walls. The assumption that David expanded the city toward the north, in the direction of the Temple Mount, has not been substantiated. Buildings were added during David's reign, but were constructed within its original confines. The Bible tells that at first David fortified the city: "And David built round about from Millo and inward" (2 Sam. 5:9) and later also built the king's palace: "And Hiram … sent messengers … and they built David an house" (2 Sam. 5:11). It would seem that the Jebusite fortress, the "stronghold of Zion," where David took refuge after the conquest of the city, was situated in the northeastern corner of the ancient City of David. This was also the site of David's palace. An artificial "tell" was discovered here, created by a system of terraces filled with stones, enclosed in box-like shapes placed one above the other. The estimated size of this structure is 39 × 66 feet (12 × 20 meters), but it could have been higher and broader. From the archaeological excavations it transpires that it was David who built these terraces, which acted as additional support for further fillings to solidify and cover over the ancient structure. (So far fifty-five such terraces have been uncovered, but further excavations will certainly uncover more.) It can be assumed that it was upon this tell surrounded by terraces that David built his palace, with the assistance of the builders sent by Hiram, king of Tyre, but the top section of the structure has not remained. Kathleen Kenyon's excavations revealed architectural remains which could well have been those of an edifice such as a palace. These included such items as a proto-Ionic capital similar to that found in neighboring countries dating to the same period. The discovery of this tremendous building project from the time of David enables us to follow the development of the center of government in Jerusalem. At first David built a palace and a center of government on this site—a "house for David" (2 Sam. 5:11)—and once the new center was built by Solomon on the Temple Mount, the old palace began to deteriorate.

The "House of David" is not mentioned again in the sources, and private dwellings were built on the terraces. There is a theory that the tremendous terraced structure is the biblical Ophel, but we are of the opinion that the

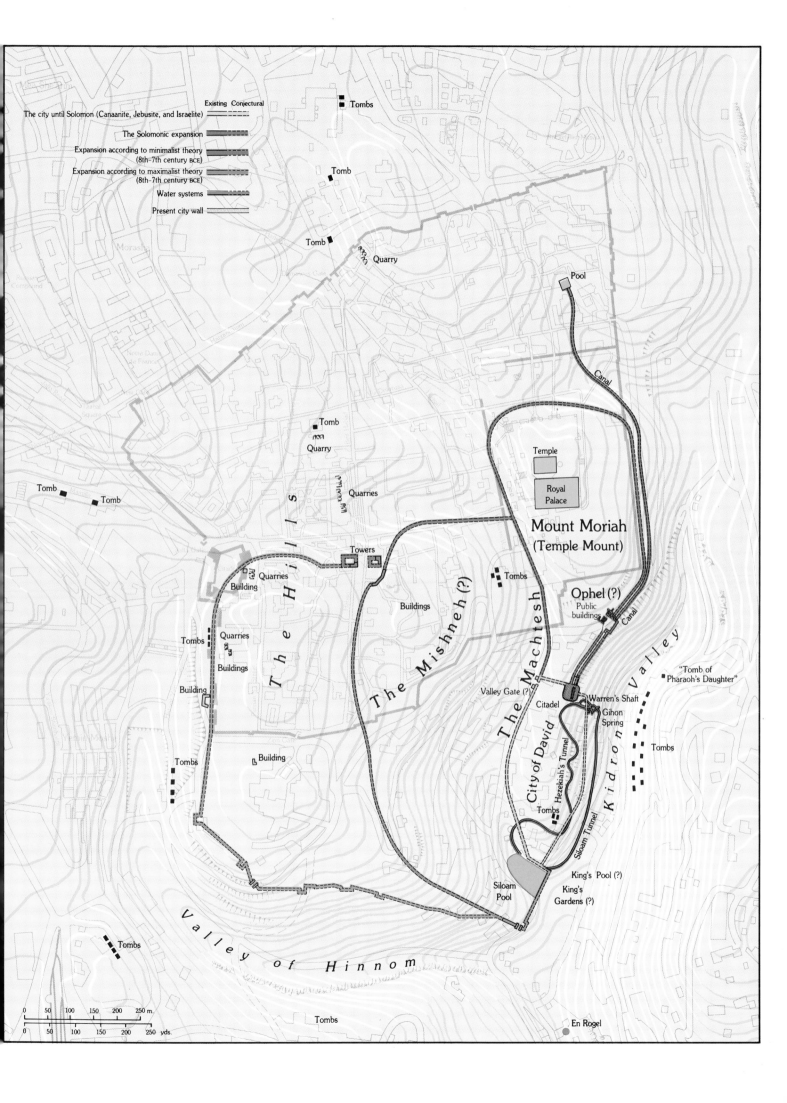

Existing Conjectural

The city until Solomon (Canaanite, Jebusite, and Israelite)

The Solomonic expansion

Expansion according to minimalist theory (8th-7th century BCE)

Expansion according to maximalist theory (8th-7th century BCE)

Water systems

Present city wall

Tombs

Tomb

Tomb

Quarry

Pool

Canal

Tomb

Quarry

Temple

Royal Palace

Mount Moriah (Temple Mount)

Tomb

Tomb

Quarries

Tombs

Ophel (?)

Public buildings

Canal

Towers

T h e   H i l l s

Buildings

T h e   M i s h n e h   (?)

"Tomb of Pharaoh's Daughter"

Quarries

Building

Tombs

Quarries

Buildings

Valley Gate (?)

Citadel

Warren's Shaft

Gihon Spring

Tombs

Building

City of David

Hezekiah's Tunnel

Building

Tombs

Siloam Tunnel

Tombs

K i d r o n   V a l l e y

T h e   M a c h t e s h

Siloam Pool

King's Pool (?)

King's Gardens (?)

Tombs

0   50   100   150   200   250 m.

0   50   100   150   200   250 yds.

V a l l e y   o f   H i n n o m

Tombs

En Rogel

term "Ophel" refers to a high feature, such as a steep slope to which one ascends, implying the sharp peak above the area at the north of David's city, beyond the southern wall of the Temple Mount. Solomon built the Temple and the royal palace beside it, north of the structure built by his father David. It can be assumed that this complex, described in detail in the First Book of Kings, was fortified when the city expanded northward and the Temple Mount was added to it. In her excavations of David's City (area P), Kathleen Kenyon uncovered a section of a possible casemate wall, of the type which was used by Solomon to fortify several of his cities. It is possible that this section of the wall is part of the system of fortifications Solomon built while expanding the city northward in order to engulf the newly built Temple. But this is not certain, and in fact hardly any remains of these fortifications have been found. One of the reasons for this is the building that took place in this area after the First Temple period, especially under Herod, which left no trace of the buildings from Solomonic times. The fortifications depicted on the map are not based on archaeological finds, but rather on the topography of the Temple Mount. This makes it possible to determine accurately the situation of the line of fortifications, since the Temple Mount is surrounded by valleys and tributaries of streams. A further allusion to the fortifications of this period may possibly be found in the deep moat discovered on the northwestern side of the Temple Mount. This moat was undoubtedly dug prior to the Herodian era, opposite the hill upon which the Antonia fortress stood in his times. Since there is no further evidence of other government-sponsored building on this section of the mountain, it would seem that the digging of the moat was in fact carried out during the First Temple period, or even during the reign of Solomon. If this is so, the area occupied by the Temple Mount during his times is highly probable and well defined.

A most impressive gate (designated in the map as the Valley Gate) and discovered by Crowfoot and Fitzgerald in 1927, was considered as having been built during the reign of Solomon. However, this is not certain, and for archaeological technical reasons it could also be dated to the Hasmonean period.

The same applies to the water system, called Warren's Shaft, which was built on the hill of the City of David, to enable water to be drawn from the Gihon Spring at times

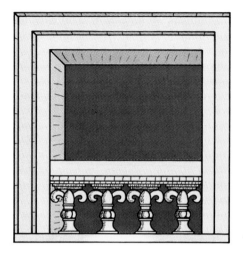

(below) **Reconstruction of a window frame** with decorations carved in stone from the First Temple period found at Ramat Rahel. The remains were in part decorated in relief and part sculpted, and apparently belonged to more than one window, which is a reflection of the quality of the structure. It is certain that this was a royal palace built in the ninth century BCE (during the reign of Asa or Jehoshaphat). The reconstruction of the window, as illustrated here, is based on a similar structure found on ivory panels dating to the same period in other places such as Calah (Nimrod) in Assyria.

The discovery of the palace in the vicinity of Jerusalem is evidence of the means of the royal family in Judah, and the sources of cultural influence upon them.

(below) One of the most ancient water supply systems in Jerusalem discovered in 1867 is called **Warren's Shaft** after its discoverer, Sir Charles Warren. The shaft was apparently dug during the First Temple period in order to enable the city's inhabitants, who were living inside defense walls, to reach the spring situated outside the walls, without exposing themselves to the enemy forces in times of siege. Similar water supply systems were found at Hazor, Gezer, Megiddo, Gibeon, and at other sites, but this seems to be the most complex. It is difficult to recreate the manner in which the shaft was constructed, but the cross-section illustration will help to do this.

The vaulted chamber is the starting point for a visit to Warren's Shaft. This chamber was probably shaped differently during the First Temple period, and there may have been a section of a tunnel by which the hill, or rather the city itself, was reached. The present chamber was built in the Second Temple period to facilitate entrance to the shaft, and a vaulted tunnel was constructed to enable easy access and exit (today this tunnel is used for exit only). At the bottom of the chamber can be seen the spot where an attempt was made to dig down to reach the water source, but for some unknown reason the work was stopped and another tunnel built instead. The tunnel begins at stepped levels, and its continuation is almost horizontal. This was done so as to make it possible to reach a particular point and then sink a vertical shaft to the spring's water level (the experimental shaft was put out of use and is now filled with soil). Above the shaft was a natural opening, a sort of cave, which was perhaps used by the workers as a source of light, or as a place in which to pile up the waste extracted during the quarrying. However, it serves no purpose within the water system. Until recently there was a supposition that this natural opening had a function during the course of the construction of the system. It was believed that when the attempt to dig the experimental shaft failed, the inhabitants of the city discovered the natural cave, sunk the vertical shaft from there, and only when the lower section was completed was the upper section of the system constructed. The purpose of all this was supposedly to guarantee the safety of the workers. However, this supposition has no substantiation.

Some two centuries after the shaft was sunk, when Hezekiah began his monumental water supply system, he made use of the tunnel connecting the shaft and the spring, thus saving himself the necessity of quarrying in the vicinity of the spring, and enabling him to begin digging his tunnel at that spot. It was only in Hezekiah's reign that Warren's Shaft fell into disuse. However, the discovery of the vaulted chamber and the determination of the date have given rise to a new problem relating to the use of this water supply system in the Second Temple period as well. It appears that the entire water system, including that of Hezekiah, was completely forgotten until the Middle Ages, and only then was the water from the Gihon Spring brought into use once more. Steps were built from the bed of the Kidron Valley, and the guardhouse was erected above them.

Vaulted chamber

Stepped tunnel

Experimental shaft

Horizontal tunnel

City fortification

Natural cave

Vertical shaft

Hezekiah's Tunnel

Connecting tunnel

Guardhouse

Spring?

Siloam tunnel

Siloam channel

Stairs (late)

(left) The **Siloam Inscription**, from the time of King Hezekiah (about 700 BCE), was discovered in 1880 not far from the southern entrance to the tunnel. Hezekiah excavated the tunnel in order to make provision for the supply of water to Jerusalem from the Gihon Spring, which was outside the city walls to the Siloam Pool inside the city. After Hezekiah built a new wall which brought the Siloam Pool within the confines of the city, guaranteeing the flow of water from the spring to the city was of the utmost importance, especially in times of siege. Hezekiah's building projects are described in the Second Book of Kings (20:20) and in the Second Book of Chronicles (32:30).

This inscription, which is in the Museum of Archaeology in Istanbul, is the longest ever found belonging to Jerusalem's biblical period. It is believed to describe the meeting between the two teams of workers excavating the tunnel, and their concern over the possibility of missing each other when they were about to break through at mid-point. Following is the text of the inscription: "[... when] (the tunnel) was driven through. And this was the way in which it was cut through: While [...] (were) still [...] axe(s), each man toward his fellow, and while there were still three cubits to be cut through, [there was heard] the voice of a man calling to his fellows, for there was an overlap in the rock on the right [and on the left]. And when the tunnel was driven through, the quarrymen hewed (the rock), each man toward his fellow, axe against axe; and the water flowed from the spring toward the reservoir for 1,200 cubits, and the height of the rock above the head(s) of the quarrymen was 100 cubits."

(right) The **terraced structure** built during the Late Bronze Age (fourteenth to thirteenth centuries BCE) on the northeastern extremity of the City of David. It was constructed by fillings of stones and soil and reinforced by thin stone walls, forming an artificial tell. This tell constituted a base upon which the acropolis of Canaanite Jerusalem was apparently built. (This was the fortified section of Jerusalem where the administration buildings of the Canaanite and Jebusite city were situated.)

After conquering the city, King David used this structure as the base upon which he erected his palace. In order to reinforce it, he encompassed it with a system of terraces, which served as additional support to the fillings. It is this complex which can still be seen on the site. This palace may well be that which Hiram, king of Tyre, helped to build (2 Sam. 5:11), or it may be David's Citadel mentioned in the Bible (2 Sam. 5:9). In the course of time, when King Solomon built the administrative center of his kingdom on the Temple Mount, consisting of a palace and Temple, the palace built by David was no longer of any significance. The terraced structure, which had served as a basis for it, turned into a tell. On this tell, and on its edges, dwellings were constructed. The result was a complete change in the terraced structure. Only a small section is still visible, enabling us to appreciate the extent of the royal construction works during the reign of King David.

The terraced structure was discovered during the archaeological excavations of the City of David which began in 1978. However, the structure had already been unearthed in the excavations carried out by Macalister and Duncan (1923–1925) and Kenyon (1967–1968), but its real significance was not appreciated at the time.

of siege. There is no conclusive proof available of the date this structure was built. However, its similarity to buildings serving the same purpose in other cities, such as Hazor and Megiddo, makes it possible to surmise that it was built at the end of Solomon's reign, or under one of the kings who reigned shortly after.

It was during this period, also, that the huge terraced structure, upon which stood the royal palace during David's reign, began to deteriorate, and whose importance seemed to have declined with the erection of the royal complex in the vicinity of the Temple.

The reconstruction of the topography of biblical Jerusalem is based on archaeological finds as well as verses in the Bible relating to various building projects within the city, and the boundaries within which it expanded. Until recently, it was considered that the Book of Nehemiah provided evidence of Jerusalem's urban structure during the First Temple period. However, from the excavations carried out in the City of David, which began in the 1960s, it became evident that the city's dimensions were greatly reduced in the time of Nehemiah when compared with those of the First Temple period, and the direction of the city walls changed accordingly. As few sources have remained (such as the descriptions in the Book of Nehemiah), it is impossible to reconstruct the topographical continuity of the area.

The third phase of Jerusalem's urban development apparently began during Uzziah's reign, in the mid-eighth century BCE. This king is referred to in the Bible as having reinforced the walls of Jerusalem and as having built its towers: "Moreover Uzziah built towers in Jerusalem at the corner gate, and at the valley gate, and at the turning of the wall, and fortified them" (2 Chron. 26:9). His son, Jotham, also continued to fortify the city (2 Chron. 27:3), and during this period—although there is no specific reference to it in the Bible—the city began to expand beyond its original dimensions.

The strengthening of Assyria, the destruction of the Kingdom of Israel in 722 BCE, the struggle between Judah and the coastal city-states for sovereignty over western Judea, and especially Sennacherib's siege of the towns of Judea, brought a stream of refugees to Jerusalem who settled in the

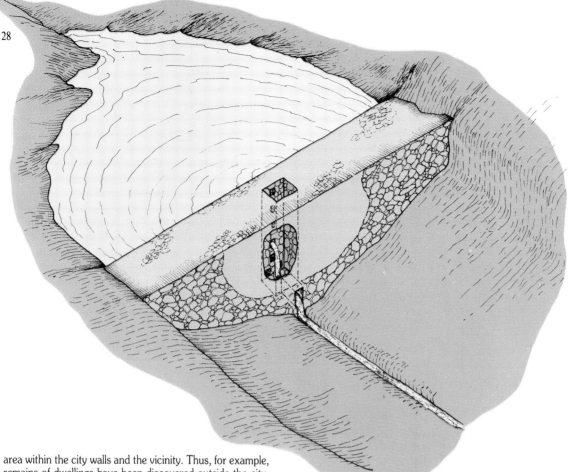

(above left) Toward the end of the kingdom of Judah a large **dam** was built across the **Beth Zetha Valley** on the site where in the Second Temple period the **Sheep's Pools** were located (today in the courtyard of the Church of St. Anne). The dam was about 131 feet (40 m.) long, 20 feet (6 m.) broad in its upper section and 23 feet (7 m.) in the lower section, and 43 feet (13 m.) high. It formed a pool which retained the waters flowing along the Beth Zetha Valley southward. This pool is situated above the second pool, to the south, and they were created at different times.

At the center of the dam a square shaft was built (3 × 3 feet [1 × 1 m.]); openings (6 × 8 inches [15 × 20 cm.]) were made in it every 6.5 feet (2 m.) connecting the shaft with the upper pool (the northern one). At the base of the shaft were two apertures the height of the base of the pool. These apertures served to regulate the draining of the waters from the pool toward the south.

It appears that the function of the dam was to accumulate the waters so as to control their flow into a conduit which apparently brought them to the northern section of the City of David. A section of this conduit, about 164 feet (50 m.) long, that ran from the dam to the south has been unearthed. It is 3 feet (1 m.) deep and 30 inches (75 cm.) wide. The scholars who discovered the conduit are of the opinion that the waters flowed from the pool to the conduit in the direction of the Temple, and were used by the people working in it. These facts were derived from the archaeological excavations carried out at the site recently by the owners of the land area, members of the Order of the White Fathers.

area within the city walls and the vicinity. Thus, for example, remains of dwellings have been discovered outside the city, in area B of the City of David excavations, in the area of Mount Zion, and on the western slopes of the Old City facing the Sultan's Pool.

The events described above occurred during the long reign of King Hezekiah (727–698 BCE), and were the motive for his great construction projects in Jerusalem, such as the new wall which also encompassed the new quarters established during this period outside the walls (Isa. 22:10; 2 Chron. 32:5), and the excavation of the tunnel which brought water from the Gihon Spring to the Siloam Pool inside the city (2 Kings 20:20). Nineteenth-century scholars and laymen alike identified this tunnel as having been built by King Hezekiah.

The wall built by Hezekiah was discovered by Prof. Avigad during his excavations in the Jewish Quarter. According to the archaeological findings, the course of the wall was based on the network of dry riverbeds in the city. The buildings constructed along the newly built wall alignment were pulled down to enable the wall to be built. Thus, in area A of the excavations of the Jewish Quarter, a section of this wall was found, on both sides of which were remains of buildings pulled down during its construction, as described in Isaiah: "And ye have numbered the houses of Jerusalem, and the houses have ye broken down to fortify the wall" (22:10). Thus it can be assumed that the wall discovered in the Jewish Quarter is a section of the wall built by Hezekiah as protection against the siege of Jerusalem by Sennacherib, king of Assyria, in 701 BCE. It has not been possible to determine the exact function of two additional sections of the fortifications found in the vicinity (area S and area 11 of the excavations) within the complex of fortifications of that period. It may well be that they are a part of the city's fortifications at a later period, during the time of the Mishnah. According to the Bible (2 Chron. 33:14), Manasseh fortified the city during his long reign over Judea (697–643 BCE), and the construction of the wall was one of his more important undertakings. A section of Hezekiah's wall was uncovered by Kathleen Kenyon during her excavations on the eastern slopes of the City of David.

The controversy over the city's dimensions during the First Temple period, which continued from the beginning of the exploration of Jerusalem, was brought to an end with the discovery of this wall. Many scholars were convinced

(center left) **Iron arrowheads** from the time of the destruction of Jerusalem by Nebuchadnezzar (586 BCE) discovered in the archaeological excavations in the Jewish Quarter. Flat arrowheads were found in the stratum of burnt materials (charred wood, ashes, and soot) at the foot of the remains of a tall tower from the Iron Age. One of the arrowheads was a Scythian arrow made of bronze, which was brought to the land of Israel by conquering armies from the seventh century BCE. It would seem that during the attack on the city flaming torches hurled by the conquerors set the buildings on fire. The siege of the tower and the tumult during the attempts to take it were indicative of the events in Jerusalem during the days preceding the destruction of the First Temple.

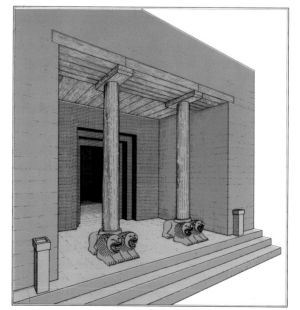

(below left) **Reconstruction of the entrance to the Tell Ta'yinat temple**, with its two pillars supporting the entrance roof. There is a great similarity between this temple and the Temple in Jerusalem as described in the Bible. The two pillars in this illustration recall Jachin and Boaz—the two pillars mentioned in the Bible (2 Chron. 3:17; 1 Kings 7:21). Lions such as those supporting the pillars are found in Syrian architecture, and were not used in the Jerusalem Temple. The illustration shows how impressive the entrance to the temple was.

(below) Section of the **First Temple period wall** of Jerusalem, discovered by N. Avigad in the Jewish Quarter. The section is about 213 feet (65 m.) long, 25 feet (7.5 m.) wide, and over 10 feet (3 m.) high.

This discovery brought to an end the long-standing controversy over the extent of Jerusalem during the First Temple period. In addition to the section of this impressive wall, two towers were discovered in this area.

This system of fortifications leads to the conclusion that from the end of the eighth century BCE, the area of the present-day Jewish Quarter was included within the walls of Jerusalem.

that Jerusalem's boundaries were the hill of the City of David and the Temple Mount. Other scholars believed that the city was much larger, and that its western boundary passed through the area of the present-day Old City. This would mean that the city was situated on the hill which today encompasses the Jewish and Armenian Quarters as well as Mount Zion. The excavations in the Jewish Quarter have established that the city did expand beyond its earlier boundaries, but this occurred only at the end of the eighth century BCE.

Some scholars are now of the opinion that the course of the First Temple period wall is identical to that of the First Wall from the Second Temple period. They argue that proof of this is provided by Josephus Flavius, who states that the First Wall was built during the rule of David and Solomon and the kings who reigned after them (*Wars* 5, 4, 1). They also base their argument on the fact that the remains discovered of the First Temple period walls were adjacent to the First Wall. However, we believe that no conclusive proof as to this has yet been provided. It is more reasonable to presume that the wall passed through what is now the Street of the Jews, since it is traversed by a riverbed which could have served as a base for the wall. It is within this area, the present-day Jewish Quarter, that a relatively dense settlement existed during the First Temple period.

The discovery of only a few houses within the confines of the Armenian Quarter and Mount Zion, as compared with a larger number of houses found in the Jewish Quarter, indicates that the situation there was similar to that which existed in the City of David (area B). In that area, too, a number of the houses of the new settlers in Jerusalem were built outside the city walls. Support of the minimalist approach can also be found in the fact that nowhere other than in the Jewish Quarter have remains been discovered of the city wall which can be definitely dated to the First Temple period. The absence of such remains in the large area excavated in the grounds of the Citadel, and along the length of the western part of the Old City walls, reduces the plausibility of the maximalist approach. The description of the construction of fortresses from the time of King Manasseh which existed outside the walls of Jerusalem can also be found in Josephus (*Antiquities* 10, 44), so that even if remains are found outside the city, this will not refute the minimalist determination of the city's boundaries.

In the northern part of the present-day Old City, remains have been found which cast light upon the expansion of the city in this direction. In the vicinity of the Muristan and the Church of the Holy Sepulcher, remains of quarries dating

(right) The **Temple at Tell Ta'yinat**. The construction of the Temple in Jerusalem was certainly one of the pinnacles of building during the First Temple period. The biblical books of Kings and Chronicles give detailed descriptions of the construction of the Temple and hardly relate to the palace adjacent to it. Both the comparison of building projects from this period in neighboring countries and our conception of the fortification of the Temple Mount lead to the conclusion that the organization of the administrative area was based on the proximity between the Temple and the royal palace. A good example of this is seen in the illustration of the administration complex at Tell Ta'yinat in northern Syria. This structure also confirms the biblical descriptions, and adds to our understanding of the complex built by King Solomon on the Temple Mount. Although the Tell Ta'yinat complex post-dates King Solomon's reign by about two centuries, it enables us to learn about the structure of the various sections of a royal palace, and the size of the palace in relation to the temple. It should be pointed out that the location of some other administration complexes of the type shown here is unknown. For example, the First Book of Kings mentions the "house of the forest of Lebanon" (7:2) and the house of "Pharaoh's daughter" (9:24). The Bible also states that Solomon built his palace over a period of thirteen years, and the Temple in only six

years (1 Kings 7:1). This fact shows that both from the point of view of time and of magnitude, the building of the palace exceeded the construction of the Temple.

Palaces of the style of this edifice have been found in the excavations at Megiddo, in the levels from the reign of Solomon, and the following elements can be discerned: the hall of columns (which served as a vestibule), an inner courtyard (termed in the Bible the "other courtyard," and which was the living area of the king and his retinue), and a large hall which is the "hall of the throne" mentioned in the Bible. The broad walls shown in the illustration were, according to the Bible, to be found in the royal palace in Jerusalem. The temple itself, whose interior measurements were 20 × 70 cubits (approximately 33 × 115 feet [10 × 35 m.]), faced toward the east, and the function of the front hall reached by a stairway, was to separate the courtyard from the sanctuary (Hekhal) itself. It would seem that in the Tell Ta'yinat temple the pillars which stood on the backs of lions fulfilled the function of the biblical pillars of Jachin and Boaz (1 Kings 7:21). From the hall, an entrance led to the sanctuary, the main part of the Temple, in which the priests carried out their duties, and where the main rituals were performed. The main difference between the Tell Ta'yinat temple and the Temple in Jerusalem was the length of the innermost section, the inner sanctuary (Debir) where

the holy ark and the *cherubim* were situated. In Jerusalem this was twenty cubits in length while in Tell Ta'yinat it was only ten cubits. The Tell Ta'yinat sanctuary was thus twice as long as the inner sanctuary of the Jerusalem Temple.

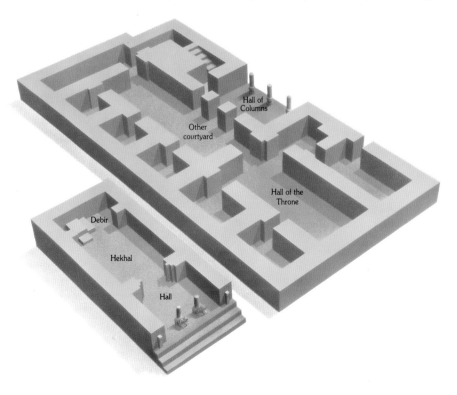

Hall of Columns

Other courtyard

Hall of the Throne

Debir

Hekhal

Hall

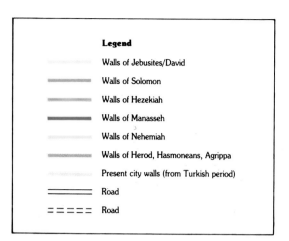

Legend

——————— Walls of Jebusites/David

══════════ Walls of Solomon

——————— Walls of Hezekiah

━━━━━━━ Walls of Manasseh

——————— Walls of Nehemiah

··········· Walls of Herod, Hasmoneans, Agrippa

- - - - - - Present city walls (from Turkish period)

═══════ Road

= = = = = Road

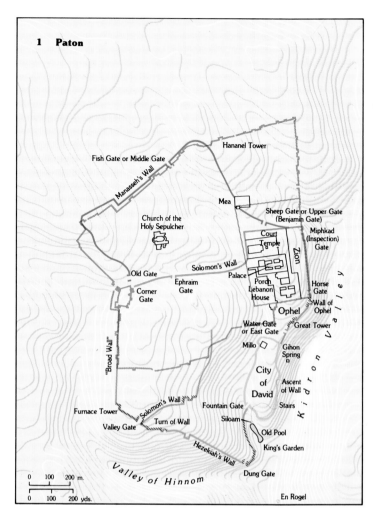

These six plans of the city of Jerusalem were drawn by the explorers **Paton** (1908), **Dalman** (1930), **Galling** (1937), **Simons** (1952), **Kenyon** (1967, 1974), and **Avigad** (1980). These maps are the result of research based mainly on details given in the Book of Nehemiah. Although the Book of Nehemiah describes the situation in the city after the Return to Zion, the scholars who were faced with the lack of sufficient archaeological evidence, tried to relate the information contained in this Book of the Bible to the First Temple period. This was the basis upon which these plans were drawn up.

Paton's map (1) depicts the city during the reign of Manasseh and Hezekiah as including the entire area of the western hill, but in Paton's opinion the course of Manasseh's wall is identical in many of its sections to that of the present-day wall of the Old City. One of the factors which brought him to this conclusion was that the Siloam Pool was included within the city walls in Hezekiah's time. It is thus obvious to him that the course of the city wall was identical with that of the present day, that is, south of the City of David and Mount Zion.

Dalman's map (2) is suggestive of contemporary theories (supporting the maximalist approach) as regards the development of the city at the end of the First Temple period. This approach to the development of the city in Nehemiah's time is found in two more maps—those of Paton (1) and Simons (4). Simons describes Nehemiah as the Josephus of the biblical era, and makes the assumption that the Book of Nehemiah provides a picture of Jerusalem before the destruction and immediately after. Despite Simons's scholarly analysis, the question arises as to the reliability of the biblical source, since the excavations in the Jewish Quarter, on Mount Zion, and in the Armenian Quarter have proved that in the time of Nehemiah Jerusalem's western hill was not inhabited, but at the time of the destruction these areas were at least partly inhabited. Thus, in actual fact, it is not possible to conceive the boundaries of Jerusalem before the destruction as being identical with those of the post-destruction period.

Galling's map (3) shows the expansion of Jerusalem at the end of the First Temple period. According to this plan the course of the wall built by Nehemiah was identical to that which existed prior to the destruction. Galling believed that the verse: "that the walls of Jerusalem were made up, and that the breaches began to be stopped" (Neh. 4:7) referred to the fact that the walls were reconstructed and repaired and not rebuilt.

Map 5 reflects two theories put forward by Kathleen Kenyon. In 1967 she estimated that the area of Jerusalem was restricted to the hill of the City of David. In her second theory posited in 1974, her point of departure was different. Not only did she base it on her own excavations, but she also referred to Prof. Avigad's findings (map 6) when he unearthed a section of the "Broad Wall" in his excavations of the Jewish Quarter. Her updated plan is similar to that of Galling, but it is difficult to comprehend the basis of her precise definition of the course of the wall.

Avigad (map 6), following his excavations in the present-day Jewish Quarter, the eastern part of the Armenian Quarter, and discoveries elsewhere, concluded that the alignment of the city wall in the later phase of the Judean kingdom is identical to that of the First Wall of the Second Temple period. This was based on the writings of Josephus, who attributed the First Wall to the Davidic dynasty, and on Avigad's own findings in which he found that at some points the two walls abutted one another. Some structures not coinciding with the general alignment of the fortifications are thought by Avigad to be of a later phase fortification scheme. The map represents the maximalist view concerning the expansion of the late pre-exilic period of Jerusalem, a theory which still requires further proof.

The lack of clarity regarding the boundaries of the city in two periods—the end of the First Temple period and Nehemiah's time—is the consequence of the scholars' assumption that the two periods were identical. This theory has existed over the decades of research of the topography of Jerusalem. However, today, after the most recent excavations, it has become obvious that the two must be separated, while still accepting that in certain places Nehemiah's wall was constructed upon the remains of the earlier wall.

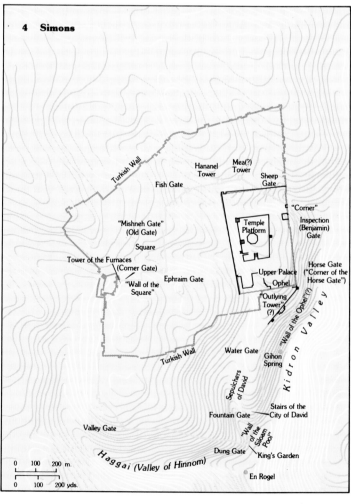

31

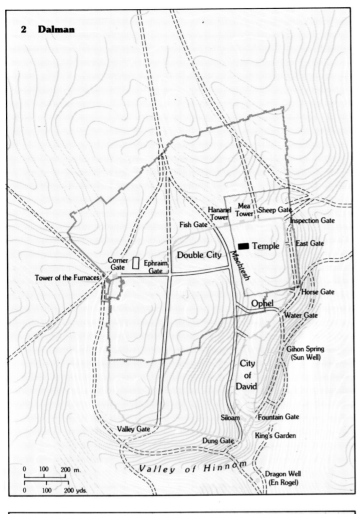

2 Dalman

Hananel Tower
Mea Tower
Sheep Gate
Fish Gate
Inspection Gate
Temple
East Gate
Double City
Makhtesh
Corner Gate
Ephraim Gate
Tower of the Furnaces
Horse Gate
Ophel
Water Gate
City of David
Gihon Spring (Sun Well)
Siloam
Fountain Gate
Valley Gate
King's Garden
Dung Gate
Valley of Hinnom
Dragon Well (En Rogel)

0 100 200 m.
0 100 200 yds.

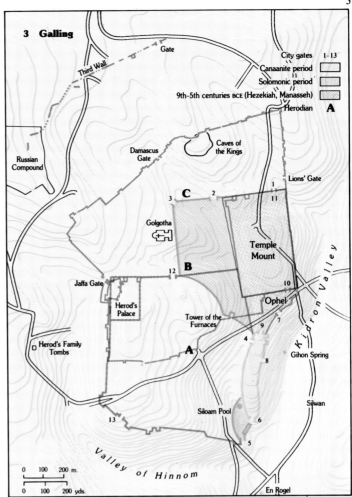

3 Galling

Third Wall
Gate
City gates 1–13
Canaanite period
Solomonic period
9th–5th centuries BCE (Hezekiah, Manasseh)
Herodian A
Russian Compound
Damascus Gate
Caves of the Kings
Lions' Gate
C 3 2 1 11
Golgotha
Temple Mount
B 12
Jaffa Gate
Herod's Palace
10 Ophel
9 7
Tower of the Furnaces
A 4
8 Gihon Spring
Herod's Family Tombs
Silwan
Siloam Pool
6
13
5
Valley of Hinnom
En Rogel
Kidron Valley

0 100 200 m.
0 100 200 yds.

5 Kenyon

Temple Platform (Herodian)
Excavated wall
1974
1967
Gihon Spring

0 100 200 m.
0 100 200 yds.

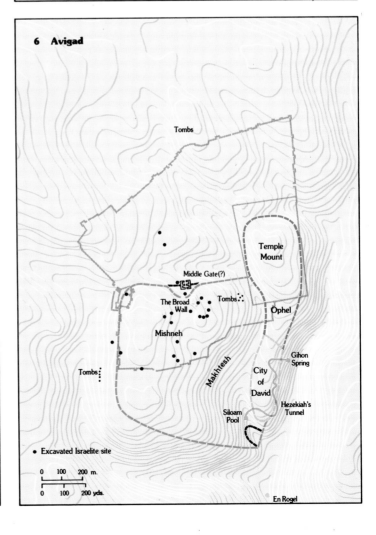

6 Avigad

Tombs
Temple Mount
Middle Gate(?)
The Broad Wall
Tombs
Mishneh
Ophel
Makhtesh
Tombs
City of David
Gihon Spring
Hezekiah's Tunnel
Siloam Pool
• Excavated Israelite site
En Rogel

0 100 200 m.
0 100 200 yds.

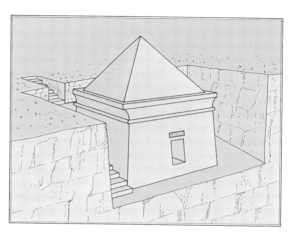

(center left) The **Tomb of Pharaoh's Daughter** in the village of Siloam, is called thus because of a tradition popular among the Arabs of the region that any strange phenomenon that occurs has to be connected to Pharaoh. Thus, for example, the "Absalom's Pillar" in the same area is called in Arabic "Pharaoh's Headdress." The biblical description of the house of Solomon's wife— Pharaoh's daughter—made it easier for the Jews to accept the designation "Tomb of Pharaoh's Daughter" (2 Kings 9:24).

This is a nobleman's tomb, expertly constructed. The structure underwent many changes during the Byzantine period, when a cell was hewn out to serve as a habitation for monks. Furthermore, the pyramid on its roof was taken down for the use of the stone, the small opening was enlarged toward the lintel, and the inscription carved above the original opening was removed. Only two letters have remained—*vav* and *reish*. They may possibly be the final letters of the word *arur* (cursed) which was part of a sentence "cursed be he who opens this grave," an inscription found on other tombs in this area from the First Temple period.

(above and below) Two **tomb inscriptions** discovered by the French scholar Charles Clermont-Ganneau in 1870 in the village of Siloam, near Jerusalem. These inscriptions are from one of the most elaborate tombs found in this area, where there is the largest concentration of tombs from the First Temple period in biblical Jerusalem.

The larger inscription reads: "This is the tomb of ... Yahu who is over the house. There is no silver and no gold here, only his bones and the bones of his slave wife (who is) with him. Cursed be he who will open this." It would seem that this is the tomb of a nobleman, and it is certainly possible that the remaining letters of the inscription—*yod, heh, vav*—are the final letters of the name Shebna which appears in Isaiah: "Go, get thee unto this treasurer, even unto Shebna, which is over the house, and say, What hast thou here? and whom hast thou here, that thou hast hewed thee out a sepulchre here, as he that heweth him out a sepulchre on high, and that graveth an habitation for himself in a rock?" (22:15-16). The second inscription was found carved in the rock at the entrance to another chamber nearby. The inscription reads: *heder be-katef ha-tzur*, meaning "a room behind the rock," or another interpretation, *heder be-katef ha-tzariah*, meaning "a room behind the cave." Both these versions show that it was the intention of the builders of the tomb to warn builders of other tombs that in addition to the large burial chamber there was another chamber, and therefore they should not excavate in that vicinity.

(bottom left) **Burial caves in the courtyard of the St. Etiénne monastery**. At the end of the nineteenth century when the Church of St. Etiénne (St. Stephen's Church) was rebuilt, two large burial caves were discovered in the courtyard. The archaeologist who excavated them did not date them accurately, and only in the course of time when the type of burial cave dating to the end of the First Temple period was identified (eighth to seventh centuries BCE) it became apparent that these burial caves belonged to a necropolis in the north of the city from this period. Characteristic of this type of tomb was the burial chamber which generally contained three shelves laid around its walls (excluding the entrance side). The corpse was placed on the shelf with its head resting in a recess in the form of a pillow hewn out of the rock. Some of these "pillows" were formed in the style of the hair of the Egyptian goddess Hathor. A further decoration in the cave was a cornice which ran along the length of the chamber walls where they join up with the ceiling. The majority of the burial chambers had pits used as receptacles for bones (the bones of the dead buried earlier were placed in them to make room for other bodies). Three stairs led to the shelf above the opening and it would seem that this was the most distinguished shelf of the three in the chamber. The second burial chamber, which is not described here, now serves as a burial cave for monks. Some renowned scholars of Palestine have also been buried here, such as Father F. M. Abel, Father L. H. Vincent, Father R. de Vaux, and Father P. Benoit.

These two caves are among the most beautiful First Temple period burial caves discovered so far. Of late, conjecture has been put forward that these might be the caves referred to by Josephus as the "Royal Caves" (in his description of the Third Wall), but so far no proof has been found to support this theory. Other burial caves have been discovered north of Damascus Gate, thus showing that this was an accepted burial ground at the end of the First Temple period.

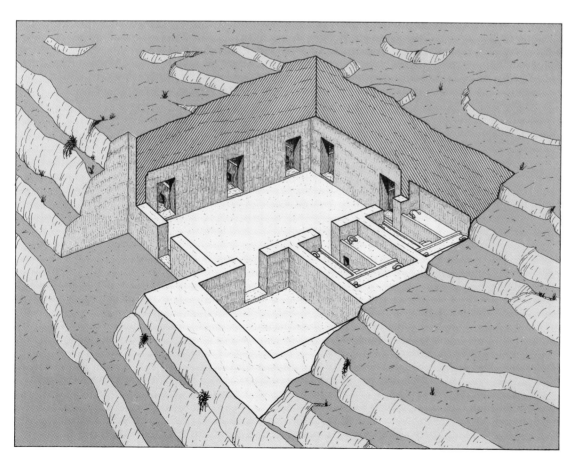

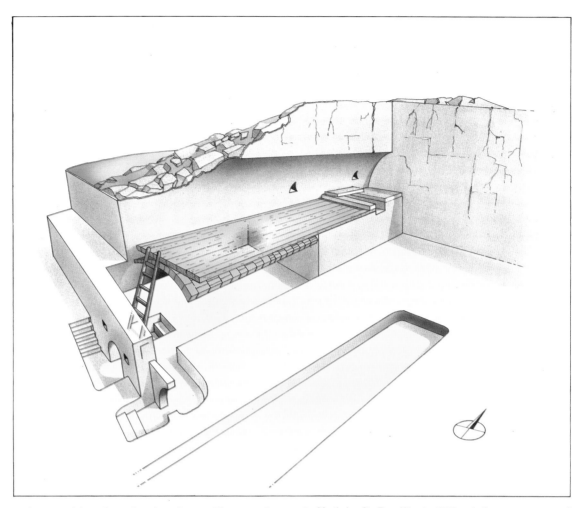

(right) **Tombs T1 and T2**.
In the excavations carried out in the City of David in 1913–1914, R. Weill uncovered stone quarries from the Roman period. These quarries damaged some areas of the City of David, then outside the walls of the Roman city. Many remains were found from the pre-Roman period which had been badly damaged by the quarrying. Among these finds were two artificially cut caves which Weill believed were the tombs of kings of the Davidic dynasty. Very little has remained of that named T2, while there are enough remains of T1 to reconstruct the outlines of the tomb.

Weill believed that there were two stages to the building of the tomb. In the first stage a passageway was excavated 52.5 feet (16 m.) long, the entrance to which was in the south. Near the northern end of the passageway, slightly above floor level, a niche was made into which the corpse was placed (or perhaps the sarcophagus). The passageway was then sealed off with stone slabs. Triangular niches were made in the wall along the passageway for candles, a fact which confirms the multiple use of the site. In the course of time, the necropolis became overcrowded, a fact that is borne out by the Bible which describes the burial place of the first kings of the Davidic dynasty thus: "And he was laid to rest with his fathers in the City of David." The later description of the burial place was the "City of David" and not "the sepulchre of the kings" (thus Jehoram and Joash). Later, the "Garden of Uzzah" is referred to as the burial place. In the second stage an additional passageway was dug and an additional opening was made under the forward section of the first passageway. Most of this opening remained, as well as the stairs that led to it. It appears that the new sarcophagus was placed at the end of the lower passageway, and obviously when this excavation was carried out, direct contact with the sarcophagus in the upper level was cut off. To this end incisions were made in the walls on both sides of the passageway which served to support a wooden dome upon which a new floor (also made of wood) to the upper passageway was laid.

As the site was turned into a quarry during the Roman period, and both parts of the passageway were broken into, all the accompanying objects in the tomb were stolen. Thus, we do not have any definitive proof of the use of this structure, its exact date, or whether this actually was the burial place of the kings of the Davidic dynasty.

(right) **"This is the tomb ... who opens it"** are the words of a Hebrew inscription carved in a rock, discovered in 1946 in the village of Siloam. The inscription was engraved above the facade of a First Temple burial cave hewn out of the rock. The villagers of Siloam sealed the cave and turned it into a water cistern, which still serves them to this day. The inscription, which was intact after the Six-Day War of 1967, has recently been despoiled by inhabitants of the village.

to this period have been found, and it would appear that they were situated outside the city confines. The assumption that many installations of the city were outside its walls is reinforced by the recent discovery that the northernmost of the two Sheep's Pools (the Bethesda Pools) was also built about the time of Hezekiah, when a dam was erected across the Beth Zetha Valley to catch the floodwaters from this valley. An opening was made in this dam for draining off waters to a conduit, which would seem to be the conduit known from the time of the Assyrian siege: "They came and stood by the conduit of the upper pool, which is in the highway of the fuller's field" (2 Kings 18:17). The biblical description of Sennacherib's siege would seem to infer that the people besieged within the city were located to the north of the Temple Mount in the vicinity of the conduit branching off the dam.

A further source for comprehending the extent of the city's expansion is to be found in the cemeteries surrounding it. Until the Six-Day War in 1967, scholars were aware of the existence of a cemetery within the City of David and one in the village of Siloam. The graves in Siloam are a particularly good example of the method of burial employed in Jerusalem during the First Temple period. In the course of the excavations carried out at the Western Wall, additional graves from this period were discovered west of Robinson's Arch. However, neither of these groups of graves has added to our knowledge of the city during the First Temple period, since geographically they were in close proximity to the hill of the City of David, and the connection between the graves and the hill was obvious.

It was only with the discovery of a group of graves in the north of the city, in the vicinity of the Damascus Gate and to the north of it, that the city had a magnificent necropolis, befitting a large and important city. Some of the graves unearthed in the north of the city—in the courtyard of St. Etiénne's (St. Stephen's) Monastery—are the most magnificent yet found in Israel. It would appear that a number of graves from this period exists in the present-day Christian Quarter (one was found in the Coptic Patriarchate near the Holy Sepulcher), and others have been discovered on the city's western slopes in the direction of the Sultan's Pool. Another cluster of graves is located in the riverbed of the Hinnom Valley, and a further one has recently been discovered on the hill upon which St. Andrew's Church stands, where a rich crop of archaeological finds has been uncovered. A number of graves were unearthed some time ago in Mamilla Street. Thus it is clear that the necropolis extended over a large area of the city. Even if this fact alone does not assist us in determining the exact boundaries, the abundance of other findings throughout the city is proof of the city's magnitude during the two centuries prior to the destruction of the First Temple.

The Second Temple Period

538 BCE – 70 CE

A coin on which the word **Yehud** is inscribed. Coins of this type, in silver or bronze, were minted in the country at the end of the fourth or beginning of the third century BCE. On one side there was an eagle with outspread wings, an owl or some other winged animal, as well as the inscription Yehud. It appears that the coins were minted in Jerusalem which was the capital of the province of Judea at that time. However, the coin does not show any particular connection to the city, nor does it have any typically Jewish symbols. Similar coins were minted in Judea at the beginning of the Hellenistic period bearing the image of Ptolemy I, who ruled over the country from 301 to 258 BCE.

The Second Temple period lasted for over 600 years, from the Proclamation of Cyrus up to the destruction of the Second Temple. In the course of this period Jerusalem's image changed, and from a small partly destroyed settlement it became one of the most important and famous cities in the Orient.

This chapter of the city's history is divided into three sections: the times of Nehemiah, the Hasmoneans, and the period of the reign of the Herodian kings.

The map at the beginning of this chapter showing Jerusalem on the eve of its destruction by the Romans, refers to all three periods. It is based on archaeological findings, historical sources and an attempt to link them together. Sites which have not been conclusively identified appear in the map by name but with no exact placement.

From the Return to Zion to the Hasmonean Period

After the destruction of the First Temple in 586 BCE Jerusalem was once again reduced to the area of the City of David and the Temple Mount. The western section (the Western Hill) was still surrounded by the remains of the city wall several feet in height, but the area within it apparently lay largely in ruins. According to the description in the Book of Nehemiah and archaeological finds, Jerusalem was a devastated city, and its demolished walls served as some sort of defense for its few inhabitants.

The Proclamation of Cyrus, given in 538 BCE, was the beginning of a process which brought about the restitution of the spiritual and political life of the Jews in their land. Cyrus gave permission for the Jews to return to Judea and to resurrect their Temple from its ruins. Twenty-two years later (516 BCE), the restored Temple was dedicated under the leadership of Jeshua ben Yozadak and Zerubavel ben Shaltiel. Huge amounts of money were contributed for the erection of the Second Temple, cedar wood was brought from Lebanon and stone and wood cutters came from Tyre and Sidon to assist in the construction work. The dedication ceremony of the Second Temple was a grand and impressive event, and the priests and Levites once more began to carry out their holy duties and the rituals were resumed. Jerusalem, now the capital of the Persian province of Yehud, was once more the center of life in Judea. Evidence of this is found in many seals from this period unearthed in archaeological excavations. Even so, it remained desolate for many years to come. From the time of the dedication of the Temple until

the arrival of Ezra the Scribe (58 years later), Jerusalem was ruled by persons who did not leave their mark on the history of the city.

Ezra the Scribe, who held a high position at the court of Artaxerxes I, king of Persia, came to Jerusalem from Babylon in the year 457 BCE at the head of a column of returnees. On the basis of the authorization granted him by the king, Ezra strove to spread the Torah, to strengthen the faith of the Jews and to renew the ritual in the Temple. It was only when Nehemiah reached Jerusalem that their joint efforts resulted in the introduction of a comprehensive reform.

Nehemiah came to Jerusalem in 445 BCE and brought about a major change in the city. Soon after his arrival he realized that it was essential to restore the walls and quickly set about putting his plan into action. The description of his nocturnal reconnaissance of the condition of the fortifications tells us of the course of the ruined walls. He began his rounds by leaving by the Valley Gate at the northwest of the City of David. From there he walked along the Tyropoeon Valley to the Dragon Well (probably En Rogel; according to this designation, the Dung Gate would be situated in the vicinity of the Siloam Pool). From the Dragon Well he turned in an easterly direction, climbed the western slopes of the Kidron Valley and looked down upon the ruined city walls lying halfway down the slope. From the northeastern corner of the City of David he turned to the west and went down the Tyropoeon Valley and returned to the Valley Gate.

The Jewish inhabitants labored fifty-two days to restore the walls of Jerusalem. Their enemies—the Ammonites, Arabians, and Ashdodites—who were living in the country at that time harassed the builders who were forced to defend themselves, as described in the Book of Nehemiah (4:17): "every one with one of his hands wrought in the work, and with the other hand held a weapon." The labor was divided among the priestly families, the inhabitants of the towns and villages in Judea, and the noble families in Jerusalem, and each group was assigned a section of the wall to be built or restored. The order of the sections enables us to trace the course of the wall at the time of its restoration. However, only a few sites along the wall have been identified conclusively. Among these are the Broad Wall, the Valley Gate, the Dung Gate, the Fountain Gate, the wall of the Siloam Pool, and the slopes of the City of David. Upon the completion of the building, a ceremony was held to mark

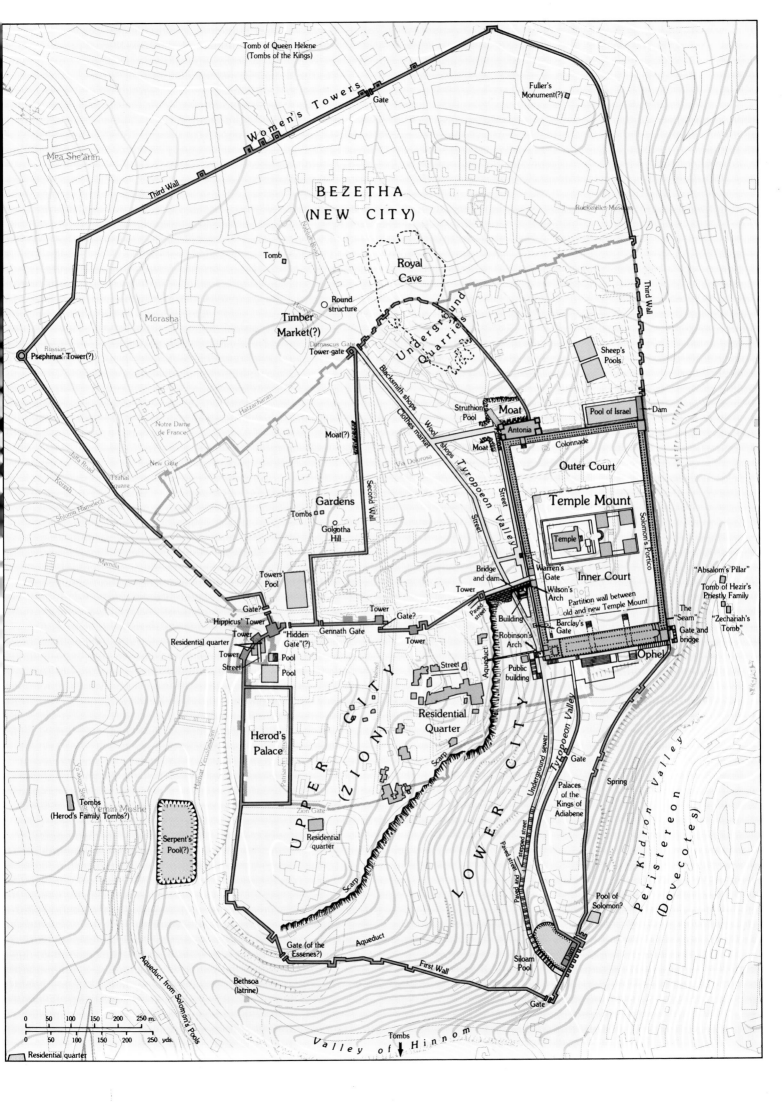

Tomb of Queen Helene
(Tombs of the Kings)

Women's Towers

Gate

Mea She'arim

Third Wall

BEZETHA
(NEW CITY)

Fuller's
Monument(?)

Third Wall

Rockefeller Museum

Tomb

Royal
Cave

Morasha

Round
structure

Underground
Quarries

Russian

Psephinus' Tower(?)

Timber
Market(?)

Damascus Gate
Tower-gate

Notre Dame
de France

Blacksmith shops

Wool shops

Struthion
Pool

Sheep's
Pools

Moat

Antonia

Moat

Pool of Israel

Dam

New Gate

Jaffa Road

Tzahal
Square

Moat(?)

Clothes market

Tyropoeon Valley

Street

Colonnade

Outer Court

Shlomo Hamelech

Gardens

Second Wall

Tombs

Golgotha
Hill

Temple Mount

Temple

Solomon's Portico

Towers'
Pool

Towers'
Pool

Bridge
and dam

Warren's
Gate

Inner Court

"Absalom's Pillar"

Tomb of Hezir's
Priestly Family

Wilson's
Arch

Partition wall between
old and new Temple Mount

"Zechariah's
Tomb"

Hippicus' Tower

Tower

Gate?

Residential quarter

Tower
Street

Gate?

Tower

"Hidden
Gate"(?)

Gennath Gate

Tower

Building

Barclay's
Gate

Robinson's
Arch

The
"Seam"

Gate and
bridge

Pool

Pool

Paved street

Aqueduct

Public
building

Ophel

Street

Herod's
Palace

U P P E R   C I T Y

(Z I O N)

Residential
Quarter

Scarp

L O W E R   C I T Y

Underground sewer

Tyropoeon Valley

Gate

Palaces
of the
Kings of
Adiabene

Spring

Kidron Valley

Peristereon

(Dovecotes)

Zion Gate

Residential
quarter

Tombs
(Herod's Family Tombs?)

Yemin Moshe

Serpent's
Pool(?)

Scarp

Paved street

Paved stepped street

Pool of
Solomon?

Aqueduct from Solomon's Pools

Gate (of the
Essenes?)

Aqueduct

First Wall

Siloam
Pool

Bethsoa
(latrine)

Gate

0   50   100   150   200   250 m.

0   50   100   150   200   250 yds.

Residential quarter

Tombs

Valley of Hinnom

(right) **Map of Jerusalem in the time of Nehemiah** based on verses in the Book of Nehemiah (2:12-15; 3:1-33; 12:31-39) and archaeological discoveries made in the City of David, especially those relating to the city wall during this period.

The course of the city wall in the map is based on that of the First Temple period wall, and the names are those mentioned in the Book of Nehemiah. Even though the First Temple period walls are not completely identical with those of Nehemiah's time, there was no significant change in certain sections, such as was made on the Temple Mount. The references in the Book of Nehemiah, and especially those describing the erection of the wall, make it possible to identify various sites, but in this map we have marked only those places which can be reasonably identified *in situ*. Thus, for example, the Water Gate mentioned in the Book of Nehemiah (12:37) was found in the City of David, in the area above the Gihon Spring. This was at the site of the Old Gate which had been demolished at the time of the destruction of the First Temple. Since a new wall was built in Nehemiah's days and no gate was found in that region, the location of the Water Gate has been marked at the spot where the remains were found.

(below right) In his description of the First Wall which surrounded the Upper City, Josephus states that the northeastern wall ended in the vicinity of the western portico of the Temple Mount, in the direction of the **Council Building**. This building was generally identified with the **Chamber of Hewn Stones**, mentioned in the sources, which was situated in the vicinity of the Temple Mount. (In the late Ottoman period, Jerusalem Jews used the name Chamber of Hewn Stones to refer to the Mahkama, a Mamluk building situated to the west of the Temple Mount, near the Gate of the Chain.)

In the course of his excavations in Jerusalem during 1867-1869, Warren discovered a hall near Wilson's Arch which he named the Hall of the Freemasons. The illustration presented here is a reconstruction of the hall based on the remains found there.

The magnificent architectural style and its resemblance to other buildings from the Herodian era make it possible to date the hall to this period. The capitals have been reconstructed here as copies of the capital situated in the far right corner, which has remained intact. An additional pillar, apparently added during the Middle Ages, is situated in the middle of the hall (not reproduced here).

It is difficult to determine whether this was definitely the council building that existed in Jerusalem under the Hasmoneans, but it undoubtedly served some public function. Hardly any vestiges of Second Temple building in Jerusalem of such grandeur have remained, and this hall is a unique example of the high standard of architecture in the city during this period.

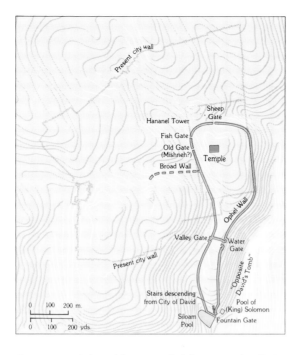

the event, and the celebrants circled the restored walls in two columns—one came down from the Temple Mount to the City of David and passed the Dung Gate, the ascent to the City of David, the Water Gate, and other sites. The second column circled the city in the opposite direction and they converged at the Temple Mount.

Even after the restoration of the walls, the city's population remained small: "Now the city was large and great: but the people were few therein, and the houses were not builded" (Neh. 7:4). The restoration of the walls was of greater importance than the provision of physical defense of the city's inhabitants. The fortifications enhanced Jerusalem's status as the nation's spiritual center, preserving its uniqueness and distinguishing it from the other peoples of the region. The description of the city in the Book of Nehemiah shows that in his time its dimensions were smaller than in the First Temple period. The new wall was built slightly to the east of the crest of the City of David, and as a result the eastern section of the hill of the City of David and the wall enclosing it were not yet included within the boundaries of Jerusalem.

We are still not certain of the course of the eastern wall

in the time of Nehemiah. It is currently considered that the remains uncovered by Kathleen Kenyon, which she believed to be the ruins of the wall, are in fact remains of quarries and retaining walls built inside them. These remains are evidence of extensive construction works carried out throughout the entire city, and it is possible that it was from here that stone was quarried for the construction of the walls. The descriptions of this period provide information about the walls only. There is almost no evidence available about other buildings or structures within the confines of the city itself. Apart from the houses of some local wealthy inhabitants mentioned in the Book of Nehemiah, a number of sites are referred to which can be identified with a certain amount of accuracy. These are the Broad Wall from the First Temple period, the Valley Gate, and the structures in the vicinity of the Siloam Pool (including the Dung Gate, the Fountain Gate, and the Siloam Pool wall). Another group of structures has been found to the north of the Temple Mount, among which were the Sheep's Gate, the Mea Tower and the Hananel Tower. However, their exact location is not known.

The hill of the City of David and the Temple Mount continued to be the focal points of the city. This is borne out by the abundance of archaeological finds dating to the fourth and third centuries BCE made in the City of David, in comparison with the scarcity of similar finds on the Western Hill. However, it would seem that the expansion in the direction of the Western Hill commenced prior to the Hasmonean period.

A number of sources, such as the Letter of Aristeas written at the end of the third or the beginning of the second century BCE, provide evidence of extensive building projects in Jerusalem during that period. The largest of all was the erection of the Birah fortress (Baris in Greek), at the northwestern corner of the Temple Mount, on the site where the Antonia fortress was built later. The Birah fortress, with its many towers, kept guard over the Temple and its surroundings. Other building projects were bound up with the provision of water for the Temple, such as the underground water supply system which brought water through conduits from the springs outside the city. It appears that at the same time the two Sheep's Pools were built (one was actually built during the First Temple period), renovations were made inside the Temple and on its paved forecourt, and the walls were reinforced.

The Book of Nehemiah, the Timocharus writings and the Letter of Aristeas are the only written historical records available relating to the history of Jerusalem from the Return

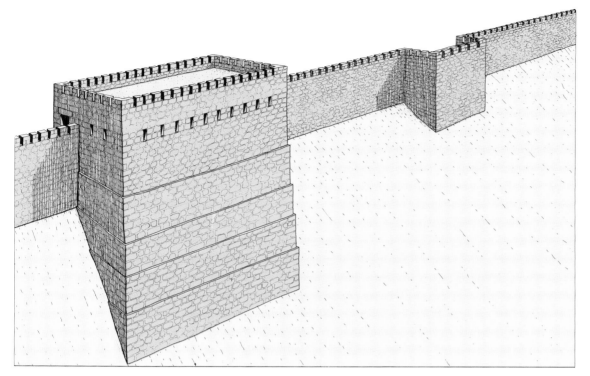

(left) The eastern section of the **First Wall** and its **two towers** in area G of the City of David. The two towers were discovered by Macalister and Duncan during their archaeological excavations of this site in 1923. They named this site the "Jebusite Bastion." From the excavations carried out here by Kenyon and Shiloh, it is now obvious that these are the remains of Hasmonean fortifications, even though Hasmonean-style cut stone such as those from the northern or western section of this wall have not been found. The Book of Maccabees makes reference to the fact that restoration work was carried out on the walls of Jerusalem on a number of occasions by the Hasmonean rulers. In addition, we find that the style of building is not always identical. This leads us to the conclusion that certain sections of the wall were built at different times. The illustration shows the glacis which was laid by the Hasmoneans, built of sloping layers of soil and limestone laid in a manner which prevented the enemy from reaching the structure's foundations. The glacis concealed the terraced structure and the remains of the First Temple buildings.

to Zion up to the Hasmonean period, a period of approximately 350 years.

The Hasmonean Period

The main source for the study of the Hasmonean period is provided by the Books of the Maccabees. Additional information is derived from archaeological excavations, as well as other sources.

The City of David area, which was inhabited at the end of the First Temple period, was abandoned after the destruction of the Temple and remained desolate during the period of the Return to Zion. At the time of the outbreak of the Hasmonean revolt (167 BCE), Jerusalem was still confined within the boundaries of the City of David and the Temple Mount as it was in the days of Nehemiah. The beginning of Jerusalem's expansion to the west on the eve of the Hasmonean period was one of the most important milestones in its development. Apparently the First Temple period walls (such as the Broad Wall) were still visible above ground and

served as the boundary for the renewed expansion of the city.

It is difficult to date with accuracy the beginning of the renewed settlement on the Western Hill, but it would appear that it commenced at the beginning of the second century BCE, after the victory of Antiochus III over the forces of the Ptolemies (200 BCE). It was during this period, under the rule of the Seleucid dynasty (whose center was in Antioch in northern Syria), that the struggle took place over the nation's spiritual image and for the control of Jerusalem. The penetration of Hellenistic culture into the country, and especially into Jerusalem was accelerated. Groups of Hellenizers, who held positions of power, assisted in this process, which was expressed in the development of the Upper City area, which at the end of the Hasmonean period became Jerusalem's main urban center.

The greatest building project during the Hasmonean period was the construction of the wall, which Josephus called the Old Wall (*Wars* 5, 4, 2). Archaeological excavations carried out on various sites in the city have provided proof that

(below right) **Map** showing the battles fought by the Maccabees to liberate Judea from the yoke of the Seleucids. The Hasmonean revolt began in Modiin, but the battles fought against the Seleucids and their allies, who sent reinforcements from outside Judea, began in the vicinity of the Gophna Hills. They then moved south to Beth Zur, and from there to the north, with Jerusalem as the focal point.

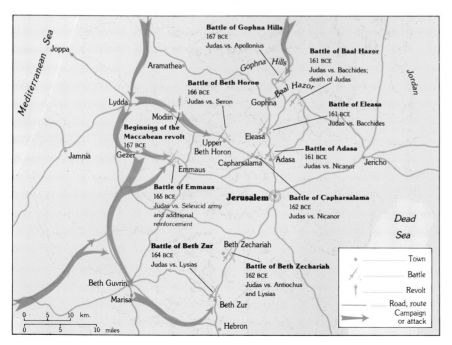
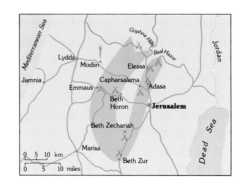

(left) **Map of the battles for the liberation of Judea** from the Seleucids. The Seleucid army was based in Jerusalem, and even though the battles took place some distance from the city, Jerusalem remained the focal point of the campaign.

The map shows the Hasmoneans' attempts to prevent the foreign forces reaching Jerusalem to join up with the Seleucids under siege in the Acra. The battles took place on the main routes leading to the city, and the Hasmonean strategy was to defend these routes. The map illustrates the vital role Jerusalem filled during the Second Temple period in general, and especially at the end of the Hasmonean era.

this wall was built in the middle of the second century BCE. This fact is supported by the Book of Maccabees (1, 10, 10), according to which Jonathan the Hasmonean began the construction of the city walls and building on Mount Zion. This project was completed by his brother Simon (Maccabees 1, 13, 1). The builders of this wall incorporated remains of the First Temple period wall, and perhaps this was the cause of Josephus' erroneous dating of the construction of the First Wall (the Old Wall) to the period of the Davidic dynasty.

It appears that the Hasmonean wall was built in stages. The first stage was the erection of the wall in the western sector of the Western Hill. The eastern side was protected by an escarpment which was cut perpendicularly (its remains are still visible underneath the houses of the Jewish Quarter facing the Western Wall square). This escarpment also protected the southern sector of the city until the completion of that section of the wall which began at the southernmost point of the City of David fortifications, near the Siloam Pool. The lack of uniformity in the building style, which can be seen in the sections themselves, is proof that it was not built at one time, and that various builders were involved in its construction.

The Upper City

The erection of the First Wall during a period in which cultural–political processes took place in Jerusalem, as described in the Books of the Maccabees, raises two questions: what were the reasons for the expansion of the city to the Western Hill; and what was the character of the Upper

(below) **Map of Jerusalem in the Hasmonean era** showing only those sites whose location has been established beyond doubt based on the results of archaeological excavations carried out in the city. Structures from this period, known from historical sources only, have not been included in the map. Thus, for example, the built-up area within the present-day Jewish Quarter does not appear. The Hasmonean dynasty palace is delineated on the map in silhouette.

The course of the First Wall built by the Hasmoneans is one of the few details on the map which is not a matter of controversy. The location of the Temple Mount and the Baris has been definitively established, but their exact dimensions and shape during this period are still a matter of contention. The dimensions of the Hasmonean Temple Mount appear in the Mishnah (500 × 500 cubits), but the topography around the Temple Mount makes it impossible to conceive it as forming a complete square, but rather a square whose northeastern boundary is curved.

The location of the Acra is also a matter of controversy among scholars. It has been marked here according to one of the theories based on the findings in excavations carried out south of the Temple Mount.

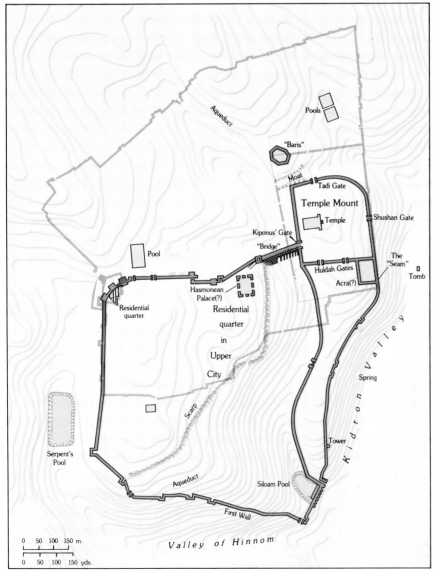

Aqueduct

Pools

"Baris"

Moat

Tadi Gate

Temple Mount

Temple

Shushan Gate

Kiponus' Gate

"Bridge"

Pool

The "Seam"

Tomb

Huldah Gates

Hasmonean Palace(?)

Acra(?)

Residential quarter

Residential quarter in Upper City

Scarp

Spring

Serpent's Pool

Tower

Kidron Valley

Aqueduct

Siloam Pool

First Wall

Valley of Hinnom

0 50 100 150 m.

0 50 100 150 yds.

City established there? One of the reasons for the city's expansion was probably the rising population density of the City of David. A further reason was the desire of the Hellenizers to make Jerusalem a city based on a Hellenistic pattern, and to this end a wider expanse was required. This was available on the Western Hill. Thus, during the Hasmonean period the Hellenistic style of building became predominant in the western sector of the city, especially in the houses of the rich. The finds from archaeological excavations uphold Josephus' accounts. In his writings mention is made of the Boule (the city council building), the gymnasium and the *kesistos* (a courtyard surrounded by pillars which was generally attached to the gymnasium). These buildings are an integral part of every Hellenistic city. The Hasmoneans also built a palace in the Upper City, in the area overlooking the Temple Mount (*Wars* 2, 17, 3). Agrippa II embellished the palace and added a special wing from which he would look toward the Temple Mount (*Antiquities* 20, 89). Because of the lack of remains from this period it is difficult to present a complete picture of the Hellenistic city established on the Western Hill. One of the reasons for this was that the city was rebuilt in Herod's time, and since the Herodian massive type of building required deep foundations, many buildings from the preceding Hasmonean period were pulled down and disappeared. Thus it can be seen that the Western Hill was settled in the Hasmonean period and played an important role in Jerusalem's urban system up to the destruction of the Second Temple.

The Temple Mount

There are no available sources for the description of the manner in which the Temple Mount was erected by the returnees to Zion. However, from the classification of archaeological finds and inferences in Josephus' writings, as well as descriptions in the Mishnah, we are able to presume that vast changes were made in the Temple Mount area during the Hasmonean period. According to Josephus, a valley to the south of the Temple Mount was closed off in order to exalt the mount itself (*Wars* 5, 4, 1). They also leveled the mountain where the Acra fortress stood

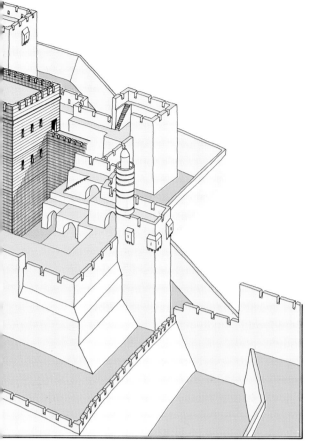

(right) A **Hasmonean period residential quarter** found underneath Herodian dwellings in one of the corners of the Citadel. The houses in this quarter were built close to the city wall, and the direction they faced was contingent upon the course of the wall. When Herod ascended the throne the entire region underwent a major change. The Hasmonean period roofs were removed, and the rooms filled up with earth. These earth-filled foundations served as the basis for a new residential quarter, facing in the general direction of the recently built houses. Herod's palace was built to the south and to the north of the Hippicus Tower, today called David's Tower. Following the destruction of the Second Temple, the Tenth Roman Legion encamped on this site.

(left) The Hasmonean period **Citadel** was situated in the northwest corner of the Upper City, after the area was annexed to Jerusalem in the late second century BCE, when the city expanded beyond the boundaries of the City of David. The First Wall built by the Hasmoneans passed through the Citadel (here it appears against the background of the present-day Citadel). The corner section

reconstructed in the illustration shows the three Hasmonean towers (shaded) which underwent significant alterations during the period of Herod's rule (see the reconstructed model from that period).

(below) **Pompey's siege of Jerusalem** in 63 BCE lasted three months, until the city wall was finally breached. From the few references made by Josephus, we learn that

Hyrcanus' men handed over the Upper City to Pompey. Thus the main effect of the siege and the thrust of the battle was concentrated around the Temple Mount. Apart from accounts of suicide carried out by civilians, who also set fire to their houses, there is no evidence of the conquest of the city's residential quarter, and it appears that the City of David was conquered only after the fall of the Temple Mount.

(see below). Contemporary scholars are of the opinion that the descriptions in the Mishnah about the Temple Mount (tractates *Kiddushim, Middot*, chapters 1, 2, 5) relate to the Hasmonean period. According to these sources, the Temple Mount was situated on a hill which had been leveled off and filled in, and on its crest was a plateau covering an area of 500 × 500 cubits (approximately 820 × 820 feet [250 × 250 meters]). There were five gates giving access to the Temple Mount: two at the south—the Huldah Gates; Kiponus' Gate at the west; the Tadi Gate at the north; and the Shushan Gate at the east. The Temple compounds described in the Mishnah are also apparently from the Hasmonean period.

During his excavations in the area of Wilson's Arch, Warren discovered the remains of a bridge constructed in the Hasmonean period, linking the Upper City with the Temple Mount. Josephus reports the destruction of this bridge in *War of the Jews* (1, 7, 2): Aristobulus burned the bridge while retreating before Pompey, and he fled from the Upper City to the Temple Mount (63 BCE). This description reveals that the Temple Mount was the site of the last stand of the defenders of Jerusalem against the Romans. The site was fortified and would seem to have been reinforced during the Hasmonean rule. Special mention must be made of the Baris fortress which existed already in Nehemiah's time (known then as the Birah) and was described in glowing terms in the Letter of Aristeas written on the eve of the Hasmonean era. According to Josephus, this fortress was built by kings of the Hasmonean dynasty (*Antiquities* 15, 403). Elsewhere he states: "When one of the priests, Hyrcanus I, built ... the Baris near the Temple, he dwelt there most of the time. ..." (*Antiquities* 18, 91). From his works it appears that the fortress served as a dwelling place for the Hasmoneans. The Hasmonean Baris was demolished and rebuilt by Herod. Only a single vestige of the Hasmonean fortress remains—a water canal hewn out of the rock below the fortress, which led to rock-cut cisterns under the present-day Temple Mount. Another point of identification, to which many legends from the Hasmonean period have been attributed, is the Acra (a Greek word meaning "the high place" or "the fortress"), built by Antiochus III. This fortress was built higher than the

Temple, so that it would be possible to observe whatever was taking place within the grounds. It was later reinforced by Bacchides. In 141 BCE it was conquered by Simon the Hasmonean and razed to the ground. Josephus relates that the hilltop on which the fortress stood was removed so that no one would even consider restoring the building.

The exact location of the Acra is unknown. Many scholars have deliberated on this problem since archaeological exploration of Jerusalem was begun. At first it was sought in the area of the present-day Jewish Quarter, at a site overlooking the Temple Mount. However, according to Josephus, the Acra stood in the place that lay between the Lower City (the hill of the City of David) and the Temple Mount (*Wars* 5, 4, 1; *Antiquities* 12, 252). If his account of the demolishing of the fortress and the removal of the hill upon which it stood is authentic, then it must be looked for in the Temple Mount area, probably in its southeastern corner. Perhaps the vestiges of an ancient building found in the vicinity of the southeastern corner of the Temple Mount are the remains of a gigantic artificial stone plinth upon which the fortress was built.

The Herodian Dynasty and the Roman Governors, 67 BCE–70 CE

Under the rule of the Herodian dynasty, Jerusalem reached the height of its prosperity as well as its optimum expansion (it was only in the nineteenth century that the city once again attained these dimensions). Archaeological findings and various descriptions from that period, mainly those by Josephus, make it possible to reconstruct one of the most magnificent construction projects ever carried out in Jerusalem.

There were a number of factors that caused Herod to embellish and fortify Jerusalem, his capital city. These were the desire to increase its economic prosperity, as well as his own personal wealth; his passion for embellishment and his desire to immortalize himself; the need to secure his sovereignty, both internally and externally; and the need to appease the people and to keep them occupied. Because of his inclination toward the Hellenistic culture and his desire to make an impression on the Roman rulers, he set out to give Jerusalem a purely Hellenistic character. This was expressed

(below) The excavations in the Jewish Quarter revealed magnificent buildings dating to the Second Temple period, attesting to the wealth of their owners. Among these edifices, the **Palatial Mansion** was most impressive.

This structure was situated on the eastern slope of the Upper City where the escarpment descends to the Tyropoeon Valley and runs between a group of magnificent

houses and the Temple Mount. The steep cliff necessitated building at different levels: the lower level held the various water installations of the house—pools, ritual baths, and cisterns—as well as storerooms. The most embellished part of the building was situated at the second level. Despite topographic difficulties, the dimensions of the building were especially large, measuring approximately 600 square meters.

The main floor was built around a central paved courtyard, underneath which water cisterns were dug. A passageway led from the courtyard to the elaborate living quarters and the servants' quarters.

The building was embellished with mosaic floors, paneled plastering, colored plastering and paneled ceilings. Few remains were found inside the building, but they bear witness to the wealth of the owners. These included tables, glass vessels, earthenware utensils, and a sundial made from soft limestone.

This building, like large sectors of the quarter, was demolished during the destruction of Jerusalem in 70 CE, when the Upper City was taken and razed to the ground on the 5th of Elul that year.

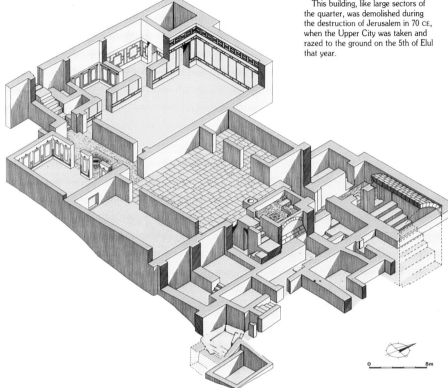

(above) **Bronze coin from the time of Matthias Antigonus**, last of the Hasmonean kings. Antigonus ruled from 40 to 37 BCE, during the period when the conflict between Herod and the Hasmoneans reached its climax. It may well be that as a result of this struggle many coins were minted during that period.

One side of the coin depicts the shewbread table surrounded by dots. Around the border is an inscription in Hebrew: "Matthias the High Priest." The inscription is distorted on most of the coins found and cannot be deciphered in the coin illustrated here.

On the obverse of the coin is the *menorah* (candelabrum) from the Temple, surrounded by an inscription in Greek: "King Antigonus." This inscription is also distorted.

(opposite below) The reconstructed room in this illustration was the largest (36 feet [11 m.] long) in the **Palatial Mansion** and it apparently served as a **reception hall** for special events.

This hall's decorations were unique: the walls were whitewashed, and adorned with large, marginally dressed stones; the ceiling was similarly decorated, but it also had triangular and hexagonal tiles. The style of decoration and construction, especially in this hall, are indicative of the Hellenistic influence, characteristic of the wealthy classes. The beauty of the structure rank it with similar buildings found throughout the Roman Empire.

in the building style, the magnitude and type of building he constructed (for example, a theater and a hippodrome). Herod built palaces, erected fortifications, reinforced the structures on the Temple Mount, and renovated the Temple, all with a magnificence previously unknown in Jerusalem. Vestiges of many of the buildings erected by Herod still remain to this day. The process of the development of the city continued unceasingly after his death (4 BCE), and building continued up to the destruction of the Second Temple (70 CE). This was especially true during the rule of Agrippa I (41–44 CE).

Herod repaired and rebuilt the First Wall, the construction of which began during the Hasmonean period. It appears that he also added the Second Wall, which accelerated the expansion of the city in a northerly direction, beyond the Upper City hill. One of the main fortifications reinforced by Herod in the First Wall was in the vicinity of the present-day Citadel. In this area, where he also built his palace (in the Upper City—*Wars* 5, 4, 3), he reinforced and embellished two towers (the Phasael and Mariamme Towers) built in the Hasmonean era. On the site of a third tower dating to that period, he built the Hippicus Tower, known today as David's Tower. Herod also fortified the Hasmonean wall south of the Citadel—originally built on a rock for the protection of the Upper City. In the course of time, he erected his palace on an elevated section in this area. The city wall became a sort of retaining wall and in order to augment it, Herod built an adjoining anterior wall. This wall was 10 feet (3.5 meters) high in some sections, and most of it later served as the basis for the Ottoman wall. Remains of these fortifications have been preserved to this day. The most striking aspect of the remains of this wall is the carved rock face surrounding Mount Zion, part of which runs underneath the Gobat School and the nearby Protestant cemetery. Archaeological finds reveal that in the vicinity of Mount Zion a gate existed in the city wall, which may well be the Gate of the Essenes through which the Essenes would emerge to relieve themselves in the Hinnom Valley at a site called Bethsoa (latrine).

The remains of the wall traced in 1894–1897 by Bliss and Dickie along the southern crest of Mount Zion, are evidence that the wall ran from the area where today the Protestant cemetery is situated, in the direction of the ancient Siloam Pool. At this point, the wall traversed the dam at the outlet of the pool, and then ran to the east and north along the eastern slopes of the City of David's hill, passed by the Ophel and linked up with the Temple Mount wall. The location of the juncture with the Temple Mount wall was found slightly to the north of the present southeast corner of the mount, called by scholars the "seam," where the two differing styles of building can be seen.

From the other side of the Hippicus Tower, the wall ran eastward in the direction of the Temple Mount. Adjacent to the tower there was a gate in the wall, which could possibly have been what Josephus called the Hidden Gate (*Wars* 5, 6, 5). East of this point, two sections were found which at the time were considered to be the First Wall. One of them was near the present-day Franciscan Information Center and the other underneath the Lutheran hostel. Wilson unearthed two towers in the second section of the wall 59 feet (18 meters) distant from each other. This discovery was in keeping with the information we have about the abundance of towers in the First Wall. However, the date of these towers is not clear. The finds which are definitely connected with the northern course of the First Wall were discovered in the Jewish Quarter. These included remains of a gate and citadel built of meticulously carved stones. According to Josephus, the wall continued in the direction of the *kesistos*, linked up with the council building, and continued to the western portico of the Temple Mount. The *kesistos* and the council building were undoubtedly situated within the area of the present-day Jewish Quarter area, but they have not been uncovered in archaeological digs, and thus it is difficult to identify them exactly.

Apparently the First Wall did not reach the western portico of the Temple Mount, but continued in the direction of a tower which we consider to have been located on the edge of the eastern ridge of the Upper City. It is difficult to believe that the wall ended here without a tower, since at the point where the wall reached the slope descending toward the Tyropoeon, there was a bridge, which carried the water conduit leading to the Temple Mount (a number of sections of the bridge have been unearthed, the most famous being Wilson's Arch, attached to the Western Wall of the Temple Mount). It can be assumed that a tower was situated at this point, with the purpose of defending the end of the wall and the bridge (it is difficult to conjecture that the wall passed over the bridge). According to Josephus (*Wars* 2, 16, 3) the bridge linked the Temple Mount with the *kesistos* near the Hasmonean palace. The ridge covering the entire Western Hill at the side of the escarpment, descending in the direction of the Tyropoeon Valley (today a section of this ridge can be discerned opposite the Western Wall square), provided a natural line of defense against the Roman attacks from the Temple Mount area, in the direction of the Upper City (as will be seen below).

As Jerusalem continued to expand to the north, a new wall was built, which Josephus calls the Second Wall. It would seem that this wall was built during Herod's rule, since it is not mentioned earlier, nor is reference to it found in the descriptions of the capture of Jerusalem, which state that only one wall surrounded the city (*Wars* 1, 17, 8–9; 18, 2). The remains of the wall, and Josephus' statement that it was connected with the Antonia fortress built by Herod, support the assumption that the wall was built in his time. An important archaeological find connected with the Second Wall is the section of the wall built from stone cut in Herodian style, discovered in the excavations carried out at the Damascus Gate in the 1930s (these remains are today covered over). The position of the wall leads to the conclusion that it was adjunct to the tower situated west of the gate in the wall. Apart from these remains, no further sections of this wall have been found, only a fleeting mention of which is made by Josephus. (Archaeological finds made in the grounds of the Church of the Redeemer and the Russian Hospice near the Church of the Holy Sepulcher, were for years considered to be part of the Second Wall, but today it is recognized that they have no connection whatsoever to this wall.)

The lack of data, which prevents the exact demarcation of the course of the Second Wall, has led to numerous speculations. We will attempt to reconstruct the course of the wall (partly according to the sites still extant), based on descriptions in Josephus' writings and the few remains discovered, and taking into consideration the topographical structure of the area. The wall began at the Antonia fortress, continued to the north along the Beth Zetha incline to the western edge of Herod's Gate; from here it continued along the present-day northern wall up to Damascus Gate. In this area the course of the wall ran alongside the moat (still visible) which was apparently excavated in the Middle Ages; from the Damascus Gate it ran south to the Muristan area, along Beit Habad Street, ed-Dabagha (Dyers' Market) Street and the Christians' Street down to the point where it meets David Street. The Gennath (Garden) Gate was situated nearby, but it has not yet been identified. However, it can be assumed that it was situated near the point where the Second Wall met up with the First Wall. The description of Jesus' Garden Tomb (John 19:41) leads us to assume that the area was rich in gardens, and this was the source of the name of the gate.

The Second Wall was shorter than the First and the Third: according to Josephus it had fourteen towers, as compared with sixty in the First Wall and ninety in the Third Wall. In the area added to the inside of the wall, dwellings and public storehouses were built. The wall ran around the middle section of the Tyropoeon Valley, from which it was possible to enter the Temple Mount (through Warren's Gate), as well

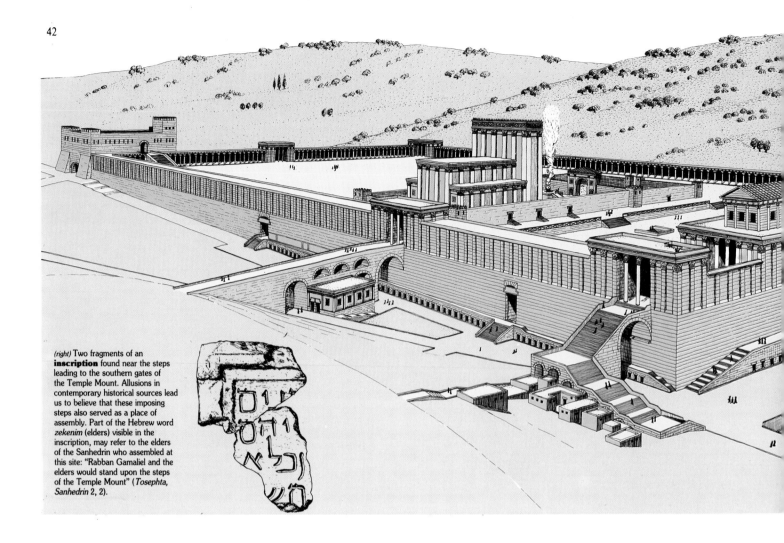

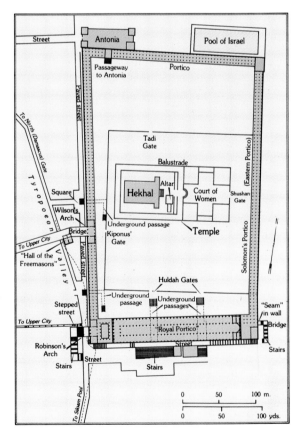

(right) Two fragments of an **inscription** found near the steps leading to the southern gates of the Temple Mount. Allusions in contemporary historical sources lead us to believe that these imposing steps also served as a place of assembly. Part of the Hebrew word *zekenim* (elders) visible in the inscription, may refer to the elders of the Sanhedrin who assembled at this site: "Rabban Gamaliel and the elders would stand upon the steps of the Temple Mount" (*Tosephta, Sanhedrin* 2, 2).

(above and right) **Plan of the Temple Mount during the Second Temple period** in which an attempt has been made to assemble all existing data about the Temple Mount from historical sources, from archaeological remains, and through comparison of buildings on the Temple Mount with similar structures in countries in the region.

In the center is the Temple, with its courtyards and buildings. The Temple is divided into two parts—in the eastern part is the women's section with its four chambers, and in the middle of the western part is the sanctuary (Hekhal), in front of which was the altar. The area around the Temple Mount is apparently the Hasmonean boundary, to which the laws of uncleanliness and purity related. For this reason it was separated by a low wall upon which were stone inscriptions warning that this was the entrance to a holy place. Herod extended the Temple Mount area beyond the Hasmonean structure, and built four porticoes around the new courtyard, thereby creating a structure of three porticoes and the southern portico which was of particular interest. It was here that Herod built the Royal Portico, a structure of the type that existed in other temples of that period. It is thought that it was in these three porticoes and the Royal Portico that visitors to the city during the pilgrimage festivals passed their time. The illustration reveals the reason that the eastern portico, called Solomon's Portico, was the earliest to be built. It was not constructed on the area added by Herod, but was erected earlier on the Hasmonean Temple Mount and later adapted to the Herodian structure.

Below the Royal Portico, underground passages can be seen, leading from the street south of the portico to the Temple Mount. To the west of the mount were two similar underground passages connecting the Temple Mount with the Upper City. There, too, two more passageways ran above the bridges between these two areas. One was the bridge above Wilson's Arch, over which ran the aqueducts bringing water from Solomon's Pools to the Temple. The second passageway ran above Robinson's Arch, and from there to the imposing steps that descended from the Royal Portico to the street. Further on was a stairway which led to the Upper City itself. In addition, there was a passage to the east, in the vicinity of the southeastern corner of the mount, evidence of whose existence is provided by the stones of the archway within the eastern wall, near the "seam." A further passageway existed in the north, leading to the Antonia fortress. Between the Antonia and the Temple Mount was a gate, but no remains of it have been found in the Temple Mount area.

The plan shows the network of streets outside the Temple Mount, whose existence has been proven by archaeological excavations. A beautifully paved street has been uncovered, running along the length of the western Temple Mount wall, and recently sections of it were found in the northwestern section of the mount. Its breadth was not uniform throughout, since a square was built (for architectural purposes) in front of each underground gate. A street ran along the Tyropoeon Valley to the present-day Damascus Gate in the north and to the Siloam Pool area in the south. From this network of streets, other streets ran to the west. One street branched off from the main street in an easterly direction, ran along the southern wall of the Temple Mount, and at certain places steps were built, as dictated by the topography of that particular section of the hill. Two sets of stairs led to this street from the City of David in the south and then to the Temple Mount through the Double and Triple Gates.

In the vicinity of the western street, a Hasmonean period structure was discovered by Charles Warren, who called it the Hall of the Freemasons. It would seem that this was an important public building. Another building was found north of Robinson's Arch facing the paved road adjacent to the western wall of the Temple Mount.

In the tractate of *Middot* of the Mishnah, it is stated that the early Temple Mount (from the Hasmonean period) had five gates: the two Huldah Gates in the south, Kiponus' Gate in the west, the Tadi Gate in the north, and the Shushan Gate in the east. In the course of extending the Temple Mount, Herod erected two gates in the south, four in the west, and an unknown number in the north. In the eastern side, in the area where Herod did not make any changes, apparently only one gate was left. The diagram points up the relationship between the proportions of the Temple and the entire Temple Mount, and for this reason the Temple has not been portrayed in detail.

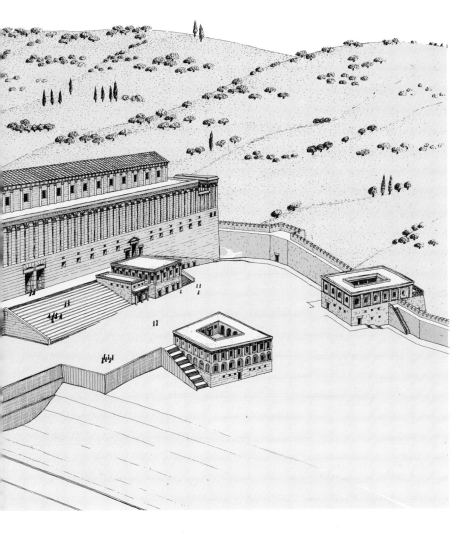

as the Antonia fortress.

Scholars are convinced that the existence of the Second Temple tombs in the Church of the Holy Sepulcher upholds the theory that in the first century CE the church area lay outside the city walls and served as a burial ground. Thus it cannot be presumed that it came within the area of the Second Wall, which served as the city wall in the time of Jesus.

The Third Wall is described in detail by Josephus (*Wars* 5, 4, 2). According to his account, it was Agrippa I who planned it and began its construction, but was forced to cease building at the order of the Romans. It was completed by the Zealots in 41–44 and again in 67–69, prior to the siege of Jerusalem.

The wall ran from the Hippicus Tower to Psephinus' Tower in the west of the city, passed opposite the Tomb of Queen Helene and the Royal Cave, bypassed the Fuller's Monument, touched the Old Wall of the Temple Mount and descended to the Kidron Valley. We still do not know how and where it linked up with the ancient walls, since its eastern and western sections have still not been found, despite the numerous excavations carried out along the course it was presumed to have followed. Perhaps the great dam built by Herod to block up the Beth Zetha Valley, thus creating the Pool of Israel just north of the Temple Mount, served as the base for the Third Wall at the connecting point with the Temple Mount wall.

Remnants of the northern section of the Third Wall have been preserved to this day. Already in the nineteenth century remains have been found in the north of the city (to the east and the west of the American Consulate in the eastern city). The sections found were about 2,950 feet (900 meters) long, and ran in an east-west direction. From the numerous archaeological finds made along the length of the wall between 1925 and 1974 (especially by E. L. Sukenik and L. A. Mayer), it has become apparent that these are sections of the wall demolished at the time of the destruction of Jerusalem in 70 CE.

In the area between the present-day Old City wall and the Third Wall, hardly any remains of Second Temple period buildings have been found. This fact shows that little construction work was carried out in the new section of the city (the Bezetha quarter, or the New City as Josephus called it), about the time of the destruction of Jerusalem.

The Temple and the Temple Mount were the focal point of religious, spiritual, and political life during the Second Temple period. The archaeological data reveal a most impressive picture of the development of the Temple Mount in this period, which reached its climax during Herod.

The topography of the Temple Mount was changed radically by Herod. He quarried into and leveled the hill northwest of the mount, and thus expanded the Temple compound and its sanctified area. He built a broad platform encompassing the mount—to the north, south, and west—upon which the portico was later erected. It would seem that from the outset the Temple Mount was built more or less in the form of a square, and according to the Mishnah its dimensions were 500 × 500 cubits (approximately 820 × 820 feet [250 × 250 meters]). The traditionally accepted description of the shape and size of the Temple Mount is quite ancient, possibly from the Persian period, and the Book of Ezekiel describes it as being square (45:2). The key to understanding the changes that were brought about lies in the "seam" in the eastern wall (105 feet [32 meters] north of the southeastern corner of the Temple Mount). As mentioned earlier, the two styles of construction merged at this juncture. The northern section was typical of the style found in other Hellenistic sites; the style of the southern section was typically Herodian. It may well be that the "seam" was the point where the Hasmonean structure merged with Herod's expansion. However, this explanation is not accepted by many scholars, and there are those who believe that the seam was the meeting point between the Acra—the fortress built by the Seleucids in Jerusalem—and the expansion carried out during Herod's rule.

(below right) The term **"Seam"** is used to describe a point in the eastern Temple Mount wall, 105 feet (32 m.) north of the southwest corner of the city wall, where two styles of dressed stones are evident. These are clearly visible in the photograph. To the north (right) of this line is the Temple Mount wall, built from coarse, marginally dressed stones, and to the south (left) are finely hewn stones, with raised smooth faces, and delicate margins along the edges.

Scholars are of the opinion that the northern part of this section of the wall is the eastern side of the southeastern corner of the Temple Mount wall from the Hasmonean period. Another assumption is that these are the remains of the Acra fortress from the Hellenistic period. The style in which the stones were cut on the section south of the "seam," and the style of building in this section, are characteristic of the Herodian period. It is now generally accepted that this section of the wall is an extension of the Temple Mount wall built by Herod when he extended the area of the Hasmonean Temple Mount toward the north, west, and south. This has strengthened the conclusion that the section north of the "seam" is part of the Hasmonean Temple Mount wall. This assumption is based on the fact that the stone-cutting and the construction at this point were done in a style similar to that of third- and second-century BCE buildings found on other sites in Mediterranean countries.

In the area south of the "seam," projections (about 40 square cm.) remaining in the wall can be discerned. These stones were used to carry the large stones to

their destination, but once the building operation was completed, these stones were not cut as was customarily done. Also visible is part of a large archway, which is evidence of the existence of a bridge which served as a passageway for persons leaving through the two gates situated above the archway. On the lower courses of this section of the wall, lying on bedrock, remains of inscriptions in ancient Hebrew were found by Warren, who sunk one of his shafts at this point. In these inscriptions, the letter *kof* recurs. This may indicate the use of the word *kadosh* (holy) by the builders of this colossal wall.

(below) **Pilgrimages** to the Temple in Jerusalem on the three pilgrimage festivals and during the rest of the year express the centrality of the city in the Second Temple period. The *Halakha* determined that the meal offerings, priestly tithes, and the sacrifices were to be from the finest agricultural produce brought from every place in the country where Jews lived. The sources list the settlements where the produce was the choicest and fit to be brought to the Temple (tractate *Minhot* 88, 1).

In Herod's time the custom of erecting temples for Caesarean worship was already popular. Temples of this type, called Caesareum (plural Caesarea), were generally large compounds in the center of which was the temple surrounded by a portico. Similar Caesarea have been found in several cities in the Orient, such as Antioch, Tadmor, Alexandria, and Cyrene. The Temple Mount compound and the Temple were built in the form of a Caesareum.

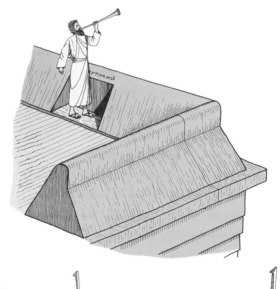

(top left) The **entrance ban inscription** was one of the inscriptions in Greek or Latin placed in the wall enclosing the sanctified area of the Temple Mount, intended to warn outsiders against entering that area. The Greek inscription presented here has been reconstructed according to an inscription found in 1871 near the "Dark Gate" (Bab el-Atm) on the Temple Mount. The section in the photograph is from another inscription discovered in the vicinity of the Lions' Gate in 1935. The text in both inscriptions is legible, stating: "Foreigner do not enter within the grille and the partition surrounding the Temple. He who is caught will have only himself to blame for his death."

(center left) **Stone of the Trumpeting Place**. The excavations of the southern wall revealed streets bordering the Temple Mount wall running from the north and west. At the time of the destruction of the city in 70 CE, gigantic blocks of stone, from which the walls of the Temple Mount were constructed, toppled onto these streets. In the vicinity of the southwestern corner of the mount, a huge stone was found on which was inscribed: **"Leveit hatekiya lehakh. ..."** (to the Trumpeting Place to ush[er]. ...). The phrase probably ended in the word *lehakhriz* (to usher). Josephus writes that the Sabbath was ushered from above the holy enclosure, and thus he may have been referring to the southwestern corner of the wall where the stone block was situated before the wall was demolished.

(bottom left) This **reconstruction of the southwest corner of the Temple Mount** depicts the magnificence of the building on the Temple Mount after the end of Herod's construction projects.

This section clearly shows the embellished western gate leading to the Royal Portico. This portico constituted the southern area of the Temple Mount, from which steps descended to the Tyropoeon Valley below. All that remains are the bases of the piers which supported the stairway as well as the springers of the upper arch called **Robinson's Arch**. From the time Charles Warren carried out his excavations at this location, it was obvious that this was not a bridge, but the scholarly literature continued to claim that a bridge existed there. Excavations carried out by Mazar in the 1970s proved conclusively that the structure portrayed here actually existed in the manner illustrated. The protruding attached pillars, which apparently surrounded the Temple Mount for decoration, have been preserved only at its northwestern corner. They were discovered and first described by Conder while carrying out the British-sponsored survey in Palestine.

The extremity of the wall and its cornerstones are restored here in accordance with the "Stone of the Trumpeting Place" found in the street abutting the wall. The assumed location of the stone, and the point where the trumpeter stood, are depicted in the illustration by a figure blowing a trumpet at the corner of the wall.

At the foot of the arch, a network of streets in this section of the city can be seen. Josephus describes the stairways and the street leading from them to the west in his *Antiquities* (15, 11, 5).

Herod began to build the Temple in the eighteenth year of his reign (apparently 19 BCE), and according to Josephus the construction work continued for a further nine years, eight of which were devoted to erecting the portico and the compound, while the building of the sanctuary itself took one year and five months (*Antiquities* 15, 420–421). The New Testament states that the construction took forty-six years (John 2:20). Apparently the project did take a considerable time, as Josephus notes that it was during the time of the governor Albinus (62–64 CE) that the building was completed (*Antiquities* 20, 209).

(above and left) Remains of **Robinson's Arch** found in the Temple Mount wall, in the southern section of the Western Wall. The arch is named after the explorer Edward Robinson, who first described it in a work published in 1838. All

that remains of the arch, which was about 44 feet (13.5 m.) wide, are the springers protruding from the Temple Mount wall and the retaining stone course below which also protrudes from the wall.

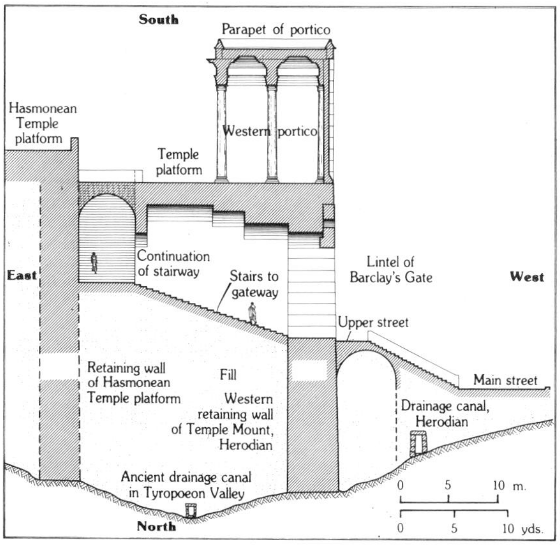

(left) An attempt to reconstruct **Barclay's Gate** (cross section) based on archaeological findings and the writings of Josephus. Over the years the original structural form of this gate has changed, but a section of it is still extant and is used as a water cistern on the Temple Mount. The original lintel and western opening can be seen in the women's section of the Western Wall prayer area.

The reconstruction shows the western stairway of the passage ascending to the Temple Mount, first going in a northerly direction and then ascending perpendicularly to the passageway. The reason for the change of direction of the stairway was apparently caused by the western retaining wall of the Hasmonean Temple platform. The change in the direction of the stairway was made to prevent visitors entering the sanctified area—the Hasmonean Temple platform—directly, which was governed by the laws of purification. These laws did not apply to the extended area of the Temple platform in Herod's time.

The cross section also shows the reconstruction of the porticoes, based on Josephus' account (*Wars* 5, 5, 2). The reconstruction of the parapet is based on the discovery of the

"Stone of the Trumpeting Place," as well as other archaeological finds. At the bottom of the mount, the riverbed of the Tyropoeon Valley can be seen, running along the foot of the western wall of the Temple Mount. A drainage canal has been found under the southern wall of the mount at the place where the riverbed emerges and continues southward. The theory that the Hasmonean Temple Mount wall was situated at this point is based on the assumption that the Tyropoeon Valley constituted the western boundary of the Temple Mount in the Hasmonean period, and it was Herod who extended the Temple Mount to the west beyond the valley. To this end he also built a new drainage scheme which can be seen on the western slope of the Tyropoeon Valley.

A street ran along the length of the western side of the Temple Mount, and this appears in the cross section diagram as the upper street. A number of entrances opened onto this street, and these were apparently used as shops which are depicted in the diagram by an archway below the street.

(above right) "**Theodotus**, son of Vettenos, priest and head of the

synagogue, son of the head of the synagogue, who was also the son of the head of the synagogue, built the synagogue for the reading of the Law and for the study of the precepts, as well as the hospice and the chambers and the bathing establishment, for lodging those who need them, from abroad; it (the synagogue) was founded by his ancestors and the elders and Simonides."

This **inscription** was written in Greek and the style of its characters dates it to the time of Herod. This is evidence that synagogues existed in Jerusalem at the time when the Temple was still standing.

The inscription was found in a large water cistern during archaeological excavations carried out by Raymond Weill in 1913-1914. The cistern contained many architectural remains of a nearby building which had been demolished. It appears that the structure was outstanding in its splendor, as evidenced by the embellished pillars and stone blocks found in the cistern. It can be presumed that the building was demolished at the time of the destruction of the Second Temple, and its remains cast into the cistern, perhaps in the hope that it would someday be rebuilt.

Cross section diagram labels:

South

Parapet of portico

Hasmonean Temple platform

Temple platform

Western portico

Temple platform

Continuation of stairway

East

Stairs to gateway

Lintel of Barclay's Gate

West

Upper street

Retaining wall of Hasmonean Temple platform

Fill

Western retaining wall of Temple Mount, Herodian

Main street

Drainage canal, Herodian

Ancient drainage canal in Tyropoeon Valley

0   5   10 m.

0   5   10 yds.

North

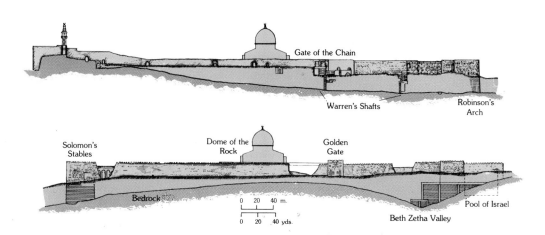

The major effort and time were devoted to the construction of the portico, one of the main architectural elements of the Temple Mount. One of the porticoes, described in full detail by Josephus, is the Royal Portico (the basilica) at the south of the compound (*Antiquities* 15, 411–420). This portico served as a commercial center for the sale of ritual articles, and may well be that called the "shops" in other sources. Perhaps also this was the site to which the Sanhedrin repaired shortly before the destruction of the Second Temple (Babylonian Talmud, *Shabbat* 16, 71). Herod linked the Royal Portico with the Upper City by a street, stairs, and an arch—today called Robinson's Arch.

With the extension of the Temple Mount area, the need arose to distinguish between the sanctified area—the ancient part—and the extended new area to which the laws of sanctity did not apply. To this end a partition wall was built, which delineated the sanctified area on the Temple Mount compound. Stone inscriptions in Greek and Latin were placed on this partition, warning gentiles not to cross beyond this point so as not to enter the sanctified section of the Temple Mount (*Wars* 5, 5, 2). The importance of the partition wall, which precisely delineated the sanctified section, is still of the utmost importance regarding the Halakhic prohibition of Jews entering the Temple Mount.

The Antonia fortress played a vital role in the defense of Jerusalem in the time of Herod. In order to maintain control over the Temple and to defend the Temple Mount at its most vulnerable point at the northwest of the mount, Herod turned the Baris (Birah in Nehemiah's time), situated at the northwest corner of the Temple Mount, into a large fortress which he called Antonia, in honor of Marc Anthony. The Antonia was apparently erected in order to replace the ancient Baris, which was demolished when Herod extended the Temple Mount northward. The Baris served, among other things, as a dwelling place for the rulers and kings of the Hasmonean dynasty. No vestiges of this earlier fortress have remained. This phenomenon—demolishing earlier structures to make way for new ones—is familiar from other sites upon which Herod built outside Jerusalem.

The Antonia was built on an elevated rocky plateau (148 × 394 feet [45 × 120 meters]), cut off on all sides by moats dug to the north and west, by a natural steep incline descending to the east, and by the leveling of the Temple Mount to the south. A tower was placed at each corner and one of them—the Straton Tower at the southwest corner—was especially well fortified. The extent to which the stone was excavated leads us to believe that it was of particularly broad dimensions, especially to the north (the tower reached the vicinity of the present-day Bani Ghawanima minaret). Josephus describes the Antonia as having bathhouses, courtyards, porticoes, and numerous rooms. Apart from this portrayal, there is no other evidence available of the interior of the fortress, especially because of the numerous structures built on the Antonia

(top left) Adaptation of the north to south **cross sections of the Temple Mount** which appeared in Charles Warren's books and atlas in which he published the summation of his exploration of Jerusalem during the years 1867 to 1870. Looking across the Temple Mount wall from the west (the upper illustration) evidence can be seen of the quarrying carried out in the Herodian period in the natural bedrock in the northwestern corner of the Temple Mount required for the construction of the Antonia fortress. The Bani Ghawanima minaret today stands in the center of the elevated rocky plateau upon which the Antonia stood.

From the eastern view of the Temple Mount wall (lower illustration) the ancient Beth Zetha Valley and the southeastern corner of the Temple Mount built upon the bedrock are easily visible. At this point, Warren dug down and reached the natural rock. It was here that he found the Hebrew letter *kof* painted on the lowest course of the Temple Mount wall. It would seem that this was the first letter of the word *kadosh* (holy).

(center left) The description of the **Antonia Fortress** in Josephus' writings (*Wars* 5, 8), and the descriptions of the Birah (Baris) in earlier sources, created the impression that the Antonia was a magnificent edifice. The various reconstructions made in the past showed that it included a large stone-paved central courtyard. However, today it is clear that the Lithostrotos, the paved area that we see today upon which according to Christian tradition the trial of Jesus took place (Mark 15:17; John 19:13), was not part of the fortress, but is to be found in the moat to the north of it. Thus, the Antonia, with its four towers, stood on the rocky surface, whose dimensions were 148 × 394 feet (45 × 120 m.), and was protected by moats surrounding it.

(top right) Reconstruction of the **Double Gate** as it was in Herod's time. From its two openings, divided by an elongated pier, two passages lead to the Temple Mount separated by a series of columns as a continuation of the pier. The ceilings of the passageways had decorated domes. The original decorations from the Herodian period have remained on three of them, partly covered with stucco in the style prevalent in Jerusalem at that time. This style can be seen in decorations in burial caves and sarcophagi dating to this period. These included grapevines, clusters of grapes, rosettas and other adornments.

According to the Mishnah (*Middot* 1) there were two gates—the Huldah Gates—in the southern wall of the Temple Mount. When Herod extended the Temple Mount toward the south, he also built two gates in the new southern wall. The eastern one is called the Triple Gate, and the western, the Double Gate. Passageways led from them directly to the interior of the Temple Mount.

Remains of these two gates can be seen in the southern wall of the Temple Mount some 558 feet (170 m.) distant from its eastern extremity.

(center right) **Decorated frame of the Triple Gate** hewn out of the stone slab surrounding the gate. The gate has remained in its original form from the Herodian era, and the decoration is the only vestige found so far of adornments of the Temple Mount gates from that period. Near the gate can be seen names of Jewish pilgrims carved in the stone while visiting the site, probably dating to the end of the Arab period.

(opposite below) A reconstruction of the **Herodian Citadel** against the background of the present-day Citadel (the Herodian sections are shaded). When Herod ascended the throne (in 37 BCE) he reinforced the section of the First Wall which included the three towers first built by the Hasmoneans. In parts of this section Herod thickened the Hasmonean wall. He also enlarged the central tower by covering its walls, and rebuilt the southern tower extending its height. In place of the northern Hasmonean tower, Herod erected the tower now known as "David's Tower" (at the left of the illustration).

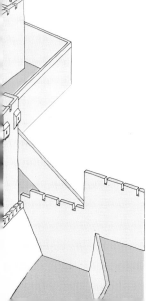

(above) The northwestern corner of the Temple Mount had always been its most vulnerable point because of the topography of the land lying to the north—a hill higher than the mount itself, to the north of which was the Antonia ridge. Evidence exists that in the biblical era a fortress was situated in this corner, for the purpose of protecting the Temple Mount. At the end of the First Temple period, the Hananel Tower was built on this site, and during the Hasmonean period the Baris stood there.

However, Herod radically changed the face of the hill. Parts of the hill were removed to bring it to the level of the Temple Mount (the lower section to the south was filled in with earth). On its north and west sides a series of moats were dug, thus forming a rock platform upon which the **Antonia Fortress** was built, in honor of Herod's patron, the military commander Marc Anthony. This rock platform is the only remnant of this stronghold. The photo shows the rocky areas exposed in the course of quarrying at the foot of the hill upon which the Antonia stood.

ridge during the Mamluk period. Stairs led down from the Antonia to the porticoes which encircled the Temple Mount (*Wars* 5, 5, 8). A number of concealed passages connected the fortress to the Temple Mount, and Josephus mentions one of them (*Antiquities* 15, 424).

In Herod's time, the Upper City was a residential quarter for the Hellenized wealthy, and Herod's palace, as well as Hasmonean and other palaces were constructed within its confines. Herod's palace, the most magnificent of them, was described in superlatives by Josephus, especially because of its gardens, porticoes, and fountains. It was divided into two sections: the Caesareon, after Augustus Caesar, and Agrippeon, after the Roman military leader Vispanius Agrippa. In the past it was assumed that the fortress and its three towers—Hippicus, Mariamme, and Phasael—seemed to protect the palace, but from the excavations it became apparent that these were part of the series of sixty towers in the Hasmonean wall (the First Wall). The palace itself was a virtual fortress because of the walls surrounding it. It is possible that it also served as the residence of Roman governors such as Pontius Pilate. According to the New Testament (John 19:13), Pontius Pilate sat in judgment over Jesus at the Lithostrotos (a place paved with stone) which is Gabbatha. This site may also be within the confines of Herod's palace.

In the area between Herod's palace and the section of the wall where the three towers stood, was the residential area. This included one street built up on both sides. The palace and residential quarter were built on an elevated plateau, which rested on retaining walls remaining from the Hasmonean period. These walls were found in the excavations carried out in the Citadel and in the present-day Armenian Garden—the only remains of this magnificent palace.

During this period there was also the Hasmonean palace, into which the Hasmoneans moved after leaving the Baris (*Antiquities* 15, 11, 410). Agrippa I and Agrippa II also inhabited this palace. It was apparently situated on the eastern slope of the Upper City, at a point overlooking the Temple Mount. Finds from archaeological excavations carried out in the Jewish Quarter reveal that in the eastern section of the Upper City there was a large concentration of public buildings. Today, there are remains of the Palatial Mansion and the Burnt House, but no vestige of the Hasmonean palace has yet been uncovered. It is almost certain that the architectural style of the Hasmonean palace was similar to that of these houses.

A further concentration of palaces known from historical sources was found on the hill of the City of David, which continued to serve as an important part of the city's municipal complex. These were the palaces of the Adiabene royal family: the palace of Queen Helene (*Wars* 5, 6, 1; 6, 6, 3); the palace of the House of Monobaz (*Wars* 5, 6, 1); and the palaces affiliated with the Graphte family (*Wars* 4, 9, 11). These palaces mentioned by Josephus have not been discovered by the archaeologists, and thus their location cannot be determined except in the most general terms. Apart from the magnificent palaces characteristic of Jerusalem under Herod's rule, other sites were referred to in historical sources. The exact location is not known (and therefore not marked in our map) of the monument to Alexander in the northeast of the city, the monument to Jonathan in the northwest, and the above-mentioned palaces of the Adiabene family. Scholars believe that a hippodrome mentioned a number of times by Josephus (*Antiquities* 17, 255; *Wars* 2, 3, 1) was situated south of the Temple Mount. Archaeological finds have not provided evidence of this, nor have they proved the assumption incorrect.

The provision of water has always been a major problem in Jerusalem. In Herod's time tremendous efforts were made to exploit to the full the many water resources available. The Gihon Spring was one of the most important of these sources. Until recently scholars believed that the spring was blocked up during the time of Hezekiah's rule, and its waters ran into the Siloam Pool. However, recent evidence has come to light showing that the Gihon Spring also served as a source of water for the City of David hill area in Herodian times.

There were also many pools in Jerusalem. The Siloam Pool, whose waters were derived from the Gihon Spring, supplied water mainly to the City of David and the vicinity. When describing the First Wall, Josephus relates to another pool in this area, which he calls Solomon's Pool. Until recently it was thought that this was an error and that Solomon's Pool was actually the Siloam Pool. However, a chance discovery revealed remains of a large pool in the riverbed of the Kidron Valley, north of the southernmost point of the City of David. This was apparently the pool Josephus was referring to.

Another pool, the Towers' Pool, was identified with what is known as Hezekiah's Pool. This identification is generally accepted, as the only reference to it is found in Josephus (*Wars* 5, 11, 4). He states that the Romans set up a siege ramp at the site called the Towers' Pool, and at a distance of thirty cubits the Roman legions set up another ramp in the vicinity of the monument to the High Priest. Elsewhere, he states that the monument to John (the High Priest) was a siege-tower opposite the Upper City (*Wars* 5, 9, 2). This pool underwent numerous transformations, but no vestiges from the Second Temple period have been found. At its eastern boundary, remains of a broad wall have been found, which in the opinion of scholars are remains of the Second Wall. However, they could be the vestiges of a broad wall that encompassed the pool itself.

Another pool dug during the Second Temple period was the Struthion Pool, which supplied water to the Antonia fortress and its vicinity. The pool was excavated near the northwestern corner of the Antonia, in the bed of the moat described above. It was a large open pool (approximately 171 × 46 feet [52 × 14 meters]), which collected the rainwater from the moat, and also apparently exploited the waters in the Hasmonean conduit, through which water from the upper section of the Tyropoeon Valley (the present-day Damascus Gate area) flowed into the cisterns on the Temple Mount. A pair of pools, which supplied the city in Herod's time, were called by explorers and Christian pilgrims the Bethesda Pools. They are identified with the Sheep's Pools (Probatica in Greek). Already in the Second Temple period

these pools were apparently considered to have medicinally healing powers. At all events, during the Roman era a temple to the god of healing was erected.

Along the Beth Zetha Valley riverbed another pool—the Pool of Israel—was situated. It was formed at the time Herod was extending the Temple Mount. A dam 46 feet (14 meters) wide was erected to block up the riverbed. It was in this manner that the largest pool in Jerusalem was created.

(left) **Hasmonean subterranean canal** through which water was brought to the cisterns underneath the Baris fortress, the seat of Hasmonean rulers. During the course of extensions to the Temple Mount, the canal was severed at various points and thus was rendered useless. The canal was discovered in October 1867 by Charles Warren (see his plan on page 46), but was blocked up in 1870 and rediscovered on March 16, 1987 by Israeli explorers. This is undoubtedly one of the most exciting vestiges of Jerusalem's past. The site is to be opened to the public in the near future.

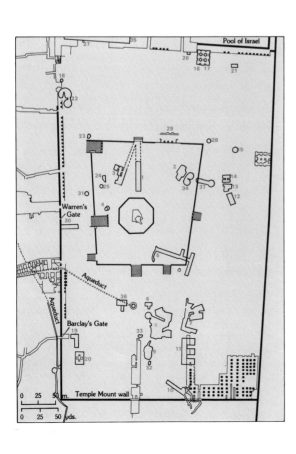

(left) The immense consumption of water at the Temple required the development of a complex **water system** on the **Temple Mount**. When the terrace was built to form the platform upon which the Temple Mount was erected, depressions were left in the filling for the express purpose of serving as water reservoirs. It is most probable that additional water cisterns were dug on the Temple Mount in later periods, but it is difficult to substantiate this assumption, since no thorough investigation has been made since Warren explored this area in the nineteenth century.

The diagram indicates the location of thirty-seven water cisterns on the Temple Mount known today. These cisterns, which all collect rainwater, were examined in the nineteenth century, mainly by Warren and Conder. The numbering of the cisterns in this diagram is that used by these two scholars, and this is the accepted numbering to this day.

Not all the cisterns were used for the accumulation of water during the Second Temple period. For example, cistern No. **19** (Barclay's Gate) and cistern No. **30** (Warren's Gate) were described by Josephus as gates which led from the Temple Mount to the street which ran the length of the Temple Mount western wall. The gates opened onto tunnels, and from there to steps going up to the Temple Mount. The entrances at

street level were sealed off and in the course of time they were turned into water cisterns. It would appear that cistern No. **5** was an installation for the draining of water from the Temple Mount platform to the lower compound, and cistern No. **10** was also part of this drainage system.

There is a theory that cistern No. **1** was the tunnel which led from the Temple compound, directly out of the Temple Mount. Another theory has it that this cistern was connected to an underground passage leading to the ritual bath (Beth Hatevila), which was the purification installation northwest of the Temple.

Cistern No. **8** is the largest of the Temple Mount water cisterns, all of which were quite large. The cistern held up to 12,000 cubic meters of water. Part of the water flowed to Jerusalem through aqueducts leading from Solomon's Pools. From the Mamluk period, the aqueducts reached the purification installation built by Tankiz en-Nasiri in the fourteenth century, near cistern No. **36**.

Cistern No. **22** was possibly the cistern dug in the Hasmonean period, to which a water conduit led from the vicinity of the present-day Damascus Gate.

(opposite below) Prior to the Herodian period the Temple Mount was bounded by a system of streams to the west, north, and east. When Herod extended the Temple Mount compound, he stopped up the course of the **Beth Zetha Valley** to the north, and the course of the Tyropoeon Valley to the west. He also set up dams along their course to collect the water.

In the northern part of the Beth Zetha Valley, dams and pools were constructed already in the First Temple period, and in the early Second Temple era the Sheep's Pools were built in its riverbed. In the southern part of the valley, which was spanned by the extended Temple Mount wall, a dam was constructed, near the northeastern corner of the mount. This dam formed the **Pool of Israel**, which was the largest of the pools in Jerusalem. It was 361 feet (110 m.) long , 131 feet (40 m.) wide, and 98 feet (30 m.) deep. In years when there was a good rainfall the pool was filled with 120,000 cubic meters of water.

The pool's huge dimensions made a deep impression on visitors to the city throughout the ages and many of them described it in detail. In the nineteenth century, it was the subject of paintings by many artists. In 1934 the Jerusalem municipality drained this pool and sealed it because it had become a health hazard. Recently a car park has been built over it.

(right) Reconstruction of the **Siloam Pool** in the Second Temple period based mainly on excavations carried out at the site by Bliss and Dickie from 1894 to 1897. Recently the tower complex (to the right of the illustration) has been uncovered once again.

During the First Temple period the pool received its supply of water from Hezekiah's Tunnel. This tunnel continued to supply the pool during the Second Temple period and later. In the riverbed a 66 foot (20 m.) wide dam was built, reinforced by a series of attached pillars erected on the extended base. These pillars were uncovered in the excavation carried out by Bliss and Dickie, when they descended a series of tunnels at various points of the structure. There are those who question the accuracy of the reconstruction based on the findings presented here. The dam's width has only been estimated, and it is possible that the dimensions of the structure as it is shown in this illustration are based on a combination of finds from the Second Temple period as well as the First Temple period, since such a dam existed during the earlier period as well. The city wall passed over the dam when it crossed the valley between the City of David (right) and Mount Zion (left), which was part of the city when the dam was built. At the foot of Mount Zion, a street was discovered paved with large stone slabs. The street led to a postern in the wall, which can also be seen in the illustration. This postern was apparently utilized again in the fifth century, when the Empress Eudocia reconstructed the southern city wall, and continued in use until the destruction of the wall in the eleventh century.

There is no available proof that the Second Temple period Siloam Pool was situated at the present-day site, and it is more plausible that the pool was situated at the location of the nearby Birket el-Hamra, where there is now a flourishing vegetable garden.

It was 328 feet (100 meters) long, 125 feet (38 meters) wide, and at its deepest point about 98 feet (30 meters). In the 1930s, the Jerusalem municipality blocked it up, and a car park was recently built above it. Apart from the Siloam Pool, we do not have any definite information about other pools located in the Tyropoeon Valley, the city's central valley. However, there are signs which may be evidence of further pools, such as a broad dam across the Tyropoeon Valley underneath Wilson's Arch (it was the same width as the Pool of Israel dam—46 feet [14 meters]). It would seem that this dam was also the beginning of a diversion canal which passed along the southwestern corner of the Temple Mount, below street level, in the direction of the Tyropoeon Valley toward the south.

Another pool that deserves mention is what is now called the Sultan's Pool, previously identified as the Serpent's Pool mentioned by Josephus (*Wars* 5, 3, 2). Trial trenches dug recently have not produced any evidence to confirm or

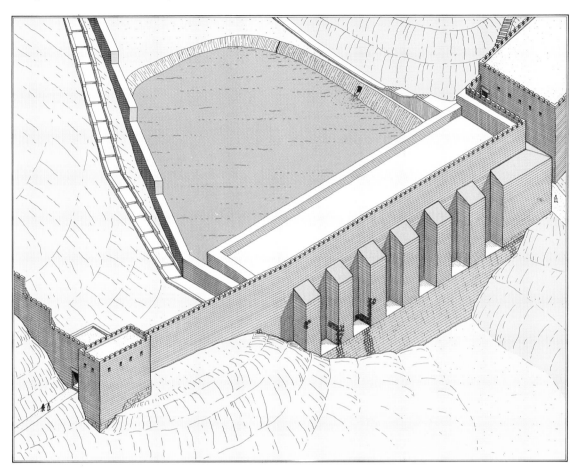

refute the assumption that this pool was in existence during the Second Temple era.

Water was also supplied to the city from springs south of Bethlehem through a system of aqueducts. The finds from the excavations in the Jewish Quarter and part of the conduit on Mount Zion have led to the conclusion that these spring waters were for the sole use of the Temple Mount. It would seem that these aqueducts were built in the Hasmonean era, at the end of the second century BCE, but were renovated over the years. The first time was apparently during Herod's rule and possibly again under the Roman governor Pontius Pilate. These aqueducts were also repaired a number of times in later eras and continued to function until the twentieth century.

Within the city itself, the use of cisterns built beneath the houses were common in Second Temple times. In the excavations in the Jewish Quarter, ritual baths, pools, and cisterns hewn out of the rock were discovered under many houses. These installations made it possible for the inhabitants to be independent of the natural spring—the Gihon Spring—and also made it possible for the city to expand in all directions. Cisterns were also sunk on the Temple Mount, and already in the Letter of Aristeas water cisterns are mentioned as being present in the lower levels of the Temple Mount. We now have evidence of thirty-seven cisterns of various sizes. Not all these cisterns were used for the supply of water during the Second Temple period. Three of them served as entrances to the Temple Mount: the first was called the Warren Gate (cistern No. 30); the second,

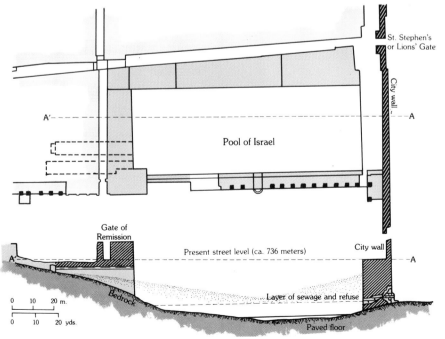

St. Stephen's or Lions' Gate

City wall

A' — — — A

Pool of Israel

Gate of Remission

Present street level (ca. 736 meters)

City wall

A' — — — A

Bedrock

Layer of sewage and refuse

Paved floor

0   10   20 m.

0   10   20 yds.

Barclay's Gate, was turned into two cisterns (cisterns 19 and 20). The system of water cisterns, which developed in the Second Temple period, was used in Jerusalem until the mid-twentieth century, and throughout the centuries served as the main source of water for the city's inhabitants. The water for these cisterns was conducted through aqueducts from Solomon's Pools and from the vicinity of the Damascus Gate (by way of the Struthion Pool). Other water cisterns were filled with rainwater.

To complete the picture of Jerusalem in the Second Temple period we must also mention its cemeteries. The pattern of the city's burial grounds is in the main well known to us, since the graves situated around it were not affected by the wars which it endured (they were ruined mainly as the result of building activities beginning from the end of the nineteenth century). In Jerusalem an amazing dispersion of graves was found surrounding the Old City itself, in localities which were outside its boundaries during the various stages of its development during the Second Temple period. The majority of the graves are groups of family burial caves hewn out of the relatively soft rock.

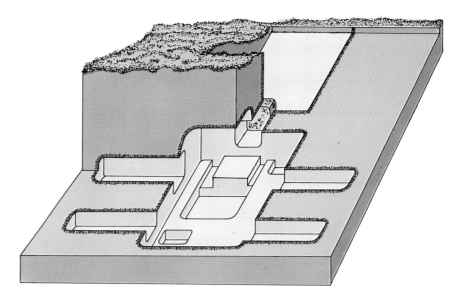

(above) This schematic diagram of a family **burial cave** is of the type found in many necropolises in Second Temple period Jerusalem. The cemeteries which surrounded the city on all sides extended during that period from present-day Romema to French Hill in the north, to Ramat Rahel in the south, from the Mount Scopus–Mount of Olives ridge in the east, and up to Giv'at Ram in the west. Wars, chaos, and destruction which the city underwent passed over the "City of the Dead" which surrounded it.

After the Six-Day War of 1967, intensive building construction took place around the city, in the course of which many Second Temple burial caves were discovered. These caves revealed names and titles of persons buried there, inscriptions and ossuaries.

The diagram shows the forecourt hewn into the rock (in the upper section), and beyond it the entrance to the burial cave, through a narrow opening blocked by a burial stone. In the center of the burial chamber was

a wide pit, in which persons carrying out the burial could stand up erect. The smaller pit to the lower left of the chamber served for the placing of bones of persons buried there previously. (In the Second Temple period the remains of the dead were collected several years after they were first buried, and preserved in ossuaries, thus making room for others in the family burial cave.) At the sides of the chambers niches can be seen where the dead bodies were placed.

(left) The **Uzziah inscription** on a stone tablet (14 × 13.6 inches [35 × 34 cm.]) with the following text in Aramaic: "Hither were brought the bones of Uzziah, King of Judah. Do not open."

From this inscription we learn that the remains of King Uzziah were reinterred here in the Second Temple period, and this stone was used to seal off the burial niche. Although there is evidence that during the Second Temple period the tombs of the Davidic dynasty were left

untouched (Tosephta, Baba Batra 1, 7), it would seem that Uzziah was buried separately from the outset. The Bible asserts this in the verse: "and they buried him ... in the field of the burial which belonged to the kings; for they said, He is a leper" (2 Chron. 26:23). Josephus states that he was "buried alone in his gardens" (Antiquities 9, 10, 227). Thus it would seem that it was possible to transfer Uzziah's remains from their original burial place.

The exact site where Uzziah was reinterred is unknown because the stone tablet was brought to the Russian Church on the Mount of Olives during the nineteenth century and placed among its antiquities collection without any reference to where it was found and how it was brought there. The tablet was identified in 1931 by Prof. E. L. Sukenik and in 1968 was purchased by the Israel Museum, where it is on display.

(right) Reconstruction of a **burial tomb** or **monument** the remains of which were discovered by Conrad Schick in 1879, about 820 feet (250 m.) north of Damascus Gate. This was a circular structure, with two peripheral walls, one inside the other. The internal walls were built by the special *opus reticulatum* technique commonly used during Herod's reign. The external part was covered in cut stone in the style commonly used in other buildings of this period. Between the two walls was a vaulted roof, and the center of the building was covered with a conical roof. Similar burial tombs were found in Rome and other locations.

The site of this monument was within the Third Wall of Jerusalem, erected by Agrippa I. As burial tombs or monuments were generally placed outside the city walls, this particular structure can be dated to the period before the reign of Agrippa I. One theory has it that this structure is "Herod's Monument" mentioned by Josephus when describing the construction of the siege wall by Titus (*Wars* 5, 3, 2; 5, 12, 2).

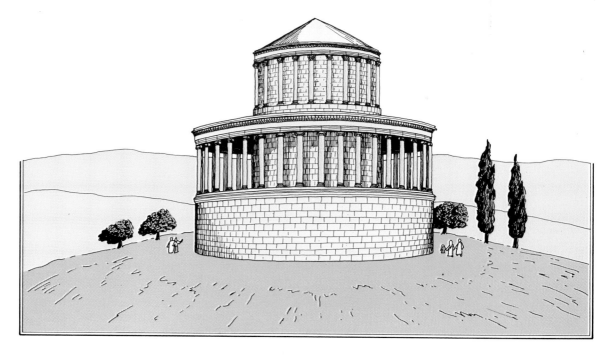

(left) The name **Absalom's Pillar** originated in a Jewish tradition which considered that the monument in the Kidron Valley was that which Absalom, King David's son, erected to himself (2 Sam. 18:18). Since in Hebrew the word for monument and hand is the same, the usual drawings of the monument will show a hand at its apex. As Absalom revolted against his father, the Jews of Jerusalem used to throw stones at this monument, and wayward sons were also brought here to show them the fate of a rebellious son.

The structure, almost certainly built during Herod's reign, is hewn out of the rock, and thus stands apart from the surrounding rockface. The structure is 26 feet (8 m.) high. In its lower section is a burial chamber also hewn out of the rock. This is a square chamber with room for two bodies.

Above the burial chamber is the circular roof built of finely-cut stone. Above that is a conical structure made out of a single stone, and at its point a calyx decorated in the shape of a flower bud.

The burial chamber was broken open in the Byzantine era, and was used by monks as a habitation, as in many of the burial caves in the Kidron Valley.

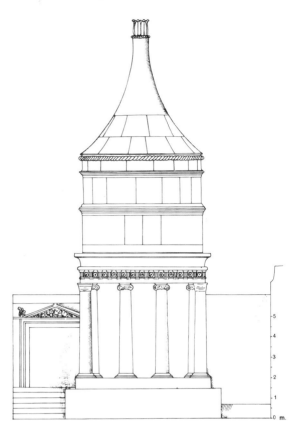

(above and below) The **Tomb of Zechariah** and the **Tomb of Hezir's Priestly Family** (cross section) are two of the most well-known burial caves in the Kidron Valley, situated opposite the southeastern corner of the Temple Mount. (The third, Absalom's Pillar, to the left of these tombs, is not included in this diagram.)

The tomb of Hezir's priestly family, from the beginning of the first century BCE (about the time of the reign of Alexander Jannaeus), is the burial cave of a family of priests known from the historical sources. An inscription on the tomb reads: "This is the tomb and the monument of Alexander, Hanniah, Yo'ezer, Judah, Simon, Johanan, the sons of Joseph, son of Oved. Joseph and Eliezer sons of Hanniah—priests of the Hezir family." The word *nefesh* (here translated as "monument") is literally "spirit," and it is possible that the tombstone was

placed to the left of the entrance with the columns. There are intimations of a structure—perhaps a pyramid—as was customary at the time in graves hewn out of the rock or built up within it.

Prior to the discovery of the inscription, Jewish tradition considered this tomb to be the "house set apart" (Beth Hahofshit), the place where King Uzziah dwelt after he was smitten with leprosy and expelled from Jerusalem (2 Chron. 26:21). The inscription confirms that this was the tomb of the Hezir family, while the names of the other two tombs are based on tradition only.

The tomb of Zechariah was apparently built at the beginning of the first century CE, but it is not known for whom it was intended. It appears that its construction was not completed and therefore may never have been used for burial.

52

(above) An engraving of a **menorah** (candelabrum), with a triangular base, 8 inches (20 cm.) high, found only a few hundred feet from the site where the Temple *menorah* stood. Additional engravings were discovered at the site depicting what seems to be the altar and the table of the shewbread. This engraving of the *menorah*, as well as that on a coin from the reign of Matthias Antigonus, and to a certain extent the *menorah* on the Arch of Titus in Rome, are the only illustrations extant of the original

menorah in the Temple, and were engraved when it was still in use there.

The engraving was made on plaster, apparently at the time of Herod's rule. It was found together with a Herodian coin beneath the floor of a building from the Herodian period, or that of one of his descendants. This was not the original site and thus it can be assumed that the building on whose wall the *menorah* was engraved was demolished during Herod's reign, or shortly after his death.

(below) **Judaea Capta** engraved on a gold coin minted in Rome in honor of the Roman victory over Judaea. On the face of the coin is the bust of the Roman Emperor Vespasian, and on its obverse is "Judaea" sitting in mourning beside a plundered statue, underneath which is the Latin inscription "Judaea."

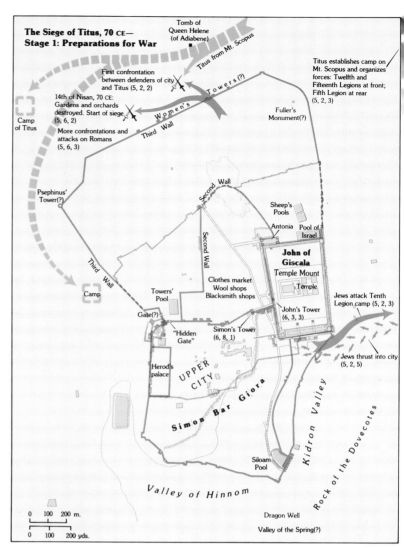

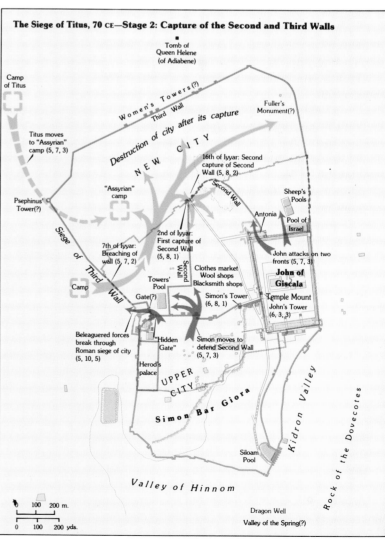

The Siege of Titus, 70 CE—Stage 3: Capture of the Antonia and Breach of the Temple Mount

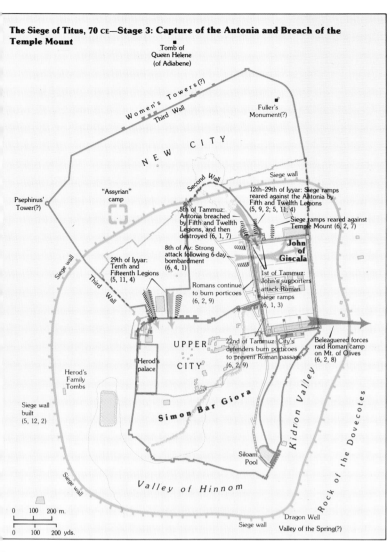

Tomb of Queen Helene (of Adiabene)

Women's Towers(?)

Third Wall

Fuller's Monument(?)

N E W   C I T Y

Second Wall

Siege wall

12th-29th of Iyyar: Siege ramps reared against the Antonia by Fifth and Twelfth Legions (5, 9, 2; 5, 11, 4)

5th of Tammuz: Antonia breached by Fifth and Twelfth Legions, and then destroyed (6, 1, 7)

Siege ramps reared against Temple Mount (6, 2, 7)

"Assyrian" camp

8th of Av: Strong attack following 6-day bombardment (6, 4, 1)

29th of Iyyar: Tenth and Fifteenth Legions (5, 11, 4)

John of Giscala

1st of Tammuz: John's supporters attack Roman siege ramps (6, 1, 3)

Psephinus' Tower(?)

Third Wall

Romans continue to burn porticoes (6, 2, 9)

22nd of Tammuz: City's defenders burn porticoes to prevent Roman passage (6, 2, 9)

U P P E R   C I T Y

Herod's palace

Beleaguered forces raid Roman camp on Mt. of Olives (6, 2, 8)

Herod's Family Tombs

Siege wall built (5, 12, 2)

Simon Bar Giora

Kidron Valley

Siloam Pool

Siege wall

Valley of Hinnom

Rock of the Dovecotes

0   100   200 m.
0   100   200 yds.

Dragon Well

Siege wall

Valley of the Spring(?)

The Siege of Titus, 70 CE—Stage 4: Capture of the Temple Mount, Upper City, and Lower City

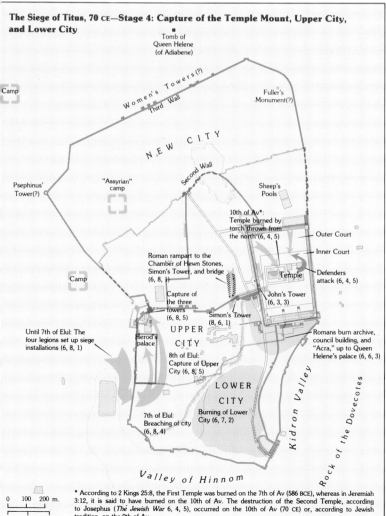

Tomb of Queen Helene (of Adiabene)

Camp

Women's Towers(?)

Third Wall

Fuller's Monument(?)

N E W   C I T Y

Second Wall

Psephinus' Tower(?)

"Assyrian" camp

Sheep's Pools

10th of Av*: Temple burned by torch thrown from the north (6, 4, 5)

Outer Court

Roman rampart to the Chamber of Hewn Stones, Simon's Tower, and bridge (6, 8, 1)

Camp

Inner Court

Temple

Defenders attack (6, 4, 5)

Capture of the three towers (6, 8, 5)

Simon's Tower (8, 6, 1)

John's Tower (6, 3, 3)

Until 7th of Elul: The four legions set up siege installations (6, 8, 1)

Herod's palace

U P P E R   C I T Y

Romans burn archive, council building, and "Acra," up to Queen Helene's palace (6, 6, 3)

8th of Elul: Capture of Upper City (6, 8, 5)

Kidron Valley

L O W E R   C I T Y

7th of Elul: Breaching of city (6, 8, 4)

Burning of Lower City (6, 7, 2)

Valley of Hinnom

Rock of the Dovecotes

0   100   200 m.
0   100   200 yds.

* According to 2 Kings 25:8, the First Temple was burned on the 7th of Av (586 BCE), whereas in Jeremiah 3:12, it is said to have burned on the 10th of Av. The destruction of the Second Temple, according to Josephus (The Jewish War 6, 4, 5), occurred on the 10th of Av (70 CE) or, according to Jewish tradition, on the 9th of Av.

53

(above) The **Tomb of the Kings** is the name by which the large burial cave is known. It is one of the most beautiful of its type in Jerusalem and it is situated some 2,625 feet (800 m.) north of the Old City wall. (The illustration shows the reconstruction of the facade of the tomb.)

According to one tradition, the kings of the Davidic dynasty were buried here. Another tradition claims that it belonged to Calba Savua, the father-in-law of Rabbi Akiva. Today most scholars agree that probably Queen Helene and members of the Adiabene royal family were buried here in the first century CE. The theory that the tomb was the burial place of royalty is supported by the fact that one of the sarcophagi found here bore the Aramaic inscription: "Queen Saddan."

Josephus (*Antiquities* 20, 4, 3)

states that the burial cave was embellished with three most impressive pyramids. Even today the magnificence of the burial cave's facade is apparent—it is decorated with a frieze, and the frame of the entrance is embossed with engravings of clusters of grapes, acanthus leaves, fruit and flower wreaths. The cave entrance was closed off with a burial stone which is still *in situ* nearby. It was moved by a secret mechanism, evidence of which was found inside the cave.

Some of the sarcophagi found inside the cave were taken to the Louvre Museum in Paris, while others were placed in various building projects on the Temple Mount when renovations were carried out during the 1860s. They were all elaborately decorated in Hellenistic style.

(above) A **decoration** typical of Second Temple period Jewish art found on one of the most splendid sarcophagi from that period. The sarcophagus was discovered in the Herod family burial tomb, which was outstanding in its magnificence. (The sarcophagus is now on display in

the Greek Patriarchate Museum in Jerusalem.) Herod's family tomb is mentioned by Josephus in his account of the siege of Jerusalem by Titus in 70 CE (*Wars* 3, 2), and this has led to its being identified with the burial cave found in the vicinity of the King David Hotel.

The Siege of Titus, 70 CE

Legend

Jews

Romans

Positioning of Roman forces

Roman camp

Battlesite

Retreat

Roman siege ramp

Siege wall

Area burned by the Romans

(5, 3, 1)   Passage from *The Jewish War*

Jerusalem at the Time of Jesus

In the beginning of the Common Era, Jerusalem generally appeared as is shown in the previous chapter during the time of Herod the Great. The king's great works—the rebuilding of the Temple and its artificial mount, the Second Wall, and all the other public buildings which he added to the city—were already in existence and serve as background to the evangelical narrative of the Gospels.

Parts of the city, shown on the map of Jerusalem at the end of the Second Temple period, were added after the death of Jesus. These include the Third Wall, and the suburb of Bezetha within it.

Although the New Testament serves as an important source for the study of Jerusalem in the time of Jesus, it is sparing in descriptive details of the city. We must therefore base our knowledge on the descriptions of Josephus Flavius and of the Mishnah, as is the case when studying Jerusalem in the year 70 CE. Usually, the New Testament mentions only the name of a place without any distinguishing feature which would help us to identify it today.

When relating to the Christian traditions surrounding the holy sites in the city, one should bear in mind that the Christian community which remained in the city after its

Map drawn in 1580 by **Heinrich Bünting** (1545–1606), a native of Hanover (whose emblem consists of clover leaves). Although a late map, it stresses the popular perception of Jerusalem as the center of the world and its significance in the life of Jesus. Its function as the pivot of three continents reflects Jerusalem's central role in world events arising out of Christ's connection with it.

America, known at the time for only about one hundred years, is here called Terra Nova, and appears in the lower left-hand corner of the map.

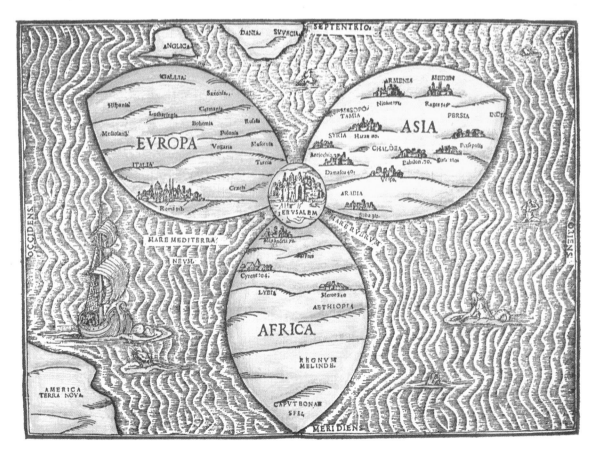

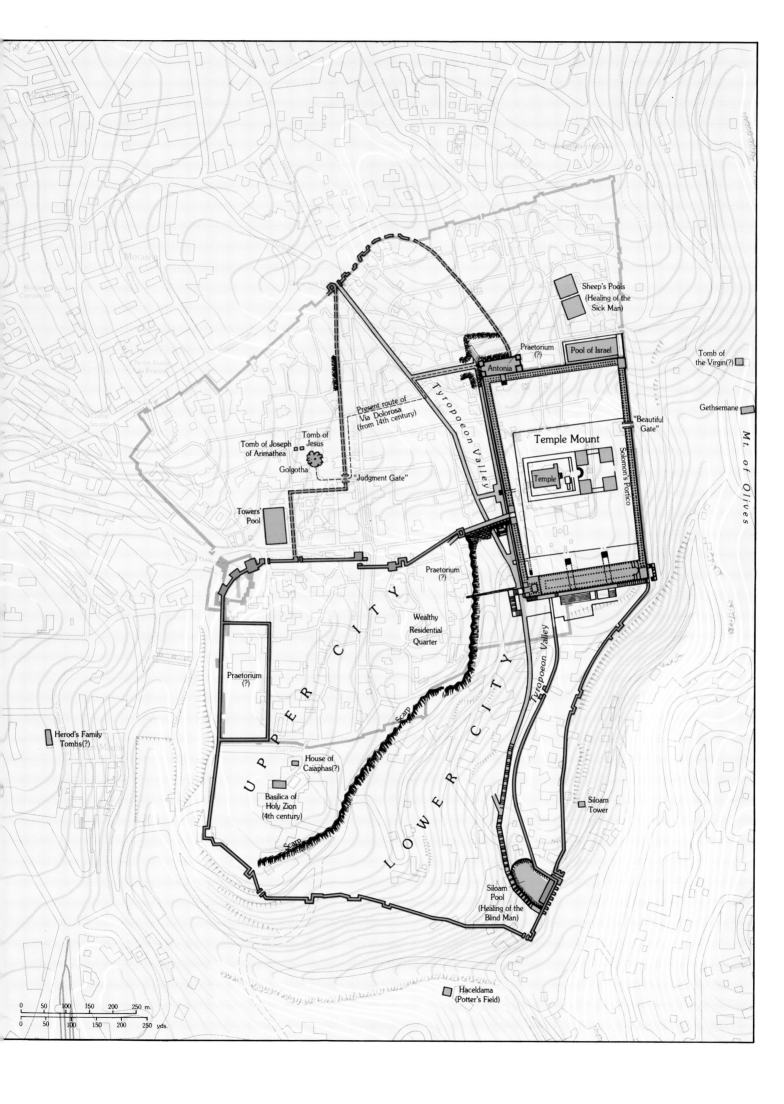

Sheep's Pools
(Healing of the
Sick Man)

Praetorium
(?)

Antonia

Pool of Israel

Tomb of
the Virgin(?)

Gethsemane

Tyropoeon Valley

"Beautiful
Gate"

Present route of
Via Dolorosa
(from 14th century)

Temple Mount

Temple

Solomon's Portico

Mt. of Olives

Tomb of
Jesus

Tomb of Joseph
of Arimathea

Golgotha

"Judgment Gate"

Towers'
Pool

Praetorium
(?)

Wealthy
Residential
Quarter

U P P E R   C I T Y

Tyropoeon Valley

L O W E R   C I T Y

Praetorium
(?)

Herod's Family
Tombs(?)

Scarp

House of
Caiaphas(?)

Basilica of
Holy Zion
(4th century)

Siloam
Tower

Scarp

Siloam
Pool
(Healing of the
Blind Man)

Haceldama
(Potter's Field)

0   50   100   150   200   250 m.

0   50   100   150   200   250 yds.

(left) Olive trees at **Gethsemane**, from an album of photographs presented to the Ottoman Sultan Abdul Hamid (1876–1909), depicting some of the curiosities in his domain he was unable to see, as he hardly ever left his palace in Istanbul. Botanists believe these trees to be about 2,000 years old, and thus could have been seen by Jesus as he reposed in the Garden of Gethsemane.

The site, still a focus of veneration to pilgrims, is located at the foot of the Mount of Olives. In the immediate vicinity, other traditional sites, such as the Grotto of the Agony and the Tomb of the Virgin, are an indication of the sanctity bestowed on the vicinity by the Christians since earliest times.

Near the small orchard, a church was first built in the Byzantine period. Destroyed by the Muslims, the church was reconstructed in the Crusader period. The present-day church, rebuilt in the twentieth century, is known as the Church of All Nations.

The well-preserved state of the olive trees in Gethsemane, some of which date to the time of Jesus, is due to the revererence that has continually been bestowed on the site by generations of believers.

The meaning of Gethsemane in Hebrew is olive-press, indicating the species of trees that has always been grown here.

destruction in 70 CE was small and poor. Furthermore, no documentation concerning the sites that were considered holy, or about their precise location, has remained. Moreover, when Jerusalem became a pagan city in 135 CE, the persecution of Christians by the Roman authorities precluded the development and maintenance of the holy places, and thus, many of the authentic sites simply disappeared, leaving no traces.

In the fourth century, when Christianity became the dominant religion and could be observed openly, the Christians built churches at various points in the city they believed to be the true sites of the evangelical events. The fact that the identification of the holy places in the first Christian period (the Byzantine period) was refuted in the second Christian period (the Crusader period), reflects the difficulties in authenticating the holy sites. The three centuries of obscurity, from the first to the fourth centuries CE, contributed to the dubiousness regarding the actual sites where the events occurred.

In addition, even to the present day, the Eastern and Western churches, as well as the various denominations, have conflicting traditions, adding to the difficulties.

The only holy site which has been thoroughly excavated and studied is the Church of the Holy Sepulcher, the traditional site of Jesus' crucifixion, burial, and resurrection. The result of the study can be summarized as follows.

During the First and Second Temple periods, the site served as a quarry, a place suitable for both executions and burials. Proof of this is provided by the numerous burial caves discovered within the premises of the church and the immediate vicinity. Moreover, the descriptions of the fourth-century church fathers concerning the works carried out at the site, first by Hadrian and then by Constantine the Great, indicate the difficulties faced by builders at this quarry. In addition, the existence of contemporary burial caves at the site is a good indication that at that time the church was located outside the city wall (that is, the Second Wall). This, therefore, adds to the authenticity of the Holy Sepulcher.

Naturally, one would expect to have the same simple explanation for the Via Dolorosa, which plays such an important role in the minds of millions of believers. However, the whole concept of the Via Dolorosa, as it is perceived today, began in the Crusader period, when on Palm Sunday the faithful would pass through the Golden Gate onto the Temple Mount, thereby imitating the triumphal entry of Jesus into Jerusalem. The pilgrims would then continue to the Church of the Holy Sepulcher through the "Gates of Sorrow" in the western wall of the Temple Mount.

This is the origin of the route of the Via Dolorosa. Its final course—as it runs today—was ascribed only in the fourteenth century. The Stations of the Cross have not been included in the map because, although the Via Dolorosa clearly ends in the Church of the Holy Sepulcher, its initial point remains obscure.

This starting point, according to the Gospels, is the site where Pontius Pilate condemned Jesus to death. The sources make no reference to the location of the site (the Praetorium). Only in John 19:13 is there a more detailed description. Even this account, however, is not sufficiently specific, and three possible locations have been considered.

The first is the Antonia fortress at the northwestern corner

(left) **David's Tower**, with the exception of the Temple Mount, is the most impressive of the remains of Second Temple period Jerusalem. In the time of Jesus, it was named the Hippicus Tower, built by Herod the Great to commemorate a friend of his by this name. Nevertheless, David's dynasty, to which Jesus is ascribed, left its profound impression on the Christians of the city. The connection between King David and his city led to the renaming of the tower already by the early community of Christians in the city, while the gate to the west of the tower had also borne the name of King David.

For the Christians, David's Tower symbolizes the "earthly" Jerusalem and during the Crusader period—when Jerusalem received its utmost expression as both the Earthly and the Heavenly City—David's Tower, as well as the Church of the Holy Sepulcher and the Dome of the Rock, became the most important symbols of Jerusalem.

Today, erroneously, the name "David's Tower" refers to the seventeenth minaret of the Citadel.

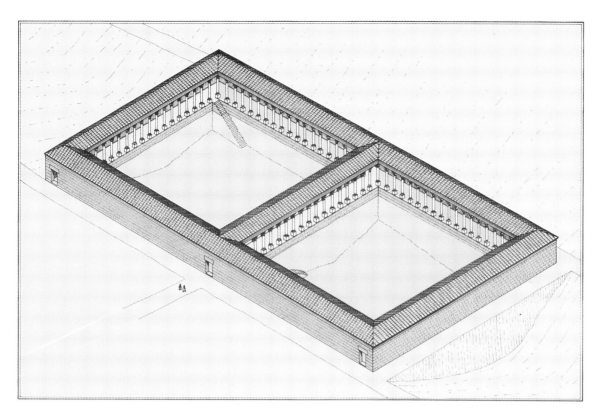

(left) The **Sheep's Pools** were built in the Beth Zetha Valley which began at the present-day American Colony, passed through the Old City wall near the Rockefeller Museum and ended in the Kidron Valley in the vicinity of the Lions' Gate. A number of dams and some of the largest pools in Jerusalem, such as the Pool of Israel, were constructed in this valley. As the archaeological evidence has shown, the northern pool was first dug at the end of the First Temple period, and the other pool was added in the Hellenistic era, at the beginning of the second century BCE, apparently at the initiative of the High Priest Simon. It continued to exist, as it is depicted in the illustration until the destruction of the Second Temple.

The reconstruction of the pools is based mainly on Christian sources. These pools were held to be holy because of the miracle attributed to Jesus at their edge, and the porticoes surrounding them are described in detail in the New Testament. It is generally believed that sheep were washed here before being offered up as sacrifice in the Temple, hence the name Sheep's Pools.

of the Temple Mount. This has been the traditional site for the Praetorium ever since Crusader times, but in the Byzantine period, and for a long time thereafter, a certain church, which must have stood somewhere near today's Western Wall plaza, was thought to have commemorated the event.

This leads us to a second possibility: Pontius Pilate used the Hasmonean palace (located in the present-day Jewish Quarter) as his residence, making this the site where the trial of Jesus took place. However, other scholars suggest he would have preferred the luxurious palace of King Herod, near the present-day Citadel.

Acceptance of any one of these theories would necessitate a change in the course of the Via Dolorosa.

A site that had an important role in both early and modern Christianity is the Basilica of Holy Zion, which served as an assembly place for the early Christian community in Jerusalem. Its long history has yet to be studied, but for pilgrims who come to Jerusalem, the Basilica of Holy Zion is second in importance only to that of the Holy Sepulcher. Remains of this fourth-century basilica were recently discovered.

But again there is a gap between the first-century residential quarter discovered on the site and the fourth-century Byzantine church, remains of which have been uncovered in a considerably preserved state. Very little is really known of events that occurred between the first and fourth centuries.

Other sites in Jerusalem mentioned in the Gospels include Gethsemane (Matt. 26:36–46, Mark 14:32), Haceldama (Matt. 27:6–8), the Siloam Pool (John 9:1–12), and Solomon's Portico (John 10:23; Acts 3:11, 5:12). All these sites are of great significance, as they provide information concerning not only the topography of the Holy Land, but also the customs and lifestyle of the communities which inhabited the city at the time of Jesus.

Although there is no doubt about the existence of the sites during this period, our knowledge is still lacking as a result of the three missing centuries of information.

(above) A **mounting stone** dating to the Crusader period, installed in the Church of Bethany, the site where Jesus began his triumphal entry into the Holy City. The stone depicts this scene (shown here) and others from the life of Christ, such as the resurrection of Lazarus.

(below) A 1922 reconstruction of **Jesus' tomb**. This is a typical burial cave with a rolling stone at its opening. The form of bedrock as shown is based on conjecture, as it is known that the area served as a quarry. Generations of pilgrims chipped away pieces of the rock as souvenirs, thus completely distorting the shape of the tombs.

Aelia Capitolina
135 – 326

(right) **Seal with the emblem of the Tenth Roman Legion**—a ship and a boar—engraved on a roof tile found in Jerusalem. In the center of the seal are the initials Leg.X.F. (Legio X Fretensis). Legions were named after the site of their most victorious battles.

(above) **Coin** from the period of the Emperor Antoninus Pius showing his image, and on the reverse side, one of the symbols of the Tenth Legion—a war vessel with oars and a battering ram on its prow.

In the process of putting down the Great Revolt, Titus destroyed Jerusalem, demolished its walls and razed the Temple to the ground by fire. He left the western wall intact, as well as the three towers built by Herod—Hippicus, Mariamme, and Phasael—to be used by the Tenth Legion as a garrison and to serve as a testament for the coming generations to the magnitude of the city he succeeded in vanquishing (*Wars* 7, 8, 1).

The archaeological finds support Josephus' account as regards the city's southwestern wall and its three towers. This wall served as the basis of all the walls built in later periods. One of its towers—the Hippicus—is still extant, and is now called the Tower of David. Another tower continued to exist until the Byzantine era, but we have no evidence as to when the third tower ceased to exist.

Scholars agree that the camp of the Tenth Legion which remained in Jerusalem, was situated within the area of the present-day Armenian Quarter in the Old City, between the Cardo and the city's western wall, and between David Street and the city's southern wall. Archaeological finds attest to the existence of the Roman camp within the boundaries of this area (approximately 820 × 1,247 feet [250 × 380 meters]). These include roof tiles, clay pipes, and bricks, generally bearing the Legion's initials Leg.X.F. (Legio X Fretensis) and its emblem—a wild boar—or maritime symbols such as ships, dolphins, or the sea god Neptune. It would seem that wooden structures and tents were erected within the area presumed to be where the camp was situated, and this explains why no remains of permanent buildings have

been found on the site. Additional support of the theory of the Roman camp's position are the remains of two streets leading to the presumed location of the entrance to the camp. These were the present-day Christians' Street, leading from the north, and part of the street discovered on Mount Zion, from the south. These streets apparently joined up with the main street which divided the camp into two equal parts.

A section of the wall discovered during the last century beneath the Lutheran hostel in St. Mark's Street, was considered by some scholars to be a section of the northern wall of the Tenth Legion's camp. However, this section was built no earlier than the Middle Ages, and thus cannot possibly be part of the Roman camp wall. There is also no foundation to the theory that the section of the wall uncovered to the west of the Cardo in the Jewish Quarter is part of the camp's eastern wall.

The activities of the Tenth Legion certainly went beyond the presumed area of the camp. This can be determined from the discovery of remains of buildings, roof tiles and clay pipes bearing the Legion's emblem. These were found in a number of locations in the region of Jerusalem: the Citadel, Mount Zion, the City of David, and in the vicinity of the present-day Binyanei Ha'ooma, Ramat Rahel, and Motza.

The soldiers of the Tenth Legion and the retired Roman soldiers Titus brought to Jerusalem, as well as Syrians and Eastern Greeks, constituted a large sector of Jerusalem's population under Roman rule. During the reign of the Emperor Septimius Severus the population increased significantly, when the soldiers of the Legion were granted permission to marry and set up families. Only unmarried soldiers continued to live in the camp. The first Christians expelled from Jerusalem to Pella in Transjordan, just prior to the Great Revolt, began to return to the city, and it seems that Jews also began to settle there once more. Epiphanius (a fourth-century Christian author) observes that seven synagogues remained standing in Jerusalem after the destruction of the city and one of them was still standing during the reign of the Emperor Constantine. If the reference is not to Christian houses of worship, this would seem to be evidence of the existence of a Jewish community in the city.

In the year 121 the Emperor Hadrian (Publius Aelius Hadrianus) set out on journeys throughout his empire, from England through Gaul and Spain up to the borders of the Parthian kingdom in the Orient. In spring of the year 130 he passed through Palestine on his way to Egypt, and decided to erect Aelia Capitolina on the ruins of Jerusalem. The name

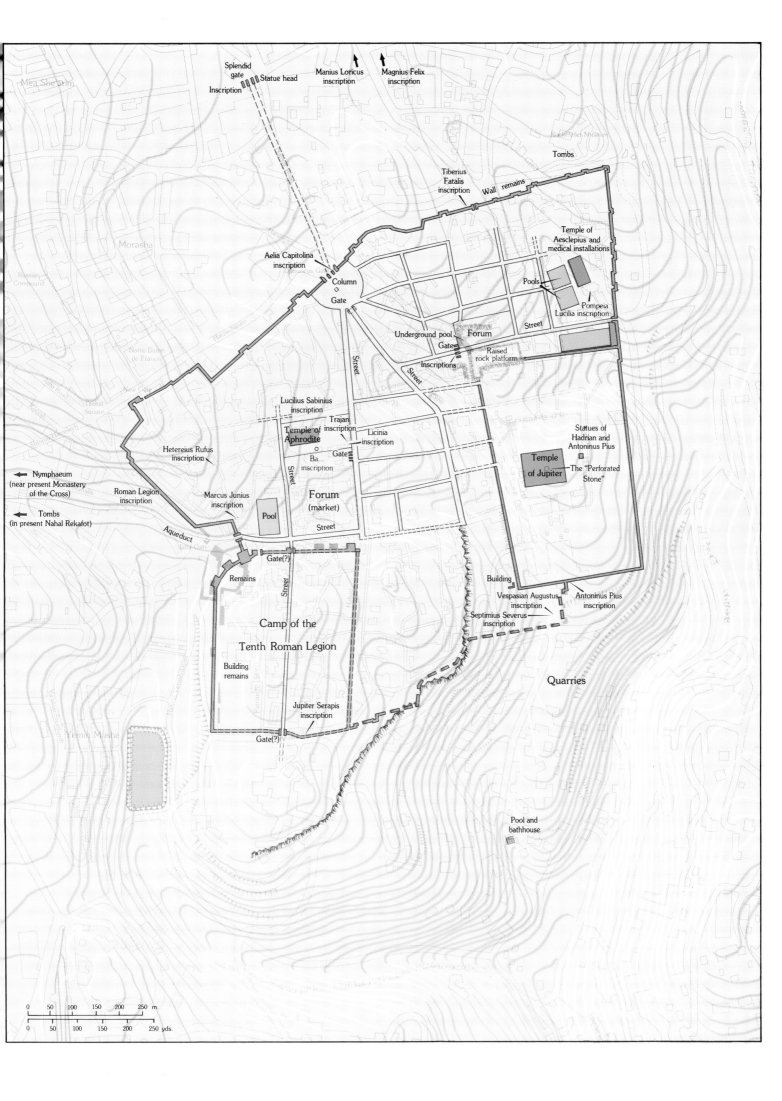

Splendid gate
Statue head
Inscription

Manius Loricus inscription
Magnius Felix inscription

Mea She'arim

Morasha

Russian Compound

Notre Dame de France

New Gate

Nahal Square

Tombs

Tiberius Fatalis inscription
Wall remains

Aelia Capitolina inscription

Column
Gate

Temple of Aesclepius and medical installations

Pools
Pompeia Lucilia inscription

Underground pool
Gate
Inscriptions

Forum
Street

Raised rock platform

Lucilius Sabinius inscription

Trajan inscription

Licinia inscription

Temple of Aphrodite

Ba... inscription

Gate

Statues of Hadrian and Antoninus Pius

Temple of Jupiter

The "Perforated Stone"

Hetereius Rufus inscription

← Nymphaeum (near present Monastery of the Cross)

← Tombs (in present Nahal Rekafot)

Roman Legion inscription

Marcus Junius inscription

Forum (market)

Pool

Street

Street

Aqueduct

Gate(?)

Remains

Building

Vespasian Augustus inscription
Antoninus Pius inscription
Septimius Severus inscription

Camp of the Tenth Roman Legion

Street

Building remains

Jupiter Serapis inscription

Quarries

Gate(?)

Yemin Moshe

Pool and bathhouse

0   50   100   150   200   250 m.

0   50   100   150   200   250 yds.

Aelia was after the family of the emperor, and Capitolina after the three Capitoline gods—Jupiter, Juno, and Minerva, patrons of the new city. A temple built on the Temple Mount—the Tricameron (see below)—was designated as a place for sacrifice to the Capitoline gods. Hadrian's desire to build a Roman pagan city on the ruins of Jerusalem was one of the main reasons for the eruption of the Bar Kokhba Revolt in the year 132. The third-century historian Dio Cassius stipulates the erection of the Tricameron on the Temple Mount as being the cause of the outbreak of the revolt. It may well be that in the first phase of the revolt, when the rebels were meeting with success, they actually conquered the city. In the few historical sources relating to this period (those that do exist are fragmentary), no mention whatsoever is made of Jerusalem, probably because of its lack of military significance. Coins from the period of the revolt often have some of the ritual vessels used in the Temple engraved on them, and all carry the inscription "For the liberation of Jerusalem," also found in many of the documents of the period. Some scholars assume that this is additional proof that Jerusalem was conquered by the Jews at that time, but it could also just be an expression of the hope in the hearts of the rebels.

After the suppression of the Bar Kokhba Revolt (in the year 135) the Romans carried out their plan to restore Jerusalem from its ruins, and to erect the pagan city of Aelia Capitolina on the site. Its erection was part of the plan to reinforce the eastern flank of the empire against foreign invaders, within the framework of which other cities were constructed and roads built. Roads were laid in Judea connecting Aelia Capitolina with Caesarea, Legio, and other cities in the land. The inscription "Colonia Aelia Capitolina condita" (the colony of Aelia Capitolina has been founded) appeared on coins of that period. They also carried the image of the emperor plowing a furrow along the course of the walls about to be built. (The furrow—*pomerium*—was the symbol of the founding of a city in the Roman Empire.) This concrete expression of the foundation of the city was considered by the Jews to be the materialization of Jeremiah's vision: "Zion shall be plowed like a field, and Jerusalem shall become heaps, and the mountain of the house as the high places of a forest" (26:18). However, the wall was erected around the city only 150 years later, and until then it was protected only by the Tenth Legion stationed there.

Aelia Capitolina was built in the pattern of a Roman colonial city—*canabea*. A Roman camp was set up and a civilian settlement grew up around it, whose economy was to a great extent dependent on this camp. It is still not clear how the new city was administered; what was the extent of the jurisdiction of the army in running it, what authority did the city council have? (Reference to the council was found in an inscription discovered on the Damascus Gate, which mentions the *decurions*—members of the council—who fixed this inscription in place.) The extent of the influence of the Roman city of Jerusalem has not yet been clarified, despite the fact that archaeological remains from that period have been found within its periphery.

In the year 195, the Second Temple aqueducts which brought water from Solomon's Pools to the city were repaired. The names of the Roman consuls of that period were carved on some of the syphon stones in these aqueducts, a fact which has made possible the dating of the repairs to the city's water supply system. It appears that it was during this period that the upper aqueduct was built, which brought water from Solomon's Pools to the vicinity of the Hippicus Tower, but there is no evidence available to substantiate this. The construction work was done by the soldiers of the Tenth Legion, as was the case throughout the empire, and the names of some of the soldiers engraved on the syphon stones have remained.

It seems that no Jews remained in Jerusalem after the Bar Kokhba Revolt, contrary to the preceding period when a small Jewish community still lived in the city following the Great Revolt. Hadrian banned the Jews from entering the city, and this ban remained in force for a long time, although there were ups and downs as regards the extent to which it was imposed. From time to time Jews were permitted to visit the site of the Temple. On the other hand, a Christian community existed in Jerusalem throughout the period of Roman rule, and was dependent upon the community in Caesarea for administrative and religious services.

In the year 235, the Roman Empire was overcome by anarchy, which lasted for about forty years. During this period the army suffered crushing defeats, and in fact ceased to exist. Tadmor (Palmyra), in Syria, exploited the empire's weakness and conquered its eastern sector, which included Palestine. It was only in the year 270, when the Emperor Aurelian ascended the throne, that order was restored and the security intensified. Aurelian fought against the internal as well as the external enemies of the empire, and conquered Tadmor in 272 in a battle in which soldiers of the Tenth Legion from Aelia Capitolina participated.

Within the framework of the reorganization introduced by the Emperor Diocletian, the Tenth Legion was transferred from Aelia Capitolina to Eilat in the year 289, after an almost two-hundred-year sojourn in Jerusalem.

(above) **Memorial to Marcus Junius** on a stone column placed in the square near the Imperial Hotel in the Old City. The monument, in memory of an officer of the Tenth Legion, was prepared by his adjutant with an inscription in Latin stating: "To Marcus Junius Maximus, commander on behalf of the emperors, of the Tenth Legion of Fretensis Antonini, (the column was prepared by)

Cassius, Domitius Sergianus, Julius Honoratus—his adjutant." This inscription is apparently from the beginning of the third century. Later (approximately 216 CE) the word Antonini was added in cursive script. This was the name the Emperor Caracalla gave to the Tenth Legion.

This column was discovered in 1885 in the course of excavations for the foundations of a nearby building. However, it seems that this was not

the original location, but that it was brought from elsewhere and here served a different purpose. This phenomenon of the use of Roman monuments for various functions other than their original purpose is found in other locations in Jerusalem (in the excavation of the northern wall, for example, some additional monuments were uncovered), but the original location of these monuments is not yet known.

(above) The **Christians' Street** is generally identified with the Patriarch's Street, well-known from Crusader sources (the street is called by this name after the Patriarch's palace which stood at its end). In the archaeological excavations carried out along this street, large serrated stone slabs were found. The stones were similar to others from the Roman era found in the Lithostrotos (the Sisters of Zion Convent) and in the Damascus Gate square. We can thus conclude that the ancient Christians'

Street was paved in the Roman era. The street was not laid when Aelia Capitolina was built, but at a relatively later phase, at the end of the third century or at the beginning of the fourth century, when Roman building in the city reached it peak.

The planner of this street was directed by two factors: the location of the Pool of the Patriarch (Hezekiah's Pool) and the site of the Tenth Legion camp. The street originated at the entrance to the camp, and from there ran

northward, bordering on the Pool of the Patriarch. Apparently an identical street ran from the southern entrance of this camp to Mount Zion, where the remains of a similar street were found. The camp of the Roman Legion was an important factor in the planning of the Roman city, and the two streets described here fit in with it well.

(above) **Coin from Aelia Capitolina** issued by Hadrian showing his image, above which is the inscription "Imperator Caesar Trianus Hadrianus." On the reverse side the emperor is seen plowing the contour of the new city with a pair of oxen, and the inscription in Latin "the colony of Aelia Capitolina has been founded." In the background is one of the legion's standards that were carried in processions.

(above) **Coin minted in Jerusalem** by the Emperor Hadrian with his bust on the obverse. On the reverse he is seen plowing the furrow for the course of the planned city walls.

The Structure of the Roman City

The dearth of historical sources and the paucity of archaeological finds make attempts to reconstruct the image of the city under Roman rule most difficult. One of the sources of information about this period are the coins minted at the time. From them it is possible to learn about the pagan rituals carried out in Jerusalem, about Roman emperors who visited it, the extent of the city's loyalty to the emperors, and the benefactions it received from them. An example of this was found on the coins minted in Aelia Capitolina on the occasion of the visit of Marcus Aurelius and his son Commodus to Palestine in the year 176. On the coins the city is designated "Commodiana Pia Felix," a title which it earned for its loyalty to the empire, and from that time the abbreviated form—Col.Ael.Cap.Comm.Pia Felix—appeared on its coins. The right to mint coins in cities was taken from them in the year 274 and remained with the emperor only. That year brought to an end this source of the city's history. Another source for the reconstruction of the city's appearance under Roman rule was the *Chronicon Paschale* (Easter Chronicle, see below).

Reliance on archaeological finds is also problematical, because the passage from the Roman to the Byzantine period was expressed in spiritual rather than physical terms, and thus there was no clear expression in the form of buildings. When Christianity dominated the city, it underwent a period of accelerated development, and the Roman structures were gradually integrated into those of the Byzantine era. Thus it is difficult to identify buildings from the period of Roman rule, unless they were not subjected to major changes under the Byzantines. It is for these reasons that the Roman period is the least well-known in the history of Jerusalem.

From the time of the destruction of the Second Temple in 70 CE, and up to the end of the third century, the city was not surrounded by walls. Anyone approaching it could easily see the walls of the Temple Mount, which stood out in the landscape. In certain places remains of the Second Temple period walls could still be discerned, but the only conspicuous section that remained was in the southwestern sector of the city. When the Tenth Legion was transferred from Jerusalem to Eilat (in the year 289), the city had no form of defense and it would seem that it was then that the wall was erected around it. The course of the new walls mainly followed that of the earlier ones.

Repair works were probably carried out on the retaining walls of the Temple Mount so as to recreate the platform upon which a temple was built. Some of the "patches" still visible in the Temple Mount walls can be related to this period. The eastern section of the city walls, which was part of the Third Wall—from the Lions' Gate to the vicinity of the Rockefeller Museum—was renovated at that time. No actual remains from the Roman period have been found, but the fact that similar remains have been uncovered along the course of the northern wall of the Old City dating to the Roman period leads to the conclusion that the course of the present-day eastern wall is identical with that of the Roman period eastern wall.

A number of archaeological excavations were carried out along the present northern wall during the 1930s and 1970s. Through them it has been established that the course of the present-day wall originated at the end of the third century, the Roman period. When the wall was erected, a triumphal arch built as a memorial about one hundred and fifty years earlier, was incorporated into it at the point where the Damascus Gate now stands (see below).

Following the excavation of a section of the northern wall, between the Damascus and New Gates, a theory was postulated that the wall was actually built in the Byzantine period. This could well have been the case, since no historical source has yet come to light which describes the erection of the walls in the third century, and archaeological finds have not made it possible to determine the exact period

the building took place. Scholars are still not agreed as to when the city wall was built: was it erected in Roman times when the Tenth Legion left the city at the end of the third century, or was it built under Byzantine rule when Jerusalem became a Christian metropolis (approximately in the year 330)?

The dating of the city's western wall—the section north of present-day Jaffa Gate—is also a matter of controversy. For some time now, scholars have tended to believe that the course of the Roman wall ran east of that of the present wall. However, the chance discovery of a section of the Roman–Byzantine wall to the west of the present-day wall may well undermine this theory. Thus, it is not possible to set the course of the walls inside the present wall, but rather outside it.

No vestiges of the city's southern wall have yet been found. The course of the wall as presented in the map at the beginning of this chapter has been determined only on the basis of information of the existence of a wall in the south of the city in the Byzantine period, mainly based on the Madaba map. It is presumed that the wall depicted in that map followed a course somewhat similar to that of the Roman southern wall, which would be near to that of the present wall.

The wall of Aelia Capitolina had four main gates, representing the four points of the compass: Damascus Gate to the north, Jaffa Gate to the west, the Lions' Gate to the east, and Zion Gate to the south. (The names of the gates in Roman times are unknown, and thus we have called them by their present names.) Of these four, only the Damascus Gate has been examined, but information regarding the structure of the other gates in the wall cannot be derived from it, since this gate was originally built as a triumphal arch when the wall was still in ruins, and was only incorporated within the wall when it was rebuilt in the third century.

The main gates served as an exit for the pattern of the city's streets, whose course has remained intact in the main until the present. The city's two main streets originated at the square near the city's northern gate (Damascus Gate). These streets were called the Cardines, in the singular Cardo, meaning axis. The remains of one of these streets were uncovered underneath the present-day Beit Habad market, while the remains of the other were found under Haggai Street. Another street that ran the length of the city, found along the present-day Christians' Street, was apparently the continuation of the main street in the Tenth Legion camp (see above). Archaeological excavations carried out there have revealed that the street was paved only at the end of the third century, or the beginning of the fourth.

An organized system of streets has been preserved from what would seem to be the Roman period in the northern sector of the Muslim Quarter of the Old City. These are streets which run parallel to one another, and intersecting at right angles. It would seem that part of the city's system of streets has been preserved in the area between the two Roman-period Cardines.

The identification of the main street that ran along the breadth of Aelia Capitolina—the Decumanus—which was built in every typical Roman city, presents a special problem. Apparently, the course of the Decumanus was from the present-day Jaffa Gate to the Temple Mount. The easterly continuation of this main road veered slightly to the north, and continued from the Cardo along Haggai Street to the present Lions' Gate, in the east. The numerous archaeological digs carried out along the course of this street have not revealed any evidence that the street existed in Roman times. It must be remembered that during this period the southern sector of the city was not inhabited, and thus there would have been no need for this street. Many scholars believed that the Tetrapylon—the gate with four openings—mentioned in the *Chronicon Paschale* was a sort of triumphal arch which stood at the intersection of the Cardo and the Decumanus.

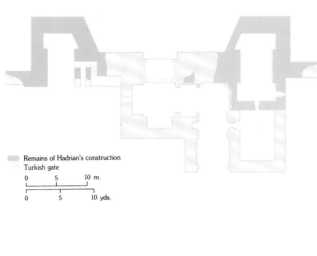

Remains of Hadrian's construction
Turkish gate

```
0        5        10  m.
0        5        10  yds.
```

(above, right, and center) The **Damascus Gate** served as the main entrance to Aelia Capitolina in the Roman period. Here began the main road to Caesarea, which served as the capital of the country at that time. The gate was built with splendor, as can be seen in the reconstruction presented here. Above the eastern entrance was an inscription reading: "The colony of Aelia Capitolina, [the inscription] was placed here by decree of the decurions [members of the city council]."

The remains of the Roman gate were first uncovered in excavations carried out in 1938 on behalf of the Palestine Department of Antiquities. The explorer Hamilton, who directed the excavations, uncovered a section of the ancient gate, and parts of the inscription and ornamental decorations. In the 1960s, the facade of the eastern entrance was found intact by J. B. Hennessy in the course of his excavations there. The finds were mainly from the Middle Ages, such as a anterior gate and adjacent buildings. The major part of the gate has been unearthed in the course of excavations carried out on the site by Israeli archaeologists from 1979. They uncovered the eastern entrance in its entirety, as well as the eastern gate tower (not shown here). This gate tower was preserved intact, except for its ceiling, which was rebuilt in the Ottoman period by Suleiman the Magnificent. This is one of the most beautiful vestiges from the Roman period preserved in its entirety in Palestine. Large sections of the gate and the tower were constructed with Herodian-style stone-dressed slabs, and were apparently taken from Herodian structures demolished at the time of the destruction of the Second Temple. The central entrance of the Roman gate has not remained, probably because it underwent many changes over the years. Only a few vestiges of the western entrance have remained.

The Madaba map shows a spacious square near the Damascus Gate and in the center of which was a large column with a statue apparently of the emperor. The two main streets (the Cardines) led from this square to the city. The excavations of the area, began in 1982, have revealed remains of sections of the square paved with large stone slabs (6.6 × 4 feet [2 × 1.2 m.]). Although the boundaries of this square have not yet been discovered, enough of its remains has been uncovered to estimate its dimensions. So far, no sign of the column shown in the Madaba map has been found.

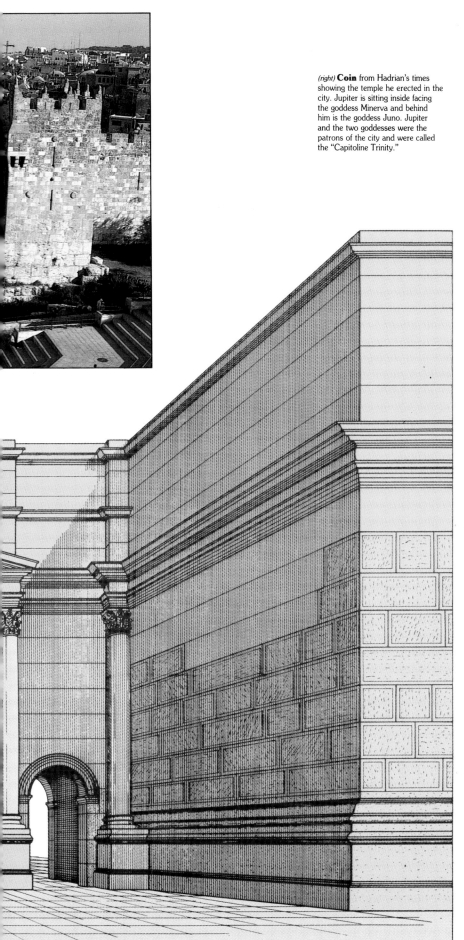

(right) **Coin** from Hadrian's times showing the temple he erected in the city. Jupiter is sitting inside facing the goddess Minerva and behind him is the goddess Juno. Jupiter and the two goddesses were the patrons of the city and were called the "Capitoline Trinity."

However, the lack of details about the Decumanus on the one hand, and the fact that in the Roman era the Cardo only reached the center of the city, on the other, did not provide a solid basis for this theory.

Archaeological excavations have revealed that the streets of Jerusalem at this time were paved. This was maintained at least up to the Arab period, and contemporary authors specifically mention this fact.

There were two main public squares in Aelia Capitolina, and they, too, were paved. The largest was situated in the present-day Muristan and was surrounded by four streets. The forum, which was the city marketplace, was situated in this square, and continued to exist until the Arab period. The area of the square was reduced when luxurious buildings were erected around it. Remains of the forum's paving stones were uncovered in the course of the many excavations carried out there.

The other forum was situated in the eastern sector of the city, near the present-day Sisters of Zion Convent. In this area is the large moat dug by Herod for the defense of the Antonia fortress, and in this period, too, the Struthion Pool was dug in the center of this moat as a water reservoir. When the Emperor Hadrian decided to set up another forum on that site, the large pool was covered over with two parallel vaults spanning its length, and the entire moat, including the area above the vaults, was paved with large stone slabs. Along the length of the main street which crossed the square, paving stones were serrated to prevent passersby from slipping on the finely hewn stones. At the northern extremity of the square was a precipice in which storerooms and water cisterns were excavated (some of these may have been incorporated in burial caves from earlier periods). No reference whatsoever to this square is found in post-Roman period sources, and thus we do not know how long it continued to exist.

Another feature of Jerusalem under Roman rule was its four monumental triumphal arches. The first was erected in the area of the Second Temple period Third Wall, about 1,312 feet (400 meters) north of the city wall. A chance discovery uncovered sections of pillars and large stone blocks, two of which bore inscriptions. One of these inscriptions is from the time of the Emperor Hadrian, and the other from that of the Emperor Antoninus Pius. Nineteenth-century explorers were of the opinion that these were the remains of a triumphal arch built by Hadrian in honor of his victories in the war with Bar Kokhba, and Antoninus Pius continued to embellish this arch. The location of this triumphal arch in the vicinity of the main entrance to the Roman city certainly stresses its great significance. This arch apparently also included the bust of an exquisite Roman statue discovered near the site where the remains of the arch were found.

South of this triumphal arch, on the site of the present-day Damascus Gate, stood another triumphal arch. Apparently erected during Hadrian's reign, this arch was also built in

64

(above) A **Roman bust** suggested
to be that of the Emperor
Hadrian found in 1873 embedded
in a wall near the Tomb of the Kings,
north of the Damascus Gate.

The archaeologist Charles
Clermont-Ganneau was the first to
describe the statue, and he reached
the conclusion that this was the bust
of Hadrian. This assumption was
accepted by many scholars, even
though it was clear that the features
on this bust differed from those on
other statues of Hadrian. Another
theory is that the indistinct symbol on
the headpiece shows this to be the
bust of a priest from one of the city's
temples.

This statue is unique among the
Roman art treasures in Jerusalem. It
is made of marble and is the size of a
human head. After its discovery, the
bust was purchased by the Russian
Archimandirate of Jerusalem, and its
whereabouts was unknown for a long
time. Only recently was it found in the
Hermitage Museum in Leningrad.

(below far right) The **Ecce Homo
Arch** is generally considered to have
been built by the Emperor Hadrian,
mainly because it has three entrances
like the other three arches built in
Jerusalem during Hadrian's rule.

In recent years a number of
scholars have questioned the dating
of this structure. When comparing
it to other buildings whose date of
construction is agreed upon, these
scholars argue that the Ecce Homo
Arch was built during the Second
Temple period and was one of the
arches in the Third Wall built by
Agrippa. Although it is difficult to
accept this argument, it cannot be
dismissed out of hand. It would seem
that the illustration presented here
was drawn by Pierotti, because an
almost identical drawing appears in
his work *Jerusalem Explored* (1864),
in which he describes the excavation
of the foundations of the Sisters of
Zion Convent. The smaller arch at
the left is situated inside the entrance
to the convent and the Via Dolorosa
runs under the larger one.

(right) The central section of the
Ecce Homo Arch as photographed
from the Via Dolorosa. The original
sections of the arch are clearly visible.
On a stone placed in the entrance
wall to the Sisters of Zion Convent,
two inscriptions in Greek can be
partly deciphered:
"... ΕΛΛΙΝΟΝ ... ΥΦ ..." and in
the second, "TOIC ... A. ..." Their
meaning is not clear.

(left) The **Ecce Homo Arch** and its surroundings (the present-day Sisters of Zion Convent on Via Dolorosa). At the right can be seen the remains of the Antonia fortress which was demolished in the year 70, during the destruction of Jerusalem. At the base of the fortress are Herodian excavations designed to reinforce the fortress. The moat between the two cliffs was dug with the purpose of protecting the Antonia fortress from the north, thus separating it from the higher extension of the ridge, upon which it was built. In the time of Herod a huge water cistern called the Struthion Pool was dug

in the moat. Josephus relates that the Romans created a siege ramp from this water cistern in the moat in order to set siege to the fortress (*Wars* 5, 11, 4). In the Roman period the cistern was covered with two vaults (shown in the illustration) which were paved over with the rest of the moat, creating the area which became the city marketplace. This pool was preserved by the vaults which have covered it to this day. At the entrance to the marketplace a triumphal arch was built with three entrances, the central one being called Ecce Homo, meaning "Behold the Man." According to a Christian

tradition which developed in the late Middle Ages, Jesus was brought out of the Antonia through this arch, and it was here that he was condemned to death. The Roman procurator, Pontius Pilate, proclaimed to the crowd pointing to Jesus: "Behold the Man (whose life you seek to take)!" In front of the facade of the arch is a broad and elongated wall, the date of whose erection is unknown, and therefore it is presented here as it appears today beneath the floor of the Sisters of Zion Convent. Another vestige shown in this reconstruction is a section of the water conduit hewn out of the rock, through which water

flowed from the Struthion Pool to the south. The conduit was apparently excavated in the Hasmonean period, and run-off waters flowed through it from the area of the present-day Damascus Gate to the water cisterns on the Temple Mount. During the reign of Herod it was cut off by the digging of the Struthion Pool, and by the construction of the western wall of the Temple Mount. Since then, its only function has been to bring water from the vicinity of the Damascus Gate to the Struthion Pool.

a magnificent style. In the center was a wide entrance and on either side were two smaller entrances. Near the arch, inside the wall, was a stone-paved square. Excavations revealed only a small section of this square, but its dimensions can be ascertained from the Madaba map. (The map shows the structure of the city in Byzantine times, but many of the sites were identical in both periods.) According to this map, a column stood in the middle of the square, upon which apparently was placed a statue of the emperor, in keeping with the practice in many of the cities throughout the Roman Empire. It would seem that in later years, when the city was under Christian domination, the statue of the emperor was removed and replaced by that of a saint.

The other two triumphal arches were adjacent to the two marketplaces (forums) of the city. The remains of one of them, which opened onto the market square from the Cardo in the vicinity of the present-day Muristan, are to be found in the Russian Hospice (or Alexander Hospice), near the Church of the Holy Sepulcher. The arch had three entrances, but it is difficult to reconstruct it with any accuracy because of the dearth of remains, and because of the fact that under the Byzantines structural changes were made, thus changing its original appearance.

The most well-known of the Roman period triumphal arches was the Ecce Homo Arch. According to Christian tradition it was at this spot that Pontius Pilate brought Jesus before the masses, proclaiming "Ecce Homo" (Behold the Man!), making this one of the most important stations in the Via Dolorosa. The central and northern sections of the triumphal arch have remained intact.

Typical Roman municipal buildings erected in Aelia Capitolina, are mentioned in the seventh-century *Chronicon*

Paschale (Easter Chronicle). According to this source, Hadrian built in the city "... two demosia (public baths), a theater, a tricameron, and a tetranymphon and a dodecapylon (also called steps), and the codra, and divided the city into seven quarters. ..."

The description of the buildings listed in the *Chronicon Paschale* provides us with information about the renovation of the Temple Mount (*codra* means square, thus implying that the intention was to the Temple Mount which was square). This source also tells us of the construction on the Temple Mount of the temple to the Capitoline gods—the Tricameron. The third-century historian, Dio Cassius, describes the erection of the temple to Jupiter on the same site. There is no evidence of the appearance of this temple since later construction (of the Dome of the Rock) has obliterated all trace of it. There has remained from this structure an inscription of a dedication to the Emperor Antoninus Pius, which has been used as a stone block in the building above the Double Gate (see illustration on page 67). Scholars are of the opinion that this inscription was originally placed at the base of the statue of Antoninus Pius. (In fourth-century Christian sources mention is made of two statues which stood on the Temple Mount—one of Hadrian and the other apparently of the emperor who followed him, Antoninus Pius. Both statues were removed after the Christian conquest of Jerusalem.)

The later sources do not specify whether the temple to Jupiter was situated on the Temple Mount compound, or on the site where the Church of the Holy Sepulcher is situated. According to the Traveler of Bordeaux, for example, the temple was situated on the Temple Mount compound, and the Jews who visited the site on the ninth of Av each year

(right) The present-day area of the **Muristan** is situated on the square designated by Hadrian for the forum (the central marketplace) and the main square of Aelia Capitolina (the area was named the Muristan during the Ayyubid period). The square is bounded by straight streets paved in Roman times, and their course exists until now: David Street to the south, the Christians' Street to the west, the Dyers' Market (ed-Dabagha) Street to the north, and the Butchers' Market Street to the east. So far, no remains have been found of the buildings that stood in the forum, but finds from archaeological excavations carried out in the vicinity of the Lutheran Church of the Redeemer (to the east of the forum) and in the vicinity of the Church of the Holy Sepulcher, reveal that most of the area was paved with large stone slabs.

The central square of the Roman city was generally built in the region of quarries and ancient

cisterns, which made the paving and construction work most difficult. Thus, supporting arches were built in some of the cisterns, while some of the others were filled with earth. According to Kathleen Kenyon, extremely large quantities of soil were brought here to fill the quarries and cisterns, in order to raise the surface level. Kathleen Kenyon discovered a drainage system below the central square. The archaeological excavations reveal that the Romans invested tremendous efforts in the construction of this square. It would appear that the square continued to exist in the Byzantine era in its original form of an open square, and it was only in the Abbasid period (the eighth and ninth centuries) that the first buildings were erected on its western side. These and others built at a later date filled in the square, and in the course of time it became a completely built-up area.

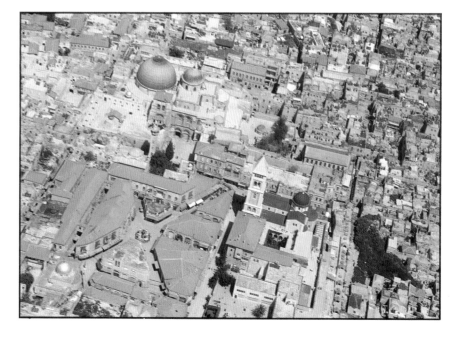

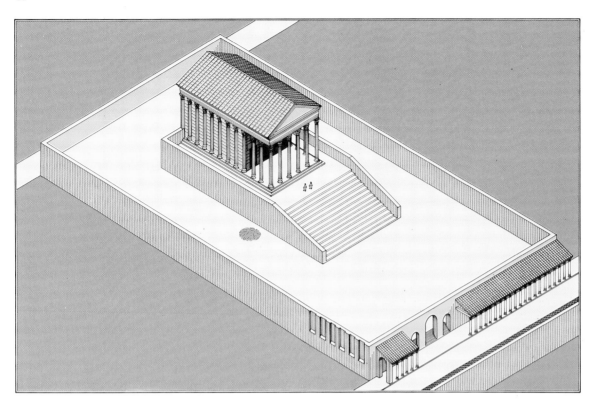

(top left) The **Temple of Aphrodite** was one of the two temples built by Hadrian in Jerusalem. In the temple courtyard the crest of the Golgotha hill can be seen. This hill plays an important role in Christian religious practice. Archaeologists who excavated the Church of the Holy Sepulcher are of the opinion that a statue of Aphrodite, who was worshipped in this temple, stood on the crest of this hill. As a consequence of inaccuracies in the historical sources, a controversy exists among scholars as to whether this temple was devoted to the worship of Aphrodite or of Jupiter.

to clean the Foundation Stone, were forced to do so in the presence of the statues of these emperors. However, reliance on the Christian sources in this matter is problematical, because they wished to create the impression that the Jews were being humiliated at that time. These sources were being written at the time the pagan temples were being demolished when the city had come under Christian dominion, and thus the information they contain may not be accurate.

The Tetranymphon mentioned in the *Chronicon Paschale* is a fountain or pool divided into four sections. This might be the Siloam Pool which had been renovated in the form of a square. The location of the other structures mentioned in this source have not yet been identified.

The main religious practice carried out in the city was the cult worship of the three Capitoline gods whose images appear on many coins of the period. But these were not the only gods worshipped in Aelia Capitolina. We know of other gods to whom temples were erected in the city. The most important of them was the goddess Aphrodite (Venus), to whom Hadrian erected a temple at the site where the Church of the Holy Sepulcher was built later. Evidence from archaeological excavations show that the site originally was a quarry and in order to enable him to build the temple, Hadrian was required to fill in depressions in the ground and to build a retaining wall. Christian tradition claims that these works were attempts on the part of Hadrian to obliterate the tomb of Jesus, which according to Christian belief at the time was located at this site. The remains of a retaining wall are evident in a number of places, especially at the Russian Hospice mentioned above. When describing the city's buildings in the fourth century, Eusebius states that the temple erected on this site was a temple to Aphrodite. However, writing a short time later, St. Jerome claimed that this was the temple to Jupiter and added that a statue of Aphrodite was placed upon the rock at Golgotha. According to reconstructions based on recent research, the filling in the plaza built by Hadrian was so high that the Golgotha protruded above the compound floor, and the statue was placed upon it. This description is surprising since there is no logical reason for the statue of Aphrodite to be placed in a temple to Jupiter. The problem of which deity was worshipped in this temple has not yet been solved. Few vestiges of the temple itself have been found, and these are mainly underground quarries, and columns which are

(center left) Remains of the **retaining wall** of the raised platform upon which Hadrian built the **Temple of Aphrodite**, as it was revealed in the grounds of the Russian (Alexander) Hospice. The hospice is part of the Church of the Holy Sepulcher complex.

In order to create the raised platform upon which the temple was built, Hadrian surrounded it with retaining walls and filled in the space between them with stones and earth. The section shown here is a vestige of one of these retaining walls. It was built with Herodian-type dressed stone blocks, and it would appear that they were taken from a Second Temple period structure and brought to the area of Hadrian's temple. The support wall was built in part in the form of forecourts and recesses in the manner of the Herodian Temple Mount wall.

Remains were also found in the grounds of the Russian Hospice of an embellished arch, built in the form of the Roman triumphal arches. The arch served as an entrance to the Roman marketplace, situated to the south of the Church of the Holy Sepulcher.

(bottom left) A Roman relief discovered in the vicinity of the Sheep's Pools, apparently connected with the worship of the Roman god **Aesclepius Serapis** (the first name being the Greek-Roman god of medicine, and the latter an Oriental deity said to have healing powers; they were unified in later Roman mythology).

After the destruction of the Second Temple, a temple for the worship of Aesclepius was built in the vicinity of the Sheep's Pools, identified in Christian tradition with the Bethesda Pools in which Jesus healed the blind, the lame, and the paralyzed (John 5:1–15). Remains were found on the site of bathing facilities, small pools, buildings, a mosaic floor, a drainage system—all part of a larger system of water works. Persons who came to be healed slept in the subterranean rooms and in the pools excavated in the rock. They believed that their sojourn at this holy place would heal their ailments.

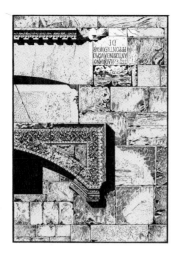

today situated underneath the rotunda of the Church of the Holy Sepulcher. Sections of other decorations which have remained in the church are cornices from the temple, which have been reused in the facade of the Church of the Holy Sepulcher in the Crusader period.

Another temple whose remains have been discovered in Jerusalem is that of Aesclepius Serapis. Coins bearing his image show that Serapis was an Oriental god who was worshipped in Aelia Capitolina. This temple was razed to the ground during the Christian conquest.

Tiche, the goddess of fortune, was also worshipped there. Her likeness appears on coins of the city, but there is no reference to the location of a temple erected in her honor.

Little is known about burial patterns in Jerusalem of the Roman era. A few graves were discovered when the Rockefeller Museum was being built; others were found in recent years in the vicinity of the Royal Tombs, in the north of the city. Perhaps what is today called the Tomb of Simon the Just, one of the most exquisite in Jerusalem, is from Roman times. The name of one of the persons buried there, Julia Sabina, appears on one of its walls.

A host of finds from this period was made in two tombs in Nahal Rekafot, situated between the Giv'at Mordechai and Bayit Vegan quarters to the west of the city. One tomb dates to the first half of the third century, and the other, a little later. Another two Roman period tombs were discovered in Shmu'el Hanavi Street, with many artifacts, especially beautiful ornaments. The two groups of tombs are similar in style, and it may well be that these were the graves of soldiers of the Tenth Legion and their wives. The wealth of expensive artifacts attest to the fact that the mid-third century was a particularly flourishing period in Roman history, about which we have further evidence from other regions of the empire.

The Roman era was an important one in the history of Jerusalem. The pattern of the streets and the general layout of Aelia Capitolina has set the character of Jerusalem up to the present.

(above and center right) A **Latin inscription** on a tablet reused in the construction of the **"Double Gate"** in the southern wall of the Temple Mount. It has been placed upside down above the decorated section of the gate. The inscription reads: "To the Imperator Caesar Titus Aelius Hadrianus, Antoninus, Augustus Pius, father of the homeland, the priest who divines the future (the tablet was placed here) by decree of the decurions."

The elegant style of the letters engraved on the tablet leads to the assumption that it was placed in a prominent position, probably some royal structure, but it is not clear where it was taken from. One theory claims that it was originally placed on the statue of Antoninus Pius that stood in the Temple Mount compound. The existence of this statue is known from the description of it recorded by the Traveler of Bordeaux (a Christian pilgrim who visited Jerusalem in the year 333). He stated that there were two statues of emperors situated on the Temple Mount.

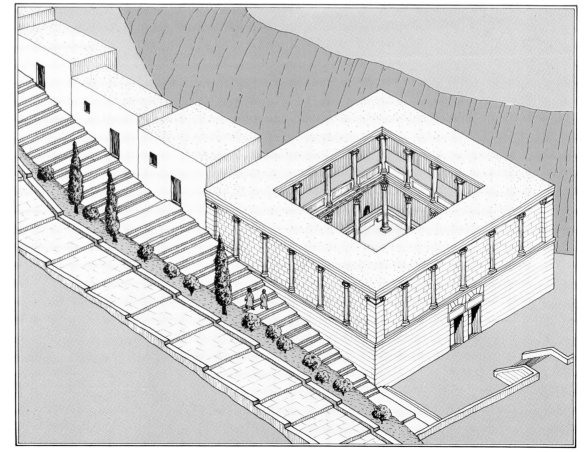

(right) A reconstruction of the **Siloam Pool** built in the southern section of the Tyropoeon Valley, above the ancient Siloam Pool, apparently during the Roman period or the beginning of the Byzantine. (In the map at the beginning of this chapter the name of the pool does not appear.)

In the First Temple period, King Hezekiah dug a tunnel through which water from the Gihon Spring flowed to the ancient pool of Siloam. However, when the new pool was built the tunnel was cut off and the water from the Gihon Spring went no further than the tunnel itself. The southern continuation of this tunnel served as a drainage canal flowing into the Kidron Valley.

A partly paved terraced road ran along the western bank of the Tyropoeon Valley. It was apparently already in existence in the time of the Second Temple. Between the road and the pool was a stairway which led to the pool, but the connection between the road and the entrance to the pool is not clear.

The Byzantine Period
326 – 638

Profile of the **Empress Helena** on a coin.

The passage from the Roman to the Byzantine period took place without an upheaval, although it brought about an important change in the structure and status of Jerusalem. The city had been governed over a long period of time by pagan rulers, for whom Jerusalem was of no religious significance. This situation changed when Emperor Constantine the Great (311–337) gained control over the eastern Roman Empire in 324. He granted Christianity priority over all other religions, and gradually made it the official religion of the Byzantine Empire. From then on, the Christian rulers of Jerusalem had new aspirations as regards its status, its outward appearance, and its function as a Christian city. This new situation sparked off an ideological struggle between the Jews and the Christians over the spiritual character of the holy city.

The Byzantine era is characterized by a tremendous momentum of building in Jerusalem. Evidence of this is found in the many written sources from that period. However, archaeological research has not yet provided sufficient evidence to make it possible to accurately site each and every building mentioned. The sources are written in a number of languages: Greek, Latin, Georgian, and Hebrew, and at the end of the period even in Arabic, Syriac, and Aramaic. They are of a variegated nature. For example, some of these writings are devoted to a particular personality, as for example Bishop Eusebius (fourth century) who chronicled the life of Constantine the Great. The historian Procopius (sixth century) described the building works of the Emperor Justinian. Other writings described the lives of the church fathers and the places in which they carried out their activities.

A large volume of written documentation was provided by the pilgrims to Jerusalem during that period, some of whom settled in the city and became central personalities in its spiritual life. The first of these pilgrims of whom we have records was the "Traveler of Bordeaux" who visited the country in the time of Eusebius, and who left descriptions of Jerusalem which were confirmed by accounts written by other pilgrims who visited the city during that period.

Religious tracts are also sources of information on Jerusalem under Byzantine rule. The most important were the commentaries on the Holy Scriptures into which comments on current affairs were incorporated. Thus, for exam-

ple, St. Jerome, a fifth-century father of the church, wrote in his commentary on the Book of Zephaniah, Chapter 1, verse 4: "And I will cut off ... from this place. ... Until this day the untrustworthy servants are forbidden to enter Jerusalem because they murdered the servants of the Lord and even the Son of God. They can enter the city only to weep for it and they redeem with money the destruction of their city." From this account we learn that the ban on Jews entering Jerusalem invoked in the second century CE was still in force during St. Jerome's lifetime, in the fifth century.

Christian prayer books and prayer charts come within the framework of this type of source. They were written in the post–Byzantine era, but from the accounts of Christian prayer services which took place at various locations, it is possible to identify Byzantine period buildings, and at times even details about them. The Georgian calendar discovered in the St. Catherine Monastery in Sinai and the Jerusalem Armenian prayer book are examples of this type of source. A further example is the *Chronicon Paschale* (Easter Calendar), from the end of the Byzantine period, which contains accounts of Hadrian's activities and building projects in Jerusalem. The calendar is of particular importance for research into the Roman era, but it also contains information about the city in the Byzantine period.

Other sources from this period relate directly to information regarding the geography of the Holy Land. The first of these was Eusebius' *Onomasticon*, in which he attempted to identify the geographical location of places mentioned in the Holy Scriptures. Another source is the account written by Thomas "the Gravedigger," who described the places where he gathered the remains of the Christians slaughtered by the Persians during the conquest of Jerusalem in the year 614.

One of the most important sources regarding the geography of Jerusalem during this period is the Madaba map, discovered in a church in the town of Madaba in Transjordan. This is a mosaic map believed to be dated to the sixth century showing the land of Israel and its settlements. Special care was given to details about the structure of Jerusalem and its buildings.

Archaeological research has also contributed to the knowledge of Byzantine Jerusalem. The excavations carried out in the city have revealed information about the Church of

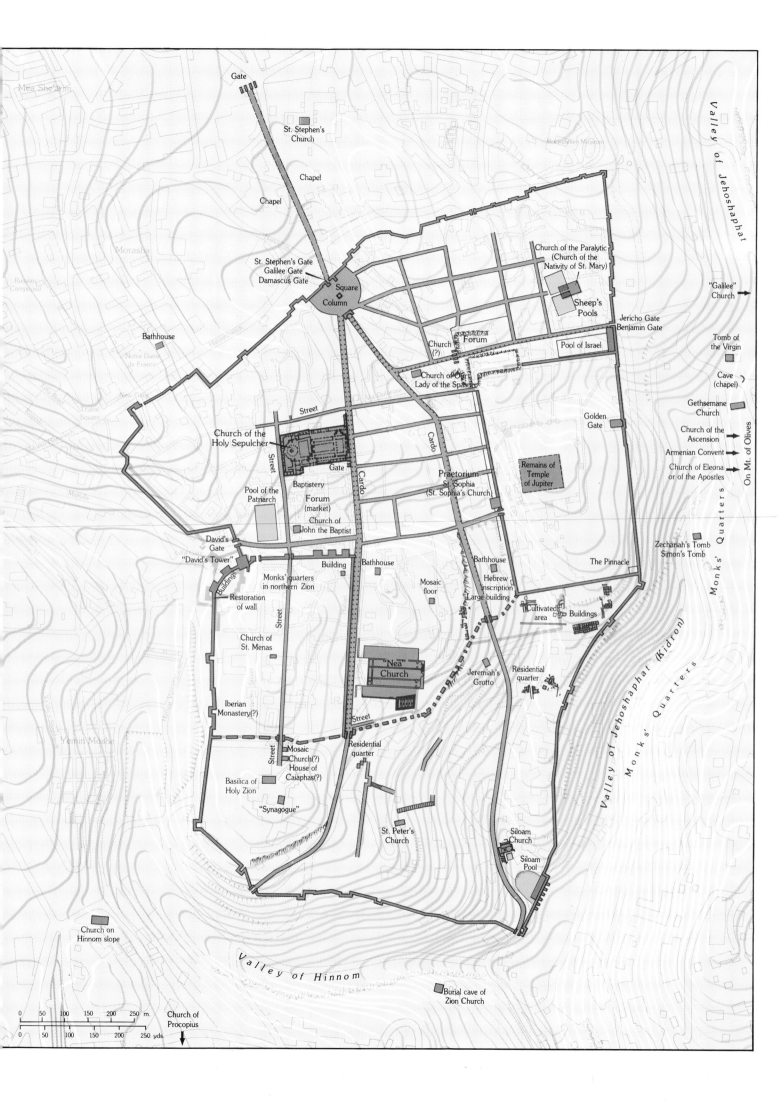

Gate

St. Stephen's
Church

Chapel

Chapel

Mea She'arim

Morasha

Russian
Compound

Notre Dame
de France

Bathhouse

New Gate

Tafta Road

Izhai Square

Mamila

Yemin Moshe

St. Stephen's Gate
Galilee Gate
Damascus Gate

Square
Column

Church
(?)

Church of Our
Lady of the Spasm

Via Dolorosa

Street

Church of the
Holy Sepulcher

Street

Gate

Cardo

Street

Cardo

Baptistery

Pool of the
Patriarch

Forum
(market)

Church of
John the Baptist

David's
Gate

"David's Tower"

Buildings

Restoration
of wall

Monks' quarters
in northern Zion

Building

Bathhouse

Church of
St. Menas

Street

Mosaic
floor

Praetorium
St. Sophia
(St. Sophia's Church)

"Nea"
Church

Iberian
Monastery(?)

Street

Bathhouse

Hebrew
inscription

Large building

Jeremiah's
Grotto

Residential
quarter

Church of the Paralytic
(Church of the
Nativity of St. Mary)

Sheep's
Pools

Forum

Jericho Gate
Benjamin Gate

Pool of Israel

Golden
Gate

Remains of
Temple
of Jupiter

The Pinnacle

Cultivated
area

Buildings

Zechariah's Tomb
Simon's Tomb

"Galilee"
Church

Tomb of
the Virgin

Cave
(chapel)

Gethsemane
Church

Church of the
Ascension

Armenian Convent

Church of Eleona
or of the Apostles

On Mt. of Olives

Valley of Jehoshaphat

Rockefeller Museum

Street

Mosaic
Church(?)

House of
Caiaphas(?)

Basilica of
Holy Zion

"Synagogue"

Residential
quarter

St. Peter's
Church

Siloam
Church

Siloam
Pool

Valley of Jehoshaphat (Kidron)

Monks' Quarters

Monks' Quarters

Church on
Hinnom slope

Valley of Hinnom

Burial cave of
Zion Church

| 0 | 50 | 100 | 150 | 200 | 250 m. |

| 0 | 50 | 100 | 150 | 200 | 250 yds. |

Church of
Procopius

the Holy Sepulcher, the Siloam Church, the chapels to the north of the northern city wall, St. Stephen's Church and many other churches. From these excavations we can also learn about the city's street pattern, its marketplaces and fortifications.

Jerusalem in the Fourth Century

In the year 326, the Emperor Constantine founded Constantinople as the capital city of the eastern part of his empire in place of ancient Byzantium, on the banks of the Bosporus. Constantine was a great supporter of Christianity, even though he took on the Christian faith only toward the end of his life. In the year 313 he published the Edict of Milan, a code of laws granting Christianity the status of a tolerated religion throughout the empire. In 344 he implemented the regulation contained in the edict in the eastern part of the empire, and throughout the years of his rule did his utmost for the progress of Christianity. In the course of the fourth century, Christianity began to be introduced gradually into Jerusalem and the land of Israel, and the city finally became an important center of the Christian religion. This was the beginning of a new chapter in Jerusalem's history.

Constantine was greatly influenced by his mother, the Empress Helena, at whose initiative he built a number of churches in Jerusalem and in other places in the land of Israel. There is a tradition that during her visit to Jerusalem in 323, she discovered the cross upon which Jesus was crucified, along with the other implements of Christ's Passion, in one of the cisterns in the vicinity of the site where the crucifixion was carried out. However, this tradition is not mentioned in any of the contemporary sources (see below). The cross upon which Jesus is said to have been crucified was apparently uncovered during the course of the construction of a church on the site, and the identification of Jesus' tomb by the construction workers is still enshrouded in traditions and legends. It would seem that it was only later that the discovery was attributed to Helena. In the year 325, Constantine ordered that the temple to Aphrodite be demolished since it stood on the site where according to the Christian tradition Jesus had been buried. He ordered that in its place the Church of the Holy Sepulcher be built. The erection of this church was one of the first major changes made in the landscape of Jerusalem in the Byzantine era. Eusebius has left a detailed account of the construction of the church which was completed in the year 335. The consecration of the church, which is marked to this day on September 14, was the occasion for the convening of the Christian Council (consilium) in Jerusalem. This council took place ten years after the first Ecumenical Council at Nicaea, the scene of a major controversy regarding the divine and human aspects of Jesus Christ and which led to the split in the Christian world. As a consequence of the Jerusalem Council, the Christian world was reunified and the holiness of Jerusalem was considered to have increased by virtue of the fact that it induced a spirit of peace among all Christians.

A pilgrim called the "Traveler of Bordeaux" visited Jerusalem in the year 333 and his accounts are an important source for our knowledge of Jerusalem in the time of Constantine. The Traveler of Bordeaux entered Jerusalem from the east, in the vicinity of the present-day Lions' Gate, and visited the Sheep's Pools. He describes the pools as being surrounded with avenues of columns. He also described the remains of the pagan temple nearby and which served as a place of healing during the Roman period, as being nothing more than a cave. He goes on to describe the Temple Mount with its subterranean structures, the water cisterns and other sites. Here for the first time we have a description of the "Foundation Stone" in the Temple Mount, to which the Jews made an annual pilgrimage on the ninth of Av. From the Temple Mount he moves on to a description of the Siloam Pool, surrounded by four avenues of columns. He also mentions a nearby pool which perhaps was the ancient Siloam Pool, the present-day Birket el-Hamra. From

Mount Zion, the Traveler of Bordeaux viewed the House of Caiaphas, and as he walked from there in the direction of the Damascus Gate, he identified the site of Jesus' trial (the Praetorium) in the Tyropoeon Valley. From there he reached the Church of the Holy Sepulcher, still in the process of construction, and describes the cave on the hill of Golgotha, where Jesus' body was kept. Among the new buildings, he described the basilica and the baptistery. He also described Second Temple tombs such as Absalom's Pillar and Zechariah's Tomb. On the Mount of Olives he saw the Eleona Church which was built at Constantine's orders.

During the reign of Julian the Apostate (361–363) there was a two-year break in the practice of Christianity into Jerusalem. This emperor, the cousin of Constantine the Great, considered paganism as the authentic religion to be followed in the empire. He set out to fight Christianity, but once he realized that he could not succeed, he granted freedom of worship to all citizens. Julian changed the official policy toward the Jews, revoking Hadrian's ban on their entering Jerusalem. In the year 362, Julian granted permission for the Temple to be rebuilt, knowing full well that its ruins provided proof to the Christians that Jesus' prophecies about the destruction of the Temple (Mark 13:2) had come true. However, Julian's order to restore the Temple and the establishment of a sort of Jewish state, was not well looked upon by the Jews, for fear that the events that occurred during his reign were no more than a passing phenomenon. In the spring of 362 building began, but soon came to a halt because of a fire that broke out, injuring building workers and ruining building materials. It is believed that the fire broke out in an underground structure (perhaps at the present-day site of Solomon's Stables), and was sparked off during an earthquake.

When Julian died on June 16, 363, he was followed by

the Christian Emperor Juvianus, and this put an end to any possibility of Jerusalem becoming a Jewish city.

During the course of the fourth century, Christianity once more deepened its roots in Jerusalem. It was during this period that churches were built and the Christian community in the city consolidated. Christian charitable institutions were established on the slopes of the Mount of Olives, and monks settled in the Kidron Valley, turning the Tomb of Hezir's Priestly Family into a church named after St. James (352). During this period, of particular interest were the activities in Jerusalem of Melania "the Elder," a Roman noblewoman who reached the city in the year 378. She built a monastery and hospice on the western slopes of the Mount of Olives. At the end of the fourth century (approximately 390), the Gethsemane Church was constructed on the slopes of the Mount of Olives.

(below) **DOMINE IVIMUS** (meaning: O Lord we have come) are the words in this inscription found in the Armenian chapel in the Church of the Holy Sepulcher. The drawing of a vessel and the words below were found inscribed on a smooth stone slab forming part of a wall of the temple to Aphrodite built by the Roman Emperor Hadrian. It appears that the inscription is an allusion to the opening verse of Psalm 122: "I was glad when they said unto me, Let us go into the house of the Lord." From this the conclusion can be drawn that the writer had come to Jerusalem from some distance, and since the inscription is in Latin, it would seem that he was a Christian pilgrim from a Western country. (If he had come from the Eastern empire he would probably have written in Greek.) The fact that the vessel was portrayed in such detail gives credit to the theory that the pilgrim came from the west by sea. The dating of the drawing and the inscription are not definite. It is generally considered that the pilgrim reached Jerusalem after the time the temple to Aphrodite had been demolished, and its foundations were revealed when Constantine the Great built the Church of the Holy Sepulcher on them. The vessel and the inscription were inscribed on the exposed section of the foundations. The location of the drawing and inscription in a remote corner of the church raises the possibility that it was executed clandestinely in the fear of being discovered by one of the priests in the temple to Aphrodite when it was still active and the practice of Christianity banned. Both of these possibilities point to the beginning of the fourth century as the time when the vessel and inscription were drawn.

Jerusalem in the Fifth Century

The end of the fourth and beginning of the fifth centuries saw a great Christian religious revival, which had its influence on the Christian character of Jerusalem. The personalities active in the city during that period brought about a major change in its status in the Christian world, raised its prestige significantly, and made a major contribution to the city's development, mainly through the construction of religious edifices.

The first major institution erected during this period was the Basilica of Holy Zion, considered to be the "Mother of all Churches." It was built in the year 390 on Mount Zion by Bishop John II on the site where the Church of the Apostles had stood from 347. The dimensions of the new church were especially large and most impressive. Its significance was mainly in the status it accorded to Jerusalem in the church hierarchy, since it was built on the site where the remains of St. Stephen, the first Christian martyr, were interred. St. Stephen's tomb was of such significance to the Christians that when it was discovered in 415 in the village of Gamla, legends were soon spread to the effect that Jesus himself had appeared once more on the Mount of Olives.

At the beginning of the fifth century, Melania "the Younger," granddaughter of Melania "the Elder" mentioned above, was most active in Jerusalem. She had monasteries built on the crest of the Mount of Olives (420), as well as other monasteries, the location of which is still unknown. There is a theory that they existed in the vicinity of the present-day Church of the Ascension.

In the year 420, Juvenalis was appointed Bishop of Jerusalem, and he later assumed the powers of Patriarch, even though he was not authorized to do so. However, in 449 he was officially appointed Patriarch, and despite the violent protests of the Christian community of Jerusalem at the devious means by which he obtained the title, Juvenalis took up residence in the city and devoted his energies to turning it into an important Christian metropolis. In the year 451, Jerusalem was awarded the status of a patriarchate at the Council of Chalcedon.

In the fifth century, it was the Empress Eudocia, wife of the Byzantine Emperor Theodosius, who made her mark in Jerusalem. Eudocia, formerly Athenaios, adopted Christianity after her marriage to the emperor in the year 426.

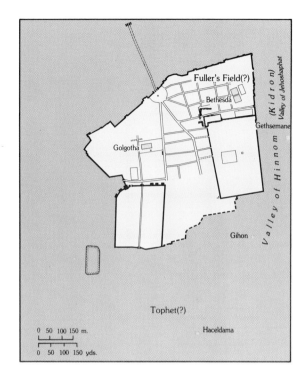

(right) **Map of Jerusalem based on the *Onomasticon*.**
The *Onomasticon* is a lexicon of all the names of sites in Byzantine Palestine compiled by **Eusebius** (lived from 260 to 340), the Bishop of Caesarea, during the reign of the Emperor Constantine the Great. The names are listed in order of their appearance in the Scriptures or the New Testament. The lexicon contains names of sites that existed in the time of Eusebius, often with a detailed description. The *Onomasticon* was written in Greek and translated into Latin by St. Jerome, who was one of the leading fathers of the church and lived in Bethlehem (347-420). The map contains the names of places in Jerusalem and its environs mentioned by Eusebius, and which can be located with some accuracy today. From the *Onomasticon* we learn that some of the sites known to have existed in Jerusalem in the Byzantine era can no longer be identified.

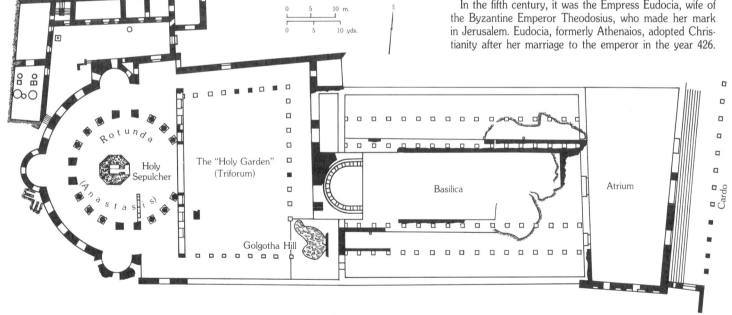

(above) The Byzantine **Church of the Holy Sepulcher** was constructed by the Emperor Constantine the Great on the ruins of the Roman temple to Aphrodite. It was consecrated in the year 335. The builders of the church used some of the remains of the pagan temple, which are visible to this day. The church was planned by a Syrian architect by the name of Zenubius.

The facade of the Church of the Holy Sepulcher in Byzantine times was on the eastern side of the building (today it is situated on the southern side). The facade pointed toward the main street—the Cardo—from which the church was approached by a number of steps.

In this section of the street the pillars on both sides of the Cardo were of granite, apparently part of the embellishment of the stairs leading to the church, while the rest of the pillars were made of limestone. Between the stairs and the eastern wall of the church was a sort of square, by way of which the building was approached through three entrances, the central one of which was the largest. The facade of the church was built entirely of Herodian-style hewn stone blocks. These stone blocks were overlaid with marble plates donated to the church by Constantine the Great. Remnants of the facade wall still exist to this day within the nearby Russian (Alexander)

Hospice, and the niches for the iron hooks with which the marble was attached to the wall are still visible.

The structure of the church was divided into four main sections of both structural and religious significance: the atrium, basilica, the Holy Garden, and the rotunda.

The atrium was an internal courtyard surrounded by porticoes, and three entrances led into the basilica.

The basilica, the large prayer hall of the church, was built in the style of other churches of the period, with five prayer aisles bounded by rows of pillars. Through the side aisles, around the main apse, access was gained to the third section of the

church, the Holy Garden.

The Holy Garden was a large colonnaded courtyard. In its southeastern corner was the hill of Golgotha, with a type of chapel opening on to the courtyard. The name, the Holy Garden, is from the New Testament reference to the siting of Jesus' tomb and the hill nearby in a garden area (John 19:41).

The rotunda, to the west of the Holy Garden, was the focal point of the entire structure. This was a circular structure, covered by a large golden dome, still somewhat extant in its original Byzantine form, except for a few changes introduced in the eleventh century. In the center of the rotunda lay Jesus' tomb, built in

Roman style. Above it was an opening through which the light filtered, and perhaps to enable the tomb to be open to the sky, since this was the site of Jesus' resurrection.

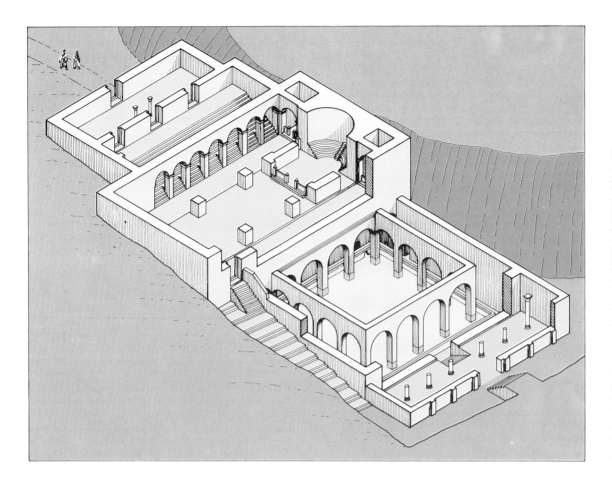

(left) The **Siloam Church** is one of the most important Christian buildings in Jerusalem. It was here that according to Christian tradition Jesus performed one of his most well-known miracles—the restoration of sight to the blind man with clay from the Siloam Pool (John 9:1-14). At the beginning of the Christian rule of the city, avenues of columns were erected around the entire pool. The church was apparently built by the Empress Eudocia (in the mid-fifth century) and existed there until it was destroyed in the eleventh century, together with the entire area south of the present-day Old City walls. The difficult topographic location of the site—in the riverbed of the Tyropoeon Valley—determined the character of the structure. Entrance was from the north, through an entrance hall to a second hall which was actually a type of staircase which led to the church itself. The church had three prayer aisles, the two at the sides being elevated. In their excavations carried out here during 1894-1897, Bliss and Dickie discovered four pillars which led them to the conclusion that above the central prayer aisle there had been a vault supported by these columns.

She made a pilgrimage to Jerusalem on two occasions, and lived in the city from 444 to 460. It was during this period that Bishop Juvenalis' activities were at their peak, and Eudocia contributed handsomely to his efforts to develop the city by the construction of churches, hospitals, and shelters for the poor.

Eudocia's name was especially connected with the construction of the southern wall of Jerusalem, which brought Mount Zion and the hill of the City of David within the bounds of the city. Up to the destruction of the Second Temple (70 CE), these hills were bounded by the First Wall, but after the destruction they were considered to be outside the city limits, and there is little evidence of habitation in this area. Eudocia rebuilt the major part of this wall, and only in a few places did she divert slightly from the original course. For her, the construction of the wall was the fulfillment of the passage in Psalms (51:18): "Do good in thy good pleasure unto Zion: build thou the walls of Jerusalem" (the Greek translation of the word "pleasure" is *eudocia*). However, her desire to accomplish this precept was not the only factor in her decision to build the wall in this area. The excavations carried out in the City of David and the Ophel have revealed that the area south of the Temple Mount was inhabited at that time, and there were a number of churches and monasteries on Mount Zion and the region to the east of it. Thus, there was a definite need to enclose them within a wall. This wall, sections of which are still extant, was demolished apparently in 1033 by an earthquake, and since then neither the City of David nor Mount Zion has been included within the city walls.

Eudocia built the Siloam Church in the southern sector of the city, including the Siloam Pool, part of which still exists. It was in this church that the city elders gathered to deliberate on the steps to be taken against Juvenalis when he appointed himself Patriarch. Eudocia also built the Church of St. Stephen, today included within the Church of St. Etiénne north of the Damascus Gate, where she was later to be buried. This church was the last in the series of prayer houses erected in honor of the first saint of the Christian church. One Christian tradition maintains that it was at the site where Eudocia erected a church in his honor that Stephen was pelted with stones. As mentioned, his remains were discovered in the village of his birth, Gamla, in the year 415. They were brought to an annex in the Basilica of Holy Zion built by Juvenalis, where they lay until 460, when they were reinterred in St. Stephen's Church. Other traditions relate that the church was built earlier, in the year 439, and that Eudocia and Juvenalis were present at the ceremony of the transfer of the saint's remains from the Basilica of Holy Zion to St. Stephen's Church. On the Mount of Olives there was a church named for St. Stephen and it may well be that St. Stephen's remains were transferred to this church from Mount Zion, and then from there to the church Eudocia erected. The multiplicity of traditions concerning Stephen's burial place apparently derives from the fact that his relics were apparently divided among a number of locations prior to their being interred in their final resting place. However, it would seem that the first tradition mentioned above describes the events as they actually occurred.

A number of scholars have attributed to Eudocia the construction of additional structures erected at various times throughout the period. One of these was the building, or shrine, called the "Pinnacle" or the "Cradle of Jesus," at the southeastern corner of the Temple Mount. They all attribute to her the construction of the St. George's Home for the Aged (together with its church), situated outside the walls. Its exact location is not known, but there are a number of possibilities. It could have been situated in the vicinity of Binyanei Ha'ooma, where the remains of a church with a mosaic floor having reference to St. George have been found. A second possible site is to the east of the King David Hotel. A further possibility is the remains of a church uncovered recently near St. Andrew's Church, to the southwest of the city.

Descriptions of most of the above-mentioned sites are

(opposite below) The **Sheep's Pools**, called by scholars and Christian pilgrims Bethesda, as they appeared during the Byzantine period. The total length of the two pools was about 312 feet (95 m.), and they were about 180 feet (55 m.) wide, and about 72 feet (22 m.) deep.

Christian tradition relates to these pools as being the pool where Jesus cured the crippled man (John 5:2-4). It is for this reason that they are mentioned by many Christian pilgrims who visited Jerusalem. It may well be that already in the Second Temple period healing powers were attributed to the waters of these pools, because a temple for healing was erected there in the Roman period following the destruction of the Second Temple.

In the Byzantine era (fifth century), an imposing church was built on the dam dividing the two pools. (This dam was begun in the time of the First Temple.) The church's two side prayer aisles were erected above the pools, supported by an impressive series of arches about 43 feet (13 m.) high. The church was reached by way of the dam itself, which continued for a further 82 feet (25 m.) to the east in the direction of the pools. The tomb of one of the bishops of this church was discovered in the 1930s outside the Lions' Gate. On its side was an inscription which stated that the church was called the Church of the Sheep or the Probatica, meaning in Greek "of sheep."

found in documents from the mid-fifth century. A typical example are the writings by Eucharius, the Bishop of Lyons, from about the year 445. From his descriptions we learn the extent to which the city underwent changes as the result of the works of Eudocia and Juvenalis. He wrote: "Mount Zion is now surrounded by a wall, although at one time it was situated outside the city." According to him, there were monks' cells on the northern sector of Mount Zion as well as around the Church of the Holy Sepulcher, which he describes in detail. Eucharius goes on to depict the ruins of the Temple buildings, apparently the Herodian retaining walls. At that time, it was mainly the remains of the southeastern section of the Temple Mount that were visible, including the "Pinnacle," which was of particular importance to Christians, because it was from that spot that James, Jesus' brother, was cast into the abyss. Eucharius also described the two Sheep's Pools and the Siloam Pool. There is no reference to the Siloam Church or the Church of the Virgin Mary, which led to the conclusion that they were built later.

In Eudocia's time, there was a certain relaxation of regulations regarding Jews visiting Jerusalem. Prior to this, Jews were barred from entering the city, except in the month of Av, when they were permitted to visit the "Holy Rock" (Foundation Stone) and mourn the destruction of the Temple. Through the intervention of the empress, Jews were granted permission to go up to Jerusalem on other occasions as well, despite the objections of fanatical Christians. One of these fanatics, Bar Zoma, organized riots against the Jews in Jerusalem. However, these concessions to the Jews did not continue after Eudocia's death in the year 460.

Toward the end of Eudocia's sojourn in Jerusalem, another important personality, Peter the Iberian, was active in the city. He was apparently a member of a royal family from the region of present-day Georgia. Upon his arrival in Jerusalem, he joined a monastery, and rose within the ecclesiastical hierarchy until he was appointed bishop of Mayumas, near Gaza. Peter the Iberian erected a monastery near David's Tower, evidence of which was found on an inscription uncovered in the vicinity of the YMCA building, as well as from other sources. Johannes Rufus, his companion during his later years, wrote a biography of Peter. This work provides information about Jerusalem during this period, about sites that existed at the time and about those that were added during the course of the fifth century. Mention is made of St. Stephen's Church, the various sections of the Church of the Holy Sepulcher, Pontius Pilate's house, the Church of the Sheep's Pools, the Church of Gethsemane, and many others. We find reference for the first time to a number of churches such as that erected on the ruins of the Praetorium, where the trial of Jesus took place. Although this site is mentioned already in the fourth century by the Traveler of Bordeaux, Rufus refers to ruins only: "In the valley below, there are walls which were at one time the Praetorium of Pontius Pilate." Thus, on the basis of the descriptions by these two

(right) **Map of Jerusalem according to Theodosius**. The writings of Theodosius, from the early fifth century, contained a guide to the visitor to the Holy Land, with special emphasis on Jerusalem and its Christian holy places. In his descriptions he referred to distances measured in double paces (a double pace = 4.86 feet [1.48 m.]). There are many inaccuracies, such as the distance between the House of Caiaphas and Pilate's house (the Praetorium) given as about 100 meters (328 feet), as compared with a distance of 200 meters between the Church of the Holy Sepulcher and Mount Zion, when in fact the distance between them is similar (700 meters compared to approximately 600 meters). It appears that these distances are not based on Theodosius' own experience but rather on information supplied by others.

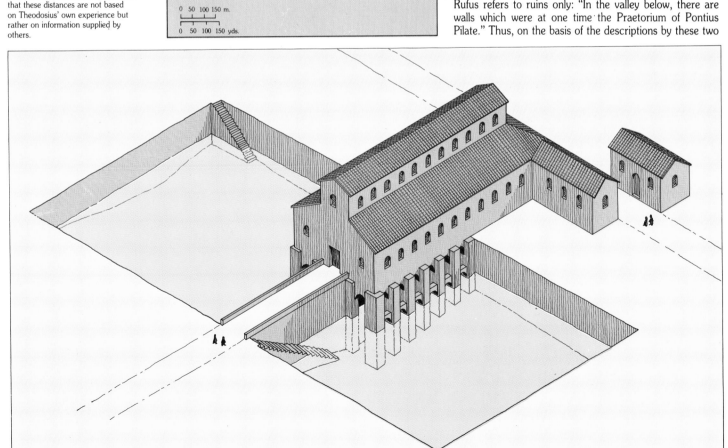

authors we may assume that the church was erected some time during the second half of the fifth century. It was in Rufus' work that the first reference is found to the church built on the dam that divided between the two Sheep's Pools.

Jerusalem in the Sixth Century

In the sixth century, Jerusalem reached the peak of its development, especially during the rule of the Emperor Justinian (527–565). This emperor was well known for his construction works throughout the Byzantine Empire, which included Jerusalem, where among other edifices he built the Néa Church and completed the construction of the Cardo. A further expression of the city's development during that period was the large number of pilgrims visiting the city, resulting in numerous written accounts of the situation they found there.

A short time after he became emperor, Justinian built a church in Jerusalem which included within its precincts a home for the aged. Evidence of the existence of this home has been found in an inscription discovered in Herod's Gate

(where it was in secondary use), with details of its construction.

Justinian built the Néa Church in 543 in honor of the Virgin Mary. It was called the "Néa" (new) to distinguish it from another church dedicated to the Virgin Mary in Jerusalem. The emperor sent the architect Theodosius to Jerusalem to plan and supervise the construction of this church. An account of its construction, which continued over a period of twelve years, is provided by the contemporary historian Procopius, who documented Justinian's building ventures. The church was built on a site with no particular holy attributes, but in order to glorify it, many legends sprung up relating to its construction with divine aid, as well as treasures from the Temple being transferred from Rome.

The Néa Church was discovered in the course of excavations of the Jewish Quarter of the Old City. The major part was uncovered in the southern sector of the Jewish Quarter, and a small part was found outside the Old City, near the present-day southern wall. The remains uncovered, in the main, sustain Procopius' description of the church and

(below) Section of an Armenian mosaic floor, typical of the Byzantine period, called the **Bird Mosaic**, because of the various species of birds depicted on it. The mosaic contains an inscription in Armenian stating: "To the memory and safety of all the Armenians, God knows their names."

The bird mosaic, whose dimensions were 12.8 × 20.7 feet (3.9 m. × 6.3 m.), was discovered by chance in 1894, inside a small chapel north of the Damascus Gate. This area was sparsely inhabited during the Byzantine period, but evidence exists that such buildings as churches, monasteries, water installations, and houses were located here.

Underneath the mosaic was a burial cave in which the bones of the dead were interred.

(below) The **Orpheus mosaic** adorned the floor of a small chapel which existed north of the Damascus Gate (in the present-day Morasha neighborhood) from the fifth to seventh centuries. It is named for Orpheus (a hero in Greek mythology with an extraordinary skill in music and song) seen in the center of the mosaic wearing a Phrygian hat and playing the harp. Around him animals listen to his charming music. A centaur and the god Pan are also depicted. In the lower part of the

mosaic are images of two women—Theodosia and Georgia—within a frame separated by a column. These, apparently, were two contributors to this chapel, within which they were buried.

This mosaic, one of the most exquisite found in this country, was discovered in 1901 and was taken to the Museum of Archaeology in Istanbul. It is similar in size to the Bird Mosaic, and this has led to the assumption that it was part of the floor of a small chapel used for burial.

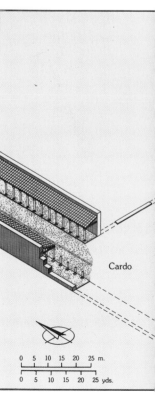

Cardo

0 5 10 15 20 25 m.

0 5 10 15 20 25 yds.

(right) **"And when ye see this, your heart shall rejoice, and your bones shall flourish like an herb."** This verse from Isaiah 66:14 was carved on a stone block in the western wall of the Temple Mount. A number of inscriptions carved by Jewish pilgrims at various times have been found in the Temple Mount area. They also generally added their names to the inscription.

There are a number of theories as to the dating of this inscription. It was first thought to have been carved by a Jewish pilgrim who came to Jerusalem during the rule of the Emperor Julian (361–363), when he granted permission to the Jews to rebuild the Temple. However, there are a number of problems arising out of such an assumption, among others

the dearth of information about the period.

Another theory believes that it was carved in the Umayyad period. In this period the street level was higher than it is today, and thus the person wishing to carve the inscription would be able to reach the stone block. It was in this period also that the Jews began to settle in the city once more, and the Jewish Quarter of the city was not far from the site of this inscription.

The most rational dating seems to be the Byzantine period. This possibility is based on the assumption that there is a link between this inscription and a letter sent by a Jew from Galilee in the fifth century. In this missive there were expressions of the feelings prevalent at the time

among the Jews that the redemption was near: "Behold, the Roman kings have ordered that the gates of Jerusalem be returned to us. Speedily come up to Jerusalem for the Festival of the Tabernacles, for our kingdom is about to be rebuilt in Jerusalem." The time the letter was written and the sentiments expressed in it, similarly to those expressed in the inscription, link them with the period the Empress Eudocia lived in Jerusalem in the mid-fifth century. It was at this time that she showed tolerance to the Jews, and even permitted them to visit Jerusalem.

It would seem that the writer worked under pressure, because he did not succeed in completing the biblical verse.

(center left) **Inscription in the Néa Church** found on one of the vaults that was part of the retaining walls of the church and its ancillary structures, at the southeastern end of the present-day Jewish Quarter. The retaining walls later became the basis of large water cisterns used to store rainwaters which ran off the roof of the church and the ancillary structures. The cisterns were lined with waterproof plaster, and on one of the walls this inscription was engraved: "And this is the work which was carried out by the generosity of our most gracious Emperor Flavius Justinianus, under the care and devotion of the most

holy Constantinus, priest and father of the church (in the year) thirteen of the indiction." From the inscription it transpires that the erection of the church was inspired and financed by the Emperor Justinian, and the construction work was directed by the church father Constantine.

The inscription, whose dimensions were 26 × 48 inches (65 × 120 cm.), belongs to one of the church's ancillary buildings, and appears to date to 549 or 550 CE. This leads us to conclude that six years after the consecration of the Néa Church in 543, work was still continuing on the construction of buildings annexed to the main church.

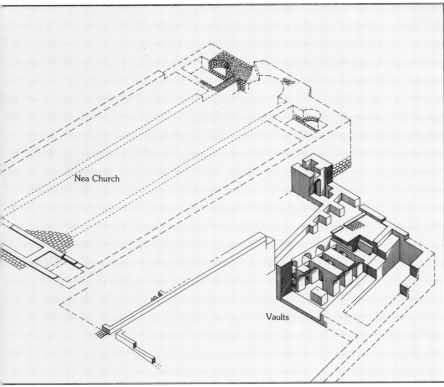

Nea Church

Vaults

(below left) The **Néa Church** was built by the Emperor Justinian and was consecrated in 543 CE. The name Néa ("new" in Greek) is a shortened form of the church's full name: The New Church of St. Mary, Mother of God.

Scholars were aware of the existence of this church over a period of many generations from the Madaba map and other sources. One of these sources was the writings of Procopius (a historian who lived in the time of Justinian) in which the church was described in detail and its magnificence praised.

From Procopius' descriptions we learn that this was a complex of buildings covering a large area and in addition to the church there was a monastery, hostel, hospital, and library. The findings in the archaeological excavations carried out on the site have confirmed these descriptions and have made it possible to establish a fairly comprehensive picture. The church was erected on the slope descending from the Jewish Quarter to the valley traversing the city from north to south. Because of the steepness of the slope, and the proportions of the church complex (its dimensions

were 187 × 377 feet [57 × 115 m.]), it was necessary to extend the building foundations. To this end a series of vaults was constructed along the slope which served as retaining walls for the buildings and later as a framework for water cisterns. An inscription was discovered on one of the vaults which was instrumental in identifying the church.

The central hall of the church was uncovered in the course of the archaeological excavations, and it was found that the eastern wall was a large retaining wall 21 feet (6.5 m.) thick. In this wall two of the three prayer apses were uncovered, the radius of the larger one being 16 feet (5 m.). The ancillary buildings have not been unearthed, but additional rooms and the series of vaults mentioned have been found.

The Néa Church was destroyed by the Muslims, apparently at the end of the eighth or beginning of the ninth century (a document called *Commemoratorium* [from 808] describes the church as having been destroyed). There is no evidence to support a theory held by some scholars that the church was destroyed during an earthquake in the mid-eighth century.

(above) The **Madaba Map** is the earliest original map of the land of Israel and of Jerusalem. It is a colored mosaic made according to general opinion in the second half of the sixth century as a section of a floor of a Byzantine church in the town of Madaba in Transjordan. The mosaic was found in 1884 during reconstruction work in the church, in the course of which parts of it were ruined.

The map faces east, and above Jerusalem is an inscription stating: "The holy city of Jerusalem." The artist created the map in the tradition of the mosaic craft in the Byzantine period, one of whose characteristics was to present the city in elliptical form, even though it was actually square.

Jerusalem is shown in the Madaba map as being surrounded by a wall in which there are a number of towers. The course of the wall has not been preserved in its entirety in the map, since the part depicting the southeast of the city was destroyed. Thus the representation of the southern section of the wall as it was then, beyond Mount Zion and south of the Temple Mount, is unknown. The city wall was breached by six gates: David's (Jaffa) Gate, St. Stephen's (Damascus) Gate, the Dung Gate, Jericho (Lions') Gate,

and two additional gates in the vicinity of Mount Zion. Inside the wall, near St. Stephen's Gate, a wide square is seen with a pillar in the center which stood there during the reign of the Roman Emperor Hadrian, upon which a statue was placed. It was from this square that the two main streets of the city—the Cardines—flanked by avenues of columns, originate.

Among the buildings inside the city it is easy to distinguish the churches whose red roofs single them out from the other buildings whose roofs are painted yellow. The structure depicted on Mount Zion in this map may be the place where Stephen's body was kept. The map also shows the baptistery of the Church of the Holy Sepulcher and a number of buildings on the Temple Mount.

The Madaba map is an excellent source for the understanding of the geographical history of Jerusalem in the Byzantine period. Evidence of the existence of the sites shown in this map is found in other historical sources, and they are often more accurate. The interrelation of the sources assists us to determine the exact location of these sites in the city.

A number of scholars are of the opinion that Jerusalem is depicted in the Madaba map on a scale of 1:1613.

its ancillary structures. Many references to this church are found in correspondence and writings from the period, from which we learn that it played an important role in the religious life of Jerusalem, until it was destroyed, generally believed to be at the end of the eighth century or the beginning of the ninth, but possibly during the Arab conquest (638). Knowledge of its importance spread beyond Jerusalem, evidence of which was found in an inscription discovered on a tomb in Jericho. This relates that the bishop by the name of Syriacus "made a contribution in favor of the new most holy church of the Mother of our Savior in Jerusalem."

In Procopius' accounts, reference is made to other monasteries and churches existing in Jerusalem at that time, such as the St. Telalius Monastery, St. George's Monastery, the Iberian Monastery, and St. Mary's Church on the Mount of Olives.

During the period of Justinian's rule, Armenian building works increased manifold in the city. The kings of Armenia obtained large tracts of land in Jerusalem for generous payments made to the emperor, and they built churches and monasteries upon them. A list exists of seventy structures built by the Armenians in Jerusalem in the sixth century. Mosaic floors containing Armenian inscriptions found in the city have remained from some of these buildings. Some of these Armenian mosaics have been found on the crest of the Mount of Olives, and one—the "bird mosaic"—has been found slightly to the north of the present-day Damascus Gate.

Toward the end of the sixth century, Pope Gregorius the Great (590–604) built a hospice for the use of the Latin clergy in Jerusalem. The location of this structure is not known, but would seem to have been where at a later date the Latin buildings were erected in Jerusalem, in the west section of the present-day Muristan quarter.

The most significant source relating to the city of Jerusalem during the Byzantine era is the mosaic map found at Madaba in Transjordan. In the opinion of the majority of scholars, the map depicts Jerusalem as it was at the end of the sixth century, when all the important Byzantine buildings already existed and the Byzantine city was at its zenith. According to this map, Jerusalem at this time was surrounded by a wall with towers—among them David's Tower and another tower nearby built by Herod—as well as a number of gates and posterns. This wall was built at the end of the third century, but its course has not been established beyond doubt, since its southern section has not yet been discovered. Attempts to reconstruct the alignment of the southern section follow that of the present-day Old City southern wall. The main difference between the two alignments is in the section between the present-day Dung Gate and the Temple Mount wall. The wall described here was in its southern section only an inner wall, since at that time the wall built by Eudocia in the fifth century was in existence. This included Mount Zion and the City of David within the boundaries of the city (this inner wall hardly appears in the Madaba map).

Inside the wall, near St. Stephen's Gate (present-day Damascus Gate), was where the city's two main streets, the Cardines (singular Cardo), divided. One of them ran from St. Stephen's Gate up to the postern in the southern (inner) wall, and the second began at the same gate and ran along the Tyropoeon Valley (present-day Haggai Street) branching off until it reached the Benjamin Gate (present-day Lions' Gate). The city's transversal road ran from David's Gate (near the present-day Jaffa Gate) to the Temple Mount. An allusion to the western section of this road is found in the Madaba map, but so far evidence has not been found that it did exist during the Byzantine era. Avenues of columns supporting roofs ran along both sides of these main streets.

The Madaba map shows the main churches of the city which existed during this period: the Basilica of Holy Zion,

(above) A **gold ring** decorated with a model of the tomb of Jesus. The structure of this tomb became one of the distinctive symbols of Christianity and appears on many objects from the Byzantine period. This ring was discovered in the excavations carried out at the southern wall in Jerusalem in 1974.

(left) The **Cardo** and the Decumanus were among the most important aspects of the plan of the typical Roman city. These were two main streets which crossed the length and breadth of the city. Cardo in Latin means "axis," and these streets were the focal axes of the city. Such main streets existed in Roman Aelia Capitolina as well as in the Byzantine city.

The original Cardo in Jerusalem was a relatively short street and ran along the northern, more populated, sector of Roman Jerusalem. It originated at a square built inside the city's main gate (present-day Damascus Gate). The Cardo was very broad and was flanked by two sidewalks covered by roofs supported by pillars. During the Byzantine period the population density of the city's southern sector increased greatly (this was the area of the present-day Jewish Quarter and the nearby sector outside today's wall), and it was necessary to lay new streets in these areas. It appears that it was the Emperor Justinian who in the sixth century built the extension of the Roman Cardo up to the vicinity of the southern city wall, and thus made the connection between the

Church of the Holy Sepulcher and the Néa Church he had constructed. To allow for this, the continuation of the Cardo deviated slightly from the original to the southwest. The direct link between the two most important churches in the Byzantine city, the Church of the Holy Sepulcher and the Néa Church, made it possible to hold religious processions between them.

The existence of the Cardo in Jerusalem was known from the Madaba map, in which it is depicted in detail. But its remains were only discovered when archaeological excavations were carried out in the Old City during the rebuilding of the Jewish Quarter. The excavations unearthed the pillars and impressive pavement, as well as drainage canals on either side. Other archaeological finds, such as pedestals and capitals, made it possible to reconstruct the imposing street.

The Cardo continued to exist during the Arab period, but gradually deteriorated. The original columns were replaced by crude pillars which blocked the wide passages and sections of the street were blocked off by structures apparently erected in the Abbasid period.

the Néa, the Holy Wisdom (Praetorium), St. Anne, and the Holy Sepulcher with its baptistery. There are also a number of churches which cannot be unequivocally identified, including the Siloam Church and the Church of St. Peter in Gallicantu.

The Temple Mount remained in ruins throughout the Byzantine period. The pagan temple built by the Romans in place of the Temple had been demolished when Christianity gained control of Jerusalem. The Christians did not erect any structures in its place as they believed in Jesus' prophecy that the Temple would be destroyed in its entirety: "There shall not be left one stone upon another, that shall not be thrown down" (Mark 13:2). However, it appears that in the corners of the Temple Mount were remains of ancient buildings, and some were even rebuilt. In the Madaba map, a chapel can be seen at the southeastern corner of the compound. This chapel was erected at the site where according to the New Testament the Satan tempted Jesus (Luke 4:9). According to Christian tradition, this is the site from which St. James was cast down into the valley beyond the wall. Another sixth-century source states that a church in the form of a cross existed on this site. At the northwestern corner of the square, a structure can be seen which has not been fully identified, and this may be a remnant of the Second Temple Antonia fortress. Between these two buildings, the map also shows the Golden Gate.

To complete the portrait of Byzantine Jerusalem as it appears mainly in the Madaba map, mention must be made of the city marketplace—the forum, from the Roman period—which continued to exist during this period to the south of the Church of the Holy Sepulcher, in the vicinity of the present-day Muristan.

Jerusalem in the Seventh Century

The seventh century saw the end of the Byzantine rule of Jerusalem. It began with the conquest of the city by the Persians in the year 614 and ended with the Muslim conquest in 638.

Already at the end of the Roman era, and throughout the entire Byzantine period, border disputes took place as part of the power struggle between the Roman–Byzantine Empire and the Persian kingdom, its eastern neighbor. At times these quarrels turned into armed encounters. In the sixth century the relations between the empires deteriorated as the result of the breach of economic agreements on the part of the Byzantines. As a consequence, the Persians invaded countries under Byzantine rule, and plundered their towns as compensation for the breaking of agreements.

In the year 611, the border disputes between the two powers reached a climax. The Persians, led by King Chosroes II (ruled from 590 to 628), carried out an invasion which deviated beyond all those that had preceded it, in the course of which they reached the land of Israel. Jerusalem had an important role in these events. The holy city was famous for its numerous treasures which had accumulated within it, especially from contributions from pilgrims and heads of the Byzantine Empire made to the holy places. Thus, this was an important objective for the Persians, who wished to enrich the royal treasury. A post–Byzantine source puts forward a premise that one of the motives of the Persian invasion of Jerusalem was the desire to overthrow Christian sovereignty and prove the inferior status of Christianity.

The conquest of Jerusalem at the beginning of 614 was carried out without any bloodshed. The inhabitants of the city acceded to the order of the Persian commander Shahr Baraz (wild boar), and threw open the city gates before him. According to Christian tradition it was the Jews who helped the Persians in their conquest of Jerusalem, and followed the conquerors into the city and settled there. The main divisions of the Persian army continued on their way, and left a small garrison to control the city.

A short while after the conquest, the Christian inhabitants of the city rebelled against the Persian conquerors, wiped out the garrison in the city, and carried out pogroms against the

Jews in revenge for their assistance in the rampages. Shahr Baraz returned to Jerusalem and on April 15, 614, lay siege to the city which lasted for twenty-one days. The Christians, in their profound religious faith, refused to open the city gates, despite attempts by the Persians to take the city in a peaceful manner. As a result of their refusal to surrender, the Persians entered the city and massacred the Christians, especially the clergy. The Persians took the holy cross from the Church of the Holy Sepulcher and carried it back to Persia, with a column of prisoners, among whom was the Patriarch of Jerusalem (Zechariah), the Persians treating them cruelly on the way. The Persian invasion and the events that followed it were given a religious interpretation by the Christians, and this is the reason for the manifold written sources relating to them. These included exaggerated accounts of the role of the Jews in the conquest of the city and the massacre of the Christians. This was a reflection of the profound hatred of the Jews by the Christians.

The ghastly massacre of the Christian inhabitants of Jerusalem was described by a monk by the name of Strategius (or Eustratus according to another version). This monk, from the Mar Saba Monastery in the Judean Desert, was taken prisoner during the Persian siege of Jerusalem, but succeeded in escaping. He left a written account of how the Christian victims of the Persian slaughter were buried by a group of persons led by Thomas "the Gravedigger." Strategius wrote in Greek, and versions of this work in Georgian and Arabic have survived, providing information about the geography of Jerusalem during that period. It is generally agreed that his description of the various sites is based on the route taken by the gravediggers, but in certain cases these routes are not in keeping with the situation that existed at the time.

The different versions of Strategius' writings give conflicting numbers of victims of the massacre; in one version it is given as ten thousand, while in another it is a sixth of this figure. It is reasonable to believe that the large numbers cited in one or other of the versions are the result of impressions gained from the immensity of the atrocity, and were not based on careful examination of the facts.

According to the Arabic version published at the end of the nineteenth century, the route taken by the gravediggers began at the altar of the Church of St. George, mentioned among the buildings erected by Eudocia. The location of the church is unknown, apart from the fact that it was situated outside the walls (see above, the section on the fifth century). From there, they continued to the House of Faith—the municipal chambers, or perhaps David's Tower. The next stop was the "cisterns" which were large water reservoirs, the location of which has not been identified with any certainty. Thomas the Gravedigger and his helpers then went to the Holy Wisdom Church (Hagia Sophia, in the vicinity of Wilson's Arch), and then to the Cosmas and Damianus Church, situated in the area between the two Cardines (some associate this with the sixth station on the Via Dolorosa). The route continued to Golgotha, which according to the Arabic version was the site of the cross, and then to other sites in the vicinity—the Church of the Redemption, the site of the Holy Sepulcher, and the greater forum, south of the Church of the Holy Sepulcher. From here the route moved outside the city walls to a place called "Samaritica." This site is identified with the location of a church dedicated to the woman of Samaria whom Jesus met (John 4:7). The church was situated near the riverbed of the Kidron Valley, and there is a theory that the allusion is to the Tomb of Hezir's Priestly Family, which Byzantine monks turned into a church. The route continued further, but we have presented only a part of it here. In the course of the description of the route taken by the gravediggers, the author stated the number of victims buried at each site. Thus at the end of the route the total figure is 62,455 and in other versions of the activities of Thomas the Gravedigger, the figures are higher.

At the beginning of the period of Persian rule over

Jerusalem, the Jews were well treated, and this led to hopes of redemption. However, a short time after the conquest, the Persians rejected the Jews in preference for the Christians who constituted the majority of inhabitants of the lands under Persian rule, and more genial relations with them made the control of the area much easier. As a result, the Jews lost the influence they had wielded at first within the Persian administration, and their hopes for redemption were thwarted.

As a consequence of the trend on the part of the Persians toward conciliation with the Christians, permission was granted to Modestos—the head of the Theodosius Monastery in the Judean Desert—to restore churches in Jerusalem. With the spiritual and material support of the Bishop of Alexandria, John the Pious, he renovated the Church of the Holy Sepulcher, restored the Church of the Ascension and the Basilica of Holy Zion. Other important churches destroyed during the invasion were not restored, and in the course of time disappeared with no further mention in the history of the city.

The Persians ruled Jerusalem for a period of only fifteen years. Already in 622, the Byzantine Emperor Heraclius set out on his campaigns to drive out the invaders from the conquered territories of his empire. Following a series of victories, he signed a peace treaty with the Persian King Kavad II, according to which the Persians agreed to withdraw from the territories of the Byzantine Empire, and the Holy Cross would be returned to the Christians in Jerusalem.

Heraclius arrived in Jerusalem with the Holy Cross at the head of a triumphal procession on March 21, 630. Christian tradition relates that the emperor and his retinue entered the city through the Golden Gate. It would appear that Heraclius erected this gate especially for the occasion, placing it in the eastern wall of the city, in his desire to retrace the steps of Jesus' entrance into Jerusalem. Since that event, Christians celebrate the day of the Holy Cross on September 14 of each year.

During the last eight years of Byzantine rule over Jerusalem, up to the Muslim conquest in 638, as far as we know, no further buildings of consequence were constructed in the city. The Byzantine character of the city, with its important buildings which filled various functions, lingered over a period of many years after the Byzantines were vanquished.

(right)The **Golden Gate** (drawing by de Vogüé) in the eastern city wall was, according to Jewish tradition, one of the gates of the Temple (perhaps the Shushan Gate), and thus in the past Jews used to pray in its vicinity. In the Ayyubid period, when the surrounding area became a Muslim cemetery, Jews were unable to pray there and they moved to the Western Wall.

In Christian tradition it is called the Golden Gate, based on the belief that this was the site of the Beautiful Gate, the eastern entrance to the Temple through which Jesus entered Jerusalem on Palm Sunday, prior to Easter (John 12:13). Another Christian tradition tells that it was near this gate that Peter miraculously healed a cripple (Acts 3:1–6). Muslim tradition links the gate with a verse in the Koran which states: "And there was set up amongst them a wall and in it a gate, toward the interior it has mercy and toward the exterior it has punishment." Thus in Arabic it is called the Gate of Mercy.

The date the gate was constructed is still a matter of controversy. Some scholars believe that it was built in the time of the Byzantine Emperor Justinian (sixth century), because of the magnificence of its structure. Another theory dates it to the early Arab (Umayyad) period, when a similar style was in use. This assumption is supported by the fact that this gate is similar to the Double Gate, which was built at that time. However, the location of this gate in the eastern wall of Jerusalem, far distant from a convenient approach to the city, bears witness to the fact that its erection was connected with a special event. Thus it is reasonable to believe that it was erected in the seventh century in honor of the Emperor Heraclius who passed through it in 629 at the head of a triumphal procession, bringing back the Holy Cross from Persia to Jerusalem.

It would seem that the Golden Gate, embellished in the best tradition of Byzantine art, appealed to the Muslims who adorned the Double Gate in the southern Temple Mount wall in a similar manner.

The Golden Gate was closed already during the Crusader period, when it was opened only on two occasions annually. It was later closed permanently, apparently in the Ayyubid period.

The Early Arab Period
638 – 1099

New coins were introduced in Jerusalem immediately after the Arab conquest of the city. This **copper coin** is probably the first to be minted in Jerusalem under Muslim rule (it is only presumed that it was minted in Jerusalem, as the place is not engraved on the coin itself). Apparently this coin was minted prior to the issue of series of coins during the Umayyad period.

On one side of the coin is the inscription: "Muhammad, Messenger of God," and on the obverse is a five-branched candelabrum. This candelabrum probably has no connection with Jewish practice, but rather seems to be an early Muslim motif, prior to the city becoming sanctified in the Islamic religion.

The conquest of Jerusalem by the Muslim Caliph Omar Ibn el-Khattab in the year 638, marked the beginning of the 450-year period of Arab rule which ended when the Crusaders took the city in 1099.

The little known about the early Arab period is based on a small number of primary sources. These include descriptions by the Jerusalem-born Muslim geographer, Shams ed-Din Ibn Abdallah, commonly called el-Muqaddasi, and the writings of the Persian traveler Nasir-i Khusraw who visited the city in 1047. There were also descriptions by Christian pilgrims as well as liturgical registers listing Christian houses of prayer throughout the city. Another important source is the Cairo Genizah, the study of whose documents has provided a wealth of information about this period. Archaeological excavations, especially those carried out since 1967, have also brought additional though limited information, since many buildings from the early Arab period were demolished in the course of the intensive construction that took place during the Crusader period in Jerusalem.

From the outset, Jerusalem has always had a special status in Islam. Muhammad tried to win over to Islam the Jews living in the Arabian Peninsula, and thus from the outset decreed that when praying the faithful should turn in the direction of Jerusalem. When he realized that he was unable to proselytize the Jews, Muhammad annulled his original decree and proclaimed Mecca to be the center of Islam. However, Jerusalem was still of the utmost importance, since the Arabs related to it as the city of the great prophets of the Jews—Joshua, David, Solomon as well as of the Christians—Mary, Jesus and other prophets. Early attempts to convince the Muslims to comply were not successful, and it was only much later that a tradition was introduced linking Muhammad with Jerusalem, even though it was not in keeping with the original intent of the Koran. The seventeenth sura of the Koran states: "Praise be the name of he who brought his servant in the night from the Holy Mosque to the furthest mosque whose environs we

have blessed." A later interpretation of this passage explains that this was the occasion of Muhammad's miraculous visit to Jerusalem riding on his legendary horse el-Buraq from the center of Islam at Mecca, to the furthest end (in Arabic, *aqsa*)—then understood as Jerusalem. It would seem that the attempt to constitute the connection with Jerusalem was made by apostate Jews, and this is expressed in the large number of Muslim sources derived from Jewish origins.

The Muslims' first victory over the Byzantines in the land of Israel took place in July 634, in the vicinity of Ijnadayn (situated according to Arab sources between Ramla and Beit Guvrin). The Muslim forces conquered the major part of the country, leaving Byzantine enclaves in Jerusalem and Ashkelon. The Arabs ravaged the villages, ruined the fields and devastated the monasteries in the vicinity of Jerusalem, but did not enter the city itself. The city's inhabitants shut themselves up inside the city and ventured forth only when absolutely necessary. The decisive battle between the Byzantine and Muslim armies took place at the Yarmuk River in the year 636. The Byzantines were defeated and forced to leave the country. The Muslims were then free to eliminate remaining Byzantine enclaves. Jerusalem remained under siege for about two years, until it surrendered in February 638.

There are no reliable sources relating to the Muslim conquest of Jerusalem, and thus it is difficult to obtain a full picture of the events of the time. A variety of traditions have evolved around the surrender of the city, such as that the Byzantines handed over Jerusalem to Khaled Ibn Tabet el-Fahmi, commander of the Muslim forces. Another tradition has it that the Patriarch of Jerusalem, Sophronius, refused to surrender to anyone but the caliph himself, and thus Omar Ibn el-Khattab was required to come to Jerusalem for the occasion.

Upon entering the city, Omar went to the Temple Mount, accompanied by his attendant Ka'b el-Akhbar, an apostate Jew. When he saw the mounds of refuse that had accumu-

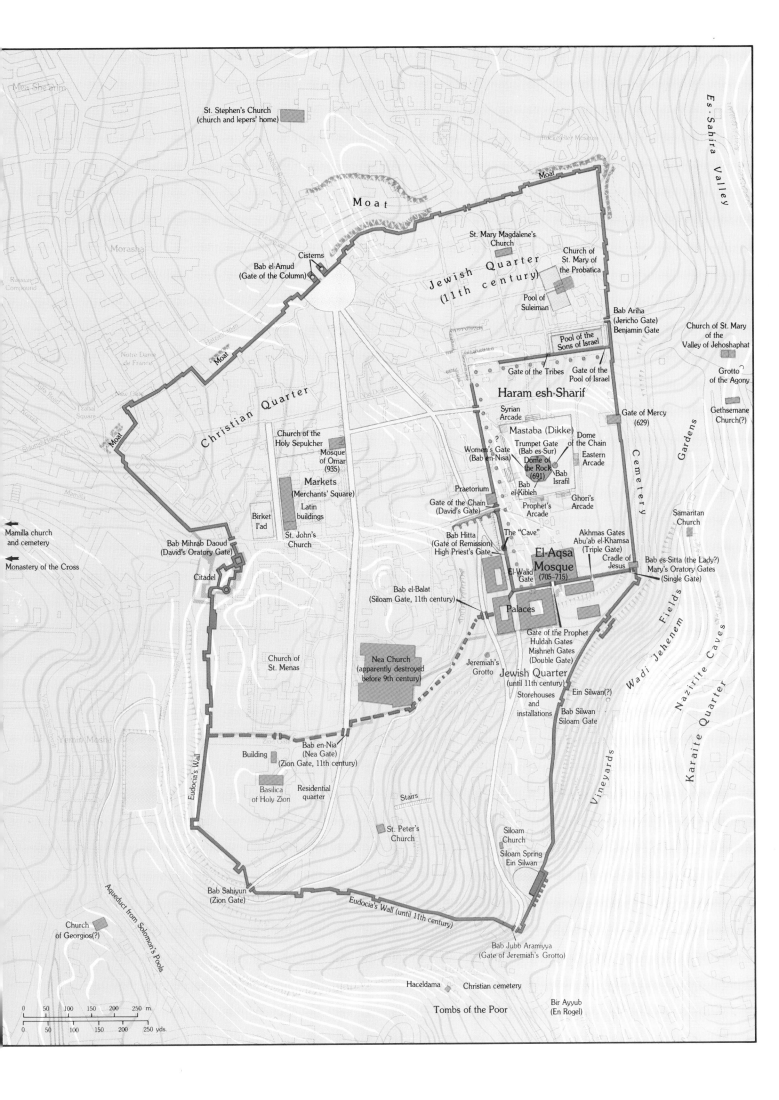

St. Stephen's Church
(church and lepers' home)

Es - Sahira Valley

M o a t

Moat

Cisterns

Bab el-Amud
(Gate of the Column)

Moat

Moat

Christian Quarter

St. Mary Magdalene's
Church

Jewish Quarter
(11th century)

Church of
St. Mary of
the Probatica

Pool of
Suleiman

Bab Ariha
(Jericho Gate)
Benjamin Gate

Pool of the
Sons of Israel

Gate of the Tribes   Gate of the
Pool of Israel

Haram esh-Sharif

Syrian
Arcade

Gate of Mercy
(629)

Church of St. Mary
of the
Valley of Jehoshaphat

Grotto
of the Agony

Gethsemane
Church(?)

Mastaba (Dikke)

Church of the
Holy Sepulcher

Mosque
of Omar
(935)

Markets
(Merchants' Square)

Latin
buildings

Birket
l'ad

St. John's
Church

Women's Gate
(Bab en-Nisa)

Trumpet Gate
(Bab es-Sur)
Dome of
the Rock
(691)

Dome
of the Chain

Eastern
Arcade

Bab
Israfil

Bab
el-Kibleh

Praetorium

Gate of the Chain
(David's Gate)

Prophet's
Arcade

Ghori's
Arcade

Cemetery

Gardens

Samaritan
Church

Mamilla church
and cemetery

Monastery of the Cross

Bab Mihrab Daoud
(David's Oratory Gate)

Citadel

Bab Hitta
(Gate of Remission)
High Priest's Gate

The "Cave"

El-Aqsa
Mosque
(705–715)

El-Walid
Gate

Akhmas Gates
Abu'ab el-Khamsa
(Triple Gate)
Cradle of
Jesus

Bab es-Sitta (the Lady?)
Mary's Oratory Gates
(Single Gate)

Bab el-Balat
(Siloam Gate, 11th century)

Palaces

Fields

Church of
St. Menas

Nea Church
(apparently destroyed
before 9th century)

Jeremiah's
Grotto

Gate of the Prophet
Huldah Gates
Mishneh Gates
(Double Gate)

Jewish Quarter
(until 11th century)

Storehouses
and
installations

Ein Silwan(?)

Bab Silwan
Siloam Gate

Wadi Jehenem

Nazirite Caves

Karaite Quarter

Eudocia's Wall

Building

Basilica
of Holy Zion

Residential
quarter

Bab en-Nia
(Nea Gate)
(Zion Gate, 11th century)

Stairs

St. Peter's
Church

Vineyards

Siloam
Church

Siloam Spring
Ein Silwan

Bab Sahiyun
(Zion Gate)

Eudocia's Wall (until 11th century)

Church
of Georgios(?)

Aqueduct from Solomon's Pools

Bab Jubb Aramiyya
(Gate of Jeremiah's Grotto)

Haceldama   Christian cemetery

Tombs of the Poor

Bir Ayyub
(En Rogel)

0   50   100   150   200   250 m.

0   50   100   150   200   250 yds.

lated on the mount, the Caliph Omar ordered the place cleaned up. As a result the revered "Foundation Stone" was revealed once again, and the caliph built a mosque to the south of it. A Christian traveler, Arculf, who visited Jerusalem in 670, described the mosque thus: "A square prayer house which they [the Muslims] built in a crude form, placing wooden boards and broad beams on some ruins. It is said that the building can contain three thousand persons."

Reports of the Caliph Omar's visit to the Temple Mount and the activities he carried out there are found in many sources, mainly Jewish, but in recent years doubts have arisen as to the veracity of the accounts of his visit to Jerusalem.

A mosque bearing Omar's name was constructed on Mount Scopus in the Middle Ages in commemoration of his visit to Jerusalem. According to tradition, Omar first saw Jerusalem and the Temple Mount from this spot when he reached the city from north Transjordan. Vestiges of this mosque could still be seen on Mount Scopus until recently.

The transition from Byzantine to Arab Jerusalem took place without any disruption. This applied specifically to the physical aspect of the city. Muslims such as el-Muqaddasi

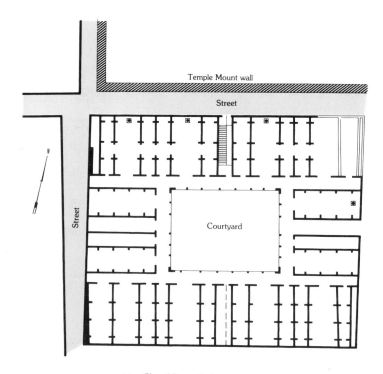

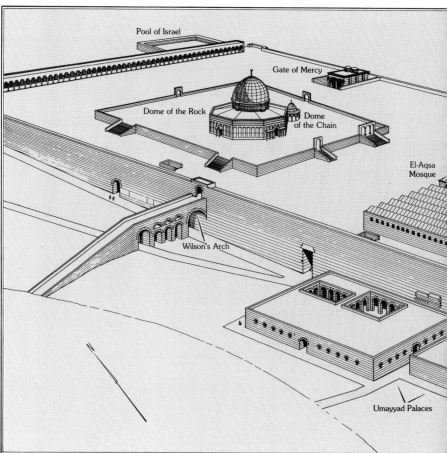

(above) Plan of the **central Umayyad palace** south of the Temple Mount. It was in the form of a square and had a large central courtyard around which were rooms divided into separate units. Buildings of a similar format were found in Syria and other countries under the rule of the Umayyad caliphate.

(left) View from the south of the Temple Mount and remains of the **Umayyad palaces** beneath it.

(right) **Reconstruction of the Umayyad building complex on the Temple Mount and to the south (view from southwest).**

In the center of the Temple Mount, the Dome of the Rock can be seen. It was erected during the rule of Caliph Abd el-Malik and inaugurated in the year 691. To the east is the Dome of the Chain which was also erected during the rule of this caliph. Both structures stood on a plateau reached by a series of six stairways.

At the south of the Temple Mount is the Aqsa Mosque, erected during the rule of Caliph el-Walid. The present-day structure is smaller than that seen in the reconstruction. To the south of the Temple Mount wall is a series of magnificent palaces erected at the same time as the Aqsa Mosque when the entire area was redesigned during the rule of el-Walid. The central palace, the most magnificent of all, served as accommodation for the caliph during his sojourn in Jerusalem. The purpose of the other palaces is not clear. They may have been used by the persons employed in the Temple Mount mosques as well as by the military personnel based in the city. Prior to the construction of the palaces, remains of buildings from earlier periods were found south of the Temple Mount. These were filled in with earth and the palaces erected on the plateau thus formed. As a result they, like the Aqsa Mosque, were susceptible to earthquakes and they remained standing only a short

while before being destroyed in the earthquake in the year 748. These buildings were repaired and served as accommodation for the simple folk. The palaces were ruined completely during the 1033 earthquake. The area was no longer inhabited and became a source for building materials and limestone prepared from the stones. At the end of the eleventh century there was no longer any sign of the region's former grandeur.

The series of palaces in the illustration differs in some details from that in the map at the beginning of this chapter. The reason for this is that the map presents only those remnants actually found on the site, while the reconstruction depicts the structures in their entirety.

On the western side of the Temple Mount can be seen Wilson's Arch, built in the Second Temple period and renovated in the Umayyad period. It appears that it took on its present form at that time, during the renovation of the city's main streets.

The gates dating from earlier times were those that opened on to the Temple Mount. A number of historical sources state that four gates existed in the southern sector of the Temple Mount: the Walid Gate, which led from the roof of the central palace to the Aqsa Mosque; the Gate of the Prophet (the Double Gate) which was also renovated during the Umayyad period; and Bab es-Sitta (the Single Gate).

and the traveler Nasir-i Khusraw, described the pleasant, paved streets and their functional drainage system.

However, the beginning of the Muslim rule of the city was a period of a decline in the number of inhabitants. Many Christians had been killed in battle, and the remaining soldiers sought sanctuary in other Byzantine countries. The Christians were gradually replaced by Muslim immigrants from the Arabian Peninsula.

After the Christian rulers had been ousted from Jerusalem the ban on Jewish settlement in the city, which had been in force during the Roman and Byzantine administrations, was revoked. The respect accorded the Jews by the Caliph Omar was a thorn in the flesh of the Christians. A Christian tradition tells of an agreement between Muslims and Christians according to which the Muslims agreed not to allow Jews to settle in Jerusalem: "And at the end of the year 948 of the Greeks and 25 of Heraclius and 15 of the Hegira, Omar the King came to the land of Israel, and Sophronius, the Patriarch of Jerusalem, went out toward him, and received a promise over all the land. And Omar gave him a written appointment and stated that no Jew could live in Jerusalem. And when Omar entered Jerusalem he ordered that in place of Solomon's sanctuary a mosque be built for their prayers." However, we learn from the Cairo Genizah that following negotiations between the Christians and the Caliph Omar, the latter granted permission to seventy Jewish families from Tiberias to settle in Jerusalem. At their request they were allowed to settle in the "south of the city, and this was the marketplace of the Jews and it was their wish to be nearby to their holy place and its gates, as well as the waters of Siloam for immersion." This leads us to the assumption that the Jewish Quarter was built south of the Temple Mount, in the vicinity of the Ophel hill. A number of archaeological finds in the area confirm this theory.

The Arab Muslim conquerors continued to call Jerusalem by its Roman–Byzantine name "Aelia," and this name appears on coins and various documents in which reference to the city is made. From the tenth century, the Arabic name el-Quds was gradually introduced, reflecting the reverence the Muslims attributed to the Temple Mount and its immediate vicinity. In the course of time the official title of Jerusalem became "the City of the Temple," which was also used by the Jews. Other names, such as the "Holy City" and the "City of the Supreme King," appear in Jewish sources from this period.

Under Umayyad Rule

In the year 661, the Caliph Ali was murdered and the governor of Syria, Mu'awiyya, was appointed Caliph of Jerusalem, where he laid the foundations for the Umayyad dynasty, which lasted until the year 750. Despite the fact that the capital of the caliphate was Damascus, the caliphs made serious efforts to develop Jerusalem and embellish it with impressive edifices, befitting the holy city of a mighty empire.

The Umayyads set out to restore the city to its former glory, and one of their first acts was to restore its main streets, which was part of the street network set up by the Romans and Byzantines. They had remained in their original form during the early Arab period. The arterial streets (the Roman–Byzantine Cardines) ran from Bab el-Amud (Damascus Gate) to Bab es-Sahiyun (Zion Gate) and to Bab el-Balat (Dung Gate), and then along the Patriarch's Street—the present-day Christians' Street. The only significant change the Umayyads made in Jerusalem's street network was in the southwestern area of the Temple Mount. It was here that the main axis leading from Bab el-Amud southward was blocked off, in the process of the construction of a series of exquisite palaces. The lanes between these palaces led to the main street which continued to Bab Jubb Aramiyya, in the vicinity of the ancient Siloam Pool. The construction of the series of palaces south of the Temple Mount may be evidence of a master plan for the city, apparently with the intention of turning it into the leading cultural center of the Umayyad caliphate.

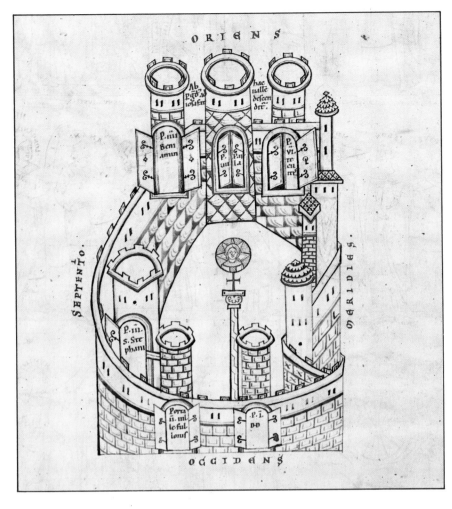

(above) **Arculf**, apparently a French bishop, sojourned in Jerusalem about the year 670 and made a plan of the city in wax which was copied by **Adamnanos** (reproduced here). The latter was the head of the Iona Monastery in western Scotland and wrote a book about the holy places. This map (from the seventh century) is reproduced from the shortened version of *Bede Venerabilis*, which included material from Adamnanos' work.

Jerusalem is portrayed in a schematic circular form, and around it are the four points of the compass in Latin. In its walls can be seen a number of towers and gates—to the west are David's Gate (i) and the Fuller's Gate (ii); to the north, St. Stephen's Gate (iii); to the east, Benjamin Gate (iiii) and the Trumpeter's Gate (vi); between these two was the "Small Gate," above which was the inscription: "From here is the descent to the Jehoshaphat Valley."

The Church of the Holy Sepulcher is denoted by a cross, above which is a portrait of Jesus enclosed in a circle. This map of Jerusalem is of the city prior to the construction of Muslim buildings, and thus the church is the focal point of the map.

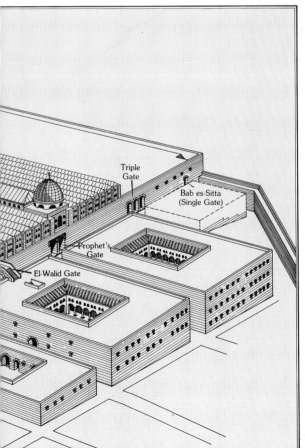

The walls of Jerusalem were renovated at the beginning of the Umayyad period, during the rule of the Caliph Abd el-Malik (685–705). Details of their course, structure and towers are known from the accounts of the siege imposed upon the city by the Crusaders in 1099. The Caliph Abd el-Malik also repaired the roads leading to the city, evidence of which is furnished by the milestones uncovered in the region.

Archaeological excavations have revealed that the Umayyads also carried out extensive building works in the area of the present-day Citadel. These buildings have been attributed to the Caliph el-Walid (705–715).

The crowning glory of the Umayyad building works was the construction on the Temple Mount. The Dome of the Rock was the first edifice built on the mount (691) by the Caliph Abd el-Malik. This building, which still functions as a cult center, was constructed more for the purpose of guarding the revered Foundation Stone than to serve as

(right) The **Dome of the Rock** viewed from the southwest.

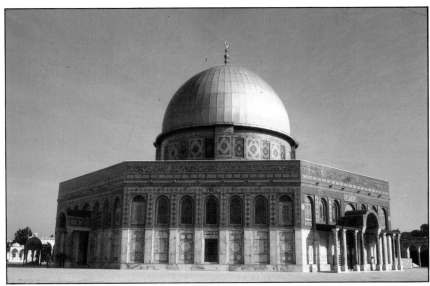

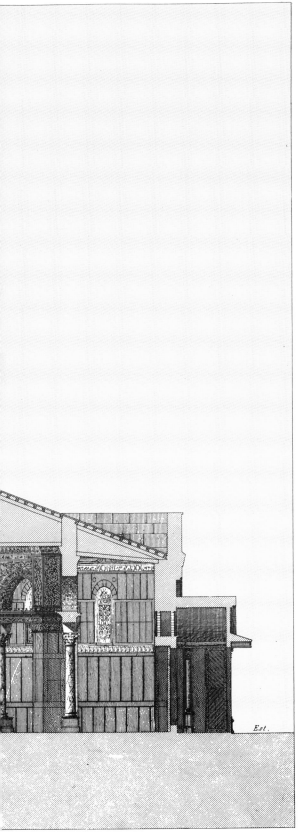

(left) A detailed drawing of a cross section of the **Dome of the Rock** from the work published in 1864 of one of the greatest explorers of Jerusalem, the **Vicomte de Vogüé**.

The cross section shows the details of construction: a double dome whose internal ceiling was embossed with decorated wooden slats. Supporting the dome is a drum (the rounded section), decorated with Byzantine-style wall mosaics typical of the Islamic art of the period. The lower section of the structure consists of a wall which surrounds a double row of columns and hexagonal portals. The internal space forms two circular passageways encompassing the Foundation Stone which can be seen in the center of the illustration. A grotto has been hewn in the rock, and between this grotto and the stoneface is an aperture. According to a recent theory this cave is the burial place of a nobleman from the Middle Bronze Age (2800–2200 BCE), and this may well be the source of the sanctity accorded the rock in later periods. Above the Foundation Stone are cloth awnings, which are described by a number of Western voyagers who succeeded in entering the building in the nineteenth century. An iron grille which surrounded the Foundation Stone during the Crusader period can also be seen, but it was removed during the Jordanian administration (it is now displayed in the Islamic Museum on the Temple Mount).

a mosque for the purpose of prayer. The reasons for the construction of this edifice have been the subject of much research, because both the Jews and Christians considered the area to be sacred. The Jews considered the Dome of the Rock to be a metamorphosis of Solomon's Temple, and it has been described in this manner in various traditions. When this shrine was erected, and the Temple Mount consecrated as a place for prayer by Muslims, the Jews were permitted to fulfil a number of caretaker functions there: to sweep it, and to clean the glass lamps and fill them with oil. The caretakers were exempt from paying the poll tax. The Jews considered fulfilling this task to be a great honor and they succeeded in maintaining this function until the Abbasid period, when they were once more forbidden to enter the Temple Mount area. The Christians also believed the Dome of the Rock to be the reincarnation of Solomon's Temple, and for this reason turned it into a church during the Crusader period. Many churches were constructed in Europe based on this model.

After the construction of the Dome of the Rock was completed, the Caliph el-Walid erected the Aqsa Mosque. The scant knowledge concerning the construction of this mosque derives from a number of papyri from Aphrodito in Egypt, which state that the builders and materials came from that country. It is possible that the reason for the lack of information about the building of this mosque is that the wooden structure previously stood on the site on which the mosque was now erected, and thus the fact of the erection of the new building was not considered of sufficient significance to be reported in contemporary sources but rather a lavish reconstruction.

The tradition of the Prophet Muhammad's ascent to heaven from Jerusalem, and the erection of the Dome of the Rock and the Aqsa Mosque, accorded the city a special status in the Islamic religion. From that time on, numerous offerings were sent to the city, which were beneficial to its economic situation. Pilgrims and tourists paid visits to Jerusalem, leaving wondrous accounts of the city's beauty, of its pleasant streets, its well-organized drainage system, and the prosperous lifestyle of its inhabitants. Obviously, some of the accounts are exaggerated, being colored by the emotional attachment of the pilgrims to Jerusalem.

Once Jerusalem became a focal point of the Islamic religion, the internal struggles between the various Muslim factions became more ardent, and relations with the Christian and Jewish minorities deteriorated.

Despite the religious significance of Jerusalem for the Umayyad rulers, it was never granted the status of a capital city. In the year 716, Ramla was established as the capital of the province of Palestine, and Jerusalem remained the spiritual center with no political significance.

The year 746 was the beginning of Jerusalem's decline.

The Muslim inhabitants of the land of Israel revolted against the Caliph Marwan II, and Jerusalem suffered more than any other city because of its importance to the caliphate. In 750 the rule of the Umayyad dynasty came to an end, and a new chapter in the annals of Jerusalem began when the Abbasids came to power.

The Abbasid Dynasty

When the Abbasids rose to power, they transferred the capital of the empire from Damascus to Baghdad (in 762), and as a result the center of power moved further away from Jerusalem, which lost its former status. Few of the new caliphs visited Jerusalem, and it was more or less neglected during that period. The Dome of the Rock was vandalized, mainly when gold and silver were removed from its doors to be used for minting coins with which to cover the costs of repairs to buildings in the Temple Mount area. (This occurred during the rule of Caliph el-Mansur from 754 to 775).

Soon after the Abbasids came to power it became apparent that the religious tolerance enjoyed by the non-Muslim minority communities was not to continue. High taxes were imposed on the Jews as well as the Christians, and at times they had difficulty in meeting demands for payment.

During this period, the prohibition imposed on Jews to enter the Temple Mount was more strictly observed. A tenth-century source describes Jews praying at the Temple Mount gates, and sources from the eleventh century state that the Mount of Olives was an important prayer site to which Jews made pilgrimages.

When the oppression by the Muslim rulers became unbearable, the Christians of Jerusalem sent a delegation to Charlemagne in the year 797 to request his intervention on their behalf. The emperor called upon Caliph Harun el-Rashid (ruled from 786 to 809) to alleviate the situation of the Christians in the city. As a sign of gratitude, the Christians sent the emperor the keys to the Church of the Holy Sepulcher, which were presented to him during the ceremony at which he was invested by the Pope in Rome. As a consequence of the cordial relations that developed between the Christians of Jerusalem and the emperor, and at the same time, between the caliph and the emperor, Charlemagne succeeded in making a significant contribution to Jerusalem's Christian community. At his initiative, a number of buildings were erected to provide accommodation for Europeans visiting the city. Evidence of this is found in the writings of the German traveler, Friar Bernard (in 870), who described the building complex erected by Charlemagne on the site of the present-day Muristan. This included a monastery for monks, a convent for nuns, a marketplace, and a hospice for pilgrims. The emperor purchased gardens in the Kidron Valley, the revenues of whose produce provided funds for the maintenance of these properties. The sales of goods in the marketplace he erected was another source of income for the maintenance of the buildings. Charlemagne also provided the funds for the construction of the Haceldama monastery in the Valley of Hinnom. A document bearing the title "A Memorandum on the Houses of God and the Monasteries," drawn up for Charlemagne in the year 808, lists the Christian buildings existing in Jerusalem at the time. This document is most valuable for the description it provides of the city at that time, since the intensive construction that took place in the Muristan Quarter during the Crusader period has made it impossible to identify the buildings erected by Charlemagne.

Today, it is assumed that these buildings were in the vicinity of the western boundary of the marketplace in the Muristan Quarter, near the Church of St. Mary la Latine, the main church within the complex. Apparently the Church of St. John the Baptist, situated at the western side of the Muristan, was part of that complex, since its construction precedes the Crusader period but is later than the Byzantine period. Buildings erected by Charlemagne were all destroyed by the zealous Fatimid Caliph el-Hakim (in 1009), but were reconstructed later in the eleventh century, when a new

European element, Italian merchants from Amalfi, settled in the city. These buildings continued to exist until they were demolished at the time of the Seljuk invasion in 1071 or 1073.

During the rule of Caliph el-Ma'mun, extensive renovations to the Dome of the Rock were carried out. It would appear that the forgery of the dedication inscription on the edifice was made at that time, when the Abbasid Caliph el-Ma'mun replaced the name of the Umayyad Caliph Abd el-Malik with his own name as the person responsible for its restoration, but without changing the date, thus leading to the discovery of the forgery.

After the end of Charlemagne's reign, the situation of Jerusalem deteriorated. A plague of locusts that struck the land was the cause of famine in the city. Numerous Muslims left Jerusalem, and as a result the balance of the communal population was tipped in favor of the Christians, who for a short while constituted the majority community in the city. They exploited the situation to obtain authorization to renovate the Church of the Holy Sepulcher. However, this situation did not last for long, and in 861 the Christian Patriarch was put to death as punishment for having carried out the renovation.

In the year 841, the inhabitants of the villages on the periphery of Jerusalem rose up in revolt against the extortion by the authorities, and they captured the city. Many buildings

were plundered and damaged, and during the year-and-a-half it took to put down the revolt, the city suffered greatly and its desolation grew. The remoteness of Palestine from the center of government in the capital, Baghdad, weakened the Abbasids' control over the country. As a result the Egyptian rulers appointed by the Abbasids won a certain amount of independence and even annexed the land of Israel and the surrounding territories to their kingdom. The first to do so was Ahmad Ibn Tulun who began to rule Egypt in 868. In 878 he annexed the province of Palestine to Egypt and his descendants ruled over it until the year 915.

The Tulunid dynasty was replaced by the Ikhshidids who found in Jerusalem a city which would accommodate their religious aspirations. Tradition has it that members of this dynasty were buried in Jerusalem. The first governor of the land of Israel appointed by the Ikhshidids, Isa Ibn el-Nushri, was buried in Jerusalem in 909, and the most famous of all the dynasty, the black eunuch Kafur, was buried there in 968. The burial place of these rulers is not known, but the general belief is that they were buried in the cemetery to the east of the Temple Mount.

Toward the middle of the tenth century the power of the central government in Baghdad declined, and extremist Muslim trends spread throughout the kingdom. These were

(left) **Jerusalem** as depicted on a mosaic floor from the **Abbasid period (785)**. The mosaic was unearthed in 1986 in archaeological excavations carried out by monks of the Franciscan Order at **Umm Rasas** in southern Transjordan. This site is 19 miles (30 km.) southeast of Madaba, on the slopes of the Arnon Valley, and it is identified with the biblical city **Mephaath** in the allotment of Reuben (1 Chron. 6:79 and Josh. 13:18). This is mainly a Byzantine city with a number of churches. The mosaic was found in St. Stephen's Church, and it is rather surprising that a mosaic floor was created in a Christian church in Transjordan during the Abbasid period. Along the length of the colonnades inside the church were panels upon which cities in the land of Israel and Transjordan are depicted. The cities in the land of Israel shown in the mosaic are Jerusalem, Shechem (Nablus), Samaria, Caesarea, Lydda (Lod), Beit Guvrin, Ashkelon, and Gaza.

The picture of Jerusalem in the mosaic on the floor depicts the major buildings in the city. The Damascus Gate appears at the bottom of the mosaic flanked by two towers. Behind the gate is a circular structure supported by three pillars. This is the rotunda of the Church of the Holy Sepulcher which contains the holy sepulcher itself. The Holy Sepulcher is flanked by two churches—one is probably the basilica of the Holy Sepulcher and the other is apparently the Basilica of Holy Zion, the Néa Church, or some other important church. Behind the structure containing the rotunda, the Tower of David can be seen standing out between other towers in the wall surrounding the city. At the top are the words in Greek "Holy City." This mosaic is the most important contribution to the plastic portraits of Jerusalem during the early Arab period, since the discovery of the Madaba map in 1897.

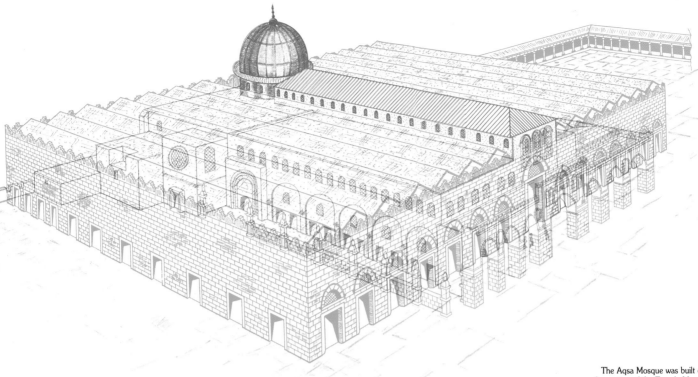

(above) **Copper coin** probably from the rule of the Caliph Mu'awiyya (661–680), depicting the image of the caliph surrounded by the inscription "Muhammad, Messenger of God." On the obverse are the names "Falastin," and "Aelia" (as Jerusalem was called in Roman times and in some places up until the Crusader period). On this side of the coin is a half moon under which is the letter "m" which may have depicted the value of the coin, as was the case in the Byzantine period.

(above) The present-day **Aqsa Mosque** (view from the north) imposed on a reconstruction of the mosque as it was in the seventh century. The reconstruction is based on descriptions by el-Muqaddasi (985) an important source of information about the structure of the mosque prior to the great earthquake in Jerusalem in 1033. It is also based on other accounts from that period.

The Aqsa Mosque is the focus of the sanctity of Jerusalem to Islam.

Already in the seventh century there are records of a large wooden structure on this site. According to the accounts of a Christian pilgrim by the name of Arculf, this mosque was able to accommodate 3,000 worshippers, and it apparently was situated to the east of the present structure, or perhaps even on the same site. During the Umayyad period the Caliph el-Walid demolished the original wooden structure and erected a magnificent new mosque, whose dimensions were particularly striking: fifteen prayer aisles, the central one of which was slightly elevated. The only vestige of the original decorations is a colorful mosaic in the section near the *mihrab*.

The Aqsa Mosque was built on the section of the Temple Mount elevated by Herod above the natural rock, and by filling it with earth and stones. Its foundations were placed on a base less solid than the natural rock, and this is the reason it was so badly damaged during the various earthquakes. The first earthquake was in 748 (Caliph el-Mansur rebuilt it in 771). The second was in 774, and it was damaged by a third earthquake in 1033. The renovated structure was narrower and longer, having been extended to the north. The present building is mainly reconstructed, but its original eleventh-century design has been maintained, with modifications introduced by the Crusaders during the twelfth century, and from time to time in later periods.

expressed by attacks upon the non-Muslim population and on its holy sites. An example of this was when in 935 the eastern section of the Church of the Holy Sepulcher was turned into the Mosque of Omar, on the grounds that this was the site at which Omar prayed upon entering Jerusalem. Three years later the church was burned down. In the year 966, the Patriarch of Jerusalem was killed during the riots which broke out against the Christians in the city.

In the year 969, the country was overrun by the army of the Ismaili Caliph el-Mu'izz, who tradition claims to be the son of Fatima, the daughter of Muhammad. This ruler established a state in North Africa, conquered Egypt, and then the province of Palestine and the neighboring territories, and founded the Fatimid dynasty which ruled for over a century (to 1071 or 1073), and later from 1098 to 1099.

At first it seemed as though the Fatimid regime would bring respite to the city which had suffered over a long period from successive changes of government and oppression. One of the signs of this was the fact that two apostate Jews held senior positions in the administration. One of them, Jacob son of Joseph, son of Khals, was the chief vizier of the kingdom, while the other, Menashe son of Abraham Ibn Alqazaz, served as collector of taxes in Syria. At that time the Karaite community grew in Palestine in general, and especially in Jerusalem, where their number at times was equal to the Jewish rabbinical population of the city. The Karaites began to migrate from Egypt to Palestine in the ninth century, and their numbers increased under the Fatimids. There is a wealth of information about this community at this time, mainly as a consequence of the conservation of correspondence between the two centers. The Karaite

center continued in Jerusalem up until it was destroyed by the Crusaders, after which time it never recovered.

However, the country was soon plunged into turmoil as the Bedouin tribes revolted, causing suffering to the inhabitants, mainly the non-Muslims. The attacks on the non-Muslim population reached a climax during the rule of the Caliph el-Hakim (996–1021), who in the year 1009 ordered all Jewish and Christian prayer houses demolished, including the Church of the Holy Sepulcher. However, in 1020 the caliph changed his mind and agreed to the restoration of the buildings, but it was only a decade later that Italian merchants from Amalfi (see above) undertook to restore the Latin center built by Charlemagne. The Church of the Holy Sepulcher was renovated only in 1048, but because of the impoverished circumstances of the Christian community, an unprepossessing building was constructed, which was rebuilt by the Crusaders fifty years later.

The Jews were apparently unable to rebuild their synagogues destroyed by the religious zeal of Caliph el-Hakim. Oppression suffered under this caliph led to the reduction in numbers of the Jewish community at the beginning of the century, and at the end of the century they were victimized by the Seljuks after their conquest of the city. The Crusader conquest put an end to the Jewish community in Jerusalem.

A major earthquake in 1033 left the country in ruins. Jerusalem's fortifications were destroyed, and in the following year the Fatimid Caliph Taher Ali set about repairing the city's walls. The caliph demolished churches situated in the vicinity of the ruined walls, and used the remaining ashlars to restore them. It would seem that the shorter alignment of the wall in the south of the city that is almost

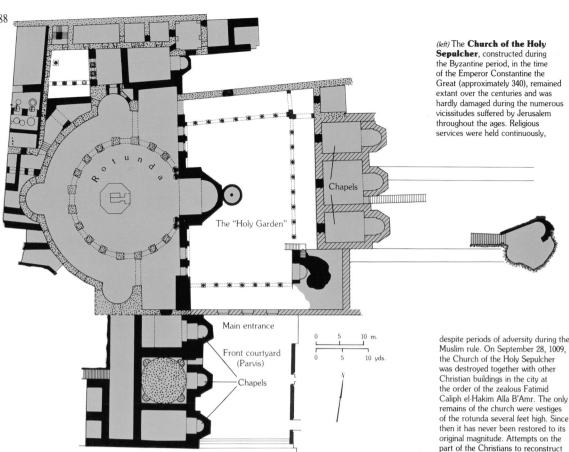

The "Holy Garden"

Chapels

Main entrance

Front courtyard
(Parvis)

Chapels

0   5   10 m.

0   5   10 yds.

N

Existed in earlier periods
and used by Monomachus

Eleventh century

Conjectural

Roofed area

(left) The **Church of the Holy Sepulcher**, constructed during the Byzantine period, in the time of the Emperor Constantine the Great (approximately 340), remained extant over the centuries and was hardly damaged during the numerous vicissitudes suffered by Jerusalem throughout the ages. Religious services were held continuously,

despite periods of adversity during the Muslim rule. On September 28, 1009, the Church of the Holy Sepulcher was destroyed together with other Christian buildings in the city at the order of the zealous Fatimid Caliph el-Hakim Alla B'Amr. The only remains of the church were vestiges of the rotunda several feet high. Since then it has never been restored to its original magnitude. Attempts on the part of the Christians to reconstruct

the church were unsuccessful. However, after intervention of the Byzantine Emperor Constantine Monomachus, who came to an agreement with the Fatimid caliph, the church was rebuilt in 1048. Constantine Monomachus made a number of important changes in the original structure of the church: he put the main entrance at the south (in the original building the entrance was at the east, facing the parvis). Near the main entrance was an inner courtyard which still serves as the approach to the building. Three chapels were built alongside the church, the central one of which previously served as a baptistery. According to one theory the colonnade at the entrance to the church compound was built at the same time, and the only vestige is the capital of one of the pillars which was repaired by the Crusaders.

At the eastern side of the Holy Garden, a large prayer niche was built which served as the main point of prayer within the church. There were also three chapels, of which no trace has remained, even though evidence of their existence is found in literary sources. The height of the rotunda was reduced, and has remained in this form until today.

The church built by Constantine Monomachus maintained its original form for only 30 years, when it was reconstructed by the Crusaders. However, its importance goes beyond this short period, because the remains of this church dictated the manner in which the later church was built.

identical to the present-day wall dates to this period. Prior to the 1033 earthquake, the southern walls built by the Empress Eudocia in the fifth century, encompassed Mount Zion and the hill of the City of David. Within these walls were important Christian buildings, such as the Church of Siloam, St. Peter's Church and the Basilica of Holy Zion. The Jewish Quarter, located south of the Temple Mount throughout the Arab period, also came within the bounds of this wall. The construction of the shorter alignment of the city wall left the Jewish Quarter outside the city limits, and the Jews were forced to move to the northeast sector, which the Crusaders later called the "Jewish Quarter."

The Christian community was assigned the construction of the walls in the northwest of the city, but as they were unable to undertake this venture they appealed to the Byzantine Emperor Constantine Monomachus. The emperor diverted his entire income from Cyprus to this purpose, and the walls were completed in 1063. Detailed data concerning the course and strength of Jerusalem's fortifications during this period, have been found in accounts of the Crusader siege of the city in 1099.

From the time the walls were completed, the Christians were required to live in the northeastern sector of the city, and the Christian Quarter built at that time has remained until this day. A Crusader source states that the majority of the Muslim inhabitants moved from the Christian Quarter to other parts of the city. This process was to the advantage of the Christians, since from that time on they were able to settle in the vicinity of the Church of the Holy Sepulcher. A number of monasteries had been built around this church in the Byzantine period (their existence is mentioned in historical, mainly Greek, sources), and many of them are still in existence. Some of them have passed from one Christian community to another.

The numerous accounts remaining from this period reveal that many churches and other religious institutions continued to exist in Jerusalem during this period. Despite the oppression suffered by the Christians from the beginning of the rule of the Abbasid dynasty, they succeeded in maintaining a considerable amount of property in the city, and apparently erected additional religious structures during the course of

(above) A **stone inscription** fixed into place in the tenth century in the Church of the Holy Sepulcher in the section appropriated from the Christians and turned into a mosque. According to Muslim tradition, the Caliph Omar came to the Church of the Holy Sepulcher after he conquered Jerusalem (638), and at the appointed time for prayer prayed on the steps of the church. This tradition was the circumstance for the appropriation of that section of the church (in 935), and for the ban on Christians entering it.

This inscription, engraved on Herodian-style cut stone, provides proof of that event: "In the name of the all merciful Allah, a supreme

decree has been issued by his immaculate highness to guard this mosque and to maintain it in good condition, and permission will not be granted to enter it by a person under his protection for reasons of taking out refuse or for any other reason. And everyone will take care not to violate this decree and he will obey the decree as regards himself, if it be the will of the Lord."

In the course of the Crusader period, the tradition regarding the praying by the Caliph Omar at this site was forgotten, and another mosque called the Mosque of Omar was erected to the south of the Church of the Holy Sepulcher.

this period. Monks continued to live their communal life in the valleys surrounding Jerusalem unperturbed, and it was only with the conquest of the city by the Seljuks that the monks were driven out of the Kidron and Hinnom Valleys.

The Seljuk invasion in 1071 or 1073, brought large-scale destruction as described in the sources: "And they burned everything and cast out all. ..." After the conquest, the Seljuks, who were Sunnite Muslims, banned the prayers recited in honor of the Shi'ite Fatimid caliphs, and reintroduced prayers for the Abbasid caliphs, who were considered by the Seljuks as being the true caliphs and Sunnite Muslims.

A revolt against the Seljuks in 1076 failed, and the rebels were massacred. In 1098 the Fatimids reconquered Jerusalem, but their rule lasted for a short while only, until the city was taken by the Crusaders in 1099.

(above) A page from **Guide to Jerusalem** discovered in the **Cairo Genizah** in the Ibn Ezra synagogue in Cairo. Letters, books and documents relating to the Cairo Jewish community and Jewish matters in general were stored in this synagogue from the ninth century. Researchers have revealed a wealth of information concerning Jewish traditions in Jerusalem during the early Arab period.

The *Guide to Jerusalem*, written in the tenth century in Arabic in Hebrew script, was designed for travelers going on a pilgrimage to the holy places in Jerusalem. It contains information about Jerusalem's buildings and topography, and thus is one of the most important sources for information about the city during this period.

The "Text of the Prayers of the Gates of Jerusalem on the Temple Mount" was written about a century after this guide appeared. This document, also discovered in Cairo's synagogue, contains prayers recited by pilgrims outside the gates of the city and the Temple Mount gates (about twenty in all).

(right) The **Double Gate** is linked with the Muslim tradition concerning the visit of the prophet Muhammad to the Temple Mount, according to which he tied up his horse el-Buraq outside and entered the Temple area through this gate. This is the origin of the name "Gate of the Prophet," which during the eighth and ninth centuries served as the entrance to the mosque and shrine on the Temple Mount from the palaces built to the south of it. Because of its importance, this gate underwent a series of modifications. One of the most striking was the decorations which are still extant in the form of two embellished lintels. This is an imitation of the Byzantine style, and is the reason that the decorations on the Double Gate are similar to those on the Golden Gate, built in the Byzantine era.

The diagram of the gate was drawn by the French architect and archaeologist **de Vogüé** who published many illustrations on the subject of Jerusalem during the second half of the nineteenth century.

The Crusader Period
1099 - 1187

The **Dome of the Ascension** is situated on the Temple Mount platform, northwest of the Dome of the Rock (the baptistery in the opening map of this chapter). In Crusader times, it apparently served as a baptistery when the Dome of the Rock functioned as a church (Templum Domini). Originally, the structure was open and overlaid with marble, and only later was it blocked up on all sides.

In Muslim tradition this structure marked the spot where Muhammad prayed before his ascent to heaven, and hence its name. A structure was erected here in the early Arab period to denote the event. This structure was demolished and the present dome erected during the Crusader period, and renovated during the Ayyubid period.

An inscription dating to 1200/01 has been placed inside the structure stating: "This is the dome of the Prophet described by historians in their records. ..." According to the inscription, its purpose was to record for posterity the dome built in honor of the prophet and which "disappeared" in the Crusader period. The decorations and the style of architecture prove beyond doubt that this is a Crusader structure.

A further inscription reveals that the structure was renovated again in 1781.

The Crusaders conquered Jerusalem on July 15, 1099, at the end of a five-week siege. The status of Jerusalem now changed from a city in an outlying province to the capital of an independent kingdom and an important center of the Christian world. It was granted this special status for it constituted the religious and emotional center of the Crusader–Christian world, despite the fact that it lacked strategic advantages and despite its remoteness from the main commercial routes and the sea, which were the main supply lines of the Crusader kingdom. The sanctity of the city attracted numerous pilgrims who brought in large amounts of money, and some pilgrims even settled there permanently. Jerusalem now enjoyed a period of prosperity, expressed in intensive construction and which brought about a change in the city's image. Many Crusader buildings have remained until today, and some even serve the very function for which they were built. The Old City of Jerusalem is in many ways a reflection of the Crusader city.

During the course of the time Jerusalem served as the capital city of the Crusader kingdom a strong link was developed with the countries of Europe, and consequently

a wealth of documentation describing the city in that period has remained. These include accounts by the numerous pilgrims who visited the city, collections of documents of some of the leading churches such as the Church of the Holy Sepulcher and the Church of St. Mary Magdalene, and documentation of the Knights Hospitallers and the Order of the Teutonic Knights. There are also the written accounts by Jewish travelers who visited the city during this period. Among the most well-known were Benjamin of Tudela (1167) and Pethahiah of Regensburg (1180). As a consequence of the abundance of maps and written sources, as well as the numerous Crusader buildings still standing in Jerusalem, the Crusader period in Jerusalem is probably the best known of all the periods throughout its entire history.

Once they had succeeded in taking the city, the Crusaders massacred the majority of non-Christian inhabitants and evicted the remainder. Since most of the soldiers had returned to Europe on the completion of their mission, Jerusalem was almost uninhabited, and the conquerors sought ways of attracting Christians to the city. They waived levies on goods brought into the city and introduced concessions on commercial transactions (especially among the Italian residents to encourage them to increase commercial ventures in Jerusalem). New laws were enacted regarding the ownership of abandoned property seized by the Crusader forces during the conquest of the city. Furthermore, persons who held property for one year, left it and then returned within the course of one year, were granted title to those holdings. In addition, Christian Arabs from the border areas of Syria and the land of Israel were resettled in the abandoned quarters of the city. As a consequence of the massacres and the Crusader government's settlement policy, the ethnic composition of the city was radically altered, becoming predominantly Christian. Religious institutions, such as the Dome of the Rock and el-Aqsa Mosque, were appropriated and handed over to the Latin church.

Godfrey of Bouillon became the first ruler of the Kingdom of Jerusalem and received the title "Protector of the Holy Sepulcher." Later, he was appointed Patriarch of Jerusalem. Godfrey's appointment gave the secular government an advantage over the religious leadership in Jerusalem, which was expressed mainly by the division of jurisdiction within the city. At first the Patriarch demanded sole authority over the entire city, but in the end accepted jurisdiction over the northwestern sector of Jerusalem (the Patriarch's Quarter).

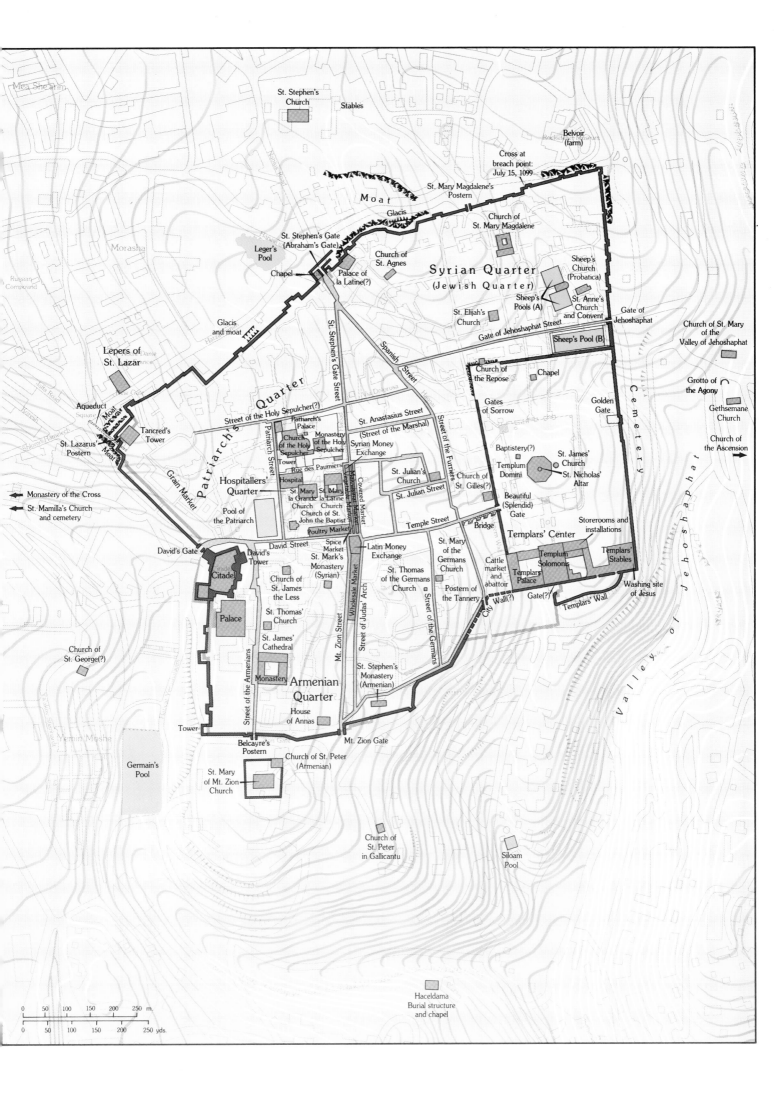

St. Stephen's Church

Stables

Belvoir (farm)

Cross at breach point: July 15, 1099

Moat

St. Mary Magdalene's Postern

Glacis

Church of St. Mary Magdalene

Church of St. Agnes

Chapel

Palace of la Latine(?)

Syrian Quarter (Jewish Quarter)

Leger's Pool

Morasha

Mea She'arim

Russian Compound

Sheep's Church (Probatica)

Sheep's Pools (A)

St. Anne's Church and Convent

St. Elijah's Church

Gate of Jehoshaphat

Church of St. Mary of the Valley of Jehoshaphat

Glacis and moat

Gate of Jehoshaphat Street

Sheep's Pool (B)

Spanish Street

Church of the Repose

Chapel

Grotto of the Agony

Lepers of St. Lazar

New Gate

Gates of Sorrow

Golden Gate

Gethsemane Church

Patriarch's Quarter

Street of the Holy Sepulcher(?)

Via Dolorosa

St. Anastasius Street (Street of the Marshal)

Church of the Ascension

Aqueduct

Moat

Tancred's Tower

Patriarch's Palace

Street of the Furriers

Baptistery(?)

Templum Domini

St. James' Church

St. Nicholas' Altar

St. Lazarus' Postern

Grain Market

Patriarch Street

Church of the Holy Sepulcher

Monastery of the Holy Sepulcher

Syrian Money Exchange

St. Julian's Church

Church of St. Gilles(?)

Cemetery

Valley of Jehoshaphat

Tower

Rue des Paumiers

Hospital

St. Julian Street

Beautiful (Splendid) Gate

Monastery of the Cross

Hospitallers' Quarter

St. Mary la Grande Church

St. Mary la Latine Church

Covered Market

Temple Street

Bridge

Storerooms and installations

St. Mamilla's Church and cemetery

Pool of the Patriarch

Church of St. John the Baptist

Poultry Market

Church of St. Mary of the Germans

Templars' Center

Templum Solomonis

Templars' Stables

David's Gate

David Street

David's Tower

Spice Market

Latin Money Exchange

Cattle market and abattoir

Templars' Palace

Citadel

Church of St. James the Less

St. Mark's Monastery (Syrian)

Wholesale Market

Street of Judas' Arch

St. Thomas of the Germans Church

Postern of the Tannery

City Wall(?)

Gate(?)

Washing site of Jesus

Palace

Church of St. George(?)

St. Thomas' Church

Mt. Zion Street

Templars' Wall

St. James' Cathedral

Monastery

Armenian Quarter

Street of the Armenians

Street of the Germans

St. Stephen's Monastery (Armenian)

Tower

House of Annas

Belcayre's Postern

Mt. Zion Gate

Church of St. Peter (Armenian)

St. Mary of Mt. Zion Church

Germain's Pool

Yemin Moshe

Church of St. Peter in Gallicantu

Siloam Pool

Haceldama Burial structure and chapel

St. Stephen's Gate (Abraham's Gate)

St. Stephen's Gate Street

0 50 100 150 200 250 m.

0 50 100 150 200 250 yds.

This quarter had formerly belonged to the church before the split and was predominantly Greek in character. Under the Crusaders, it passed to the Latin church.

Shortly after the Crusaders conquered Jerusalem, the Greek Patriarch Simon and the Greek bishops left the city and moved to Cyprus. In 1099, the Greek Patriarch was declared dead, and as a result a Latin Patriarch was appointed and Latin bishops replaced the Greek bishops. The Greek Orthodox community lost the status it had prior to the arrival of the Crusaders, and the church property it controlled was taken over by the Latins. At the same time, it appears that the other Christian orders were granted permission to celebrate their festivals at their altars in their chapels in the central houses of prayer such as the Church of the Holy Sepulcher. However, the former tension between the various Christian sects continued, and attempts to reduce it were made throughout the entire period of the first Crusader kingdom.

The Appearance of the City

The fortifications that protected Jerusalem during the early Arab period continued to guard the city during the Crusader period as well. The Crusaders did not reinforce the fortifications, and it was only toward the end of the period of the Crusader kingdom that the city's barons contributed the funds to secure them. It appears that the only significant change made in the fortifications during this period was the reinforcement of the Citadel, and the digging of the moats around it in the 1160s. The Citadel Valley was included within the network of moats, and a wall was built within the riverbed which joined the northwest corner of the Citadel to the continuation of the city wall to the northwest. David's Gate (the present-day Jaffa Gate) was moved to the west from its original site, and was reconstructed as part of the new wall. David's Tower was reinforced, and was given its impressive features which was to become one of the city's emblems and appeared on its king's seals.

The network of moats excavated in the eleventh century in the north of the city continued to function. On this side of the city wall there were three gates: to the east was the St. Mary Magdalene's Postern (Herod's Gate)—on one of the towers east of the gate was a huge cross marking the site where the Crusaders breached the walls when conquering the city; in the center was St. Stephen's Gate (Damascus Gate); to the west was the St. Lazarus' Postern, which led to the leper hospital.

Both the eastern and western walls were constructed on the ruins of the ancient walls. The eastern wall had one gate only, the Gate of Jehoshaphat (present-day Lions' Gate), which led to the Valley of Jehoshaphat, which was the Kidron Valley.

Little is known about Jerusalem's southern wall in the Crusader period, but the prevalent theory is that in the main its course was identical to that of the present-day wall. From historical sources we have evidence of three gates in

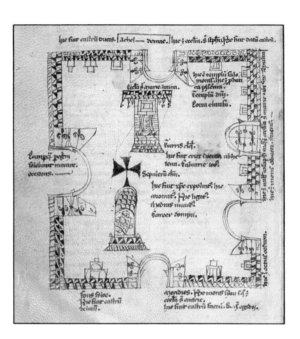

(above left) A graphic description of the **Crusader siege of Jerusalem** on a map showing the city in the year 1099. (The map is now in the library of L'école de Médecine in Montpellier, France).

The map shows the position of Raymond of St. Gilles or the army of Godfrey of Bouillon. It does not show any events taking place in the city itself, but depicts the buildings best known in the Western world at the time: the Church of the Holy Sepulcher and the complex known as St. Mary la Latine. It would seem as though the cartographer was not familiar with the internal aspect of Jerusalem, perhaps having left the forces besieging the city prior to its surrender.

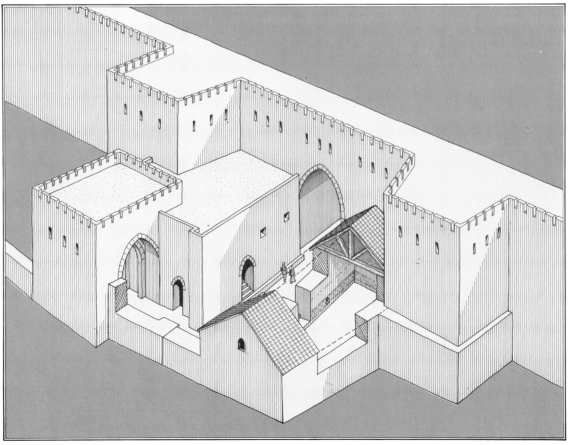

(below left) Reconstruction of **Damascus Gate** in the Crusader period. The upper segment depicts the Roman gate with its two towers, and part of the wall which continued to exist up to the Ottoman period. The Damascus Gate, known in the Crusader period as St. Stephen's Gate stood where the Ottoman gate is situated, but at a lower level. During the Crusader period, a wall was erected adjacent to the western tower, thus reinforcing it. In addition, a number of structures were built, surrounded by a wall parallel to the gate wall. Near the eastern tower an external gate-tower was built leading to the main gate. A huge building was erected alongside the tower, reached by stairs shown in the illustration, and it apparently was used for administrative purposes. The building had an additional entrance, to the north, which seemingly led to an Umayyad period water cistern, which continued to serve the city's inhabitants during the Crusader period. This cistern was a sort of basement of the administration building, and the above-mentioned stairs were built to facilitate passage over the cistern's vaults. Near the western tower can be seen a chapel, not mentioned in historical sources. This chapel was wide and short, embellished with colored plaster, part of which has remained. In this illustration, part of the chapel roof has been "removed" and some of its walls lowered.

(right) **The Crusader siege of Jerusalem** lasted from June 7 to July 15, 1099. It ended with the surrender of the Citadel to Raymond of St. Gilles. This siege must be examined in the light of the fortifications erected by the Fatimids and possibly also by the Seljuks in the eleventh century. The line of fortification included a main wall, an anterior wall, in front of which was a moat. The lack of archaeological finds from this period makes it difficult to establish the full details of these fortifications. However, considerable data on the siege are available, especially from the records kept by persons accompanying the commanders of the Crusader forces in the camps outside the beleaguered city.

Despite the fact that the Crusader siege lasted for no more than five weeks, it had a major impact on the contemporary society, as well as on the following generations. For centuries after the siege, Europeans endeavored to organize further Crusades in their desire to conquer Jerusalem once more.

(above) **The royal seal of King Baldwin I**, the first Crusader king. On one side the Tower of David is depicted between the dome of the Church of the Holy Sepulcher at the left, and the Dome of the Rock at the right. This image of Jerusalem appeared on most royal seals of the Crusader period, surrounded by the inscription "Civitas Regis Regum Omnium" (the city of the king of all kings), which stresses the supremacy of Jerusalem over all other cities in the Crusader eastern kingdom. On the obverse of the seal, King Baldwin I can be seen seated on his throne.

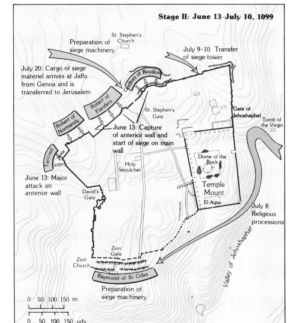

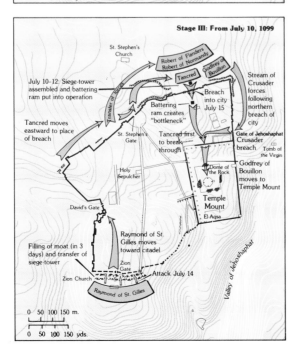

the southern sector of the city: the Postern of the Tannery, which was apparently located on the site of the present-day Dung Gate; Zion Gate; and Belcayre's Postern.

The Temple Mount was fortified during the Crusader period. Its three southern entrances—today called the Double Gate, the Triple Gate, and the Single Gate—were well fortified by the Templars' wall which enclosed them from the south. A further outer gate was part of the structure adjacent to the southern side of Templum Solomonis (present-day el-Aqsa Mosque).

Jerusalem's four principal gates—St. Stephen's Gate, Gate of Jehoshaphat, Zion Gate, and David's Gate—led to the city's main streets, which were called by these names. In actual fact, the network of streets laid at the end of the early Arab period continued to exist throughout the Crusader period as well. The impressive Roman-Byzantine pavements in the main streets deteriorated in part and were refurbished in the early Arab period, and once again in the Crusader period. This process became evident from the archaeological excavations carried out in the Cardo, and in other sites in the city. The Cardo, the main street of Byzantine Jerusalem, was partly built up in the Abbasid period. Along its course, north of the market intersection, the Crusaders built three parallel streets, each with its own marketplace. These streets are still extant. During this period also, an additional marketplace was built south of the intersection, and new streets were laid from two of its extremities: Mount Zion Street (present-day Habad Street), and the Street of Judas' Arch (present-day Street of the Jews). The name Judas' Arch originates in a Christian tradition, according to which Judas Iscariot hanged himself on one of the arches in this street after having betrayed Jesus.

The city's other main street, today called Haggai Street, was divided into two sections: the northern one was called Spanish Street probably after the origins of its inhabitants, while the southern section was called the Street of the Furriers. In this section of the street the furriers and tanners labored in the workshops situated under the huge bridge (a section of which is today called Wilson's Arch), near the municipal abbatoir on the site of the present-day Western Wall plaza. The tanned hides were taken out through the Postern of the Tannery.

To the west of St. Stephen's Gate Street was Patriarch's Street (present-day Christians' Street), which also followed the course of the Roman street. It was named for the Patriarch's mansion situated at the end of the street. The Roman-Byzantine pavements in both streets remained intact during the Crusader period.

Two streets led to the Church of the Holy Sepulcher. These were the Street of the Holy Sepulcher, whose course can be seen in the map at the beginning of this chapter, and to the south, the Rue des Paumiers (Street of the Date Palms; today, ed-Dabagha Street). In this street souvenirs were sold to pilgrims, as well as date palm fronds used in the Palm Sunday procession held the Sunday before Easter.

Other Crusader streets are named for the various buildings situated in them. One of them, St. Julian, was identified by the church by that name discovered nearby. Another was the Street of the Germans (present-day Misgav Ladach Street), named for the origin of the inhabitants of the area. Their main church—St. Mary of the Germans Church—was located on this street.

The network of main streets divided Crusader Jerusalem into a number of quarters, onto which fronted the majority of the buildings. The Patriarch's Quarter, which was administered by the Patriarchate, was autonomous in the Crusader city. It was more or less identical to the present-day Christian Quarter. It was first established in the eleventh century, when the Christians were required to fortify the walls in this area of the city. The Byzantine emperor came to the assistance of the Christians in this undertaking, and the boundaries of this quarter were defined in the agreement drawn up in 1063 between the emperor and the Fatimids. The Muslim inhabitants moved to other areas of the city, and from *(right)* The **facade of the Church of the Holy Sepulcher and its entrance compound** reflect the various stages in the history of this building.

The facade in the photograph presented here is from the Crusader period which incorporated the remains of the temple to Aphrodite built by the Roman Emperor Hadrian on that site. The cornices at both levels are probably remains from this temple.

During the rule of Constantine the Great (fourth century), a postern led to the baptistery situated to the left of the left-hand portal. Constantine Monomachus (eleventh century) placed the main entrance to the church at this spot. In the Crusader period there were two wide portals, of which the left one is still in use, and the right-hand one was blocked off during the Ayyubid period. An additional entrance built at the end of the staircase (at the right) leads to the Franciscan chapel, which serves as an approach to the Chapel of the Hill of Golgotha. This entrance was still in use in the sixteenth century, but there is probably no record of when it was closed off.

The parvis in front of the church's facade was built as an approach compound, and was repaved in the eleventh century and again in the twelfth century. It was bounded by a row of columns crowned with Byzantine capitals, shown here in their secondary usage during the Crusader period (one of these columns can be seen at the right, beside the stairs).

Below the parvis are remains of water cisterns and burial caves, some of which date to the Second Temple period. Two of the three chapels built by Monomachus in the eleventh century can be seen at the left of the photograph. The chapel adjacent to the church facade served as the base for the belfry erected upon it during the Crusader period. The chapel at the left was built as an addition to the Byzantine period baptistery.

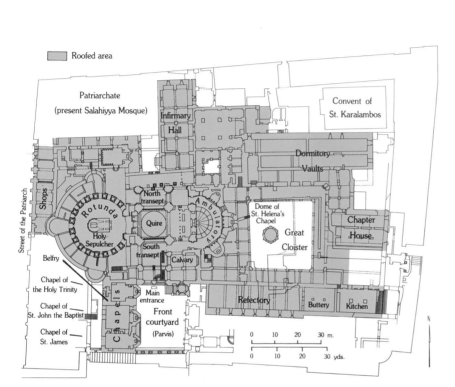

Roofed area

Patriarchate
(present Salahiyya Mosque)

Infirmary
Hall

Convent of
St. Karalambos

Dormitory

Vaults

Shops

Street of the Patriarch

Rotunda

Holy
Sepulcher

North
transept

Quire

Ambulatory

South
transept

Calvary

Dome of
St. Helena's
Chapel

Great
Cloister

Chapter
House

Belfry

Chapel of
the Holy Trinity

Chapel of
St. John the Baptist

Chapel of
St. James

Chapels

Main
entrance

Front
courtyard
(Parvis)

Refectory

Buttery

Kitchen

| 0 | 10 | 20 | 30 m. |
| 0 | 10 | 20 | 30 yds. |

(above) The **Church of the Holy Sepulcher** was the most important edifice in Crusader Jerusalem, and its liberation from the hands of the infidels was the main goal of the Crusades. When they reached Jerusalem, the Crusaders found a church with a number of chapels and the rotunda rebuilt by the Byzantine emperor, Constantine Monomachus, in 1048. In order to create a consolidated structure, the existing complex was integrated into the magnificent edifice constructed to unite under one roof all the holy sites connected with the crucifixion and burial of Jesus. The rotunda reconstructed by Constantine Monomachus was left intact, except for additions to the galleries which encompassed the holy sepulcher, and which were embellished with mosaics and decorated floors.

In their determination to erect a building in the Romanesque style prevalent in Europe during that period, the Crusaders concentrated on construction in the area of the Holy Garden, to the east of the rotunda. They built the transept and the quire (now called the Catholicon) at the end of which stands the altar. Today the Catholicon serves as the prayer hall of the Greek Orthodox community. Around it was built the ambulatory, access to which was gained from the various chapels, which are traditionally bound up with the crucifixion and resurrection of Jesus. Of special interest is the Chapel of Adam. According to Christian tradition, the skull of Adam was buried in the Hill of Golgotha, which is the origin of its name. The Crusader kings of Jerusalem were buried in this chapel, but hardly any vestiges of their graves have remained. On the second level, the Chapel of the Hill of Golgotha was erected to mark the site of Jesus' crucifixion. The only remains of the magnificent mosaic in this chapel is the section probably depicting the ascension of Jesus to heaven, as only the upper part of Jesus' body is preserved. To the east of the Catholicon, in the area where the basilica was standing in the Byzantine period, the great cloister was built for the Canonics (the monks who guarded the Church of the Holy Sepulcher), and it was from here that a passageway was opened to the ambulatory.

The Crusaders used the southern portal as the main entrance to the church, as built by Constantine Monomachus, and embellished it with a beautiful facade. During the Crusader period, an additional entrance, to the right of the main portal, led to the Chapel of the Franks. Through this chapel it was possible to gain access to the Chapel of Golgotha. Beneath the Chapel of the Franks was the Chapel of Mary the Egyptian, a sinful woman who according to tradition was prevented from entering the church by Mary, mother of Jesus. As a result she led a life of abstinence and was sanctified by Christianity.

Between the facade and the rotunda were three chapels built in the time of Constantine Monomachus. One of them was rebuilt by the Crusaders, another served as the base for the belfry erected by the Crusaders after the dedication of the church. The restored structure of the Holy Sepulcher was dedicated in the year 1119. The Church of the Holy Sepulcher was dedicated on the fiftieth anniversary of the Crusader rule of Jerusalem on July 15, 1149, and it has remained in this form, apart from minor modifications, to this day.

(bottom) The **Church of St. Agnes** (named for a fourth-century Roman saint) situated in the north of the present-day Muslim Quarter, is a typical medium-sized (33 × 41 feet [10 × 12.5 m.]) Crusader church. Although the building itself has been well preserved, no vestiges of the original embellishments have remained. Reference to the existence of this church is found in a document from the year 1165, which refers to a furnace belonging to the Church of the Holy Sepulcher, "to the east of St. Agnes' Church."

In the nineteenth century, scholars tended to identify it with St. Peter's Church, but no definitive proof has been forthcoming to support this.

Until the 1930s, the church served as a center for the "Whirling Dervishes." Today it is the Ma'ulawiyya mosque used by the inhabitants of the area.

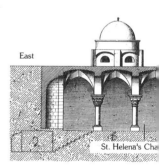

East

St. Helena's Cha

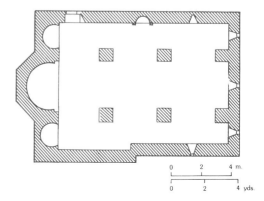

| 0 | 2 | 4 m. |
| 0 | 2 | 4 yds. |

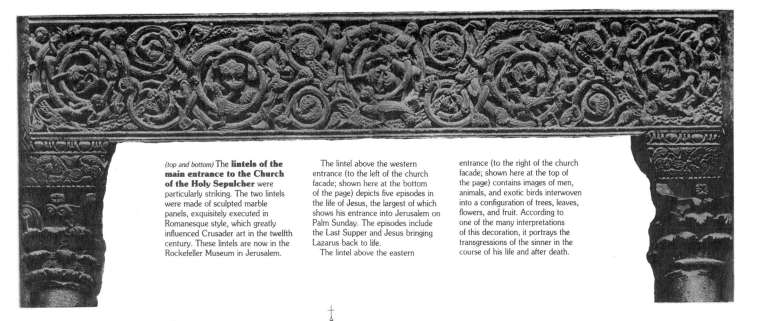

(top and bottom) The **lintels of the main entrance to the Church of the Holy Sepulcher** were particularly striking. The two lintels were made of sculpted marble panels, exquisitely executed in Romanesque style, which greatly influenced Crusader art in the twelfth century. These lintels are now in the Rockefeller Museum in Jerusalem.

The lintel above the western entrance (to the left of the church facade; shown here at the bottom of the page) depicts five episodes in the life of Jesus, the largest of which shows his entrance into Jerusalem on Palm Sunday. The episodes include the Last Supper and Jesus bringing Lazarus back to life.

The lintel above the eastern entrance (to the right of the church facade; shown here at the top of the page) contains images of men, animals, and exotic birds interwoven into a configuration of trees, leaves, flowers, and fruit. According to one of the many interpretations of this decoration, it portrays the transgressions of the sinner in the course of his life and after death.

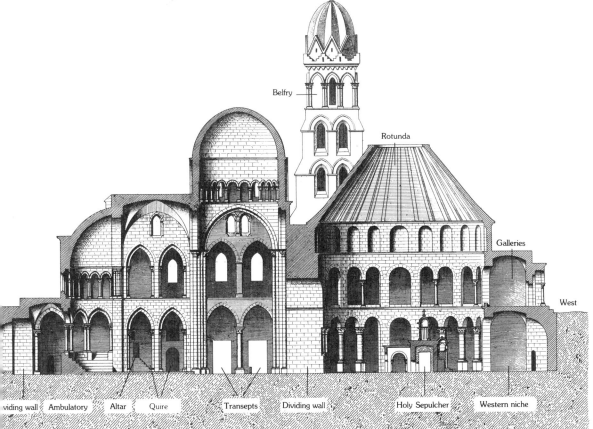

Belfry

Rotunda

Galleries

West

viding wall | Ambulatory | Altar | Quire | Transepts | Dividing wall | Holy Sepulcher | Western niche

(left) **Cross section of the Church of the Holy Sepulcher** from the northern view reproduced from the work of the Vicomte de Vogüé (1860) on the churches in the Holy Land. This is a reproduction of the church as it appeared during the Crusader period, without any of the additions made in later years. At the right extremity is a niche, one of the three constructed by Constantine the Great in the rotunda to the north, the west, and the south. To the left of it is the impressive two-storied rotunda. Under the Crusaders, the conical roof of the rotunda was truncated and open to the sky (it was replaced by a circular dome only in 1808 in the course of renovations carried out after the great fire that damaged the church building). The upper section of the high belfry reproduced here was destroyed in an earthquake in 1545, and it was only in 1719 that the Greek Orthodox were granted permission to reconstruct part of it, which still exists.

Between the rotunda and the Holy Garden is the dividing wall built in the fourth century, renovated by Constantine Monomachus in the eleventh century, and continued to be used by the Crusaders.

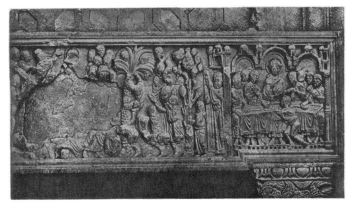

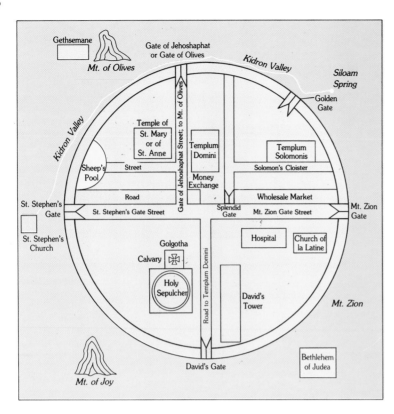

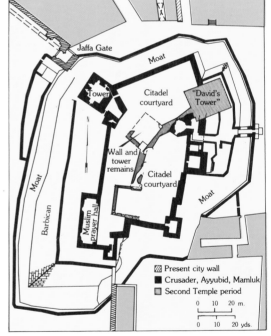

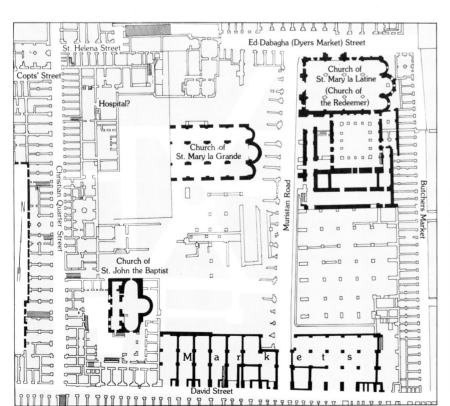

(below) The **Citadel** was one of the important building complexes in Crusader Jerusalem, and was used to symbolize the city on seals of that period. In some of the historical documents it is called "David's Tower," but it is not always clear whether the reference is to the Tower of David itself or to the entire citadel complex.

Following the Crusader conquest of Jerusalem, Godfrey of Bouillon handed over the Citadel to the Patriarch of Jerusalem, Daimbert of Pisa (this may be the reason why the Citadel was at times referred to as the "Citadel of the Pisans"). During the Crusader period it served as the citadel of the city and was administered by the Castellan, the official appointed by the king. From the year 1118 the site was the seat of the Crusader kings of Jerusalem, after their residence had been transferred there from the Aqsa Mosque on the Temple Mount. Some remains of the royal palace in the vicinity of the Citadel have been recently found (in 1989). This palace appears in the Cambrai Map as "Curia Regis."

A number of outstanding events took place within the Citadel during the Crusader period. In 1152 Queen Melisande fortified herself within its walls when she refused to hand over the rule of Jerusalem to her

son, the crown prince Baldwin III. In 1177 many of the city's residents took shelter in the Citadel before the onslaught of the Muslims, thereby enabling us to estimate its dimensions (probably near its present-day size).

Very few finds from the Crusader period have been uncovered in the archaeological excavations carried on the site, and thus it is not possible to reconstruct it with any accuracy. The lack of remains is due to the fact that in the Ayyubid period the Citadel was destroyed and renovated, and later it was damaged extensively during successive earthquakes or destructions.

(above) This **schematic diagram of circular maps of Jerusalem** contains all the elements common to most of the maps presented in the following pages. The recurring errors lead to the conclusion that they were all copied from the same anonymous source. For example, in the original map some lines of explanation appeared next to the Sheep's Pool, but the copyists did not connect it to the pool. Thus in each of the circular maps the pool appeared as an oval in one of its corners, and the explanation was printed elsewhere in the map.

The original map was apparently drawn during the Crusader period—the twelfth century—and the other circular maps mostly in the fourteenth century. However, because of the fact that they were copied from the Crusader original, they depict Jerusalem as it was in the twelfth century. It is possible that during the fourteenth century the need arose to provide a map for the increasingly large number of pilgrims from European countries who began to visit the city. To this end, an earlier map was copied and distributed throughout the cities of Europe. This would be a feasible explanation of

how the circular map of Jerusalem came to be distributed in so many different centers in Christian Europe. The circular maps printed in the following pages are to be found in libraries in Brussels, Copenhagen, Florence, the Hague, London, Stuttgart, and Paris as well as in other cities in France.

(left) The **Muristan Quarter**, situated within the bounds of the ancient Roman forum, was the city's central marketplace under the Romans and the Byzantines until the beginning of the early Arab period. During the Crusader period the quarter underwent a major change. Most of the area was handed over to the Knights of the Order of **Hospitallers**, and the entire area was named for their order during that time. The Hospitallers renovated a number of central buildings in the quarter and constructed new ones. They erected a hospital, hostels, markets, and monasteries. They also built churches not belonging to their order such as the Church of St. Mary la Grande and the Church of St. Mary la Latine.

The buildings in this quarter

continued to be used in the Ayyubid period, especially the hospital from which the name of the quarter was derived—Muristan in Kurdish means hospital. During the course of the Mamluk and Ottoman periods, the quarter deteriorated and was completely destroyed, but was rebuilt in 1869, when part of it was handed over to the Germans. They erected the Church of the Redeemer and a number of other buildings on the ruins of the Crusader Church of St. Mary la Latine. Later, the western section of the quarter was handed over to the Greek Patriarchate who set up the Aftimos market (1905).

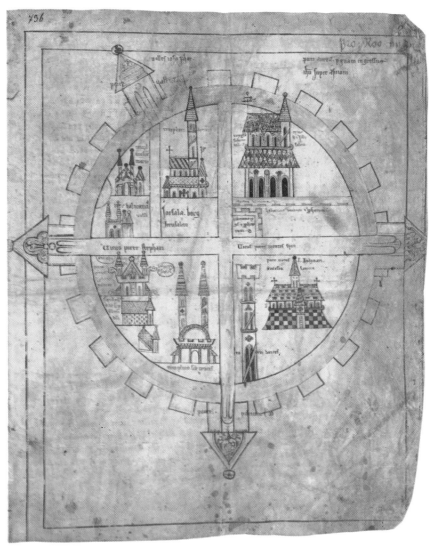

(above) **Jerusalem in the Copenhagen Map**

then on the entire area was predominantly Christian. According to a contemporary historian, William of Tyre, the wall that ran from David's Gate in the west, past Tancred's Tower and up to St. Stephen's Gate to the north, constituted the "external boundary" of the quarter. The "internal boundary" was marked by St. Stephen's Gate Street which ran "directly to the money-changers booths and from there further to the Western Gate" (David's Gate). The main buildings within the Patriarch's Quarter were the Church of the Holy Sepulcher, monasteries and the Patriarch's mansion.

Other quarters were named for the community's living in them. The Syrian Quarter in the northeast of Jerusalem was named for Christians who were placed there from the border area between Syria and Transjordan. This quarter was formerly inhabited by Jews, until they were massacred or evicted during the Crusader conquest of the city. Armenians had for generations settled in the Armenian Quarter around their main church, and in the German Quarter, in addition to the church, there were a hospice for German pilgrims, public buildings, a hospital, and several other churches.

Knights of the various Christian orders had their own neighborhoods. The largest and most important order was the Hospitallers, whose members settled in the present-day Muristan Quarter. The Hospitallers' Quarter was allocated to them by Pope Paschal II in 1113 from lands appropriated from the Patriarch of Jerusalem. The horses and donkeys of the knights of this order were placed in stables outside the city's limits, in the vicinity of the present-day St. Stephen's Church.

The Order of the Knights Templars, founded in the land of Israel in 1118, settled on the Temple Mount when King Baldwin I vacated his quarters in the Aqsa Mosque in favor of the members of this order and moved to the Citadel. The mosque was renovated and became the center of the Templars, who called it Templum Solomonis (Solomon's Temple) from which they derived their full name—Order of the Poor Knights of the Messiah and of the Temple of Solomon. At this time, the Dome of the Rock became the Templum Domini (Temple of the Lord). The Templars did not alter the structure of this building, merely adding a metal grille around the sacred rock. Northwest of the Templum Domini they erected an elaborate baptistery, known today as the Dome of the Ascension. To the north of the Temple Mount, a monastery was built which provided accommodation for the Canonics who served in the area. The Templars turned the subterranean halls into stables which are called to this day Solomon's Stables. In the southern wall of the Temple Mount openings were built to provide access to the stables, and a wall was erected to guard against incursion from the outside. To the west of Solomon's Temple, an administration center was constructed, and the remaining southern section today serves partly as a women's mosque and partly as a museum for Islamic art. The Templars also erected structures adjacent to the eastern side of Solomon's Temple, which served as storehouses. These structures were demolished at the end of the British Mandate period. According to a traveler of the Crusader period the foundations for a large church were begun on the Temple Mount, but it appears that it was never completed. It is most difficult to obtain an accurate picture of the structures erected by the Templars on the Temple Mount, because so few of them have remained. However, contemporary accounts lead to the assumption that during the Crusader period the Temple Mount was a magnificent site which attracted numerous Christian pilgrims. Architectural elements from Templar buildings were later introduced into Ayyubid and Mamluk buildings on the Temple Mount.

The Order of the Teutonic Knights was a branch of the German section of the predominantly French Hospitaller Knights. Accounts exist of the organization of Knights of German origin beginning from 1128, but the order was given official recognition by the Pope only in 1198, when Jerusalem was under Muslim domination. The Teutonic Knights' center, including a hospital and the St. Mary's hostel and church, was in the present-day Jewish Quarter. The buildings held

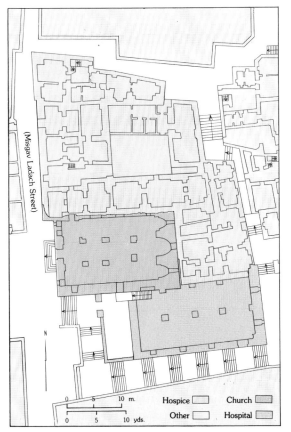

(left) **St. Mary of the Germans Church** was first discovered in the course of the British survey of Palestine during 1867–1869, but no further attention was paid to it. However, it was rediscovered in 1968 during the rebuilding of the Jewish Quarter. The church was situated in the center of the German Quarter of the Crusader city. For some time, the Germans endeavored to establish an order of their own so as to disassociate from the Hospitallers Order, which was French in spirit and language. The Germans wished to set up their own welfare organizations and to work in their own language, but all their efforts failed. The church was erected at the beginning of the Crusader period (1127–1128) in the artistic style of the period. The street in which the church was situated was called the Street of the Germans—the present-day Misgav Ladach Street.

Remains from the Crusader period were also found in the area south of this complex. It appears that this complex existed until Saladin's conquest of Jerusalem, and was rebuilt in the Mamluk period when it functioned as a *khanqah* (a hospice and prayer house of the dervishes).

by the order were appropriated by Saladin in 1187, and have since never been returned to the order.

In the 1120s, the Order of St. Lazarus was established in Jerusalem. A comparatively small order, it was founded by knights who considered their mission to include the care of pilgrims suffering from leprosy. They set up their center at the lepers' home in northwest Jerusalem (a few vestiges of the building have been uncovered recently near the New Gate), and they erected a church, a monastery and other buildings. Members of the order later formed a military order. They entered the city from their center by way of the St. Lazarus' Postern in the city's northern wall. The scant remains of these buildings have precluded their exact reconstruction, and the location of the postern is unknown.

An important element of the city was its marketplaces. At the southern extremity of St. Stephen's Gate Street (in the Roman Cardo) were three markets: the western one was the "Vegetable Market" (or the "Spice Market"); nearby was the "Market of Evil Cooking" (Malcuisinat), named for the eating places for pilgrims situated in the marketplace. The third was the "Covered Market." West of the Spice Market, running the length of David Street, was the "Poultry Market." In this market apart from poultry were to be found eggs, cheeses, and other milk products. Money-changers'

(below right) **One of the three Crusader capitals** embellishing the facade of the Bani Ghawanima minaret in the northwest corner of the Temple Mount. These three capitals, as well as a fourth one now in the Islamic Museum on the Temple Mount, were apparently part of a small Crusader chapel near the Temple Mount. They were salvaged from its ruins and reused in the present structure.

The chapel—the Church of the Repose—in the area of the present-day Umariyya school, near the northwest corner of the Temple Mount, marked Jesus' arrest prior to his being brought for trial before Pontius Pilate. A thirteenth-century account states: "It is said that this was the spot where Jesus rested when they brought him to be crucified."

All the capitals portray the identical occurrence of Jesus' immersion in the Jordan River, well known in Christian iconography. Jesus is seen sitting on stones, tended by two angels holding his clothes. This conventional motif may refer to another metaphorical theme—the description of Jesus at the time of his arrest, when he was "protected" by two angels.

The Bani Ghawanima minaret is an example of a particular architectural style developed in Jerusalem during the Crusader period. This is a blend of Oriental and Western art, whereby Crusader architectural motifs are introduced into Muslim structures.

(below left) **Jerusalem in the Brussels Map**

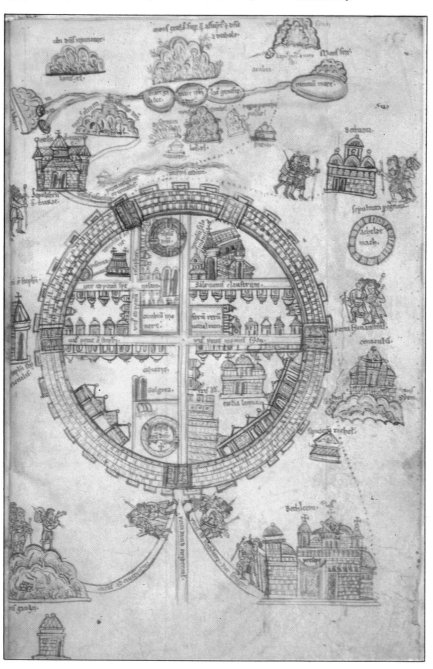

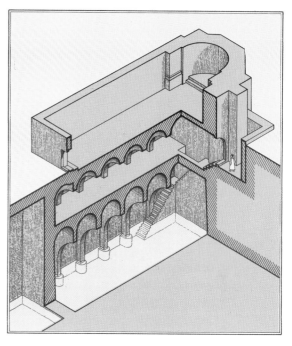

(top right) The **Church of St. Anne** is one of the most exquisite examples of Crusader architecture in the country. According to Christian tradition, this church was erected on the site of the house of Anne and Joachim where their daughter the Virgin Mary was born. The Church of St. Anne, built in the vicinity of the fifth-century Byzantine church named for St. Mary (the Church of Probatica), was maintained by four nuns until the Crusaders reached Jerusalem. The latter introduced structural changes in the church and convent in which the nuns lived. In 1104, the first Crusader king of Jerusalem, Baldwin I, banished his Armenian wife Arda to this convent. The Crusader kings of Jerusalem made munificent donations to the convent, including property such as the three marketplaces in the city center, where the sign "Santa Anna" was prominently placed. The revenue from these properties accrued to the benefit of the convent. In the year 1130, the daughter of Baldwin II lived in the convent for a short time, and later, Theodora, widow of Baldwin

III, spent some time there. The fact that women of the Crusader royal household inhabited the convent increased its prestige and the church institutions heaped riches upon it, and continued to embellish it. The Crusader church and the adjoining convent were erected in 1140, but was destroyed in the nineteenth century. The church was famous for its splendor, and already in 1165 it is described in detail by Johannes of Würzburg, one of the important visitors to Jerusalem.

(opposite below) Reproduction of the **Church of Mary of Bethesda** erected in the Crusader period near the Church of St. Anne, on the ruins of a Byzantine church. The church was built on the wall separating the two pools of Bethesda. The archaeological excavations carried out at this site reveal that the pools were almost completely blocked up at that time, although they were apparently well known to pilgrims, who reported having seen vestiges of them.

The reproduction shows the church with its single prayer aisle built over a series of arches. This created a lower vault which served to support the structure and an upper vault which served as a crypt for the upper church. Little mention is made of this church in historical sources, and thus the information about it is scant.

(right) The **Crusader candelabrum** is in the upper left corner of this etching of the inside of the Dome of the Rock, as depicted in Wilson's *Picturesque Palestine* in 1880.

After the Crusader conquest of Jerusalem, the Dome of the Rock became the Templum Domini church, and an altar devoted to St. Nicholas was erected above the Foundation Stone. The rock was surrounded by an iron lattice-work grille, decorated with leaves and branches. The altar was also encompassed by an iron grille on which the date of its creation (1162) was engraved. The two oil candelabra, also made of iron, were placed in the corner southwest of the Foundation Stone, near a lattice-work cell whose function is not known. These candelabra were transferred, apparently during the British Mandate, to the Islamic Museum on the Temple Mount. The photograph *(above)* is of one of these candelabra in the Islamic Museum.

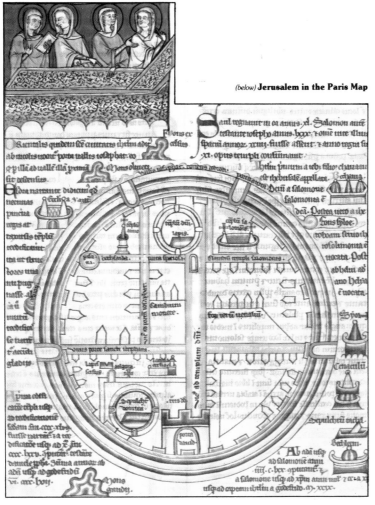

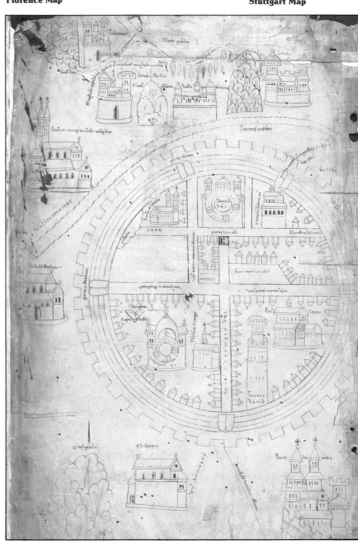

(below) Jerusalem in the Paris Map

booths were situated in the squares that led to the three main marketplaces, and it was here that pilgrims changed their money when they reached the city. In the northern square was the Syrian Money Exchange run by Christian Syrians, found in the vicinity of the souvenir shops near the Church of the Holy Sepulcher. In the southern square was the Latin Money Exchange (manned by money-changers from Europe). The money-changers generally sat on benches placed in the squares, but in recent excavations carried out in the square north of the "Wholesale Market," four shops were found which could possibly have been used by the money-changers. This marketplace, erected (apparently in 1152) in the southern section of the Byzantine Cardo, is depicted in Crusader maps as part of the network of markets in the center of the city. North of David's Gate, and adjacent to the western wall was the spacious Grain Market. In this area, too, was a flour mill belonging to the Order of St. Lazarus. However, in the year 1151, the mill was demolished to facilitate the flow of traffic in the street. As compensation, the members of the order received lands in the region of Bethlehem.

During the Crusader period, a great variety of peoples of different nationalities inhabited Jerusalem. There were Spaniards, after whom Spanish Street was named; French who mainly inhabited the Hospitallers' Quarter; Germans living in the German Quarter; and Syrians and Armenians who inhabited the Syrian and Armenian Quarters respectively. There is also evidence of the existence of a Hungarian hostel in the city, and the presence of English aristocrats and Italian merchants from various cities.

(below left) Jerusalem in the Florence Map

(below) Jerusalem in the Stuttgart Map

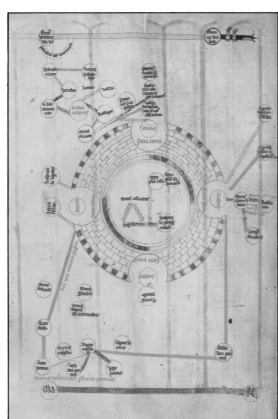

(above) **Jerusalem in the London Map**

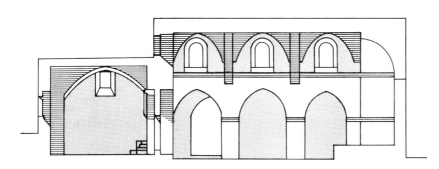

(above) Cross section of the **House of Annas Convent** (or Convent of **Deir Zeituna** [the Olive Tree]), situated in the southeastern corner of the Armenian Quarter. According to Christian tradition this was the house of the High Priest before whom Jesus was brought to trial. The Armenians believe that it was in the courtyard of this house that the olive tree grew to which Jesus was bound during his trial. The convent is also known as the "Convent of the Angels," to mark the appearance of the angels Michael and Gabriel when Jesus was struck by Annas' servants.

The present structure was erected in the twelfth century, and additions were made in 1286 by King Levon III of Armenia. In the seventeenth century a convent was built which surrounded the present structure. A large number of Crusader architectural elements have been introduced into the church inside the convent. This fact has led to a controversy between those scholars who believe that the church was built in the Crusader period and those who argue that it is from a later period, and that the Crusader elements have been added. Recent reconstruction works (in 1990) in the church have shown that the former theory was correct.

(below) **Jerusalem in the Saint-Omer (France) Map**

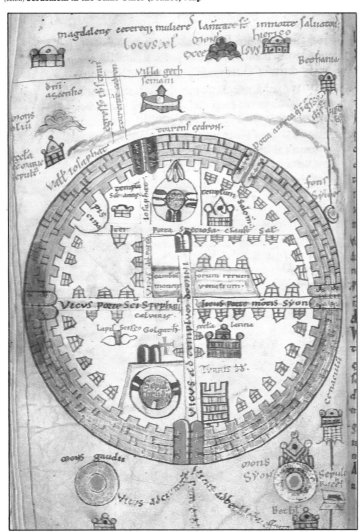

The Crusader era in Jerusalem was a period of great thrust in building enterprises in the city. Churches and monasteries were constructed, and churches that had been demolished were rebuilt. These included the Church of the Holy Sepulcher, St. Anne's Church, and the Church of John the Baptist. The map at the beginning of this chapter is an attempt to present the majority of the churches, monasteries and central structures built or renovated during this period. The map also reflects the upsurge of building so characteristic of Crusader Jerusalem. The majority are still extant, although some are used for purposes different from those for which they were originally intended.

Fall of the Jerusalem Crusader Kingdom

The decline of the Jerusalem Crusader kingdom began with the defeat of the Crusader forces by Saladin at the Horns of Hattin (July 4, 1187). Saladin then moved southward and nearly all the cities and Crusader strongholds surrendered before his onslaught. After the conquest of Ashkelon on September 4, 1187, Saladin turned toward Jerusalem, which he reached on September 17, 1187. On their way, the Muslims destroyed the Christian churches on the outskirts of the city, so as to prevent the Christians from attacking the lines of communication of the forces mounting the siege of Jerusalem. These structures included the Church of St. Mary of the Valley of Jehoshaphat, the Gethsemane Church, and the St. Mary of Mount Zion Church. Jerusalem refused to surrender, and the siege of the city began. The city abounded with refugees who had fled from Judea and Samaria, as well as about five thousand Muslims taken prisoner by the Crusader forces. There were also many Christians belonging to the Eastern church, on whose loyalty the Frankish forces could not rely. The remaining Crusader forces in Jerusalem were led by Balian d'Iblin, a survivor of the battle at the Horns of Hattin, who was the ruler of Nablus and a scion of one of the leading families of the Crusader kingdom. The forces at his disposal were limited, since the majority of the knights and soldiers had been killed or taken prisoner during the battle at the Horns of Hattin. To this end, he

102

created knights from among the younger members of the nobility and aristocracy in order to provide a military force for the defense of the city. Gold and silver ornaments from the Church of the Holy Sepulcher were used to pay their salaries.

At the beginning of the siege, Saladin concentrated his forces on the western side of the city, mainly opposite the Citadel, and stationed smaller forces at various points around the city. After besieging the city for about a week, during which skirmishes took place between the Muslim and Christian forces, Saladin moved his forces to the north, and stationed them in the area between Tancred's Tower and the northeastern tower. The Christians followed a "scorched earth" policy, during the course of which they demolished St. Stephen's Church (St. Etiénne) situated in the north of the city. The city was taken on October 2, 1187, after Saladin's forces tunneled under the anterior wall, pulling it down into the empty space created. Once Saladin's forces reached the main city wall, the Crusaders agreed to negotiate. At first the Christians threatened to destroy the city completely, but it was finally agreed that the Crusaders would be granted status of prisoners of war, and specific amounts were set as ransom money.

Columns of ransomed soldiers made their way to cities still under Christian rule, and Jerusalem reverted to the Muslims after eighty-eight years of Christian domination.

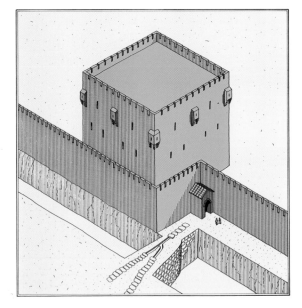

(left) Reproduction of the **Tower of Goliath** located in the northwestern corner of the city wall. According to Muslim tradition, this was the site of the duel between David and Goliath. In the Crusader period it was known as **Tancred's Tower**, after the prince whose forces were stationed in this area during the siege of Jerusalem in 1099.

The tower was built 10 feet (3 m.) inside the city wall, near one of the weakest spots of its defense. Its dimensions were 115 × 115 feet (35 × 35 m.), and the date of its erection is not known, although it is generally believed that it dates to the Crusader period. Crusader sources describing the conquest of 1099 make mention of a tower in the corner of the wall (or perhaps a tower with corners), in connection with the Crusader siege of the city. This leads to the conclusion that a tower did exist in the vicinity, prior to the Crusader period. Archaeological excavations have revealed two towers built one upon the other. It would seem that the earlier one dates to the Crusader

(above) The **Tomb of the Virgin Mary**, in the Crusader church in the Valley of Jehoshaphat. According to Christian tradition, Mary, mother of Jesus, was buried here. A church was erected on this site in the fifth century, but it was destroyed by Muslims when the Crusaders were approaching Jerusalem, to prevent them from using it as a stronghold at the approaches to the city.

During the Crusader period, the church was rebuilt and a Benedictine monastery constructed adjacent to it. Voyagers of the period mention especially the impressive crypt in which the queens of the Crusader kingdom were buried, among whom was Queen Melisande, whose tomb is known to us.

Both the church and monastery were destroyed once again during the conquest of Jerusalem by Saladin, and its stones were used to reinforce the city wall. Only the crypt remained, but many of the decorations of its facades were removed and placed in other buildings in the city.

(right) **The Cambrai Map** is the most important illustration of Jerusalem during the Crusader period. It appeared in the *Exegesis of Brother Angelomus to the Four Books of Kings*, now in the library of the city of Cambrai in northern France. The sites depicted in the map date it to the end of the Crusader period (even though the library catalogue gives the date as 1150). The Cambrai map differs from the other maps from this period, since it does not derive its information from the same source as the circular maps.

Furthermore, this map points to the north, while the circular maps point east.

It seems, though, that the person who drew this map had not visited Jerusalem himself, and this would explain the erroneous placing of several of the city's buildings. Thus, for example, in the Muristan (the Crusaders' Hospitallers Quarter) the order of the churches is inaccurate and the Hospitaller Order's hospital has been misplaced. Similar mistakes have been made in the area of the Citadel.

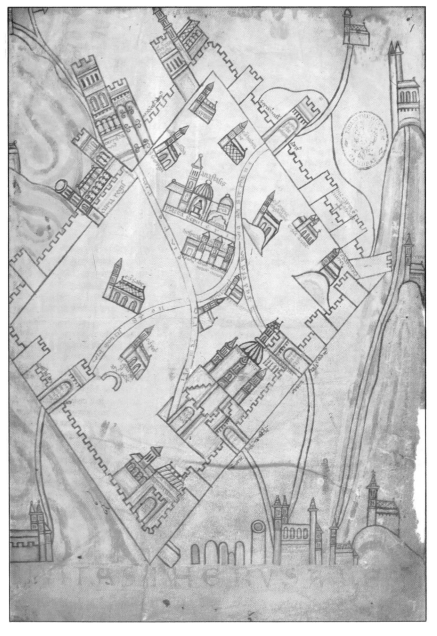

period and the later to the Ayyubid period.

When a wall was built in this area at the end of the early Arab period, a deep moat (see illustration) was excavated out of the rock alongside this and other sections of the wall. Near the tower a path at ground level was left to carry the aqueduct which brought run-off waters into the city. In the nineteenth century, a small postern was discovered in the side of the tower, which may be the St. Lazarus Postern. Its location intimates that it could have led to the bridge carrying the aqueduct.

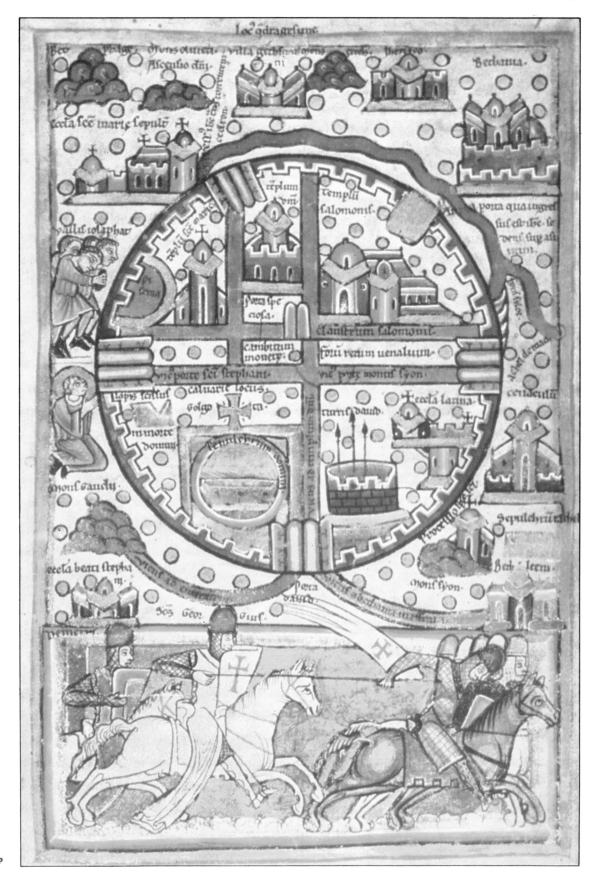

(right) **Jerusalem in the Hague Map**

The Ayyubid Period
1187 – 1250

Saladin entered Jerusalem on October 2, 1187, at the exact spot where the Crusaders entered it (in the year 1099), opposite the present-day Rockefeller Museum. A huge cross had been placed at this point by the Crusaders at the beginning of their rule, to mark the site at which they penetrated the city.

After paying ransom money to the Muslims (ten Byzantims per male, five per woman and two for each child), the non-Muslim residents of the city left through David's Gate (present-day Jaffa Gate). They left in three columns: the first was headed by the Templars, the second by the Hospitallers and the third column was headed by the commander of the city, Balian, and the Patriarch of the city. They reached the ports, and then embarked for Europe. Those unable to pay the ransom money were taken prisoner and deported to other Muslim cities.

Saladin was magnanimous toward the conquered city, and once the first elation was over, he began to develop it in accord with the needs of the Muslims. The Christian manifes-tations were eliminated, and el-Aqsa Mosque and the Dome of the Rock on the Temple Mount once again functioned as Muslim prayer houses. The cross at the apex of the Dome of the Rock was removed and dragged through the city streets as a sign of degradation. The Crusader adornments, paintings and mosaics were removed from these buildings or covered over with layers of plaster. The mosques were purified by the sprinkling of rose water brought especially for this purpose from Damascus. A prayer pulpit, prepared by Nur ed-Din of Aleppo a few decades earlier, was placed in el-Aqsa Mosque as a sign of the renewal of Muslim worship there. A few years after the conquest of the city, the Church of St. Anne and its monastery were converted into a Shafi'i Muslim school, which continued to benefit from income from those properties put at the disposal of the church during the Crusader period. Saladin also fixed a Muslim inscription at the entrance to the church which is still extant. He also appropriated the northeastern section of the Church of the Holy Sepulcher, which had belonged to the Patriarchate

The Church of St. Anne in about 1860, as drawn by Pierotti. One of the most important and elaborate Crusader churches in Jerusalem, Saladin was attracted to it after conquering the city (1187). Saladin converted the church into a Shafi'i Muslim school, since called el-Madrasa es-Salahiyya. An inscription, which still exists, was fixed at about this time in the facade, above the entrance, describing the change in function in 1192. It appears that the building served as a Muslim school until 1761, when a rumor spread that it had been invaded by evil spirits. The Muslims were so stricken with fear that in that same year they sold the building to the Franciscan Order, who after much deliberation decided not to restore it. The monks marked St. Anne's day there annually, but the building was mainly used as a hostel by camel drivers entering the city through the nearby Lions' Gate, and they added to the deterioration of the structure.

From a number of drawings of the church, it has become apparent that up to 1820 it had a magnificent belfry, and to the south there was a convent (its ruins disappeared after another building was later erected on the site). In 1835 the governor of Jerusalem demolished part of the church and used its stones to build the Ottoman barracks (today the Umariyya School). The Muslims made a further attempt to restore the building and reopen it as a mosque in 1842. They even began to erect a minaret, but the work was discontinued and the

believed that the building project was suspended because the Christian laborers refused to cooperate in converting the Christian building into a Muslim school and a mosque, and they even sabotaged the work.

In 1856 the Sultan Abdul Mejid handed over the church to the French government, which arranged for the dilapidated convent to be demolished, and for another to be built in its place. The church was renovated and its facade altered. Pierotti's drawing shows the church prior to its renovation, when vestiges of the later Crusader period walls could be seen.

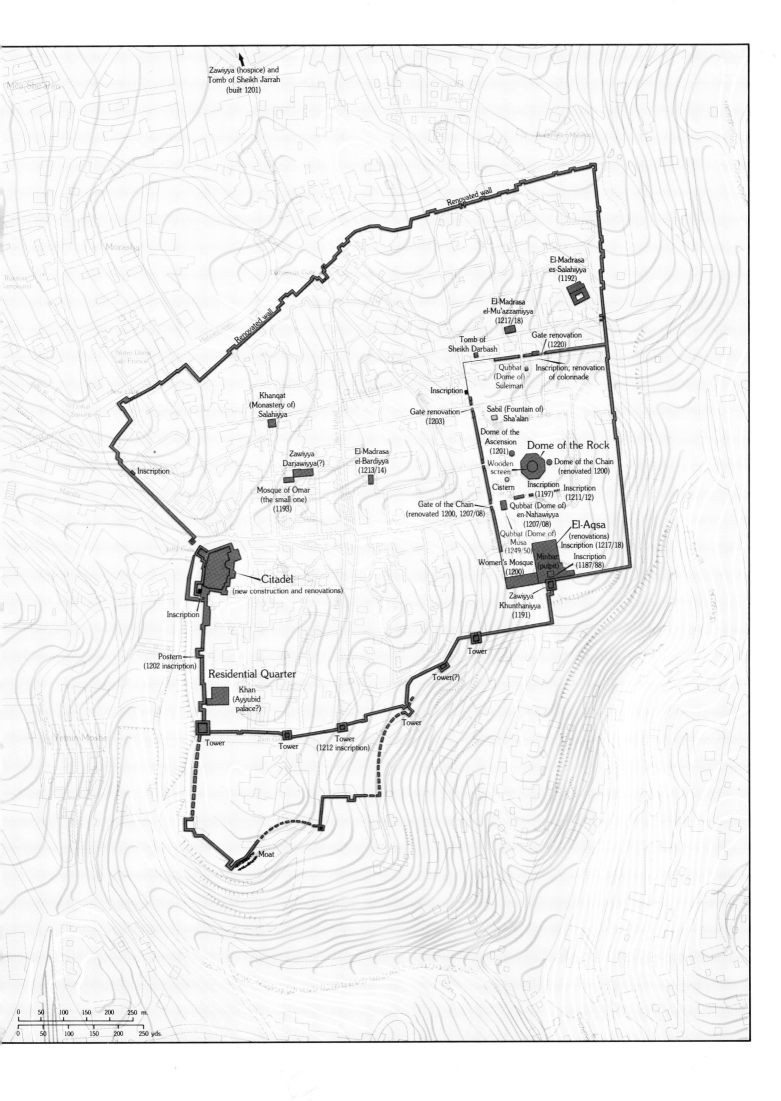

Zawiyya (hospice) and
Tomb of Sheikh Jarrah
(built 1201)

Renovated wall

Renovated wall

Renovated wall

El-Madrasa
es-Salahiyya
(1192)

El-Madrasa
el-Mu'azzamiyya
(1217/18)

Tomb of
Sheikh Darbash

Gate renovation
(1220)

Qubbat
(Dome of)
Suleiman

Inscription; renovation
of colonnade

Inscription

Khanqat
(Monastery of)
Salahiyya

Gate renovation
(1203)

Sabil (Fountain of)
Sha'alan

Dome of the
Ascension
(1201)

Dome of the Rock

Dome of the Chain
(renovated 1200)

Wooden
screen

Inscription

Zawiyya
Darjawiyya(?)

El-Madrasa
el-Bardiyya
(1213/14)

Cistern

Inscription
(1197)

Inscription
(1211/12)

Mosque of Omar
(the small one)
(1193)

Gate of the Chain
(renovated 1200, 1207/08)

Qubbat (Dome of)
en-Nahawiyya
(1207/08)

El-Aqsa
(renovations)
Inscription (1217/18)

Qubbat (Dome of)
Musa
(1249/50)

Women's Mosque
(1200)

Minbar
(pulpit)

Inscription
(1187/88)

Inscription

Citadel
(new construction and renovations)

Zawiyya
Khunthaniyya
(1191)

Inscription

Tower

Postern
(1202 inscription)

Tower(?)

Residential Quarter

Khan
(Ayyubid
palace?)

Tower

Tower

Tower
(1212 inscription)

Tower

Moat

0   50   100   150   200   250 m.

0   50   100   150   200   250 yds.

(left) Reconstruction of the **Ayyubid tower** built in the time of el-Malik el-Mu'azzam Isa east of Zion Gate (in 1212). It seems that this sultan, who erected many buildings in Jerusalem (evidence of this has been attested by many of his inscriptions found in the city), set the course of the present-day southern walls of the city. One inscription refers to the erection of a tower, but no reference is made to the construction of a gate. This fact is surprising, since the tower was erected at the southern extremity of the Cardo, on the very site where the city's southern gate has been situated since the Byzantine period.

There is also additional evidence that no gate existed here during the Ayyubid period. The vestiges of the tower found on the site have not revealed any proof of the existence of a monumental gate, as would be expected at the entrance to the city. Perhaps the gate that existed at that time at the south of the city was situated within the Ayyubid tower, found underneath Zion Gate.

In 1219, el-Malik el-Mu'azzam Isa ordered the demolition of the city's fortifications, which included this tower, in the fear that the Crusaders might return to Jerusalem and take refuge in its fortifications.

(below) **The el-Malik el-Mu'azzam Isa inscription**, one of the most exquisite Ayyubid period inscriptions, fixed in the Ayyubid tower in the year 1212 by Saladin's nephew. Remains of the tower were found in the vicinity of the Zion Gate, partly outside the Old City wall, and partly inside it, in the Jewish Quarter. The inscription was engraved on Herodian-period stone and stated the date the tower was erected.

of Jerusalem, and handed it over to the dervish community (a mystic Muslim cult). They settled there and benefited from the income from the Patriarch's bathhouse (in the present-day Christians' Street). Saladin banned the Christians from entering the Church of the Holy Sepulcher for some time, until the members of the Eastern church were granted permission for four monks to run services in the church. Christians were once again permitted to visit the church after 1192, and these pilgrimages became an important source of income for the Muslims.

Saladin's conquest of Jerusalem also brought the repeal of the ban on Jews settling in the city imposed by the Crusaders. Jews came to Jerusalem from coastal towns destroyed by Saladin himself (in 1191), mainly from Ashkelon. Later, Jews from Morocco and the Yemen settled in the predominantly Muslim city of Jerusalem, and in the year 1211 Jews came there from England and France.

During the Crusader period, the walls of Jerusalem were apparently neglected and the situation was such that the Muslim conquerors were required to undertake a construction and fortification program. We are able to reach this conclusion from the fact that shortly before Saladin's conquest of the city, the Crusader barons collected monies for the purpose of fortifying the walls, but we have no confirmation that the walls were actually reinforced. A few years after the conquest, Saladin carried out a thorough examination of the walls and began rebuilding them, participating personally in the work so as to set a good example to his sons and the commanders of his army. These works on the fortifications were carried out at the time of the Third Crusade in 1192 led by the colorful personality of Richard the Lion-Heart,

who threatened the city's safety. The building project was not restricted to the erection of the walls, but to the digging of moats as well.

Literary sources as well as an inscription provide evidence that Saladin's brother, el-Malik el-Adil, continued the construction of the fortifications. Later, Saladin's cousin, el-Malik el-Mu'azzam Isa, changed the course of the southern wall, and built a wall following a shorter course, which is that of the present-day wall. He built a number of huge, strong towers in this wall. Inscriptions from the time of el-Mu'azzam's reign reveal that he built fortifications during the years 1202 and 1212, and possibly a year or two later.

In the year 1219, the city underwent a radical change. The Ayyubid rulers of Jerusalem feared a further sudden attack on the city by the Crusaders, such as that of 1099, and therefore decided to follow a "scorched earth" policy. To this end, el-Malik el-Mu'azzam Isa demolished the city walls. Jerusalem was no longer a fortified city, and remained so throughout several centuries, until after the conquest by the Ottoman Turks. The destruction of the walls led to a substantial reduction in the number of inhabitants in Jerusalem, since many were afraid to remain in an unfortified city.

During the first phase of the Ayyubid period (1187–1229), the rulers erected a number of buildings, and added to existing structures, especially those used for religious purposes. The inscriptions from this period reveal that major construction works were carried out on the Temple Mount. Thus, for example, the Aqsa Mosque was renovated and reconverted from serving as a church. During the years 1196 to 1199, a wooden screen was built to encompass

(above) **Philip d'Aubingni** was the personal aide of John Lackland, king of England, and tutor to his son, Henry III, as well as governor of the Channel Islands. He visited Jerusalem a number of times as a pilgrim, and in 1236 during one of these visits, he died and was buried there. His grave is located in the entrance to the Church of the Holy Sepulcher, to the right of the main portal. The d'Aubingni family crest and an inscription have been engraved on the tombstone. The grave was discovered in 1867 when the bench upon which the church guards rested was removed.

(above left) **Khanqat Salahiyya**. In preparation for the visit to Jerusalem of the German Emperor Wilhelm II (1898), the Ottoman authorities repaired and tidied up the sections of the city which he was to visit. One of these buildings was Khanqat Salahiyya, named for Saladin, which still constitutes the northwestern corner of the Crusader Church of the Holy Sepulcher complex.

According to Crusader period sources, the *khanqah* served at that time as the palace of the Latin Patriarch of Jerusalem. Proof of this was found with the discovery of a Latin inscription during the renovations carried out in the building prior to the visit of the German emperor. The inscription reads: "The Patriarch Arnolfus erected this building." Arnolfus served as the fourth Latin Patriarch of Jerusalem in 1099 and from 1112 to 1117, the year in which the building was constructed. After the inscription was discovered, it was despoiled by the Qadi of the *khanqah*, for fear that the Christians would demand they be given repossession of the building. However, a Dominican monk succeeded in making a copy of the inscription.

In 1187, Saladin converted the building into a *khanqah* (a hospice and prayer house for dervishes) named for him. The building was renovated by the Mamluk Sultan en-Nasir Muhammad Ibn Qalawun in 1341, and it would seem that the minaret was erected at this time. Few Crusader period remains are extant, and what is visible is mainly from the fifteenth-century Mamluk restoration work.

the holy rock in the Dome of the Rock. The baptistery of the Templum Domini church (the Dome of the Rock) was converted into a Muslim building marking the Prophet Muhammad's ascent to heaven, and to this day it is called the "Dome of the Ascension" (the Crusader elements are still evident in the structure). Some of the Crusader hospital buildings located south of the Church of the Holy Sepulcher were converted by el-Malik el-Afdal into the Mosque of Omar.

The Ayyubid rulers also built water installations at various points in the city. One of the characteristics of Ayyubid building works in Jerusalem was the recurrent use of sections of buildings from the Crusader period.

In 1229, Jerusalem once more became a Christian city, as a consequence of an agreement between the Ayyubid Sultan el-Malik el-Kamil and Frederick II, emperor of Germany and king of Sicily. By the terms of this agreement, much of the city was returned to the Christians, but Frederick was not permitted to restore the fortifications, demolished a decade earlier. However, it would appear that in spite of the ban, the king repaired the Damascus Gate and reinforced the fortifications around the Citadel. These fortifications withstood a number of attacks, until they were completely demolished in 1239 by another Ayyubid ruler, el-Malik en-Nasir Daoud, the ruler of Kerak (biblical Kir Moab). The short period of Crusader rule in the thirteenth century (1229–1244) was not sufficient for them to erect any important public buildings.

With the renewal of Crusader rule of Jerusalem, the few remaining Jews were expelled, and were permitted to return only after the city reverted to Muslim rule.

During the last year of Christian rule, 1243–1244, the Khwarizmians (invaders who came from the east of the Aral Sea in southern Russia) invaded Jerusalem, massacred the Christian inhabitants, destroyed church buildings, and burned Christian holy relics in them. During the last six years of the Ayyubid rule of the city the only structures to be added were the Qubbat (Dome of) Musa on the Temple Mount (1249–1250), and the first phase of the burial chamber Barka Khan in the Street of the Chain.

(above) **The el-Malik el-Adil inscription** found at the foot of the mosque tower in the course of the Citadel excavations carried out in the 1930s (by C. N. Johns). The text reads: "Our lord the magnificent Sultan el-Malik el-Adil Abu Bakr Ibn Ayyub," apparently Saladin's brother and heir. From various historical sources we learn that el-Malik el-Adil (ruled 1200–1218) fortified Jerusalem, and this inscription is the only evidence that these descriptions of his fortification works are authentic.

There is no definite knowledge in which of the buildings constructed by el-Malik el-Adil the inscription was fixed, since it has been reused in another building. However, it is possible that it was introduced into one of the structures built by the sultan in the Citadel, destroyed together with all Jerusalem's fortifications by his son, el-Malik el-Mu'azzam Isa, in 1219.

An inscription attributed to another Ayyubid ruler who built in Jerusalem—Uthman (he ruled in Banias and Subeiba during the years 1193–1198)—was also of secondary use when it was found in 1927 beside the Third Wall during the excavations by Sukenik and Mayer.

(right) A large **public building** discovered in the area of the **Armenian Garden** in the Old City, together with other buildings in which one side was the city wall. In the many rooms within the wall, ledges were found which were used for sleeping, and in some there were stoves for heating. These finds have led scholars to believe that the structure served as a khan in which visitors slept while their pack animals were tied up outside. This khan was apparently built by the Sultan el-Malik el-Mu'azzam Isa, but served for only a short period, since it was destroyed soon after by that sultan (as were the Ayyubid towers).

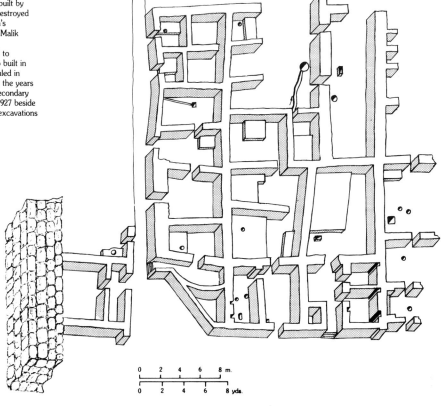

```
0    2    4    6    8 m.
0    2    4    6    8 yds.
```

The Mamluk Period
1250 – 1517

(above) **Minbar Burhan ed-Din** is an open-air pulpit on the Temple Mount platform, also called Minbar es-Seif, meaning the summer pulpit. During the summer, when numerous believers assemble on the Temple Mount during the Muslim festivals, this structure serves as a preacher's pulpit.

In the past, the structure was apparently connected with the ritual for prayers for rain. A mobile wooden structure on wheels was erected here at the end of the twelfth century, and according to historical sources, the present one was built by the Qadi Burhan ed-Din Ibn Jama'a, who lived from 1325 to 1388.

The prayer structure was built with stone and marble, and architectural details from both Crusader and Mamluk period buildings have been introduced into it. Renovations carried out in the nineteenth century can still be discerned.

The Mamluk period began with the fall of the Ayyubid dynasty in Egypt in the year 1250 and ended with the Turkish conquest in 1517. The significance of Jerusalem as the focal point of political and spiritual contention waned during this period, but its status as an important religious center of Islam was maintained. It was during the Mamluk period that the Muslim character of the city developed, tangible evidence of which still exists in the form of many exquisite structures from that period.

The most important written source remaining from that period is the work of the Jerusalem-born Qadi Mujir ed-Din el-Ulaymi (1456–1521), titled *The Wonderful Guide to the History of Jerusalem and Hebron*. This work contained the history and a detailed description of these two cities.

After the Mamluks vanquished the Ayyubid empire, the remaining Crusader strongholds in the coastal region of the land of Israel were systematically wiped out, and by the end of the thirteenth century, the Crusaders had been finally expelled from the country. From 1260, the year the Mamluks succeeded in repelling the invasion of the Mongols, there was an augmented feeling of security throughout the Mamluk empire, and there was no danger of attack throughout the entire region until the Turkish conquest. During this period, the country was nothing but a remote and politically insignificant outpost of the Mamluk empire. Entire areas of the country were ruined and abandoned by their inhabitants, for the coastal settlements were systematically ravaged by the Mamluks so as to prevent the Crusaders from returning and fortifying them once again. This was also the reason that Jerusalem's fortifications, demolished in 1219, were never rebuilt, and it remained an unwalled city throughout the

Mamluk period. The only fortification remaining in Jerusalem, and reinforced by the Mamluks in 1310, was the Citadel (the Tower of David). From inscriptions dating to this period, we learn that it was the Sultan en-Nasir Muhammad Ibn Qalawun who reconstructed the Citadel in approximately its present shape. However, it is not absolutely certain that the purpose was the defense of the city against enemy incursions. According to one theory, the sultan reinforced this citadel at the time he repaired other citadels throughout the kingdom as defense against internal adversaries. A small military force was resident in the Citadel under the command of a local governor appointed by the governor of the province of Damascus.

Jerusalem's remoteness from the main transport routes reduced its political and strategic significance within the Mamluk kingdom, in which the roads, hostels and postal service were of the utmost importance. This situation was reflected in the low status it had in the administrative hierarchy of the kingdom. At first it was a district capital in the province of Syria, and the governors of Damascus were responsible for its administration (evidence of this is found in the inscriptions on buildings erected during this period at the order of the rulers in Damascus). It was only in 1376 that the city's status changed when it was declared a province and its governors appointed directly from Cairo. However, Jerusalem never succeeded in attaining the status of capital city of a province, at the same level as Damascus.

During the Mamluk period, Jerusalem was administered by a governor whose seat of office was in the Citadel, and by a governor for religious affairs. The governor was responsible for internal security, the collection of taxes and municipal services such as the supply of water, garbage collection and sewage. Under the jurisdiction of the governor for religious affairs were the holy sites of the Temple Mount and the Cave of the Patriarchs in Hebron. He was responsible for the property of the *waqf* and the distribution of income from these holdings for the various religious requirements. In addition, he was responsible for the pilgrims visiting Jerusalem. The division of responsibility between these two functionaries was clear, but at times the governor took upon himself tasks that came within the domain of religious affairs, and sometimes even served as a sole governor, filling both functions.

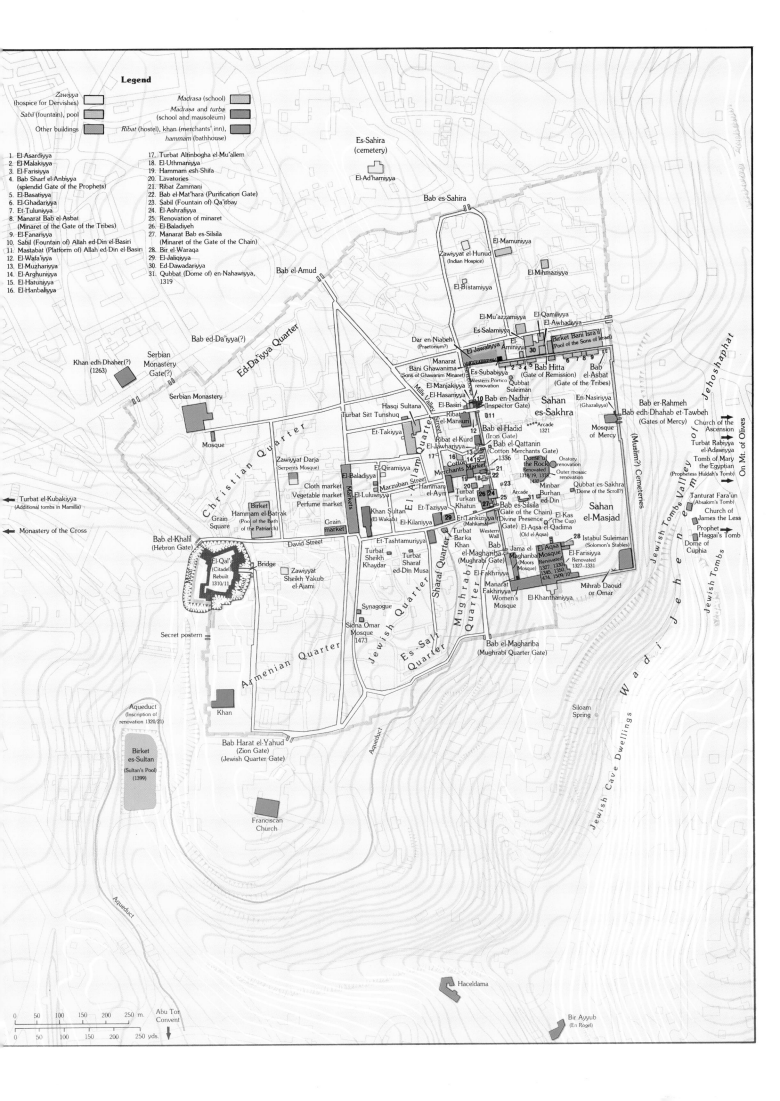

Legend

Zawiyya (hospice for Dervishes)
Sabil (fountain), pool
Other buildings
Madrasa (school)
Madrasa and *turba* (school and mausoleum)
Ribat (hostel), khan (merchants' inn), *hammam* (bathhouse)

1. El-Asardiyya
2. El-Malakiyya
3. El-Farisiyya
4. Bab Sharf el-Anbiyya (splendid Gate of the Prophets)
5. El-Basatiyya
6. El-Ghadariyya
7. Et-Tuluniyya
8. Manarat Bab el-Asbat (Minaret of the Gate of the Tribes)
9. El-Fanariyya
10. Sabil (Fountain of) Allah ed-Din el-Basiri
11. Mastabat (Platform of) Allah ed-Din el-Basiri
12. El-Wafa'iyya
13. El-Muzhariyya
14. El-Arghuniyya
15. El-Hatuniyya
16. El-Hanbaliyya
17. Turbat Altinbogha el-Mu'allem
18. El-Uthmaniyya
19. Hammam esh-Shifa
20. Lavatories
21. Ribat Zammani
22. Bab el-Mat'hara (Purification Gate)
23. Sabil (Fountain of) Qa'itbay
24. El-Ashrafiyya
25. Renovation of minaret
26. El-Baladiyeh
27. Manarat Bab es-Silsila (Minaret of the Gate of the Chain)
28. Bir el-Waraqa
29. El-Jaliqiyya
30. Ed-Dawadariyya
31. Qubbat (Dome of) en-Nahawiyya, 1319

Another important function in the Mamluk administration was that of the chief of police who was responsible for the internal security of the city and the local prison, situated near the Church of the Holy Sepulcher. The functionary responsible for the city's economy during this period was the Muhtasib ("Protector of the City's Morals"), whose tasks also included the prevention of fraud.

Another important function in the Mamluk administration was held by the Qadi, who was the chief justice. Trials in Jerusalem during this period were held according to the Shafi'i tradition of Islamic law, and at times according to other traditions. The above-mentioned Mujir ed-Din was one of the Qadis who judged according to the Maliki tradition.

(below left) Second Temple period **aqueducts** running from Solomon's Pools to the Temple Mount served Jerusalem until the twentieth century. At various times throughout this long period, repairs were carried out as required. The aqueducts crossed mountains, ran through tunnels and across bridges. The longest bridge they traversed was above the Hinnom Valley, slightly to the north of the Sultan's Pool. In the photograph (taken during the 1880s), the top of the arches supporting the bridge can be seen (the lower section is buried below), which was traversed by the aqueducts.

Above the arch at the left is an inscription in Arabic which states: "The order was given to repair this blessed conduit by our master the Sultan el-Malik en-Nasir, Sultan of Islam and of the Muslims, Muhammad son of the Sultan el-Malik el-Mansur Qalawun in the month of the year 720 (=1320/1) to the glory of our master el-Malik en-Nasir." From this inscription we learn that it was the Sultan en-Nasir Muhammad Ibn Qalawun who repaired the aqueducts during the Mamluk period.

(far right) The legend relating to the **Lions' Gate** tells that Suleiman the Magnificent dreamt that he would be devoured by lions unless he built the walls of Jerusalem. Thus, when the walls were erected he commanded that lions be placed at one of the gates, in memory of that dream. However, the four animals on either side of the gate are panthers, the heraldic insignia used by the thirteenth-century Sultan Baybars. They were apparently removed from one of the large public buildings he erected. This could have been the elaborately decorated Khan edh-Dhaher built in 1263–1264, whose doors were brought from the Fatimid palace in Cairo to add to the building's beauty. It would seem that this structure was demolished during the course of the building of the city walls in the sixteenth century. Its stones were apparently reused, and the panthers which had decorated it were transferred to the Lions' Gate.

(above) **The Lions' Gate.**

(below) **Et-Turbat el-Kubakiyya** is the tomb of the Mamluk Emir Allah ed-Din Aydughdi Ibn Abdallah el-Kubaki. Aydughdi was an Ayyubid official stationed in Syria, appointed during the course of Baybar's rule as governor of Safed and later of Aleppo. His fate was similar to that of many other officials in the Mamluk administration. He was arrested and exiled to Jerusalem where he died in 1289.

This tomb is located in the Mamilla cemetery in the center of Jerusalem. Although it was built in characteristic Mamluk style, many Crusader period architectural elements have been included, possibly taken from a Crusader tomb in the vicinity.

Administrative decrees relating to all residents of Jerusalem were placed on a stone notice-board at the entrance to the Gate of the Chain, through which the majority of the residents passed on their way to prayer on the Temple Mount.

The economy of the land of Israel during the Mamluk period was adversely effected by the fact that the Mamluk rulers did not attribute particular political significance to the country, and thus took no measures to develop it or improve the welfare of its inhabitants, except where the interests of the government were concerned. The country's agricultural produce was exported to Egypt, and the heavy taxes and levies imposed on the inhabitants were exploited mainly for the benefit of the Mamluk military forces. Jerusalem, too, suffered economic decline and impoverishment during this period. In addition, the city's remoteness from the main international and internal trade routes had a detrimental effect on the city's income. Furthermore, its agricultural hinterland was unable to supply its needs. As a consequence, it was dependent upon food being brought over long distances, which often led to dire shortages. Jerusalem's economy was based on various crafts, such as carpentry, shoemaking and weaving, as well as on small businesses. Agricultural produce from the surrounding villages was processed in olive oil presses, wine cellars and soap factories.

The city's desolate economic situation was worsened by the fact that its rulers extorted its inhabitants. These

(below right) One of the four early fourteenth-century **maps of Jerusalem** from the book by **Marino Sanuto** of Venice. He first visited the country in 1285, when Acre was still the capital city of the Crusader kingdom. He came back to the country several times after that and wrote a number of books about it.

Marino Sanuto was one of the many Christians who dreamed of organizing another Crusade to liberate the Holy Land from the Muslims, and his work, *The Book of Secrets of the Defenders of the Cross*, set out his proposal for this Crusade.

As a consequence of the author's idealistic conception of Jerusalem, the map is full of inaccuracies. For example, he depicted the fortifications around the city as being complete, when in fact they were in ruins at that time. However, this map is an important historical source for information about Jerusalem at the end of the thirteenth century, prior to the time when many Mamluk buildings were added to it.

(below) Lithograph of a section of the **Turbat Barka Khan** from the book by Pierotti printed in 1864. Several parts of the facade illustrated here were taken from Crusader buildings demolished by Mamluk builders. Examples are the central arch, the adornments on the gadroons and the ledges on both sides of the entrance.

This is a small thirteenth-century Mamluk structure situated in the Street of the Chain. It now houses the library of the Khalidi family established here in the year 1900. The reading room was originally the tomb of Barka Khan, the father-in-law of the Sultan Baybars (who ruled from 1260 to 1277).

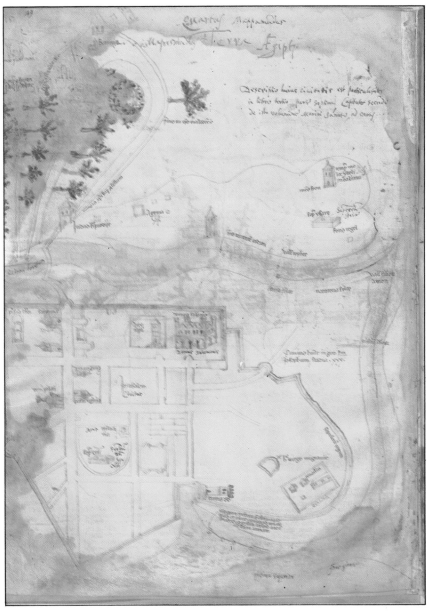

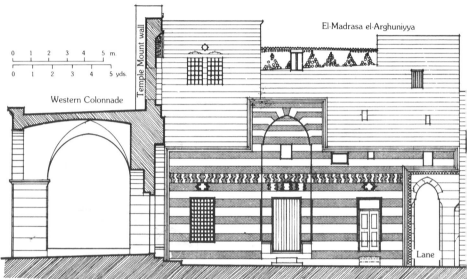

(left) The tomb of the Emir **Baybars el-Jaliq—Turbat Jaliqiyya**—situated at the intersection of the Street of the Chain and Haggai Street. This is a simple unadorned structure. Above the burial chamber window is an inscription referring to the burial of Rukn ed-Din Baybars el-Jaliq es-Salihi who died on November 4, 1307. He was the keeper of the clothes and one of the bodyguards of the Sultan Baybars. Baybars el-Jaliq's personal insignia (a lily with eleven leaves) can be seen on the inscription. During the Ottoman period, the structure was called Dar el-Baskatib. The building also has a dwelling section without any embellishments.

El-Madrasa el-Arghuniyya

Temple Mount wall

Western Colonnade

Lane

(bottom) An illustration by **Pierotti** made in 1864 of the two gates of the **Palace of Sitt Tunshuq** located in Ma'alot Hamadrasa Street. The noblewoman's tomb is on the other side of this street. These two structures, dating to the end of the fourteenth century, are the most elaborate examples of the art of Mamluk building works in general and in Jerusalem in particular. The palace, one of the most exquisite in the city, was erected by the noblewoman, Tunshuq, daughter of Abdallah el-Muzaffariyya, to serve as a hostel for dervishes. Little is known about this noblewoman apart from the fact that she was a liberated female slave who married a wealthy man. There is a theory that her husband was the Mamluk Sultan el-Malik el-Muzaffar Hajji (ruled 1346–1347). The noblewoman died in Jerusalem in 1398, and was buried in a tomb whose decorations were similar to those on the palace built by her.

Because of the dimensions of these structures, many of the city's inhabitants and visitors believed that they had been built by some eminent personality such as Hasqi Sultana, the most loved wife of the Sultan Suleiman the Magnificent, or Queen Helene of Adiabene, and others. The Christians believed that this was a hostel built by Helena, mother of the Emperor Constantine, to accommodate the building workers engaged in the construction of the Church of the Holy Sepulcher. Once the church was completed, the building became a shelter for indigent pilgrims, and is thus portrayed in the pilgrim literature. The building now serves as a trade school for children from the villages on the outskirts of Jerusalem.

Pierotti illustrated the embellishments of two sections showing the doors of the building. On both sides were wooden "wings" that had remained from the Mamluk period and two stone benches at the entrance. The facade, enclosed in a frame, is composed of stone layers in a variety of colors—black, white or red—characteristic of Mamluk building. Above the entrance is a lintel made from a single stone, and above it is the relieving arch designed to protect it from cleavage. It was concealed by dressed stones in the form of interlaced leaves in various colors.

Above the eastern entrance is an exquisite square adornment made of mosaic of different inlaid stones and colors (an identical but smaller panel exists in the facade of the nearby tomb). The transition from the square form of the entrance niche to the semicircular dome at the top, is done with beautiful dripstone. This style is called *muqarnas*, and is one of the most beautiful contributions of Islam art to architecture in general.

The western gate is different from the eastern one. Passages from the Koran surround the window decorated with a series of rosettes. Noticeably absent is the inscription bearing the names of the donors which is found in most buildings devoted to the needy erected in Jerusalem during the Mamluk period.

Fig 1   Fig 2

(below) The southern streetfront of the **Street of the Iron Gate** leading to the Temple Mount. Like all the streets leading to the Temple Mount built in the Mamluk period, this street is a good example of the buildings erected at that time.

The tallest building in the street was el-Madrasa el-Arghuniyya, which according to an inscription in the building was built in 1358 by Arghun el-Kamili, the governor of Syria who

was exiled to Jerusalem. The building is now known as Dar el-Afifi.

At the side of this building is an entranceway opening on to an alley leading to el-Madrasa el-Hatuniyya adjacent to the Temple Mount. Madrasa el-Muzhariyya was erected at the order of Zayn ed-Din Abu Bakr Ibn Muzhir el-Ansari esh-Shafi'i, and was completed in the year 1480/81. Abu Bakr (1428–1488) was the secretary of the Chancery Bureau

(Diwan) of the Egyptian kingdom and responsible for the sultan's stables. He visited the land of Israel for the purpose of recruiting soldiers from Nablus to fight against the Turkish sultanate which had begun to expand. It is possible at this time that he visited this building, erected several years earlier. The three *madrasas* in this illustration are now residences.

El-Madrasa el-Muzhariyya   El-Madrasa el-Hanbaliyya

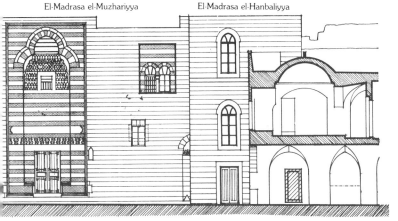

(right) **El-Madrasa el-Ashrafiyya** is situated in the area between the Cotton Merchants Gate and the Gate of the Chain, on the western boundary of the Temple Mount. According to the works of Mujir ed-Din el-Ulaymi, the *madrasa* was erected by the Emir Hasan Ibn Tatar ez-Zahiri, keeper of the Temple Mount and the Cave of the Patriarchs in Hebron. The structure was erected in 1465 for the Sultan el-Malik Zahir Khushqadam (ruled from 1461 to 1467). After the sultan's death, el-Malik el-Ashraf Qa'itbay came to Jerusalem and ordered the building demolished and rebuilt (1479–1482). Since then it has been considered the third most beautiful building on the Temple Mount, after the Dome of the Rock and the Aqsa Mosque. Like the majority of buildings of this period, most of its adornments are concentrated in its facade, and most especially in the entrance. Many of the architectural and artistic elements of Mamluk building are evident. Examples of this are the *muqarnas* (the pattern of stepped stones), the *ablaq* (the course of stones with recurring colors), the joggling (the decoration of interlacing stones in a variety of colors), and the relieving arch.

The inscription inside the building records the names of the first builders.

officials would gain their positions through bribery, and once they attained power, imposed heavy taxes in order to compensate themselves for the initial outlay, and even to make a handsome profit. The tax burden suppressed any economic initiative. An example of the extortion was the monopoly the city rulers held over the production of oil and its byproducts. The rulers claimed the right to sell these products at exorbitant prices and forced the inhabitants to purchase them in order to finance the wars being fought against the Ottomans during the course of the fifteenth century. The difficult economic situation and the oppressive policy of the governors of Jerusalem led to a considerable reduction in the number of inhabitants of the city, evidence of which can be seen in the population censuses held during this period.

One of the major changes that occurred in Jerusalem and in the country during the Mamluk period was the ascendancy of Islam. Most of the Christians were expelled once the Mamluks had occupied the country, and Jerusalem became a focal point of pilgrimage and attracted numerous Muslim settlers who soon constituted the major component of the population. As the city became a religious center for Muslims, both its rulers and residents set about erecting buildings there, and the city underwent a major transformation in its outward appearance, changing from a cosmopolitan center to a religious Muslim city. Thus, despite its impoverished economic situation, Jerusalem underwent a period of Muslim religious growth. In addition to repairing and expanding the water installations, building marketplaces and erecting public buildings, the Mamluks constructed numerous religious institutions, to the extent that the Christian and Jewish (to a lesser extent) character of the city's buildings was no longer discernible. It was no accident that the Mamluk architects made use of adornments taken from demolished Crusader structures.

During the Mamluk period, Jerusalem received numerous Muslim pilgrims from countries with Muslim populations: Afghanistan, Anatolia, Egypt, Morocco, Spain (from where Muslims fled after the Christian conquest), and many other countries. Muslim religious functionaries moved into the many institutions for religious studies and the hostels built in the vicinity of the Temple Mount, especially in the streets leading to it. In many locations, sometimes even in cemeteries, special retreats were set aside where Muslims could be in solitude. Hostels were constructed for poor pilgrims, the majority being close to the relevant holy sites in the Temple Mount area. The main buildings of a religious nature in Jerusalem were the *madrasas* which served as seminaries for the study of religion. These were erected both by the sultans themselves and by leading personalities from among the governing bodies. During this period, the great *madrasas* were constructed in the Street of the Chain, in the vicinity of the Iron Gate and other locations. The most well-known were el-Madrasa el-Arghuniyya and el-Madrasa et-Tankiziyya.

As Jerusalem was far from any significant political development, it often served as the place to which dignitaries who had fallen into disfavor with the Mamluk government were exiled. They were termed *batal* (meaning unemployed). Some of these dignitaries, who wished to protect their property from being expropriated by the authorities, erected religious buildings which they donated to the Muslim *waqf*. The donors were allowed to live in these buildings and on no account could they be evicted by the authorities from *waqf* property.

Some Muslim buildings were erected by persons who were not Mamluk citizens. For example, the Ottoman ruler, Murad II, constructed buildings in Jerusalem, and others were erected by the sultan of the small state of Du el-Qadir. A Turkish princess built a *madrasa* in Jerusalem, and a representative of the Persian royal family built a hostel there.

It was in the Mamluk period that the Muslim style of architecture developed which is still visible to this day.

114

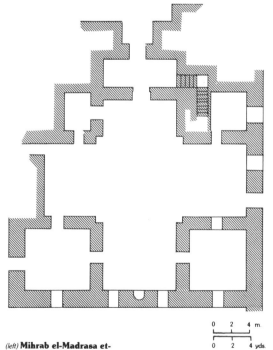

(left) **Sabil (Fountain of) Qa'itbay**, one of the most beautiful structures on the Temple Mount, and an example of the magnificent Mamluk buildings in Jerusalem. The Mamluk Sultan el-Ashraf Inal (ruled 1453–1461) built the fountain whose waters were brought to it from the main aqueduct from Solomon's Pools.

Sultan Qa'itbay (ruled 1468–1496) renovated the structure in 1482, and it has been named for him. In 1883, it became necessary to renovate the fountain once more, since the ravages of time were beginning to have their effect on it. It was then that the original inscription was removed and replaced by the present one, bearing the name of the last person to repair it, the Turkish Sultan Abdul Hamid. The original inscription placed in the structure by Qa'itbay was copied at the end of the nineteenth century, and reads as follows: "This blessed place has been built by the Sultan, King el-Malik el-Ashraf Abu en-Nasir Qa'itbay...on the date, the blessed month of Shawal of the year 879 [1474]." Two dates—1474 and 1482—are mentioned, but this apparent contradiction derives from an error made by the person who copied it.

(below) **El-Madrasa et-Tankiziyya** is located in the square near the Gate of the Chain and surrounded by other Mamluk buildings. The Emir Seif ed-Din Tankiz en-Nasiri erected the *madrasa* building named in his honor. The emir's insignia, a goblet enclosed by a circle, and the date of construction (1328–1329) are incised on the facade of the building. The building's facade is typical of Mamluk buildings in Jerusalem, as is the plan of its interior. It has a hall with four square "bays," and in the center is a pool with a fountain, an unusual architectural element in Jerusalem. Water reached the fountain from the main aqueduct that brought water from Solomon's Pools.

In the course of time, a dervish monastery and elementary school for orphans were added to the *madrasa*. This was the reason that it was called a *madrasa*, even though the name does not appear in the inscription on the building's facade. The building's prestige was enhanced when the Sultan Faraj (ruled 1406–1412) stayed there during his visit to Jerusalem.

At the end of the fifteenth century, the building began to be used as a courthouse, and it was later (apparently from the nineteenth century) called the Mahkama (court). According to Jewish tradition the building served as the Chamber of the Hewn Stone (the seat of the Sanhedrin in the Second Temple period), and was thus referred to by travelers in the literature of the time.

(left) **Mihrab el-Madrasa et-Tankiziyya**, adorned with a mosaic, is similar to many other Muslim religious structures from the Mamluk period, as for example, el-Madrasa el-Hasaniyya, the Dome of the Rock, and others. Mosaics were used to decorate many parts of the buildings, and in the majority the motifs were taken from the plant world. This art was a continuation of the tradition of mosaic art from the early Arab period in Jerusalem.

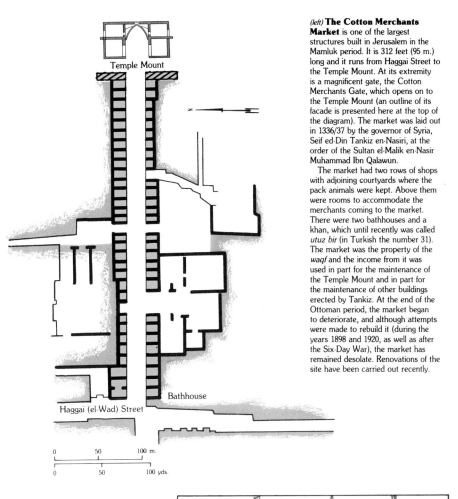

Temple Mount

Bathhouse

Haggai (el-Wad) Street

```
0        50        100 m.
|____|____|

0        50        100 yds.
```

(left) **The Cotton Merchants Market** is one of the largest structures built in Jerusalem in the Mamluk period. It is 312 feet (95 m.) long and it runs from Haggai Street to the Temple Mount. At its extremity is a magnificent gate, the Cotton Merchants Gate, which opens on to the Temple Mount (an outline of its facade is presented here at the top of the diagram). The market was laid out in 1336/37 by the governor of Syria, Seif ed-Din Tankiz en-Nasiri, at the order of the Sultan el-Malik en-Nasir Muhammad Ibn Qalawun.

The market had two rows of shops with adjoining courtyards where the pack animals were kept. Above them were rooms to accommodate the merchants coming to the market. There were two bathhouses and a khan, which until recently was called *utuz bir* (in Turkish the number 31). The market was the property of the *waqf* and the income from it was used in part for the maintenance of the Temple Mount and in part for the maintenance of other buildings erected by Tankiz. At the end of the Ottoman period, the market began to deteriorate, and although attempts were made to rebuild it (during the years 1898 and 1920, as well as after the Six-Day War), the market has remained desolate. Renovations of the site have been carried out recently.

(right) **Glass lamp** from the Mamluk period used in the Cave of the Patriarchs in Hebron. It is now in the Islamic Museum on the Temple Mount. Lamps of this type were used in mosques, and mention is made of similar lamps in descriptions of buildings on the Temple Mount.

On the lamps is the personal insignia of Seif ed-Din Tankiz en-Nasiri, the Mamluk governor of Syria from 1312 to 1340. The insignia, a goblet within a circle, was engraved on some of the buildings erected by this governor in Jerusalem (similar insignia can be found on other Mamluk buildings in the city). A passage from the Koran is engraved on the upper section of the lamp, and another inscription around the center which reads: "On behalf of the school of his eminence, the Emir Seif ed-Din Tankiz, governor of the splendid kingdom in the protected city of Nablus."

The many public buildings erected during this period have their own distinctive, easily recognized style. They were simple in design, and the decorations were concentrated in their unique facades. An inscription constituted part of the embellishment of the building. It included passages from the Koran, a description of the structure, information about the builder (and often his insignia), as well as the date of construction.

The dates appearing on the buildings reveal that hardly a decade went by during the Mamluk period without a single building being dedicated. However, during certain periods an upsurge of building activity took place. An example of this was during the rule of the Sultan en-Nasir Muhammad Ibn Qalawun, which was a particularly peaceful period. The governor of Syria at that time, Tankiz en-Nasiri, under whose jurisdiction Jerusalem came, erected many buildings in the city, including the city Citadel and a *madrasa* named for him—et-Tankiziyya (from the nineteenth century it was re-named Mahkama). In addition, he opened two markets, one of which was the Cotton Merchants Market, and he built water installations on the Temple Mount, as well as el-Kas (the Cup), an installation for purification between the Aqsa Mosque and the Dome of the Rock. Tankiz also renovated the Dome of the Rock and repaired its roof and part of the Aqsa Mosque. Building activity in Jerusalem was also rife during the rule of Sultan el-Malik el-Ashraf Qa'itbay (1468–1496). During this period, the sultan himself supervised the building works. He repaired the water conduits in Jerusalem, and an exquisite fountain was built and named for him. He also rebuilt the *madrasa* called in his honor, el-Ashrafiyya. This *madrasa* is considered to be the most beautiful building on the Temple Mount, after the Dome of the Rock and the Aqsa Mosque.

Jerusalem had many scholars, many of whom taught in the *madrasas*. The Muslim tradition most prevalent at the time was the Shafi'i, to which the majority of the inhabitants adhered. However, other traditions were also followed in the city, such as the Hanbali, whose adherents had strong connections with the authorities in Damascus, or the Maliki tradition followed by North Africans. The study of Muslim religious law was stressed in these institutions of learning, but in some of the *madrasas* the Koran and the oral law were also taught. The teachers themselves studied at the *madrasas* a number of times each week. After the formal lessons, the students were assisted by the preceptor, a type of tutor who would elaborate on the lesson and assist the students in understanding it. Generations of scholars and writers educated at these institutions wrote exegeses on the Koran and interpretation of Muslim law. Although many of the authors did not live in Jerusalem throughout their entire lives, Jerusalem played an important role in their education. These writers earned a very high income, since they benefited from the revenue gained from the properties donated to the *madrasas* over the years.

A special place in the life of Jerusalem was held by the dervishes, a mystic Muslim cult similar to the *hasidim* in Judaism. Influenced by the Christian ascetic monastic movement, the dervishes devoted themselves to prayer, playing musical instruments and in executing mystic dances. Many of them lived in seclusion. The city's inhabitants believed that they had miraculous powers and requested their intervention in times of distress. The leader of the dervish movement was called the "Sheikh of Sheikhs."

The dervishes had a number of centers in Jerusalem, the most important of which was the Khanqat Salahiyya, formerly the palace of the Crusader Patriarchs of the city. Another center was el-Madrasa es-Salahiyya, the dervish school (the former Crusader Church of St. Anne). Adherents to this sect lived in types of hermitages, constructed especially to enable them to seclude themselves for extended periods. The most well-known of these hermitages (*zawiyya* in Arabic) were the Zawiyya Yunusiyya in the present-day Inspector Gate Street and the Zawiyya el-Bistamiyya, in today's Muslim Quarter.

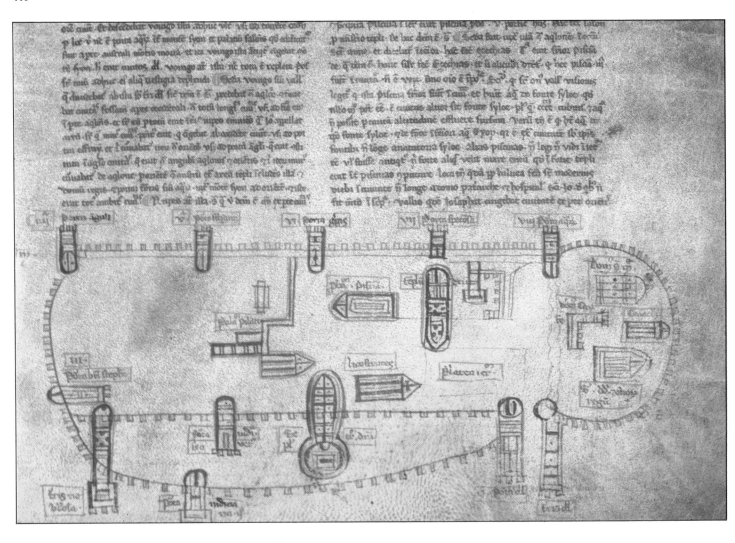

(right) The tomb of **Turkan Khatun** is a small structure used for burial situated in the Street of the Chain in the Old City of Jerusalem. Its facade is ornamented with leaves and palmettos. In the lintels are rosettes and ornamented panels, which provide a good example of Mamluk art. Similar decorations appeared on the binding of books and on wooden elements in architectural patterns of prayer pulpits, and in other places.

The inscription on the pillar records the building of the tomb for Turkan Khatun, daughter of the Emir Tuqtay Ibn Saljutay el-Uzbaki, in the year 1352/53. The names of the father and grandfather of the deceased are mentioned, and they too came from Asia. It is not clear, therefore, why the daughter of an emir from Central Asia was buried in Jerusalem.

After the consolidation of the Mamluk rule in the land of Israel, and when the Crusaders had been driven out of the country, the Jewish community was revived in Jerusalem. The tiny Jewish community that remained in the city, information of which exists in a letter written by Nahmanides (in 1267), was augmented in the fourteenth century and attracted Jews from countries of the Orient and from Europe. Many scholars arrived in the land of Israel during this period, such as Estori Haparhi who became famous for his works on the geography of the country. Estori Haparhi lived in Jerusalem for only a short while, and left it for Beit She'an during the controversy in the city over a work by Maimonides, and because of the despotic ways of the Jewish community leaders. Reference to the despotism of the Jewish leadership is found in letters written by Obadiah of Bertinoro during 1488–1490, according to which many Jews left the city as a consequence of the actions of the "Elders," who were greatly feared. Despite this, the Jewish community which had been so tiny at the beginning of the Mamluk period, became a significant factor in the city at the close of the period. It had its own internal leadership and institutions, and was firmly established in Jerusalem.

During the Mamluk period, the Jews of Jerusalem lived mainly in the vicinity of Mount Zion, according to an account written by Jacob of Verona, who visited the city in 1335. Apparently, this area was more protected than other parts of the city at this time. Another source states that Jews lived in caves in the Kidron Valley, and engaged in the manufacture of pottery. Following the advent of a large number of Jewish immigrants in the fourteenth century, the community's residences extended to include the present-day Jewish Quarter.

The authorities were most stringent with the minorities, including the Jewish minority, and from time to time were

(opposite above) **A fourteenth-century map of Jerusalem.**
This map reflects the knowledge of Jerusalem in Europe at this time, but is full of inaccuracies because of the artist's Christian religious tendencies to depict the city as it was in the time of Jesus. Since the map was based on twelfth- and thirteenth-century sources, it shows the city surrounded by walls, even though in the Mamluk period the greater part of them had been demolished. Mount Zion is also encompassed by a wall, and the wall which separates the mount from the rest of the city is only hinted at in this map. Jerusalem is similarly depicted in Marino Sanuto's map. Furthermore, five gates appear in the map, but it is difficult to identify them accurately since no data remains from this period. The interior city wall is also drawn according to the New Testament tradition, according to which the hill of Golgotha and Jesus' burial place were outside the wall.

A number of sites holy to Christianity appear in the map: Pontius Pilate's palace (Palacium Pilatt); the Lithostrotos (which appears as Licostrates in the map); and the Bethesda Pool (Probatico Piscina). There are also sites on Mount Zion: the House of Mary (Domuss. Marie); the House of Caiaphas (Domus Cayfe); the Room of the Last Supper (Cenaculum) and the Tomb of David and of other kings (Sepulca David et aliorum Regun). The map is now housed in the library of Florence.

provoked by zealous religious upsurges on the part of the Muslim masses to introduce harsh measures. References are found in the pilgrimage literature to the fact that both the Jewish and Christian minorities suffered from the harsh policy of the authorities, and that they were not permitted to enter the Temple Mount area. At the beginning of the fourteenth century decrees were issued requiring the Jews to wear distinctive clothes, prohibiting them from riding horses and imposing a special head tax upon them. Toward the end of the period, the authorities became more charitable, even though these decrees were not annulled. Sultan Qa'itbay expressed his annoyance at the destruction of a synagogue in Jerusalem in 1474.

A small Christian community remained in Jerusalem from the Crusader period, and during the Mamluk period was concentrated in the area of the Church of the Holy Sepulcher. The most active members of this community were the Armenians and the Greek Orthodox, as well as the Franciscans who settled in Jerusalem in the fourteenth century, mainly on Mount Zion. The Franciscans fulfilled an important function in the city, even though they constituted a minority in the city, as well as within the Christian community. They were given the task of guarding the places holy to Christianity, organizing religious services and providing services to pilgrims visiting Jerusalem.

The Christian influence in Jerusalem continued throughout the entire Mamluk period, mainly because the interest of the Christian countries in the city did not wane. The Christian rulers endeavored to influence events in the city, and at times even succeeded in doing so. These activities and the constant friction between the Jews and Christian communities continued throughout the entire Mamluk period. One of the striking examples of the continuing controversy between the Jews and Christians was the dispute over Mount Zion and the Franciscan monastery there. Even European rulers such as Jaime II, king of Aragon, intervened in this matter. He endeavored from 1327 to obtain for the Franciscans the right to occupy the Mount Zion Monastery and to gain possession of David's Tomb and the Cenacle (the Room of the Last Supper). He succeeded in this only after the king of Naples, Robert of Anjou, obtained rights for the Franciscans in other places holy to Christianity, such as the Church of the Holy Sepulcher and the Tomb of the Virgin Mary. In the year 1428, the Jews endeavored to purchase the building which housed David's Tomb on Mount Zion, but

failed as this site included the Room of the Last Supper, and thus was of great significance for Christianity. The Muslims ended the dispute by taking possession of the building and converting it into a mosque. The Franciscans succeeded in repossessing it once more, but for a short time only. After the accession to the throne of Sultan Jaqmaq (1438–1453), a most devout Muslim, riots broke out against the infidels, during the course of which the Mount Zion Monastery and the Church of the Holy Sepulcher were ravaged. A few years later, the Christians once more attempted to restore the holy places including the Church of the Dormition. However, violence broke out once again in 1452, and the Muslim zealots destroyed the buildings. During the reign of Sultan Khushqadam (1461–1467), attempts by the Christians to rebuild the Mount Zion Monastery were thwarted by irate Muslims, who demolished it once again. In 1489, when the Mamluk empire was ruled by Sultan Qa'itbay, the Franciscans built the Holy Zion Church, and once more applied to the authorities for the rights to the holy places on Mount Zion. However, after protracted deliberations among the various Muslim groups, a decision was taken to demolish the church. The Christians left one of the stones of the church as an altar to mark the exact location on Mount Zion of the site of Mary's repose, and it remained thus until the arrival of the Turks.

The Muslims considered the Franciscans to be the representatives of the country's Christian community, and from time to time punished them as retaliation for harassment of Muslims by Christians in European countries. This was the reason for the arrest in 1365 of all the monks on Mount Zion, and their eviction to Damascus, where they remained until their death. A similar event occurred in 1422, when in retaliation for a Catalonian attack on Mamluk vessels, Franciscan monks were arrested and exiled to Cairo. These actions were not restricted to Christians alone. In the drought year of 1491, the Muslims destroyed the wine cellars belonging to Jews as well as Christians, claiming that they were the cause of the drought that had struck the city.

Jerusalem as a predominantly Islamic city, the massive building of Muslim religious institutions, the Muslim–Jewish–Christian relations, the city's decline as a political factor— these were the dominating features of the Mamluk period in Jerusalem. The period of Sultan Qa'itbay's rule were the last great days of the Mamluk empire. It then began to decline until it was finally conquered by the Turks.

The Ottoman Period
1517 – 1917

An **ornamental inscription** found on the side of the stone bridge leading to the Citadel. The inscription bears the name of Suleiman the Magnificent and reads: "Glory to our master Suleiman el-Malik el-Muzaffar Abu en-Nasir Suleiman Shah Ibn Uthman."

The inscription is decorated in the style similar to that of the Mamluk inscriptions of this type, and was probably influenced by them. The gate, the gate tower, the drawbridge, the external fortifications and the internal stone bridge on which the inscription was found, were repaired during the renovations carried out by Suleiman the Magnificent.

The members of the Pro-Jerusalem Society, who carried out extensive repair work in the Citadel from 1918 to 1920, claimed the discovery of the inscription. However, it seems that it was known to scholars already in 1914, but as it was concealed by the foliage which covered the bridge rail, its existence was forgotten.

The latter years of the Mamluk rule of the land of Israel was a period of the degeneration of the security situation and the deterioration of the economy. These factors also had their effect on the situation in Jerusalem, where the decadent government was no longer able to maintain a stable administration.

During these years the Ottomans began to constitute a threat to the Mamluk empire, and already in the fifteenth century Bayezid II tried to conquer it, but failed to do so. A tiny state, Du el-Qadir (in northern Syria between the Euphrates River and the Mediterranean Sea) acted as a buffer between these two empires. The conquest of Du el-Qadir by the Ottoman Emperor Selim I (ruled from 1512 to 1520) paved the way to the conquest of Syria, Palestine and Egypt. In August 1516, Selim vanquished the Mamluk army under the command of the Sultan Qansuh el-Ghori at Marj Dabek (north of Aleppo) and conquered Syria and all of Palestine. The Ottoman sultan continued to Egypt, and after a further battle near Cairo, put an end to the Mamluk empire. At the end of December 1516, Selim I entered Jerusalem at the head of his cavalry as the inhabitants joyously welcomed him. The sultan scattered coins to the cheering crowds and thus obtained their approbation.

During the early years of Ottoman rule, Jerusalem remained as neglected as it had been under the Mamluks, and its status was lower than that of other cities in the country. It was symbolic that the Sultan Selim I was not presented with the key to the city of Jerusalem when he entered it, but received it in Gaza together with the keys of other cities.

Some time after the Turkish conquest, the country underwent a major transformation after which it became an integral part of the Ottoman Empire. An organized administration was introduced, and the economy began to improve as agriculture, trade and commerce flourished. The Ottoman authorities invested great efforts in developing the country, and especially Jerusalem. There was a significant increase in the number of pilgrims visiting the city as a result of the improved security and economic situation. The population also grew apace.

The country under the Turks became part of the Province of Damascus. New administrative divisions were introduced after the Ottoman conquest, but some vestiges of the Mamluk period still remained. Some of the local governors retained their posts in Palestine and in Syria. Jerusalem itself was not accorded a special administrative status, and constituted the district of Jerusalem together with the sub-district of Hebron.

The governor (or pasha) of Jerusalem appointed by the Turks had his office in the Jawiliyya (in the northwest corner of the Temple Mount), which had served as the residence of the ruler of the city since 1427. He had a small military force at his command which was garrisoned in the Citadel (an account written in 1660 states that there were no more than ninety soldiers stationed there). The Citadel was renovated a number of times during the Ottoman period, and became the symbol of Ottoman dominion over the city.

A basic change was brought about in the city under the rule of Suleiman the Magnificent (1520–1566). This sultan fought wars throughout Europe, and once he had extended the borders of his empire to the west, he devoted his efforts to its internal development. Under his rule, the empire reached a peak in its cultural development, an expression of which was his great building works, such as the erection of the walls of Jerusalem.

To the sultan's credit also was the improvement of the city's water system which began in 1532. The aqueducts from Solomon's Pools were repaired, and six fountains drawing their waters from these aqueducts were built in the city. These fountains were decorated with architectural details derived from Crusader edifices and introduced into Muslim structures, thus creating a special kind of building style. The improvement of Jerusalem's water supply made it possible to establish public gardens in the city.

The greatest of Suleiman the Magnificent's ventures in Jerusalem was undoubtedly the reconstruction of the city walls during the years 1536 to 1541. The erection of these walls was considered to be an important architectural achievement. There were few places where the Ottomans built fortifications on such a great scale and embellished them in such a manner. There is a theory that the famous architect of the period,

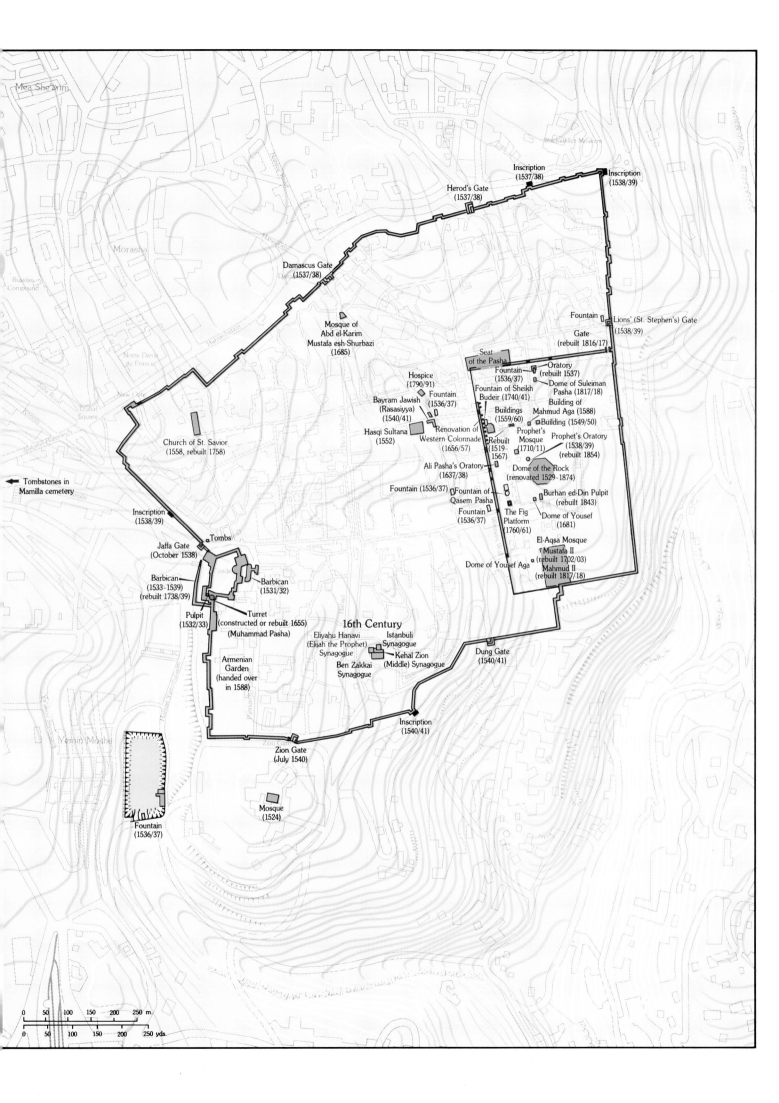

Mea She'arim

Morasha

Russian Compound

Notre Dame de France

Inscription (1537/38)

Inscription (1538/39)

Herod's Gate (1537/38)

Damascus Gate (1537/38)

Mosque of Abd el-Karim Mustafa esh-Shurbazi (1685)

New Gate

Fountain

Lions' (St. Stephen's) Gate (1538/39)

Gate (rebuilt 1816/17)

Seat of the Pasha

Hospice (1790/91)

Fountain (1536/37)

Oratory (rebuilt 1537)

Dome of Suleiman Pasha (1817/18)

Bayram Jawish (Rasasiyya) (1540/41)

Fountain (1536/37)

Fountain of Sheikh Budeir (1740/41)

Buildings (1559/60)

Building of Mahmud Aga (1588)

Building (1549/50)

Hasqi Sultana (1552)

Renovation of Western Colonnade (1656/57)

Prophet's Mosque (1710/11)

Prophet's Oratory (1538/39) (rebuilt 1854)

Church of St. Savior (1558, rebuilt 1758)

Rebuilt (1519-1567)

Ali Pasha's Oratory (1637/38)

Dome of the Rock (renovated 1529-1874)

Tombstones in Mamilla cemetery

Fountain (1536/37)

Fountain of Qasem Pasha

Burhan ed-Din Pulpit (rebuilt 1843)

Dome of Yousef (1681)

Inscription (1538/39)

Fountain (1536/37)

The Fig Platform (1760/61)

El-Aqsa Mosque

Mustafa II (rebuilt 1702/03)

Tombs

Dome of Yousef Aga

Mahmud II (rebuilt 1817/18)

Jaffa Gate (October 1538)

Barbican (1533-1539) (rebuilt 1738/39)

Barbican (1531/32)

Pulpit (1532/33)

Turret (constructed or rebuilt 1655) (Muhammad Pasha)

16th Century

Eliyahu Hanavi (Elijah the Prophet) Synagogue

Istanbuli Synagogue

Kehal Zion (Middle) Synagogue

Dung Gate (1540/41)

Armenian Garden (handed over in 1588)

Ben Zakkai Synagogue

Yemin Moshe

Inscription (1540/41)

Zion Gate (July 1540)

Mosque (1524)

Fountain (1536/37)

0   50   100   150   200   250 m.

0   50   100   150   200   250 yds.

Sinan Pasha (also called Koja Mimar, meaning the Great Architect), passed through Jerusalem on his way to Egypt, and it was he who built the Damascus Gate.

During this period, many religious buildings were renovated, as for example the central dome of the Dome of the Rock edifice. These renovations and the improvements in the water supply provided ameliorated facilities for those coming to pray on the Temple Mount.

As part of the reorganization of commerce in Jerusalem, new marketplaces were set up, and those still existing from Mamluk times were improved, as for example the Cotton Merchants Market. The city's commerce developed, especially the trade in spices. Various industries began to develop, such as the weaving of flax and the manufacture of soap, which used the oil produced in the area.

The improvement of the inhabitants' economic situation is described in contemporary writings. A Jewish document written soon after the Ottoman conquest refers to the rise in prices of goods in the markets, testifying to the improved standard of living of the city's population. Moses Basola, who visited Jerusalem in 1520, sang the city's praises when describing its pleasant houses and busy markets. Apparently his allegations of destruction and desolation referred mainly to the city's fortifications which had been demolished centuries earlier.

The changes in the life of Jerusalem's Jews during this period raised their hopes for a better future. An expression of this feeling is found in their reaction to an occurrence which caused excitement among the city's inhabitants. When the crescent above the Dome of the Rock keeled over on the Feast of Weeks festival (in 1520), they considered this to be a sign heralding the advent of the redemption.

Evidence of the improved situation of the inhabitants of Jerusalem at the beginning of the Ottoman period is found in the growth of the city's population as well. Proof of this is provided by the population censuses carried out by the Ottoman authorities for the purpose of the collection of taxes. (Four censuses were conducted between the years 1525 and 1563.) The Muslims constituted the largest community in the city, and from the beginning of the sixteenth century the Jewish community was the second largest.

Jerusalem under the Ottomans during the first half of the sixteenth century reached previously unprecedented heights. However, its prosperity within the Ottoman Empire was short-lived. Suleiman the Magnificent was succeeded by his son Selim II, and already during the period of his rule (1560–1574) the decline in the economic, social, cultural and political aspects of the empire was manifest. The cause was mainly his defeat in battle, and his inefficient methods of tax collection. This development was evident in Jerusalem as well, where the sewage and water systems were despoiled, the state of the roads deteriorated and the number of inhabitants declined.

The Ottoman administration was no longer concerned about the development and maintenance of the city. One of the reasons for this was the procedure whereby the governors of the city procured their positions of office, and during the course of their administration they used the monies collected in taxes to recoup their outlay as well as to make a profit. An extreme example of this was the actions of one of the despotic governors of Jerusalem, Ibn Farouk (a Mamluk of Circassian extraction who ruled the city between 1603 and 1625). He extorted monies from the inhabitants and as a result of the intervention of the Jewish community of Istanbul was dismissed from his position.

The city's deterioration is also reflected in the decline in the numbers of its inhabitants. The heavy burden imposed by the local rulers led to the reduction in numbers of Jerusalem's Jewish community, and already in 1578 there are records of complaints by Jews against governors who extorted monies from them, and of the deterioration of their economic situation. Jews abandoned the city and many moved to Safed, and by 1677 there were no more than fifteen thousand inhabitants in Jerusalem. Because

(top left) The **Fountain of Qasem Pasha,** an octagonal structure on one side of which is an installation for purification prior to prayers, and on the other a marble pool in the center of which is a fountain for washing the hands. The structure is covered with a broad lead-plated dome, in keeping with the Ottoman-style architecture on the Temple Mount.

According to the inscription on the western facade, the fountain was erected in 1527 by Qasem Pasha, a high official in the court of Suleiman the Magnificent and also Governor of Egypt.

Apparently this is one of the earliest Ottoman structures in Jerusalem. It was built prior to all the other fountains, even before the Turkish walls and gates of the city.

(center left) The **Inspector's Gate Fountain** situated at the intersection of Haggai Street and Allah ed-Din Street in the Old City. As in the five fountains erected by Suleiman the Magnificent, here too use has been made of architectural elements from the Crusader period. The main arches have been assembled from the adornments of a window or gate and brought here from an unknown site. The rosette and the inscription are Turkish. The inscription reads: "The command to erect this blessed fountain was given by our master the Sultan, the great king and illustrious ruler, ruler of peoples, the Sultan of Byzantium [the Turks], the Arabs and the Persians, the Sultan Suleiman son of the Sultan Selim Khan, and would that Allah perpetuate his kingdom and his sultanate, dated the second month of Ramadan in the year 943 [February 12, 1537]."

(bottom left) The **Gate of the Chain Fountain** built by the Sultan Suleiman the Magnificent. Crusader elements have been introduced into it. The embellished trough is actually a Crusader period sarcophagus transferred from an unknown site. The upper section of the prayer niche is adorned with a rosette, which is a beautiful example of Crusader stonecutting, and was apparently taken from an ancient church. In the center is a smaller rosette surrounded by small pillars, the bottom one having been removed to enable it to be adapted to the structure of the niche. The capitals of the pillars are sculptured in the characteristic style of twelfth-century Jerusalem.

The fountain received its waters from the aqueducts from Solomon's Pools. From the aqueducts the water ran through a pipe which passed along the Street of the Chain, and near the fountain there was a division so that most of the water went to the Temple Mount. Part was used for the Mamluk Tankiziyya building and the rest for the fountain. Few changes have been made to the fountain since it was built. The exquisite rosettes originally set on either side of the prayer niche have been removed and replaced by an inscription which reads: "The Muslim Waqf." The inscription inside the prayer niche is identical to those on the other fountains erected by Suleiman, except for the date of its construction— January 1537.

(above right) The **Citadel Gate** built by Suleiman the Magnificent as drawn by Wilson in 1864. The gate and the minaret are the most important elements of the Citadel remaining from the Ottoman period, during which the eastern section was renovated. The illustration depicts the gate at the extremity of

a drawbridge. This was attached to the Citadel's anterior fortification system. Turkish soldiers are seen guarding the entrance to the Citadel. The wooden drawbridge which can be seen in the background was removed in the Mandate period and replaced by the present concrete bridge. An inscription on the gate structure

praises Suleiman the Magnificent and states the date the Citadel was renovated—938 in the Hegira (1531/1532). Beneath this inscription is a plaque bearing passages from the Koran (verses 1-3 of sura 48). The inscription is written in Kufic square script, and is a very special example of Ottoman architecture in Jerusalem.

(right) The **Citadel** seen from the east, as drawn by E. Pierotti in 1864. The illustration depicts the Citadel as it appeared throughout the Ottoman period, even though there are a number of errors in the sketch.

The present-day Citadel is a mixture of structures from various eras, beginning from the Second Temple period. In the illustration we can see "David's Tower," whose lower section dates to Herodian times and is identified with the Hippicus Tower—one of the three towers built by Herod on this site. The majority of the structures seen here are from the end of the Middle Ages. From the end of the Crusader period (1187), up to the time when the Mamluk sultans were firmly entrenched, the Citadel was destroyed and rebuilt many times, and it is therefore impossible to accurately determine the period in which each building was constructed. The various stages of building which began during the rule of the Mamluk Sultan en-Nasir Muhammad Ibn Qalawun (he reigned a number of times during the years 1293-1341) can be discerned. The Citadel's external section, including the walls, is mainly Mamluk and the restoration is from the Ottoman period. Descriptions by a German pilgrim to Jerusalem at the end of the Mamluk period lead us to the conclusion that the Citadel was almost identical to the present-day structure, apart from the Turkish additions such as the minaret and the gate tower.

The gate tower built by Suleiman the Magnificent in 1531/1532 can be seen in the illustration. One can also see the bridge which passed over the inner moat and entered the Citadel gate, also built by this ruler. The original gate was apparently erected by the Sultan en-Nasir Muhammad Ibn Qalawun during the years 1310 to 1311. A wooden structure was erected above the entrance during the Ottoman period, but was removed by the British in the course of renovations of the Citadel. Some scholars believe that the lower section of the tower, to the left of the gate, dates to the Crusader period, but no proof of this has yet been produced. The upper sections of this tower shown in the illustration also probably date to the Mamluk period. The retaining walls in the foreground of the sketch, between the gate tower and the figures walking in front of it, have not been depicted accurately, although they are shown as they were from the Ottoman period down to the present.

of their impoverished situation, the remaining Jews were dependent upon aid from Jewish communities overseas. However, despite this situation, Jews continued to visit the city and some even settled there, reflecting their readiness to undertake the burden of heavy taxes and other hardships in order to enable them to live in the holy city. In the eighteenth century there was a considerable increase in the community's size, especially after the arrival in the year 1700 of Judah Hehasid and his followers. However, after his death, the group he headed became a burden on the already impoverished Jewish community.

The disintegration of the central government also had a detrimental effect on Jerusalem's Christian community, and already in 1522 there was evidence of the Ottoman authority's harassment of some of the city's Christian communities. The Franciscans were evicted from the Cenacle (Room of the Last Supper) on Mount Zion, and they were forced to seek an alternative center for their activities. They purchased the St. John Monastery from the Georgians in the northwest of the city, and in 1558 it was consecrated as the Church of St. Savior, which is still extant. The Franciscans' success in making this purchase was the result of pressure being brought to bear on the Georgians by the Ottoman authorities. During this period of recession, the situation of most of the Christian orders in the city declined,

reflected in the constant change of ownership of church property. Thus the Serbs were constrained to sell their Mar Saba monastery to the Greek Orthodox (1623), who also purchased property owned by the Georgians, including the Monastery of the Cross (1558). The Greek community succeeded in maintaining its status in the city as a result of its influence at the sultan's court. Pilgrims who visited the city during this period complained of the large sums demanded from them as payment for entrance to the city and for admission to the Church of the Holy Sepulcher and other holy sites, including some outside the city.

The weakness of the central administration led to a situation in Jerusalem, as in other cities in the country, whereby power was concentrated in the hands of a few local families holding government offices which were handed down from father to son. These were families such as the Nashashibis, the Husseinis, the Alamis, the Khalidis, and others.

Jerusalem ceased to develop in the mid-seventeenth century, and the Ottoman authorities did not initiate any new construction work during this period. The only building that did take place was renovation and repairs to buildings on the Temple Mount, carried out for purely religious reasons. The city was described as being a ghost town, depressing and filthy, many sections of it lying in ruins, its houses neglected and disintegrating.

Jerusalem in the Nineteenth Century: The City Comes to Life, 1830–1917

(above) **Jaffa Gate at the end of the nineteenth century.** During this period all the city gates were closed at sundown, except for Jaffa Gate which remained open. The military force which guarded it checked everyone entering or leaving through this gate. Near the gate, outside the city wall, was the station for carriages leaving for Jaffa, Bethlehem and Hebron.

The nineteenth century is the turning point in the history of Jerusalem. During this period, which lasted from the 1830s to the British conquest in 1917, Jerusalem underwent a major change. Its population grew eightfold and its Jewish community was twenty times greater than before. The city moved out from between the ancient walls and expanded to the north and west of the Old City. Impressive buildings were erected, and public and religious institutions were established. Its economy developed and transport and communications systems improved.

This transformation began with the conquest of Palestine by the Egyptians in 1831, which brought about a reformation in the administration, and the rights of the country's inhabitants. It was especially the non-Muslim citizens of the country who benefited from these changes as a result of the repeal of the regulations which had discriminated against them in relation to the Muslims. The Egyptians introduced these reforms in the attempt to win the support of the European powers, and in the desire to attain the cooperation of the local population. The Egyptian rulers annulled the administrative division of the country introduced by the Turks, and Jerusalem was granted a special status. A city council (*majlis*) was established, consisting of representatives of the local population. The non-Muslim communities were granted permission to build and renovate prayer houses, and thus during the years 1835 to 1836 the four Sephardic synagogues were renovated, the Menahem Zion synagogue was erected in the "Hurvah" compound, and Jews were allowed to pray at the Western Wall without obtaining prior permission to do so. During the period of Egyptian rule, there was an upsurge of building in the city, buildings on Mount Zion were restored and military barracks (the Kishleh) were erected beside the Citadel.

This process of change in the appearance of the city continued after the return of the Turks in 1840. During this period, known as the "Tanzimat period," the Sultan

Abdul Mejid issued two royal decrees introducing reforms in the administration and in citizens' rights: the *khatti sherif*, issued in 1839, and the *khatti humayun*, issued in 1856 in pursuance of the Paris agreement following the Crimean War. These decrees included regulations relating to the equal rights of non-Muslim citizens. They granted permission to foreign residents to purchase land, and guaranteed freedom of worship (and also the erection and renovation of houses of prayer). The special status of the consuls of foreign powers was enhanced. The new regulations (Capitulations) granted tax exemption to European nationals and guaranteed that litigation against them would not be held without the presence and full protection of the consular representatives of their countries. This status granted persons holding foreign citizenship the right to function anywhere throughout the Ottoman Empire. The majority of the Jews of Jerusalem came under the protection of the various consuls, and this enabled them to carry out activities in many areas within the city. Jerusalem was made into a special administrative unit (the *mutasarif* of Jerusalem) directly responsible to the central administration in Constantinople (from 1873).

Other factors that influenced the rapid changes that took place in the city was the opening of the Suez Canal and the resulting prosperity in the region. There were also improvements in the transport system, and increased settlement of Jews in the city.

Until the early 1860s, building activities were concentrated mainly within the city walls. However, the shortage of housing among the Jews, the importance of the holy places to the Christian communities, and the building opportunities that opened up at this time, were all factors leading to the founding of new neighborhoods and the erection of institutions outside the city walls. These building activities expanded greatly from the early 1860s until the outbreak of World War I, and changed the appearance of Jerusalem radically.

Christian construction within the confines of the Old City of Jerusalem was mainly concentrated in the vicinity of the Church of the Holy Sepulcher, the Via Dolorosa and the Armenian Quarter. The Church of the Holy Sepulcher underwent extensive renovation after the fire that broke out in the building in 1808. The various Christian orders purchased plots of land available for building surrounding the church and erected their own institutions. The greatest of these was the Church of the Redeemer, which was consecrated in an impressive ceremony in 1898 in the presence of the German Emperor Wilhelm II and his wife. The German Archaeological Institute and a hospice were erected close by. During this period, the Greek Orthodox Church built the Muristan Quarter, and opposite it the Russian Alexander Nievsky Church was constructed in 1887, upon archaeological remains discovered there.

Christian building activity took place along the length of the Via Dolorosa, and the majority of its churches were built or reconstructed during the nineteenth century. The first of these, the Church of the Flagellation, was built by the Franciscans in 1839. Other Christian buildings are the Sisters of Zion Convent (1868), the Church of St. Anne (renovated in 1860), the Greek Orthodox Praetorium and the Austrian Hospice (1856). In the mid-nineteenth century the consulates of the Western powers were concentrated in this area. On one side of the Armenian Quarter, a number of educational institutions were established, and on the other side, the Protestant Bishopric built the Christ Church, as well as the English Hospital and the Diocesan Sisters hospital. On Mount Zion, the Church of the Dormition was built and the Bishop Gobat School (1855). Within the Christian Quarter, the Latin Patriarchate complex was set up (1864) and nearby were the buildings erected by the Greek Church including a school, hospital, a shopping arcade, a hotel, the Spiridon Monastery, and the St. Spirito Monastery near the Damascus Gate.

The Jews concentrated their building projects mainly within the Jewish Quarter. They erected a number of syn-

agogues, the best known being the Hurvah of Rabbi Judah Hehasid (Beit Ya'akov, 1864), Doresh Zion (1857), Menahem Zion (1837), Tiferet Israel (Nisan Bak, 1872). Numerous educational institutions were founded, including yeshivas, the Laemel School (1856), and the Evelina de Rothschild School for Girls (1857). On the outskirts of the Jewish Quarter, the English Hospital was erected with the purpose of providing medical services for the Jewish inhabitants of the city. This led to the speeding up of the establishment of Jewish medical institutions. The first Jewish institution of this nature was a clinic opened by Dr. Frankel who had been

Development of the Built-up Area, Late Ottoman Period. Neighborhoods and Year of Establishment:

1. Beit Kerem Avraham (1855)
2. Bishop Gobat School (1855)
3. Russian Compound (1860)
4. English Hospital
5. Mahane Israel (1868)
6. Nahalat Shiv'a (1869)
7. Beit David (1873)
8. Mea She'arim (1874)
9. Even Israel (1875)

10. Mishkenot Israel (1875)
11. Kirya Ne'emana (Nisan Bak) (1875)
12. Beit Ya'akov (1877)
13. Mazkeret Moshe (1883)
14. Ohel Moshe (1883)
15. Beit Shmu'el (1884)
16. Mishkenot Hatemanim (1884)
17. Sha'arei Moshe (Batei Württemberg) (1885)
18. Ir Shalom (1887)
19. Nahalat Tzvi (1888)
20. Sha'arei Pina (1888)

21. Mahane Yehuda (1888)
22. Succat Shalom (1888)
23. Sha'arei Tzedek (1889)
24. Zichron Tuvya (1890)
25. Benei Moshe (1891)
26. Batei Ungarin (1891)
27. Knesset Israel "A" (1891)
28. Sha'arei Yerushalayim (1891)
29. Ohel Shlomo (1891)
30. Kerem Shlomo (1891)
31. Jorat el-Anab (1892)
32. Batei Milner (1892)
33. Kolel Horodna (1892)

34. Kolel Vilna (1892)
35. Ezrat Israel (1892)
36. Shevet Ahim (1892)
37. Eshel Avraham (1893)
38. Nahalat Zion (1893)
39. Kolel Warsaw (1894)
40. Even Yehoshua (1894)
41. Ohalei Simha (1894)
42. Neveh Shalom (1896)
43. Batei Minsk (1898)
44. Batei Yosef Ha'amerikai (1900)
45. Batei Werner (1902)
46. Batei Kronheimer (1902)

47. Batei Broida (Ohel Ya'akov, Knesset Hadasha) (1902)
48. Batei Jacobson (1902)
49. Batei Neitin (1903)
50. Hatzer Harav Miublin (1903)
51. Sha'araim (1903)
52. Zichron Moshe (1906)
53. Ahva (1906)
54. Batei Hornstein (Kolel Volyn) (1908)
55. Batei Rand (1910)
56. Batei Saidoff (1911)
57. Ethiopia Street

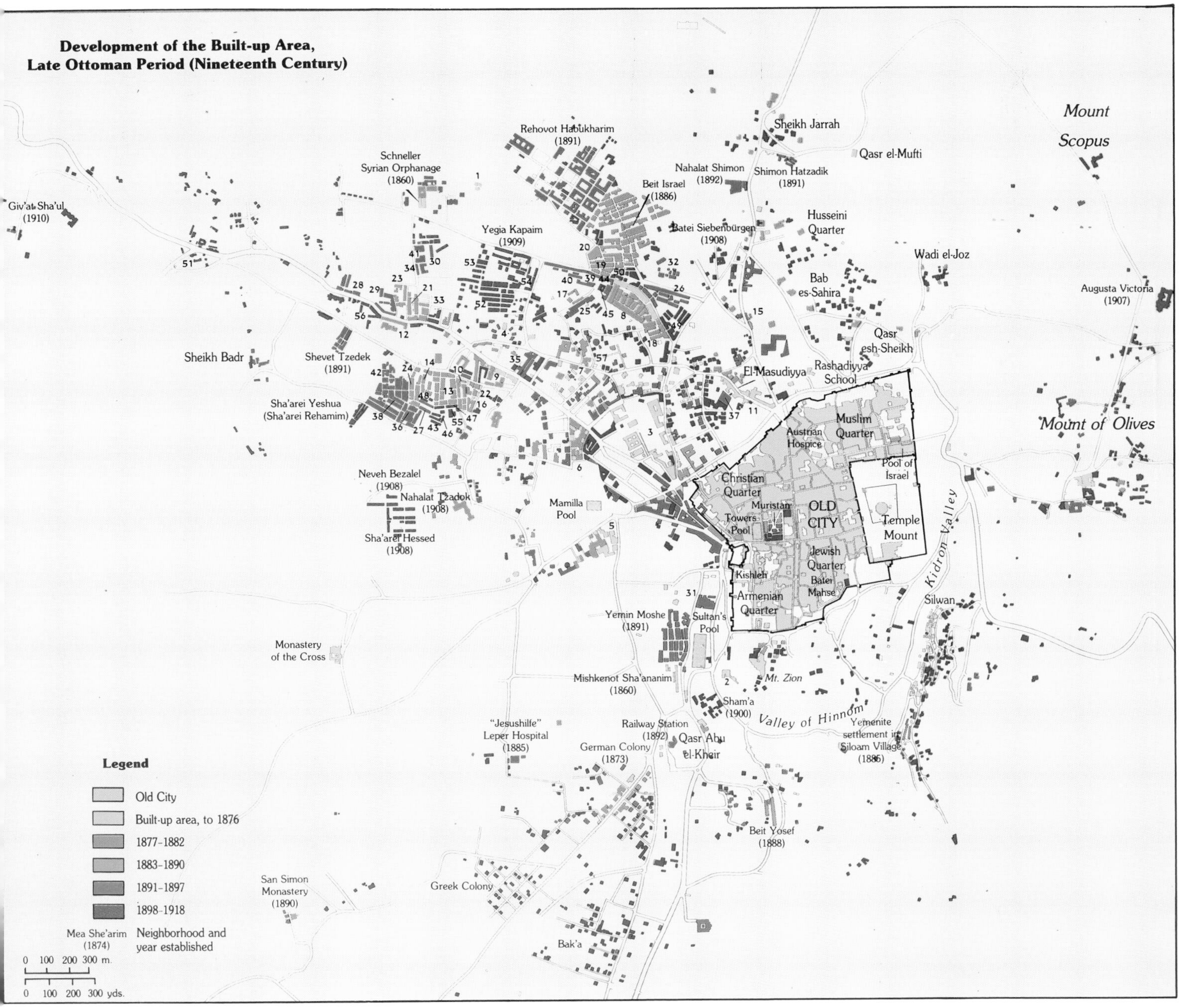

Development of the Built-up Area, Late Ottoman Period (Nineteenth Century)

Legend
- Old City
- Built-up area, to 1876
- 1877–1882
- 1883–1890
- 1891–1897
- 1898–1918

Mea She'arim (1874) Neighborhood and year established

0 100 200 300 m.

0 100 200 300 yds.

124

(left) **Map of the Mea She'arim neighborhood**, the main part of which was completed by 1881. The quarter was planned by the architect Conrad Schick, who created a wall by building a line of attached houses along the perimeter of the area. The protected inner section served for the erection of public buildings, a park and a courtyard which was the center of communal activities.

The adjacent neighborhoods of Batei Ungarin and Batei Neitin were built later, following a similar plan.

○ Well/cistern
▨ Residential area
□ Courtyard
▓ Balcony or vaulted pasageway, stairs

(below) **Gateway to Mea She'arim** built in 1875. The gateway, the wall, the courtyard and alley are typical of Jerusalem which throughout its long history has been an Oriental city whose internal security was precarious, and ruled by an unstable regime. These manifestations were also evident in the first neighborhoods built outside the city walls.

sent to Jerusalem by Moses Montefiore with the intention of providing alternative services to those given by the Anglican mission. In 1845, the Rothschild Hospital was opened, and in 1857 the Bikur Holim Hospital was founded. Later, the Misgav Ladach hospital was built to serve the needs of the inhabitants of the Jewish Quarter, where it functioned as the only hospital until the surrender of the quarter in May 1948. In an effort to alleviate the housing problem, the Kolel "Hod" (an association of immigrants from Holland and Germany) set up a housing project called Batei Mahse (1860) in the southeast corner of the Jewish Quarter. This quarter expanded to the north into the Muslim Quarter in the vicinity of the Temple Mount. Jewish families resided in the Bab el-Hitta area, in Hebron Road and in Ma'alot Hamadrasa Street. They built synagogues, opened yeshivas and other institutions, such as a printing press and the offices of the Hebrew periodical *Havazzelet*.

One of the important processes that began in Jerusalem during the nineteenth century, and which brought about a radical change in its appearance, was the move outside the city walls. The modifications to the Ottoman laws enabling residents who were not Turkish citizens to make land purchases, the improvement in the economic situation, and the overcrowding in the city's housing were all factors in this process which dominated the development of the city during this period and culminated in the building of the "New City."

Building outside the city walls began in the early 1850s. The first building to be erected apparently was built by the British consul, James Finn, as a summer house on the hill of Talbieh, and he was followed by Bishop Gobat, who built the Protestant school on Mount Zion. In that year, Consul Finn built Beit Kerem Avraham (now 24 Ovadiah Street), which became the Finn residence. Orchards were planted on the grounds of this house, and this became a source of income for some Jews. Nearby, Johann Ludwig Schneller built the Syrian Orphanage (1860). In 1857, the Palestine Pravoslavic Society purchased a plot of land near the northwest corner of the city wall, and in 1860 began to build a complex which included a church, a hospital, hostels and buildings to house religious and consular missions. This complex is called the "Russian Compound."

The paving of the Jaffa–Jerusalem road, the opening of the Suez Canal in 1869, the improvement of maritime communications, and facilities for steamships to call at Palestine ports, especially Jaffa, brought Jerusalem closer to Europe. Eminent personalities visited the city, such as the Emperor Franz Josef in 1869. Members of the Templer Order settled in the south of the city and established a small neighborhood, called the "German Colony" (1872). The colony was situated on both sides of a main road, and its houses were surrounded by fruit trees and well-kept gardens. The Christians also built houses along the road that ran from the northwestern corner

of the city wall past the Russian Compound and along the Street of the Prophets (Hanevi'im). One of the best known buildings in the city was the German Talitha Kumi School for Girls (1861). The Pater Noster Church was erected on the Mount of Olives in 1868, and in 1876 construction of the Ratisbon Monastery was begun in 1876. Many private residences were built outside the walls, including that of the British consul in the upper part of Jaffa Road (the present-day Mahane Yehuda Police Station).

Construction of Jewish building mainly for living accommodation was begun at about the same time. During his fourth visit to Palestine, Moses Montefiore purchased land on a hill in the western part of the city with the intention of building a hospital there. However, this plan was not carried out, and instead in 1860 the Mishekenot Sha'ananim neighborhood was built, with a windmill to provide a livelihood for the inhabitants. This was the first residential quarter built outside the city walls. Jewish building increased apace toward the end of the 1860s. In 1867, Rabbi David Ben-Shimon ("Davash") purchased a plot of land near the Mamilla Pool, and erected housing units for impoverished members of the North African community—the neighborhood was called Mahane Israel. In 1869 seven members of the Ashkenazic community purchased land upon which they built the Nahalat Shiv'a neighborhood. A Jewish philanthropist, David Reiss, provided the funds for the establishment of the Beit David neighborhood (1873).

In 1874 the construction of the Mea She'arim neighborhood was begun. The group setting up this quarter introduced new methods of organization, which were emulated by the majority of neighborhoods founded later. This included prior registration by persons wishing to join the project. Purchase of land and the building of housing units was to be financed by the residents themselves (members of the Ashkenazic community). Monies collected during the course of the year were to be used for the construction of additional units for which lots would be drawn by persons registered for the project. The neighborhood was to be run by an elected committee which would include residents as well as public figures. A constitution was drawn up, which included the detailed plan of the neighborhood, regulations applying to relations between the residents, allocation of the housing units and methods of organization. Emphasis was placed on the allocation of land for parks, public amenities such as synagogues, a yeshiva, water cisterns, a bathhouse, an oven to serve the inhabitants and accommodation for visitors. Some of the original plans were altered as the situation required. As a result of the pressure of the demand for additional housing by candidates wishing to dwell in the neighborhood, houses were often constructed on sections originally intended as open spaces. Building societies, such as that which established Mea She'arim, provided an expedient

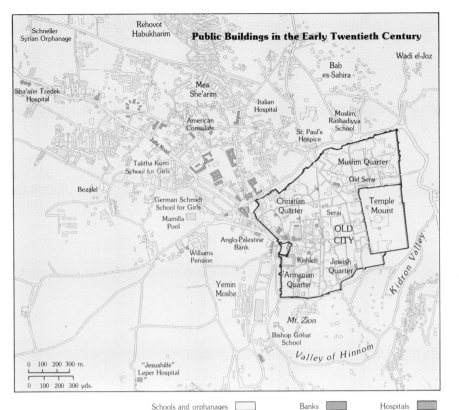

Public Buildings in the Early Twentieth Century

Schneller Syrian Orphanage · Rehovot Habukharim · Wadi el-Joz · Bab es-Sahira · Mea She'arim · Italian Hospital · Sha'arei Tzedek Hospital · Muslim Rashadiyya School · American Consulate · St. Paul's Hospice · Muslim Quarter · Old Serai · Talitha Kumi School for Girls · Bezalel · Christian Quarter · Serai · Temple Mount · German Schmidt School for Girls · Mamilla Pool · OLD CITY · Anglo-Palestine Bank · Williams Pension · Kishleh · Jewish Quarter · Kidron Valley · Yemin Moshe · Armenian Quarter · Mt. Zion · Bishop Gobat School · Valley of Hinnom · "Jesushilfe" Leper Hospital · Jaffa Road

0 100 200 300 m.
0 100 200 300 yds.

Schools and orphanages · Banks · Hospitals
Christian schools and orphanages · Post offices · Pharmacies
Government institutions · Consulates · Hotels

solution for the purchase of living accommodation on easy terms. The establishment of Mea She'arim was followed by an upsurge of construction of residential neighborhoods, and during the next two years four housing estates were built along Jaffa Road and another near Damascus Gate.

In 1877, the neighborhood building projects faced a crisis. The initial cause was the Russo-Turkish war, and then later the objections voiced by overseas donors to the distribution monies being "wasted" on the construction of housing estates. As a consequence, construction work was slowed down, and in a number of areas it ceased completely.

At the beginning of the 1880s building recommenced. The Mazkeret Moses Fund assisted in the construction of nine new Jewish neighborhoods and in the renewal of building in existing neighborhoods. Housing was provided for the Yemenite community which arrived in Jerusalem in 1882, in the Mishkenot Israel neighborhood founded in the village of Silwan, and Nahalat Tzvi (1881) was built near Mea She'arim. During this period, a number of commercial companies were established for the purchase of land and the construction of housing units which were sold at a profit to Jewish residents of the city. The neighborhoods of Beit Yosef (1868), Batei Perlman (Ya'ar Shalom, 1887) and Mahane Yehuda (1888) are examples of this type of neighborhood.

A second center of Jewish life began to be created in the "New City" of Jerusalem, which included educational institutions as well as hospitals, some of which were transferred from the Old City. In the 1890s, the number of Jewish neighborhoods was doubled, notwithstanding the financial problems resulting from crises faced by some banks, and despite the administrative difficulties imposed by the Ottoman authorities. Each quarter in the New City developed its own peculiar characteristics. The Jewish neighborhoods and institutions developed around Mea She'arim and the upper part of Jaffa Road. The Street of the Prophets became the "European Center," containing churches, hospitals, consulates, Christian schools and homes of intellectuals of all religions.

The Muslims began to build to the north of the Old City, opposite Herod's Gate and Damascus Gate, and the

Jaffa Gate area became a center of commerce. The existing markets of the Old City expanded and almost reached the city gate. Hotels (the Grand and the New Hotel) were built inside the gate and along Jaffa Road (Fast Hotel and others). Banks were also established in this area of closely built commercial buildings.

The municipal buildings, the Turkish post and telegraph services and the other foreign postal services were concentrated in the area from Jaffa Gate to the vicinity of the Russian Compound. Photographic studios, souvenir shops and workshops opened in the vicinity. During the first decade of the twentieth century, a number of new neighborhoods sprung up on the outskirts of the existing ones.

At the end of the nineteenth century and the beginning of the twentieth, the neighborhoods began to develop along community lines. The Christians built mainly churches and monasteries. These buildings were beautifully constructed in European style, and manifested the wealth and power at the disposal of these communities. Their buildings were monumental, and were concentrated around the Old City as well as at sites held holy by their religion, such as Mount Zion and the Mount of Olives. The Christian population increased from 3,000 at the beginning of the period to about 13,000 on the eve of World War I. Apart from the German Colony and the tiny American Colony, no Christian neighborhoods were established outside the city walls.

The Muslim community increased during this period from about 4,000 at the beginning of the nineteenth century to about 12,000. Muslim building works were centered around the north of the Old City, in the vicinity of Herod's Gate up to Sheikh Jarrah. Their buildings spread over a wide area, and they built mainly elaborate villas, richly adorned in oriental fashion. In the course of time, these houses were formed into spacious neighborhoods.

The Jewish population grew from about 2,000 at the beginning of the nineteenth century to about 45,000 at the end of the Ottoman period. This vast increase was expressed in the construction of extensive and closely packed living quarters, in inexpensive, functional and nonluxurious buildings. About 30,000 Jews inhabited the New City prior to the outbreak of World War I. They lived in densely built apartment blocks, most of which were established to the north of the Old City because the land was more suitable for building and was cheaper than those plots nearer the city wall on which the Christians erected their buildings.

The Jewish neighborhoods existed in two large blocks. The Mea She'arim block was concentrated around the Mea She'arim neighborhood, and extended northward to the end of the Bukharan Quarter. The Jaffa Road block extended westward from the Even Israel neighborhood up to the old Sha'arei Tzedek hospital. In the course of time, the space between the two blocks was built up, and they fused into a single block. Other neighborhoods were spread throughout the city, ranging from the Yemenite quarter in the village of Silwan, to Beit Yosef in Abu Tor and as far as Shimon Hatzadik in the north. Certain neighborhoods were inhabited by members of specific Jewish communities only, while others had a mixed Jewish population, but each quarter had its own particular character and lifestyle.

There was a great improvement in the sanitation system in the New City. The streets were wide and clean, and large water cisterns were built in the neighborhoods. Regulations were laid down for the keeping of order and cleanliness.

The second half of the nineteenth century brought technological innovations in various fields. The main route between Jerusalem and Jaffa, which passed through Sha'ar Haggai, could not carry wagons and carriages until the 1860s. The journey was fraught with danger and took some sixteen hours, with an overnight stay on the way. With the opening of the Suez Canal in 1869, and in preparation for the visit of the Austrian Emperor Franz Josef, the sultan ordered that a road be built between Jerusalem and Jaffa. The time required for the journey was reduced to ten hours, but was still physically exhausting. In 1878 public transport was introduced for the first time. With the laying of a railway line between Jaffa and Jerusalem (in 1892), the journey was now reduced to four hours, and stiff competition was created between the carriages and the trains. As a result, the prices of the journey by carriage were reduced, the conditions of travel improved, and attempts were made to reduce the traveling time by changing horses midway at Sha'ar Haggai. The improvement of the connection between Jerusalem and the coastal plain made traveling for pilgrims and tourists to Jerusalem more attractive. Inside the city itself, the streets between the Old City and the outlying neighborhoods were paved.

The use of kerosene was introduced in the 1860s and glass-covered street lamps were placed in a number of main streets in Jerusalem. During the 1920s, a number of the city's institutions began to use electricity for lighting.

The postal services which were dependent upon the transport facilities available were also improved. This was the result of competition between the various postal services introduced into the country, and the inefficient Turkish mail that existed in Jerusalem in the 1830s. The first of these was the courier service introduced by the Anglican mission. However, the first modern postal service in Jerusalem was inaugurated by the Austrians in the early 1850s and was based on the connection with an office in Jaffa which collected sacks of mail from the steamships calling at the port. Other postal services were opened by the Germans, Italians, French and Russians. Both Jews and Christians used the various postal services to maintain contacts with their brethren overseas. The Jewish communities in Europe took advantage of these services to transfer monies for the support of the Jews of Jerusalem. In 1865, the first telegraph connection was set up between Jerusalem and Beirut, and from there via Constantinople to the countries of Europe.

Modernization, increased economic development, and land and sea communications with Europe expanded the possibilities of employment for the city's inhabitants. In addition to the usual trades—tailoring, shoemaking, carpentry, tinsmithing, goldsmiths and silversmiths, as well as the manufacture of quilts and mattresses—new areas were opened up. A number of printing shops were opened, the most well-known being the "Havazzelet," and a few score Jews were employed in this trade. The building trade and stonecutting were learned from European craftsmen, and this became an important section of the economy. The tourist trade was a source of income for many inhabitants of the city who provided services to the thousands of pilgrims and tourists who visited Jerusalem. A number of hotels were opened in the vicinity of Jaffa Gate and in other parts of the city, such as the Kamenitz Hotel in the Street of the Prophets. The manufacture of souvenirs developed apace, and Jewish artisans working in stone and wood entered the field previously dominated by Christian craftsmen. They opened workshops for the production of ornaments made of shell, olive wood, lace and copper.

The Templers who were expert in many fields—carpenters, blacksmiths, gardeners, metalworkers and locksmiths—brought technological innovations in the field of mechanization and made a valuable contribution to the development of crafts in the city.

Toward the end of the nineteenth century a number of Jewish workshops existed in Jerusalem for weaving, dyeing of fabrics, metal casting, and the production of floor and roof tiles. There were also schools for training artisans, such as the Alliance Israélite Universelle and Bezalel, and crafts were also taught in the Ezra schools and the Laemel School.

The most explicit expression of the city's economic development was the large number of banks that opened in Jerusalem during this period. The most well-known were the Valero Bank, which also represented the interests in Jerusalem of the German emperor; the Hamburger Bank, which handled the monies of the *kolels*; and the Bergheim Bank, belonging to the apostate Bergheim family, which provided credit and was involved in industry. After the crash of the private banks at the end of the 1890s, a number of

(opposite above) **Jerusalem stonemasons** and porters helping them move the finished product.

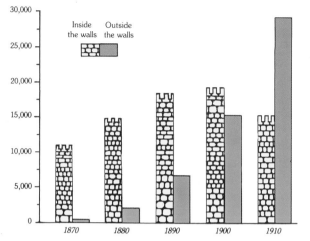
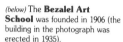

(left) **Population of Jerusalem inside/outside the city walls, 1870–1910.**

(below) The **Bezalel Art School** was founded in 1906 (the building in the photograph was erected in 1935).

international banks opened branches in Jerusalem. These included the German-Palestine Bank (1897), the French Crédite Lyonnais Bank (1900) and the Anglo-Palestine Bank (1902). In 1905, the Royal Ottoman Bank opened a branch in Jerusalem.

In the 1870s, the Jews constituted a majority in Jerusalem. The enhancement of Jewish settlement in the northwest sections of the city determined its character for generations to come. The Mea She'arim and the Street of the Prophets area, for example, developed at this time the character it still maintains to this day. On the other hand, the Old City has undergone very little change from the end of the nineteenth century until the present. Modernization and improvement in transport and communications have reflected the transformation that has taken place in the city during the nineteenth century.

The First World War and the consequent famine that struck the city, and the attempts on the part of the Turks to recruit the inhabitants for their army, reduced the population to a certain degree. The war years were particularly difficult from the material aspect. The Turks were extremely harsh on the population, and the contact with Europe was severed.

The conquest of Jerusalem by the British troops on December 9, 1917, brought this period to a close.

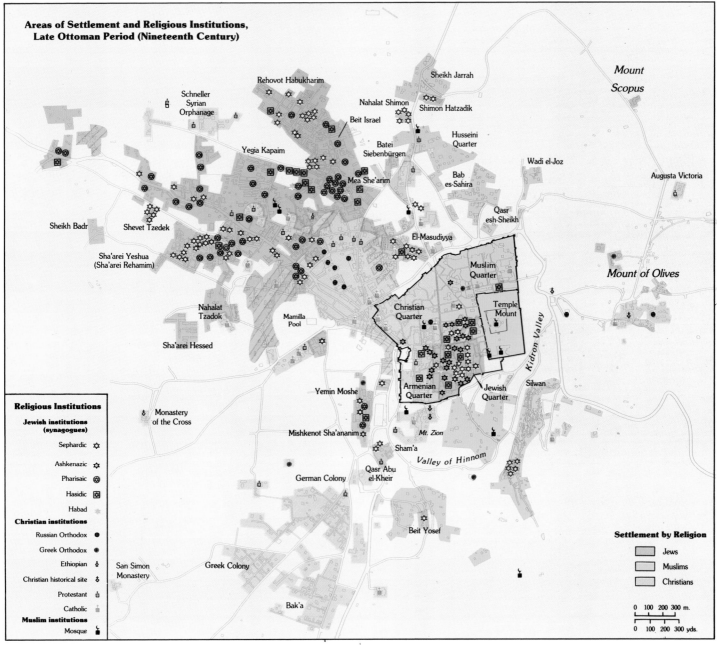

Areas of Settlement and Religious Institutions, Late Ottoman Period (Nineteenth Century)

The British Mandate
1917 – 1948

The conquest of Palestine by British forces in 1917 and the mandate granted Britain in 1920 opened the "modern era" in the history of the country. Jerusalem became the seat of government and benefited greatly from this change in its status. The city expanded as a result of the intensive building that took place during the 1920s and 1930s. The water supply was augmented and electricity brought to it. New buildings housing a host of institutions lined the streets. The concentration of the British Government departments and the offices of the Executive of the World Zionist Organization in Jerusalem formulated the city's economic and municipal character. Attention was now given to municipal planning, and to the preservation of the architectural features pertaining to its status as the city holy to a number of religions. Jerusalem's cosmopolitan population constituted the basis for political processes and tension between peoples who left their mark on it during this period.

The British Conquest

In the course of World War I, after having crossed the Gaza–Beersheba line, the British troops rapidly moved northward and on November 16, 1917, they reached the Yarkon

(below) **British monument** erected in Romema on the site the last Turkish mayor of Jerusalem, Hussein Selim el-Husseini, handed over the flag of surrender to the British commander. The inscription in English reads: "Near this spot the Holy City was surrendered to the 60th London Division, 9th December 1917. Erected by their comrades to those officers, N.C.O.s and men who fell in fighting for Jerusalem."

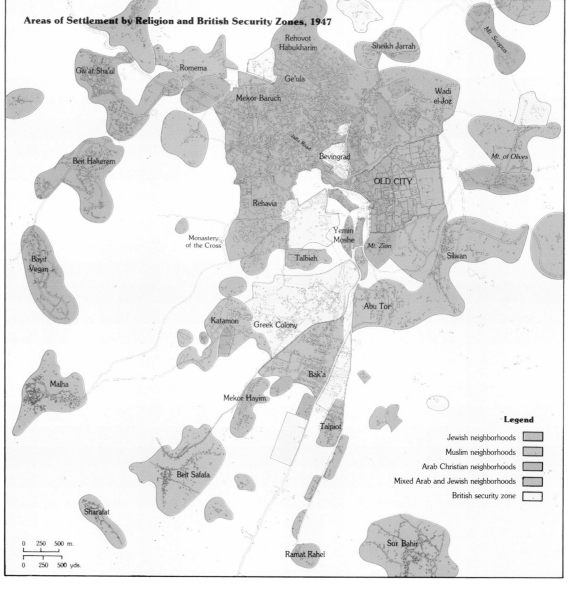

Areas of Settlement by Religion and British Security Zones, 1947

Mt. Scopus

Rehovot Habukharim

Sheikh Jarrah

Giv'at Sha'ul

Romema

Ge'ula

Wadi el-Joz

Mekor Baruch

Jaffa Road

Bevingrad

Mt. of Olives

Beit Hakerem

OLD CITY

Rehavia

Yemin Moshe

Monastery of the Cross

Mt. Zion

Silwan

Bayit Vegan

Talbieh

Abu Tor

Katamon

Greek Colony

Bak'a

Malha

Mekor Hayim

Talpiot

Legend

Jewish neighborhoods	
Muslim neighborhoods	
Arab Christian neighborhoods	
Mixed Arab and Jewish neighborhoods	
British security zone	

Beit Safafa

Sharafat

Sur Bahir

Ramat Rahel

0   250   500 m.

0   250   500 yds.

(left) **General Allenby** addressing representatives of the local population from the steps of the entrance to the Citadel.

(below) **Map showing Allenby's campaign of the capture of Jerusalem**, December 8–9, 1917.

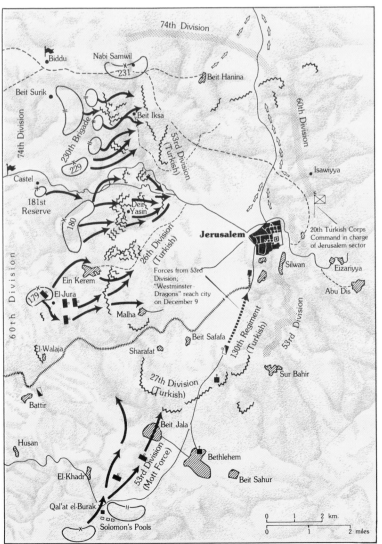

Consolidation of British forces after the city's capture

→ Assault routes, December 8

▸ Penetration of first organized British forces into Jerusalem

⇨ ⇨ Withdrawal of Turks

◯ Area of formation or initial gathering of troops

× Brigade

River. While the Turks were trying to gather their forces which were in disarray, General Allenby decided to exploit his advantage and move toward Jerusalem.

The attack was mounted by the 21st Corps, in three divisional spearheads which fanned out from the Jaffa-Jerusalem road to Ma'aleh Beit Horon. An additional division (the ANZACs) set up a defense line on the plain in order to secure the main communication lines. The British encountered resistance from the Turkish Seventh Army which was defending Jerusalem. It was also impeded by the inclement winter weather. On November 29, the British corps halted north of Jerusalem along the Nabi Samwil-Kiryat Anavim line.

After the attack on el-Jib failed, the 21st Corps was replaced by the 22nd which succeeded in capturing Beit Iksa–Deir Yasin–Beit Masmil, and on December 8 attacked Jerusalem along a broad front (see map on this page). During the night, the Turks fled from the city and on the following day, the mayor surrendered to General Shay, commander of the 60th Division. On December 9, the British advanced and took up positions east of the city, along the Tell el-Ful–Mount Scopus–Mount of Olives–Jebel el-Mukaber ridge. On December 28, after a counterattack had been rebutted, the British moved to the north and the new frontier was relocated to the north of Ramallah.

On December 11, 1917, General Allenby entered Jerusalem through the Jaffa Gate and received the formal surrender in front of a large gathering. In his address, General Allenby stated that the status quo in Jerusalem would be maintained and that martial law would be enforced in British-occupied territory.

The British set up a military government in the occupied territory called the "Administration of the Occupied Territories in the South," which governed the country up to the time the civil administration took over in July 1920. Because of the importance of Jerusalem, a military governor was appointed for the city, Colonel Ronald Storrs, and in summer 1919 military headquarters moved to the Augusta Victoria building on Mount Scopus. When the British troops entered the city they found a shortage of food and other essentials, and immediately set about bringing in food and vital goods, improving the municipal services, setting up a basis for the economy and finding means of livelihood for the poor. One of Colonel Storrs' first acts was to publish an ordinance forbidding structural changes—construction or demolition of buildings—within a radius of 2,730 yards (2,500 meters) of the Damascus Gate, and the construction of buildings not faced with stone within the city limits. This led to the preservation of the city's appearance up to this day. In March 1918, the city engineer of Alexandria, W. H. MacLean, was appointed to draw up the first master town plan for Jerusalem.

The military forces spread out through the city. In Talpiot there was a landing strip for the planes of the Royal Air Force. A field hospital was organized in the Ratisbon Monastery and the city's military administration set up offices in the Schmidt College building, opposite Damascus Gate. A railway line was laid from the Jerusalem railway station to the front lines at Ramallah.

On July 1, 1920, the military government was handed over to a civil administration headed by a British high commissioner who served as both the legislative and executive arm of the government. The first high commissioner was Sir Herbert Samuel, who set up residence in Jerusalem, in the building of the German hospice, Augusta Victoria, on Mount

Scopus. With the transfer of the center of government to Jerusalem, the city became the functional capital of Palestine. The commands of the army and the police were based there, and it became the seat of the supreme court. From November 1926, Jerusalem was part of a special district which included Ramallah, Bethlehem and Jericho. The only administrative area common to both the Jews and Arabs in Jerusalem was the municipal authority.

Administration of the City During the Mandate

With the conquest of the city by the British, the Turkish city council ceased to function, and the military governor appointed a council consisting of six members—two from each religious community—headed by the outgoing mayor, Hussein Selim el-Husseini. Upon his death, Hussein el-Husseini was replaced by his brother Musa Kazim el-Husseini. However, the latter was dismissed by Storrs for engaging in political activity. He was replaced by Raghib Nashashibi, who filled the position until 1927.

The municipality was responsible for the smooth running of the city's commerce, the cleanliness of its streets and the general welfare of the public. Storrs founded the Pro-Jerusalem Society to serve as an advisory body to the municipality and an instrument for collecting funds on behalf of the city. In April 1927, the first municipal elections were held. A Muslim mayor, and two deputies, a Jew and a Christian, were elected by all the Jewish votes, a majority of Christian votes and half the Muslim votes. The political tension between the Jews and Arabs, which welled up during the riots in the 1930s, was evident in the administration of the city. The Jews demanded that the Jewish majority should be reflected in the number of representatives it had in the administration. Their demand was granted only partially, when it was agreed that the Jewish deputy mayor would be the senior functionary.

From March 1930 to summer 1945, the municipality (or later the city council) functioned only sporadically. During this period the British high commissioner and the represen-

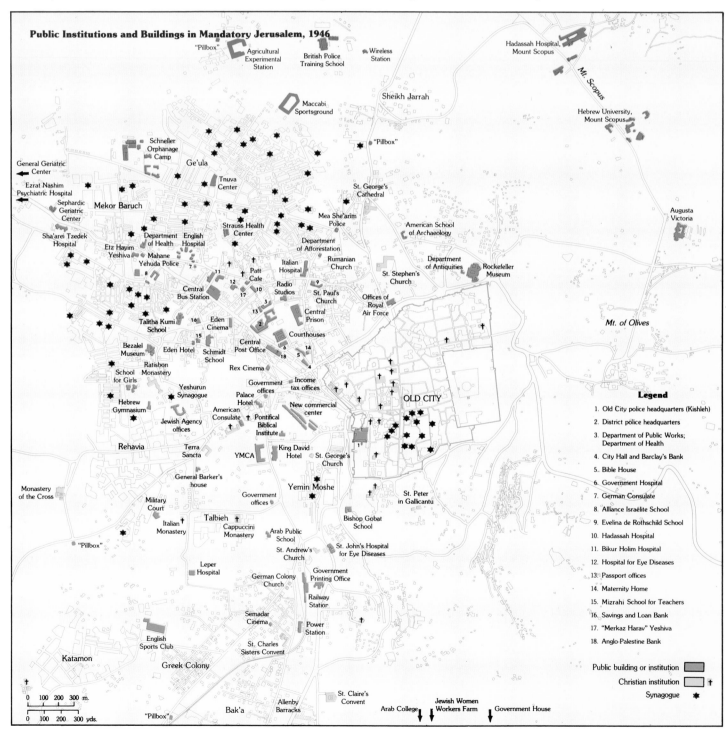

Public Institutions and Buildings in Mandatory Jerusalem, 1946

Legend

1. Old City police headquarters (Kishleh)
2. District police headquarters
3. Department of Public Works; Department of Health
4. City Hall and Barclay's Bank
5. Bible House
6. Government Hospital
7. German Consulate
8. Alliance Israélite School
9. Evelina de Rothschild School
10. Hadassah Hospital
11. Bikur Holim Hospital
12. Hospital for Eye Diseases
13. Passport offices
14. Maternity Home
15. Mizrahi School for Teachers
16. Savings and Loan Bank
17. "Merkaz Harav" Yeshiva
18. Anglo-Palestine Bank

Public building or institution
Christian institution
Synagogue

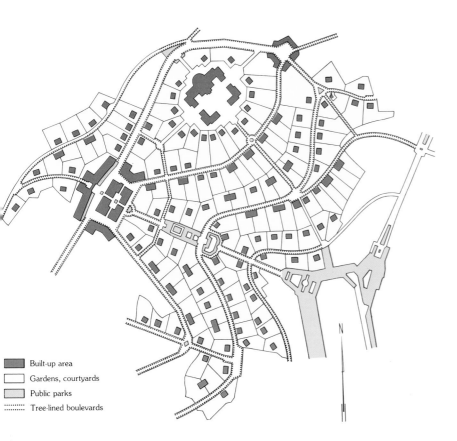

■	Built-up area
□	Gardens, courtyards
▨	Public parks
⋯⋯⋯	Tree-lined boulevards

(above) The neighborhood of **Beit Hakerem**, a good example of the garden suburbs built during the British Mandate period, and planned by R. Kaufmann. Other garden suburbs of this type were Talpiot, Rehavia, Bayit Vegan and Kiryat Moshe. The school, the neighborhood's most important institution, was placed at its highest spot. On the second highest point, at the end of the park area, the synagogue was built.

tatives of the various communities held ongoing discussions, under constant intercommunal political tension, which prevented them from cooperating in the running of the city. Throughout this entire period, elections were held only once (in 1934).

At the beginning of summer 1945, the British High Commissioner Lord Gort announced the termination of the city council's term of office and the appointment of a (British) ad hoc committee to run the city's affairs, which functioned up to the end of the mandate (1948). He also appointed an enquiry committee to examine Jerusalem's administrative problems.

Urban Planning

The British drew up a number of master plans for Jerusalem, and in all of them the historical significance of the city to the three religions was stressed. The town planners also considered the Old City as the focal point of their work, desiring to preserve its special character through placing limitation on the height and style of the buildings to be constructed, and through the allocation of open areas in the city and its environs.

The municipal building regulations remained in force after the establishment of the state of Israel until the Planning and Building Law was passed in the Knesset in 1966. The building regulations in Jerusalem ensured that construction would remain within the confines of the city's master plan. It was only after the Mandate civil administration took power that the Land Registry Office was opened (October 1920) and the Urban Building Regulations for Palestine were issued. In February 1921, a municipal committee for planning and construction was set up, and every building plan, or plan for the establishment of a new neighborhood, was required to be submitted to it for approval.

In 1918, the architect W. H. MacLean submitted the first master town plan for Jerusalem designed to provide a legal framework for the city's development. The direction of this development was mainly to the west. In the course of time, further master plans were submitted by P. Geddes, C. R. Ashby and C. Holliday. Following a basic survey of various aspects of the city, Holliday's town plan was submitted in 1944 (at the height of World War II), and was the most detailed

and most professional of all the master plans for Jerusalem. The plan stressed the city's topographical contours and their effect on its skyline. The valleys were to be devoted to parks and the mountain ridges to building, ideas which were put into practice by Israeli planners in years to come. This town plan had a profound effect on the town planning and Jerusalem's development from the mid-twentieth century. It was used by the Israeli planners as well as by the Jordanians, since Holliday served as town planning consultant to the Jordanian government after 1948.

Development of the Built-Up Area

During the Mandate period, the built-up area of Jerusalem grew fourfold, and there was a threefold increase in the population. During the 1920s, the construction of new neighborhoods extended beyond the built-up areas that existed before World War I. Building was also begun in the areas between the existing neighborhood blocks, as for example between Katamon and Sha'arei Hessed and between Zichron Moshe and the Bukharan Quarter. The houses were mainly one-family structures.

In the 1930s, building was mainly concentrated in the vicinity of the city center and the commercial center in the triangle constituted by Jaffa–Ben-Yehuda–King George Streets. Buildings with five or more storeys were erected despite the municipal regulation limiting buildings in residential areas to three storeys and in commercial areas to four.

The building regulations required buildings to be constructed from stone or faced with stone, but in some of the neighborhoods beyond the municipal boundary (Talpiot, Mekor Hayim, Beit Hakerem, and others) permission was granted for the use of bricks or to be finished in sprayed plaster. Between the 1936 riots and the War of Independence there was a lull in building, both because of the unstable security situation and because building came to a standstill during World War II. The building that did take place was mainly in the Arab quarters of Bak'a and Katamon, and in the southern sections of Rehavia, Kiryat Shmu'el and Merhavia.

The major building thrust took place during the first decade of the British Mandate. A number of new neighborhoods were established in the north of the city, and houses were added to existing ones, especially in Mea She'arim, Batei Warsaw and Beit Israel. The Romema neighborhood was built near the Allenby monument in 1921, and the city's water reservoir was constructed nearby (see below). Private Muslim building was concentrated mainly north of the Old City, as it was in the Ottoman period. Sheikh Jarrah, Wadi el-Joz, Bab es-Sahira and the American Colony were built in this period. In the city center, Ben-Yehuda and King George Streets were paved, and the Palestine Land Development Corporation planned and constructed high-rise buildings with a row of shops in this area. The open spaces between Nahalat Tzadok and Sha'arei Hessed were soon built up to relieve the congestion of these neighborhoods populated in the main by members of the Oriental communities. The Sha'arei Hessed and Knesset Israel neighborhoods, which had been constructed during the last years of the Ottoman period, expanded greatly.

On the outskirts of the city, neighborhoods of a new type were established. These were the "garden suburbs" designed by the architect Richard Kaufmann. They were based on the principle of building beyond the city center, with plenty of open spaces, each housing unit being allocated a plot on which to build a single-storey house surrounded by a garden. The public areas were designed as parks with public amenities in its center, such as a synagogue, community hall, and so on. The garden suburbs developed a character of their own, and the neighborhood committees carefully supervised the planning and quality of the building. The first of these garden suburbs was Talpiot. The land was bought by the Palestine Land Development Corporation for officials of the Anglo-Palestine Bank, and a settlers' committee was set up to supervise the construction.

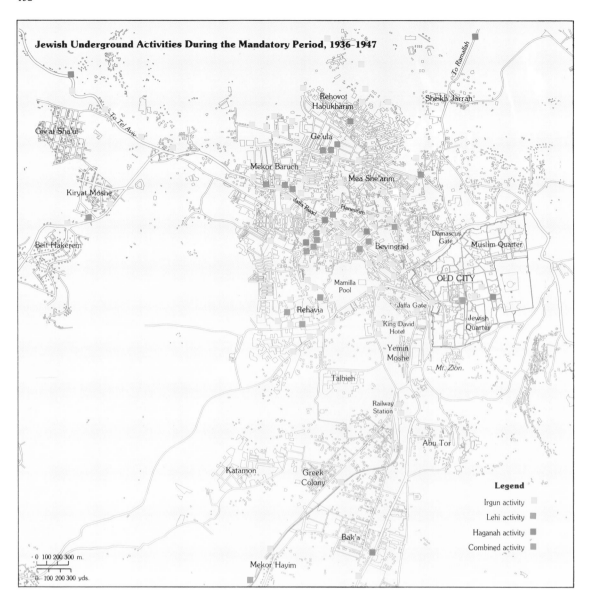

Jewish Underground Activities During the Mandatory Period, 1936–1947

Legend
Irgun activity
Lehi activity
Haganah activity
Combined activity

(below) **The Rockefeller Museum** was built opposite the northeast corner of the city wall by the British Mandatory government, with funds donated by the American millionaire John D. Rockefeller, Jr. The building was designed by the architect A. Harrison to house the museum and the offices of the British Mandatory Government Department of Antiquities which was established in 1920. Construction was begun in 1930, and the museum was opened officially in 1938.

On lands acquired by the Palestine Land Development Corporation from the Greek Orthodox Church, a commercial center was built on Ben-Yehuda Street and nearby, and on the Janzariyya land the first houses of Rehavia went up in 1924 and was populated by many of the leaders of Jerusalem's Jewish community. A mutual society supervised the building, but as this was a private venture, the construction was determined by the means at the disposal of the owner of each plot of land. The neighborhood was built within the Jerusalem city limits and thus was subject to its building regulations. It soon benefited from the city's municipal services, and Mamilla Street was extended to within the neighborhood (present-day Ramban Street). Rehavia was joined to the city water system (electricity was received from the nearby Ratisbon Monastery). The neighborhood was completed in 1930 and the construction of Rehavia "B" was begun (between Ramban Street and Gaza Road [Derech Azza]). Other garden suburbs (planned by Kaufmann) were Bayit Vegan, Kiryat Moshe, Shoshanat Zion and Yafeh Nof. On the open area south of Rehavia, the neighborhoods of Talbieh, Katamon and Bak'a (the residents were mainly non-Jews) went up, and on its northern boundaries, Kiryat Shmu'el and Merhavia were built. In Talbieh magnificent houses were built by Christian Arabs, Greeks and Armenians, and many consulates moved from the Street of the Prophets (Hanevi'im) to this area.

The Katamon neighborhood was established in 1924 near the San Simon Monastery. Its residents, mainly upper-middle-class Christian Arabs, built spacious and elaborate houses, compared to those surrounding it. In the German Colony and the Greek Colony many houses were built in the 1920s. Many British officials lived in these neighborhoods and they even set up an English sports center in the vicinity. The area south of the railway line was built up by Muslim Arabs. In the 1930s, a number of small neighborhoods were established around Talpiot such as North Talpiot, Arnona and "Binyan Umelacha." During this period, roads were paved with asphalt and the public services improved. In the 1930s, residential building expanded and many public institutions were built throughout the city (see below).

Jerusalem's main commercial center moved westward, from the area of Jaffa Gate to the Jaffa–Ben-Yehuda–King George Streets triangle, where the banks were also concentrated. A second commercial center began to develop on the edge of this area. This was the Mahane Yehuda market to the west, the Bukharan market to the east, the textile shops in Mamilla, and the market in Mea She'arim.

At the outbreak of World War II, most of the building activities ceased in Jerusalem and were renewed only after the War of Independence.

Population and Economy

Since Jerusalem served as the capital of Palestine during the Mandate period, many public, religious and educational institutions were established there. Over half of the city's population were employed in the provision of services, and only about one-quarter earned their living from trade and industry. During this period, Jerusalem functioned as the religious, administrative and educational center of the country and less as an industrial city. Heavy industry was never developed in Jerusalem, and the only industry was in the form of small factories and workshops in the fields of textile, leather, food and printing. The British administration preferred to employ Arabs rather than Jews. For example, despite the fact that 75 percent of the city's taxpayers were Jews, 66 percent of the municipal employees were Arabs. The number of Jews employed in industry and in the professions was larger than the number of Arabs in this field. The Arab sector supplied agricultural produce, and were laborers and employees in the various services. Many of the city's residents were employed by the World Zionist Organization, while others worked in education and allied fields.

Even though the Jewish population of the country was doubled during the 1920s and 1930s by the waves of immigration, Jerusalem did not benefit from this influx of immigrants. Throughout the entire Mandate period there was a constant growth in the Jewish population of Palestine, and there was also a relative increase in Jerusalem. In 1922, the Jews constituted 54 percent of Jerusalem's population, while in 1947 they constituted 60 percent. The total number of Jews in the city was 99,320 at the end of 1946, compared with 34,124 in 1922, an almost threefold increase during the period of the Mandate.

Education and Culture

Jerusalem was the center of education and religious learning, both for the "old" and for the "new" Jewish communities.

Alongside the veteran yeshivas, such as Etz Hayim and Hayei Olam, new yeshivas sprang up, such as Knesset Israel, which moved from Hebron to Jerusalem after the 1929 riots.

In April 1925, the cornerstone of the Hebrew University was laid on Mount Scopus. The Institutes for Jewish Studies, Science, Mathematics, and Oriental Studies were opened and by 1945 the student enrollment was 650. The Hebrew University became the intellectual and cultural center of Jerusalem. The National and University Library was established in 1938 in its own building on Mount Scopus. Research in the fields of the history and archaeology of the land of Israel, which flourished during this period, was carried out at a number of institutions established in the city. These included the Department of Archaeology at the Hebrew University, the British Palestine Exploration Fund, the American School of Oriental Research, the British School of Archaeology (transferred from Egypt in 1916) and the Pontifical Biblical Institute. The Rockefeller Museum was opened in the 1930s, and was run by the British Mandatory Government Department of Antiquities.

The center of book publishing moved during this period from Jerusalem to Tel Aviv, and even the *Haaretz* newspaper which at first appeared in Jerusalem moved to Tel Aviv. The veteran daily newspaper *Doar Hayom* closed down, and in 1931 the English-language daily, *The Palestine Post* (later *The Jerusalem Post*) began to appear in Jerusalem.

Musical and theatrical life was also concentrated in Tel Aviv. However, Jerusalem remained the center of art, mainly through the efforts of the Bezalel School of Art. The governor of Jerusalem, Storrs, persuaded a group of Jewish artists, such as Zaritzky, Tajar, Rubin and Guttman, to mount an exhibition of their works in David's Tower regularly from 1923 to 1928.

Many educational and cultural institutions erected their buildings in Jerusalem during the British Mandate period, designed by well-known architects. These included the King David Hotel and the YMCA (A. L. Harmon); the central post office (A. Harrison) and the Anglo-Palestine Bank next door (now Bank Leumi LeIsrael; A. Mendelssohn); the high commissioner's residence (A. Harrison) at Jebel Mukaber; the Jewish Agency compound (Y. Rechter) on the edge of Rehavia; the Schocken Library and Academy of Music (A. Mendelssohn) in Rehavia; the Hebrew University complex, the National Library building, and the Hadassah Hospital (A.

Mendelssohn) on Mount Scopus; the Scottish Hospice (C. Holliday); and the Pontifical Biblical Institute and the French Consulate.

The City's Water Supply

Jerusalem under the Turks obtained its water supply from cisterns and an ancient pipeline from Solomon's Pools. The Mandatory authorities set out to ameliorate the water supply and laid a pipeline from Solomon's Pools to the city. Later, a second pipeline was built from the Ein Fawar and Ein Fara springs in Wadi Kelt. The waters from these springs flowed into the reservoir built near Romema. In 1935, another pipeline was laid that brought water to Jerusalem from the springs at Rosh Ha'ayin. Prior to the building of this line, water was rationed and allocated once every few days. To this end water tanks were placed on the rooftops and they are part of Jerusalem's skyline to this day.

The Riots and Jewish Underground Organizations

The development of the city was accompanied by outbursts of violence against the Jews and Zionism. The first outburst during the Mandate period was on Passover (in April) 1920, on the eve of the San Remo Conference. The riots were designed to create irrevocable facts before the international institutions took decisions as regards the future of the mandate over Palestine.

The riots broke out in the Jordan Valley and in Jerusalem. They began at the annual Nabi Musa celebrations in the Old City of Jerusalem, in the course of which six Jews were killed and over two hundred wounded. The Jewish inhabitants of the Muslim Quarter were the main victims of these attacks. British military forces intervened only after three days of rioting, arrested the leaders of the Jewish defenders, headed by Zev Jabotinsky, who was sentenced to fifteen years imprisonment with hard labor. As a consequence of the 1920 riots, the Jewish community in Jerusalem set up a defense organization to cope with such outbreaks, and when the force defending the Jewish Quarter was attacked on November 2, 1921, the attackers were repulsed with the aid of a hand grenade thrown by the Haganah (defense) unit.

The extremist Palestinian Arabs received additional support with the appointment of Hajj Amin el-Husseini as the Mufti of Jerusalem and his election as head of the Supreme Muslim Council. The alleged reason for the outbreak of the riots was the dispute over Jewish rights at the Western Wall, which began with the tearing down of a dividing wall erected on the eve of the Day of Atonement in 1929. However, there is no doubt that the Arab leaders exploited the dispute to arouse the passions of the Arabs against the Jewish community. In the riots, which began on August 23, 1929, and continued throughout the week, 133 Jews were killed and 339 wounded in Jerusalem and its environs (Motza and Hebron). In the city itself, Jews living in the Muslim Quarter were assaulted and, as a consequence, Jews moved out of this quarter and abandoned it almost completely. Jewish neighborhoods contiguous upon the Arab quarters were attacked, such as the Georgian quarter near Damascus Gate and Mea She'arim, as well as neighborhoods on the outskirts of Jerusalem. The riots were put down by British military and police units who were called in for this purpose.

A group of defense fighters (Irgun "Bet") broke away from the Haganah defense organization because of their feeling of frustration and ineffectuality during the riots. This organization continued its activities against the Arabs and British in Jerusalem throughout the Second World War years.

At the beginning of 1944, the commander of the Irgun (Irgun Zevai Leumi) organization, Menachem Begin, proclaimed the renewal of the struggle against the British, and during the years 1944 to 1946 the organization carried out a number of large-scale attacks, some of them jointly with the Lehi fighters (see map on page 132).

In the summer of 1945 the Jewish underground movement

was set up as a joint military body encompassing the Irgun, Lehi, and Haganah, and a number of attacks were carried out under the aegis of this body.

The blowing up of a wing of the King David Hotel in Jerusalem by the Irgun forces, in which 91 civilians were killed, led to the breakup of this organization. The Irgun and Lehi continued their activities in Jerusalem and functioned independently during the War of Independence as well.

The political and military events during this period had its effect on the city's population distribution. The activities of the underground organizations also enhanced the tension. A number of neighborhoods were evacuated by the Jews as a consequence of the 1929 riots. The residents of the Old City left it in large numbers, and the Jewish residents of the Muslim Quarter continued to abandon it until none were left. The Jewish Quarter also suffered from the fact that many Jewish families were moving out, and the number of inhabitants declined from about 15,000 when the British first arrived to about 1,800 about the time they left. This phenomenon had adversely effected the demographic balance between Jews and Arabs in the various sectors of the city, and was reflected in the course of events during the War of Independence.

As a consequence of the Jewish underground activities, and especially the blowing up of the King David Hotel (July 22, 1946), the British authorities decided to close off sections of the city in which the British military installations and government offices were located. These zones were fenced off with barbed wire, the majority of their inhabitants were forced to vacate the area, and unauthorized entrance was forbidden. In the center of Jerusalem, the law courts, the central prison and the main post office were fenced off into an area called "Bevingrad." The introduction of security zones divided the city and caused a split in the Jewish residential sectors. This fact had its adverse effect on the placement of Jewish Haganah forces on the eve of the War of Independence.

The War of Independence, from November 29, 1947 to the Invasion of the Arab Armies on May 15, 1948

The Haganah's "Etzioni" district comprised the city of Jerusalem and fourteen villages that were divided into four sectors. These were Neveh Ya'akov and Atarot in the north; Beit Ha'arava and the Dead Sea Potash Plant in the east; the Etzion bloc in the south; and Motza, Kiryat Anavim, Ma'aleh Hahamisha and Har Tuv in the west.

In the "Etzioni" district there were 102,000 Jews (one-sixth of the Jewish population of Palestine) as opposed to 300,000 Arabs (in Jerusalem and the Arab villages in the area). The majority of the Jewish population were residents in the city of Jerusalem, and because of the city's economy and the type of Jewish inhabitants, it was almost totally dependent upon the import of goods from outside the city. The roads connecting the city to the Jewish communities in the coastal plain mainly passed through Arab-controlled areas, as for example from the outskirts of Tel Aviv up to the present-day Neveh Ilan.

In the city itself, Jewish and Arab quarters were contiguous upon one another. Some of the Arab quarters and the British security zones cut off some of the Jewish neighborhoods from the majority of the Jewish community, a situation which led to difficulties in the organization of defense by the Haganah. The 3,000 fighters of the Jewish defense forces belonged to the Haganah (the majority), Irgun, and Lehi, and functioned under clandestine conditions.

During the first phase of the war, Jerusalem and its environs were attacked by Arab semiprofessional military gangs led by local leaders, the most outstanding of whom was Abdul el-Qadir el-Husseini. In addition, the Arab Legion, some of whose forces were stationed in Palestine, supported the gangs in their attacks on the Jewish settlements. The British, who had begun to withdraw their forces from most parts of the country, remained in Jerusalem until the day the mandate ended on May 14, 1947. The British soldiers

secluded themselves within the security zones, and left the arena open to the combatting forces. They continued to maintain control of the road out of Jerusalem to the north, to keep it clear for their withdrawal from the city, but stopped patrolling the other roads where fierce battles were fought between the warring sides.

The First Incidents: November 29, 1947 to April 1, 1948

The day after the United Nations passed the resolution calling for the partition of Palestine into a Jewish and an Arab state, a bus traveling to Jerusalem was attacked in the vicinity of the Lod airport.

The Arab Higher Committee called a three-day strike from December 1, 1947. On the following day, an Arab mob streamed out through Jaffa Gate to the nearby Jewish commercial center and looted and burned the stores. Attempts on the part of the marauders to advance into the nearby Jewish neighborhoods were repulsed.

The Arabs began to carry out terrorist raids against the Jews in Jerusalem, as well as in other cities throughout the country. The raids were more or less regular, including sniping from the Arab quarters into the Jewish quarters. Grenades were thrown into populated areas, and car bombs exploded in strategic places. The most destructive of these events were the blowing up of *The Palestine Post* building (February 21), the explosion of a car bomb on Ben-Yehuda Street (February 22), the explosion of car bombs in the Jewish Agency compound (March 11), and in the Yemin

(below) **"Bevingrad,"** as the British security zone in the center of Jerusalem was named by the inhabitants, where the main government departments were concentrated. In response to the

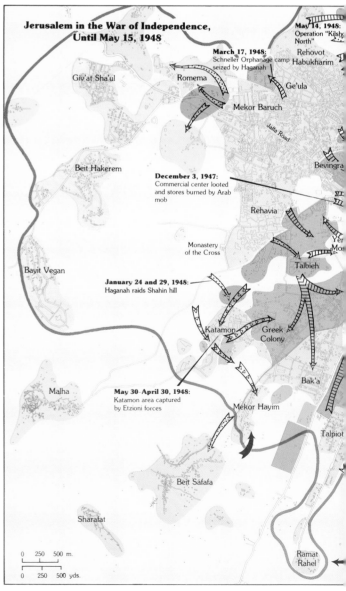

underground raids carried out in the city, the British cordoned off the area toward the end of the mandate. The buildings in the photograph are typical of the building style of the period.

April 13, 1948:
Hadassah convoy attacked by Arabs

February 12-13, 1948:
Haganah raids Sheikh Jarrah

Wadi el-Joz

Mt. of Olives

Silwan

May 13, 1948:
British positions seized after evacuation, within framework of Operation "Shefifon"

Legend

Jewish neighborhoods	
Muslim neighborhoods	
Arab Christian neighborhoods	
Jewish and Arab neighborhoods	
British security zone	
Jewish raids at start of war	
Operation "Yevusi"	
Operation "Kilshon"	
nt line after Operation "Kilshon," May 14-15	
Repulsed Arab attacks	

Moshe quarter (March 23).

The Jewish defense forces quickly retaliated. The Irgun bombed Jaffa Gate (December 13 and 29) and Damascus Gate (January 7), blew up the Samiramis Hotel in Katamon, which served as the headquarters of the Iraqi forces (January 5), and bombed buildings in the Sheikh Jarrah quarter in the north and Shahin Hill in the south.

The Arab attacks escalated from the beginning of January, and in addition to firing into the neighborhoods in the city area, they carried out raids on the outlying suburbs. On January 14, attacks against Ramat Rahel and the Etzion bloc were successfully repulsed, and in February, Mekor Hayim and Yemin Moshe came under fire. The Jewish Quarter was subject to attack a number of times during this month.

In March, the situation in the city deteriorated. Public transport vehicles were attacked; the Jewish Quarter, which had been virtually isolated since the beginning of December, could only be reached by a convoy protected by British troops; vehicles making their way to the Hadassah Hospital and the Hebrew University on Mount Scopus were ambushed by snipers; the southern neighborhoods—Talpiot, Ramat Rahel, Mekor Hayim and Yemin Moshe—were cut off from the rest of the city by the Arab quarters of Bak'a and Katamon and by the British security zones around the railway station and the King David Hotel, which could only be entered in armored cars.

The Jewish inhabitants of Jerusalem were subject to constant Arab fire, and at the same time were faced with a dire shortage of food and water as the result of the Arab siege of the city. The Jerusalem Committee had already begun to function in December 1947, in anticipation of such a siege. It made plans for laying in supplies of food, water and fuel, carried out a survey of the city's water cisterns, and stored 115,000 cubic meters of water in cisterns which had been cleaned out for this purpose. Meat, flour and sugar were rationed and allocated by government departments. There was only a small reserve of supplies in the city itself, and additional quantities were brought in by train or lorry. From the end of March, when the city was completely cut off from the rest of the country, there was no natural protein in Jerusalem, but the Jerusalem Committee had prepared a stock of vital foodstuffs sufficient to supply the Jewish community for a period of fifteen days. At the beginning of May the Electricity Company had enough fuel to last three weeks only, and that after drastic cuts in the supply of electricity. Food and water supplies were radically reduced. The daily water ration per person at first was two gallons (eight liters) and then reduced to one-and-a-half gallons (six liters). Contact with the outside world was by light planes which landed on improvised landing strips in the Valley of the Cross (lane 1) and at Giv'at Sha'ul (lane 2). Within the course of Operation Harel, on the eve of Passover 5708 (April 15-20, 1948), the soldiers of the Harel-Palmach Brigade succeeded in bringing three large convoys of supplies into the city, which helped to alleviate the crisis situation.

The Battle for the Road to Jerusalem

From the month of December 1947, Jewish vehicles on the roads leading to Jerusalem came under constant attack. The city was in danger of being cut off from Tel Aviv, as well as from the nearby settlements and its outlying suburbs. Entire sections of the roads leading to and from Jerusalem passed through Arab-controlled territory. In order to bypass the section of the Tel Aviv–Jerusalem road between Holon and Latrun, cars and buses traveled via Hulda. Vehicles were then organized into convoys with armed security guards, and traveled along the Wadi Serar–Latrun road, climbed the ascent from Sha'ar Haggai to Kiryat Anavim and from there to Jerusalem.

In the course of time the situation deteriorated. Transport from Jerusalem to the Etzion bloc was constantly subjected to harassment, and even convoys came under severe attacks. One of the convoys was attacked in the vicinity of Solomon's Pools, and ten passengers were killed (December 11, 1947).

Another convoy was attacked near Bethlehem and thirteen passengers were killed (January 13, 1948). At the end of March numerous attacks were mounted against convoys. One of these, the Nabi Samwil convoy, was attacked on the road from the Etzion bloc (March 27), and after a lengthy battle in which fourteen of the Jewish fighters were killed and forty wounded, the survivors were rescued by British troops, not before Jewish armored cars had been captured by the Arabs. On March 31, another convoy on its way to Jerusalem was attacked near Hulda with the loss of seventeen fighters.

Jerusalem was now completely cut off from the coast. Haganah headquarters realized that the system of convoys was no longer practical, and it was decided to take the offensive, and Plan D was put into operation. Plan D set goals for a general offensive throughout the country in order to improve the position held by the Jewish forces before the British withdrawal. In Operation Nahshon (April 5-16, 1948) large numbers of troops were amassed to launch a two-pronged attack. On the eastern front, after an arduous battle, the Arab villages of Castel and Colonia were captured and in the west, forces moved from Hulda to Deir Muheisin. The plan was to capture strategic points which would make it possible to bring up a number of convoys to break the siege of Jerusalem. Further convoys reached the city during Operation Harel (April 15-21) and Operation Maccabee (May 8-18), when areas controlling the road to Jerusalem were taken.

On the eve of the invasion of the Arab armies, the Harel Brigade held strategic positions between Neveh Ilan, Sha'ar Haggai and Beit Mahsir, and the Givati Brigade controlled the western slope of the Ayalon Valley. However, the Arab Legion troops based in the Latrun area, and the Egyptian forces which reached Isdud, prevented these advantages from being exploited to keep the road to Jerusalem open. The road was cut off once again in the Latrun area.

Conquest of the City's Strategic Points

The aim of Haganah's Plan D was to gain control of those areas which had been allocated as part of the Jewish state by the United Nations resolution for the partition of Palestine.

In mid-April the struggle for Jerusalem reached a climax with the attack on Deir Yasin by the Irgun and Lehi and the attack by Arabs on a convoy on its way to the Hadassah Hospital on Mount Scopus (April 13, 1948). The situation was relieved to a certain extent by the Nahshon and Harel Operations and by the fact that some of the soldiers of the Harel-Palmach Brigade were brought in to bolster up the Portzim Regiment manning the city's defenses. These forces mounted an attack as part of Operation Yevusi (April 21-30, 1948) with the aim of gaining control of the northern entrance to the city, as well as the southern neighborhoods. The operation was only partially successful. The Fourth Regiment failed in its attack on Nabi Samwil on the night of April 22, while the British forced the Fifth Regiment to withdraw from Sheikh Jarrah (April 26-27). On the southern front, the Fourth Regiment succeeded in taking the San Simon Monastery in a bloody battle (April 30), thus opening the way for the capture of Katamon, and thus creating territorial connection with the southern neighborhoods of Mekor Hayim and Talpiot (May 2).

In Operation Kilshon, the Haganah, Irgun and Lehi forces succeeded in gaining control of the security zones vacated by the British. Sheikh Jarrah was captured by the Irgun and in Operation Shefifon, the defense lines in the Jewish Quarter was improved considerably.

The major part of Jerusalem, from Mount Scopus in the northeast up to kibbutz Ramat Rahel in the south, was now under the control of Jewish forces. On the other hand, the settlements on the outskirts of Jerusalem were still cut off. The Etzion bloc in the south fell on May 14 and its members were taken prisoner. Neveh Ya'akov, Atarot and Beit Ha'arava were evacuated a few days later. Within the city, the Jewish Quarter was still cut off.

Divided Jerusalem
1948 – 1967

The War of Independence

When the establishment of the state of Israel was declared on May 14, 1948, the division of Jerusalem became a fact. The British, who had evacuated the city the day before, left the Jews and Arabs to battle against each other. In Operation Kilshon, the Jewish defense forces succeeded in gaining control of most of the security zones abandoned by the British in the center of the city, and thus created a continuous strip of Jewish-held areas from Mount Scopus in the northeast to the Talpiot neighborhood in the south. The scant defense forces were sparsely spread out along this border in an effort to withstand the onslaught of the irregular forces, and in readiness for the anticipated invasion of the Arab armies. The Jewish Quarter, which had been under siege for almost half a year, was completely cut off from the Jewish sector of Jerusalem.

As for the road to Jerusalem, Operation Maccabee "B" was called to a halt before the forces were able to attain their final goal. The Givati Brigade, which was in the middle of a flanking action in the Latrun area, was ordered to call off the operation and move to the south to stop the advance of the Egyptian army. The Harel Brigade captured all the mountain ridges controlling the road to Jerusalem from Sha'ar Haggai to the east. The road to Jerusalem, which had been severed at the end of Operation Harel (April 20), still remained cut off. Only a few small convoys succeeded getting through before the Arab Legionnaires began to move forward along the Ayalon mountain ridge.

The Month-Long Invasion

At the end of Operation Kilshon, there were clashes between the Jewish and Arab forces along the entire city border. But the most harsh battles took place in the Jewish defense's most vulnerable point, the Jewish Quarter. On May 17, Arabs began to pound the western side of the quarter incessantly, and succeeded in capturing the major part of those areas held by the Jews. Attempts were made to relieve the beleaguered Jewish defenders who fought with hardly any ammunition for their few weapons. The Haganah endeavored to break into the city in the area of the Citadel (May 17–18). This attempt failed, but a unit of the Palmach's Fifth Regiment, which mounted a diversion in the region of Mount Zion, succeeded in capturing the Arab positions and taking the mountain. The following day Palmach forces broke through the Zion Gate and joined up with the defenders of the Jewish Quarter. Members of the Home Guard (Mishmar Ha'am) were brought in as reinforcements, and supplies were brought to the Jewish Quarter. Arab Legionnaires succeeded in regaining the Zion Gate the next morning, and once again the quarter was besieged.

The Arab Legion, which invaded Palestine on May 15, entered Jerusalem from the east and the north. The Sixth Regiment entered the Old City from the east, and joined the irregular forces in their attack on the Jewish Quarter. The Fifth and Third Regiments attacked Sheikh Jarrah and the Police School in the north on May 19, and succeeded in capturing them. During the following four days attempts were made by the Arabs to break into the Jewish part of the city along the entire frontier, from the "Pagi" neighborhood in the north, the Mandelbaum Gate intersection in the center, and Suleiman Street in the south. All these attacks were repulsed by the few Jewish defenders, who included young teenagers serving in the ranks of the Gadna. The defenders succeeded in reinforcing the center of the front line—in the Musrara quarter—and thus held the northern region.

In the south of the city semiregular Egyptian forces, aided by the Arab Legion, attacked kibbutz Ramat Rahel, with

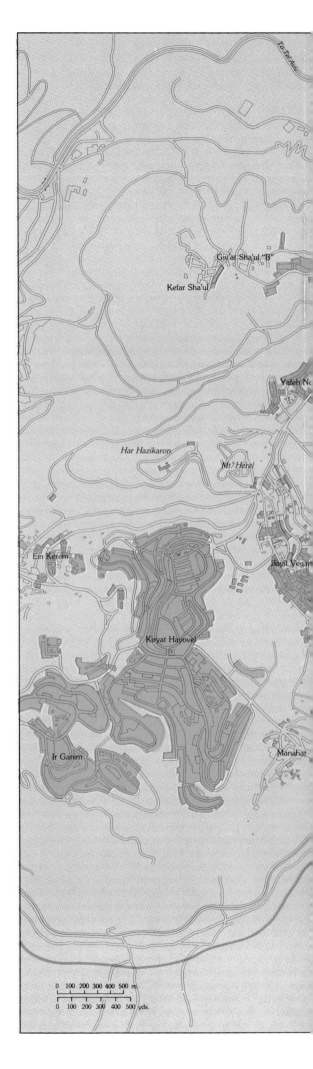

Sanhedria

Romema
Illit

Industrial Area

Romema

Mekor Baruch

Bukharan
Quarter

Ge'ula

Sheikh Jarrah

Wadi el-Joz

Mt. Scopus

t Sha'ul

Kiryat
Moshe

Hamekasher

Binyanei Ha'ooma
(Convention Center)

Jaffa Road

Mea She'arim

Zion
Square

Hakerem

Hakirya
(Government
Center)

Knesset

Rehavia

YMCA

OLD CITY

Hebrew University

Israel Museum

Neveh
Sha'anan

Neveh Granot

Nayot

Kiryat Shmu'el

Komemiut

Yemin Moshe

Sham'a

Silwan

Giv'at
Hanania

Abu Tor

Giv'at Mordechai

Rassco

Gonen

Emek Refa'im

Ge'ulim

Gonen "Heh"

Gonen "Vav"

Gonen

Gonen "Het"

Gonen "Dalet"

Gonen "Aleph"

Mekor Hayim

Government House

Headquarters of the
United Nations Truce
Supervision Organization
(UNTSO)

Gonen "Tet"

Gonen
"Gimel"

Gonen "Bet"

Talpiot

Beit Safafa

Arnona

Ramat Rahel

Built-up area, 1949–1967

Armistice line, 1949

the aim of capturing the southern ridge of the city (May 22). Kibbutz Ramat Rahel changed hands a number of times, until it was finally recaptured by members of the infantry and the Palmach (May 25).

The ever-decreasing number of Jewish defenders in the Jewish Quarter still succeeded in withstanding the heavy attacks. A regiment of Legionnaires and three companies of irregulars mounted an assault against a few score exhausted Jews who were defending 1,300 Jewish inhabitants who had crowded together in the area of the Sephardic synagogues and the Batei Mahse compound. Attempts to come to their aid were unsuccessful. Under inordinately difficult conditions, with inferior numbers, and fighting from house to house, the defenders of the Jewish Quarter succeeded in holding out for two weeks until they had no choice but to surrender on May 28. Two hundred and ninety persons were taken prisoner (69 were soldiers), and the rest of the residents were transferred to the New City.

There were no further dramatic events in the city until the first cease-fire came into effect on June 11. The few attempts to capture Arab positions in Musrara, Sheikh Jarrah and Sur Bahir were only partially successful. Until the first cease-fire approximately 10,000 mortar bombs were fired on the city, causing 1,222 civilian casualties (204 of whom were killed). Despite the austere conditions prevailing in the city (the water ration had been reduced to 1.5 gallons [6 liters] per person per day and bread to 5 ounces [150 grams]), the civilian population remained steadfast. The members of the Home Guard continued to ensure that the city functioned under the constant bombing, and especially ensuring that the water rations were distributed to the civilians regularly throughout the city. During this period, Jerusalem was completely cut off by the Arab siege, and the major battle was being fought to free the approaches to the city.

The Battle for the Road to Jerusalem

At the end of the Operation Maccabee "B," a number of small convoys succeeded in breaking through to Jerusalem at night. One of these consisted of a lone armored car. On May 17, the Arab Legion's Fourth Regiment took up its position at Latrun, and in the course of a few days the Legion's Third Brigade had fanned out over the Ayalon ridge and was finally entrenched by May 25. On May 30,

the Legion's soldiers succeeded in staving off the attack of the new Israeli Seventh Brigade (Operation Bin Nun A and B) and on June 6 repulsed a further attack by the Harel Brigade (Operation Yoram), leaving the section of the road between Deir Muheisin and Sha'ar Haggai still under control of the Arabs. In the course of the fighting, the stretch of land between Deir Muheisin, Beit Susin and Beit Jiz was captured by Israeli troops, thus joining up the area held by the Harel Brigade in the east with that controlled by the Seventh Brigade in the west. A convoy comprising five jeeps succeeded in getting through to Jerusalem on the night of June 1, thus bringing to an end the one-and-a-half-month siege of the city. Working at night so as not to be spotted by the Legionnaires on the nearby Ayalon ridge, a road (called the "Burma Road") was rapidly cut through the mountains to bypass the section of the Jerusalem highway held by the Arabs near Latrun. By the time the first cease-fire came into effect, a week and a half later, the road was being used regularly, and convoys bringing heavy equipment to Jerusalem were able to get through and avoid the closed section at Latrun. Pipelines for water and fuel were laid along this road as well.

The First Cease-Fire (June 11 to July 8)

Major changes were brought about in the city during the period of the first cease-fire. With the opening of the "Burma Road," which was not under United Nations surveillance, vast quantities of food, fuel and military equipment were brought into the city. The fighting forces were reorganized and equipped with arms, including machine guns, mortars and artillery.

The Ten-Day Battle (July 8–18)

The first cease-fire came to an end on July 8 at 10 a.m. During the period between the first and second cease-fire, no major battles took place in the city. On July 10, Khirbet el-Hamama (present-day Mount Herzl) was captured in the western part of the city. On July 10–11, Israeli forces took Beit Masmil (Kiryat Hayovel), and on July 14, Malha (Manahat). A fierce battle was waged with Arab Legion forces in the Mandelbaum Gate area (July 16–19). An attempt by joint forces of the Israel Defense Forces, the Irgun and Lehi to retake the Old City (Operation Kedem, July 16–17) met with failure. Miss Carey ridge and Ein Kerem were captured on July 17–18. Operation Dani was carried out on July 10–18, during which the corridor leading to Jerusalem was widened, and the area south of the "Burma Road" in the vicinity of Ramla and Tzova were taken. On the following day, at 7 p.m., the second cease-fire came into effect.

The Second Cease-Fire (to October 15)

During the course of the second cease-fire progress was made mainly in exchanges between the commands of the forces, and on the political level. Agreements between the Arab Legion and the Israel Defense Forces were signed during the course of the month as follows: on July 7, the agreement on the demilitarization of the Mount Scopus enclave (earlier, in May, it was agreed to demilitarize the Government House area, where the Red Cross mission had its headquarters); on July 22, an agreement was made for the marking out of the no-man's land area. These agreements constituted the basis for relations between the Arab Legion and the Israel Defense Forces, and both sides did their utmost to contain any local incidents.

A number of minor operations were carried out in Jerusalem during the period of the second cease-fire. In August, following a number of breaches of the cease-fire agreements, a regiment of the Etzioni Brigade tried to repel Arab forces who had moved forward along the slopes of the Government House ridge. The attack failed and the Israeli troops were forced to withdraw (August 16–17). In October, a number of installations were blown up in the southern sector of the city, and in Operation Yekev (October 19–20) the area controlling the railway line came under Israeli control. The Beit Jalla ridge, which was the operation's final

(far left) **The Turjeman building** in the northeast of the city, near the former Mandelbaum Gate. This building served as an Israel Defense Forces' border position until the Six-Day War. It now houses a museum depicting Jerusalem during the period the city was divided.

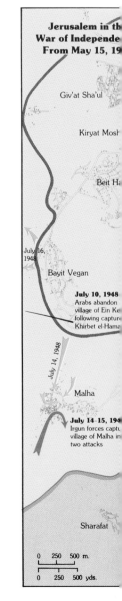

Jerusalem in the War of Independence From May 15, 19...

Giv'at Sha'ul

Kiryat Mosh...

Beit Ha...

July 16, 1948

Bayit Vegan

July 10, 1948
Arabs abandon village of Ein Ke... following capture... Khirbet el-Hama...

July 14, 1948

Malha

July 14–15, 194...
Irgun forces captu... village of Malha in... two attacks

Sharafat

0   250   500 m.

0   250   500 yds.

(below) One of the **concrete barriers** erected after the War of Independence between the two sectors of divided Jerusalem (Mamilla Street) to protect the Jewish inhabitants of the city against Jordanian snipers. These barriers were demolished when the city was united after the Six-Day War.

goal, was not captured. On the following day, in Operation Hahar, the Jerusalem corridor was widened extensively, and areas south of the Jerusalem–Latrun highway were captured by the Israel Defense Forces.

The Armistice Agreement and the Status of Jerusalem

In June 1948, the United Nations intermediary, Count Bernadotte, put forward a proposal for the solution of the Israeli–Arab conflict. The proposal included a clause by which Jerusalem would be included in the Arab territory, with autonomy granted to Jews. The Israel Government rejected this proposal out of hand. When he arrived in Israel at the end of July, Count Bernadotte then proposed that Jerusalem be demilitarized. On September 17, Count Bernadotte was murdered by members of the National Front organization, which included members of Lehi. As a consequence of this act, the government decided to disband the independent Irgun and Lehi forces in Jerusalem.

On November 30, 1948, the Armistice Agreement was signed by Colonel Moshe Dayan, commander of the Israeli forces in Jerusalem, and Abdallah et-Tal, the commander of the Jordanian forces. At the end of December, the Road of Heroism, which bypassed Latrun, was opened. On February 2, 1949, the government proclaimed the end of military rule in Jerusalem and on April 3, the Armistice Agreement with Jordan was signed in Rhodes. The agreement provided for the renewal of railway traffic to Jerusalem, and for a joint committee to arrange access to the holy places and to the

enclave on Mount Scopus. This latter clause was never implemented and was the cause of dissension between Israel and Jordan up to 1967.

The Jewish City

Following upon Count Bernadotte's proposals, the Israel Government decided to proclaim Jerusalem as a military area and appointed Dov Joseph as military governor. This was the city's status until the military government was revoked in February 1949.

On December 9, 1949, the United Nations passed a resolution to the effect that Jerusalem should be an international city. The government of Israel, preferring that it remain divided between Israel and Jordan, decided to take steps to proclaim Jerusalem the capital of the nascent Jewish state. Thus, it was decided to move the Knesset and the government offices to Jerusalem. The prime minister's office was transferred on December 16, 1949, followed by the Knesset which began to function in its temporary quarters in the city center (Beit Froumine) on December 26. This process of moving the government offices was completed with the transfer of the Foreign Office in July 1953.

On January 17, 1949, the Jewish City Council, appointed in December 1948, held its first session. Shlomo Zalman Shragai was elected mayor. The office was then held by Avraham Yitzhak Kariv (September 1952–April 1955), Gershon Agron (1955–1959), Mordechai Ish-Shalom (1959–1965) and by the present incumbent Teddy Kollek (from 1965).

The Municipal Boundary

The positions held by each side at the end of May 1948, with a few minor adjustments, constituted the Israel–Jordan armistice line. The borderline was drawn on the map which was attached to the Armistice Agreement signed on November 30, 1948, and was termed the municipal boundary. This map, which was considered by those who prepared it to be temporary until replaced by a permanent peace agreement, became the only binding document in effect up to 1967. This fact led to many complications because the line had been rapidly drawn with a thick wax marker on a map whose scale was 1:20,000. When the municipal boundary began to be translated into reality, it led to conflicts between the sides because of the differing interpretations given the map by the Israelis and the Jordanians. In reality the borderline was 98–131 feet (30–40 meters) wide, and it included entire buildings and even whole streets. Many areas became no-man's land, and the borderline often ran right through the skeletons of ruined buildings. The municipal boundary, which began on the slopes of Ammunition Hill, was about 3 miles (5 kilometers) long. An Israeli unit of some 70 soldiers, manning about 14 posts, faced Jordanian soldiers at 36 posts along the border. Many of these posts were located in stone houses whose doors and windows were blocked up with concrete, leaving narrow apertures to fire through. Defense walls were erected along the borderline as protection against sniping, both on the Israeli side (along Shmu'el Hanavi and Mamilla Streets) and on the Jordanian side (Damascus Gate and along the road leading to Sheikh Jarrah). The close proximity between the sides and the areas in no-man's land, whose ownership had not been finally established, led to numerous incidents incurred by both sides. During the first years, there was intermittent sniping and bombing from the Jordanian side, but in 1952 the Israel Defense Forces retaliated with a concentrated barrage which settled matters.

The Israel–Jordan Armistice Commission was responsible for dealing with disputes arising in relation to the municipal boundary. Among the typical problems on its agenda were complaints of violation of the Armistice Agreement as regards building in no-man's land, the throwing of stones by Jordanian soldiers, the return of stolen property, the return of infiltrators and persons who inadvertently crossed the lines, and the spraying of crops in no-man's land. Following an incident in 1954, the sides agreed to improve the communications between the commanders on either side, both by telephone

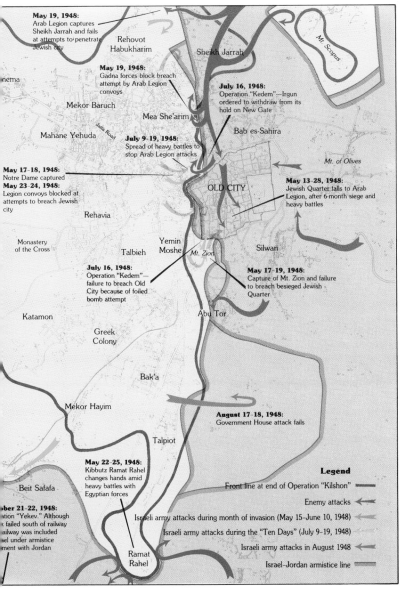

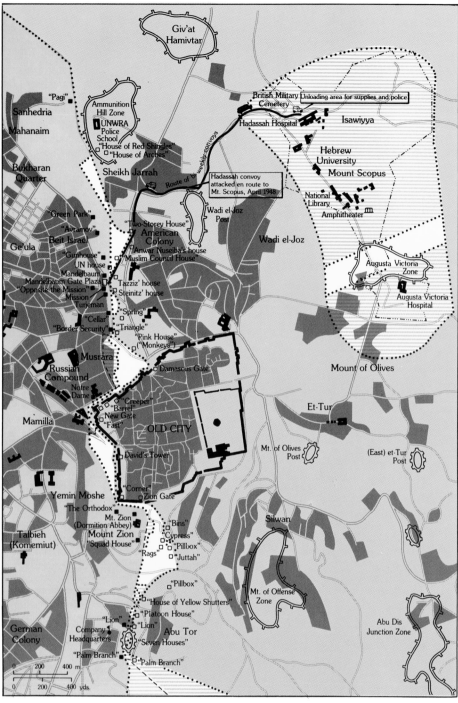

.... Armistice line, 1949

-----.---- Armistice line on Mt. Scopus,
according to Jordan and UN

▭ No-man's land

▧ Israeli territory

▨ Israeli demilitarized zone

▩ Jordanian territory

▤ Jordanian demilitarized zone

■ Israeli position

□ Jordanian position

(above) **The city boundary**, running
along the border set by the Armistice
Agreement between Israel and
Jordan, divided the city into two
sectors. Many incidents occurred
along this boundary, and this was
reflected in the city's appearance: the
no-man's land areas were piled up
with refuse and junk, and minefields,
barbed-wire fences and concrete walls
were scattered along the border.

tanker, a lorry carrying equipment and supplies, and an
ambulance. The convoy went through Mandelbaum Gate,
which was the only crossing point between the Jordanian
and Israeli sectors of the city. Pilgrims also passed through
this point on their way to the Church of the Holy Sepulcher,
and it also served United Nations personnel and tourists.

The Mount Scopus enclave was guarded by a company
of Israeli soldiers in police uniform. A convoy of these "po-
licemen" went up to Mount Scopus every two weeks to
replace half the company stationed there. The convoy and
the equipment it was carrying were carefully scrutinized by
United Nations Observers, and these inspections were the
cause of intermittent disputes. One of the causes was the
attempt by the Israelis to send through military equipment
in various guises. On one occasion, a jeep on which a
recoilless gun was mounted had been dismantled and its
parts concealed in the double roof of the armored bus. A
number of convoys which attempted to slip through at night
were caught by Jordanian patrols and forced to return.

A number of battles broke out over the disputes concerning
the no-man's land areas. The worst occurred in May 1958,
in the course of which a United Nations Observer, Colonel
Flint, and four Israeli soldiers were killed when Jordanian
soldiers opened fire on an Israeli patrol. During the tense
period preceding the Six-Day War, the Jordanians requested
that the convoys to Mount Scopus be cancelled. At midday
on June 6, 1967, Israel Defense Forces broke through to the
mount, after having captured Ammunition Hill and Giv'at
Hamivtar.

Development of the Municipal Area

Jerusalem's development after the War of Independence
depended greatly on the existence of the municipal boundary
which divided the city into two sectors. Along the length of
the frontier, which constituted a physical barrier of barbed
wire and mines, as well as an area of shooting and sniping,
there remained a number of abandoned houses which were
occupied by some poverty-stricken families. Those families
who were better off moved away from the border areas,
and these were inhabited by families of a low socioeconomic
level.

After the War of Independence, Jerusalem expanded
mainly toward the west. Building was carried out mostly on
the mountain ridges and on the city's uppermost slopes. The
new neighborhoods built in the western sector of the city were
designed mainly for new immigrants who came to Jerusalem
during that period. These were mass building projects being
hastily developed at the lowest possible cost. In 1949, building
was begun in Kiryat Hayovel on the site of the Arab village
of Beit Masmil. At first, duplex single-storey houses were
built, and then followed by high-rise apartment buildings
built in close proximity. In the veteran neighborhoods, such
as Kiryat Moshe, Katamon, Talpiot and Giv'at Haveradim
(Rassco), long concrete structures, not faced with hewn
stone, were built to provide rapid and cheap solutions to
the urgent need for accommodation.

The areas where the city was able to expand to the
north were also constrained by the armistice line. In the
area between Romema and Sanhedria, apartment blocks
were built to supply accommodation for the ultra-Orthodox
inhabitants.

Arab neighborhoods abandoned during the War of Independence were adapted to provide accommodation for
new immigrants, as for example, Musrara, Bak'a, and Ein
Kerem. In the southern sector of the city, in the British
el-Alamein Camp sector, a huge immigrant camp was set
up, which was vacated only during the 1960s (it is now part
of the Talpiot industrial area).

The city center, which during the Mandate period constituted the triangle of Ben-Yehuda–Jaffa–King George Streets,
was not badly damaged in the course of the battles (apart
from the middle of Ben-Yehuda Street), and continued to
function. But as a consequence of the city's economic slowdown, the commercial center was unable to develop. Few

and through weekly meetings. It was also agreed to tighten
up control over the forces, and both armies agreed to ensure
the rigid implementation of standing orders.

A regular point of friction between the two sides was Mount
Scopus. According to the agreement signed on July 7, 1948,
the area was to be demilitarized, and it was to contain
Augusta Victoria, the Hebrew University, the Hadassah
Hospital and the Arab village of Isawiyya. The number of
Israeli civilians was restricted to 33, and the area was divided
between Israel and Jordan. It was also agreed that the area
would be under United Nations jurisdiction, and UN forces
would make provision for the supply of food and water and
the change of personnel. These matters were not included
in the Israel–Jordan Armistice Agreement. The demilitarized
zone of Mount Scopus was referred to in clause 8, but the
sides were unable to reach agreement on it. The result was
a long-standing argument between Israel and Jordan which
lasted until the Six-Day War. In actual fact, the directives
issued by the head of the United Nations Observers in 1950
were binding: a convoy went up to Mount Scopus once
every two weeks, consisting of two armored buses, a fuel

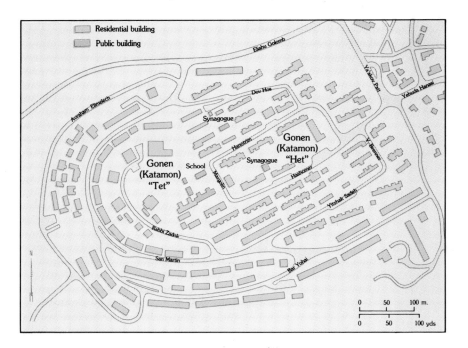

Residential building
Public building

Gonen
(Katamon)
"Tet"

Gonen
(Katamon)
"Het"

School
Synagogue

Synagogue

(above) **Gonen Het and Gonen Tet**, typical neighborhoods built in the western city during the 1950s to accommodate the numerous new immigrants who arrived in the city during that period. This was mass construction under adverse conditions according to specially designed plans. The immigrant housing projects were built on the slopes of the hill, and the public amenities, such as the school and the synagogue, were built on the uppermost part.

buildings were constructed, and its general appearance did not change from the Mandate period up to the Six-Day War.

The Jordanian City

The eastern sector of the city which was under Jordanian control, did not develop at the same pace as the Israeli sector, mainly because the Hashemite Kingdom of Jordan devoted its resources to the development of the capital city, Amman. The population of East Jerusalem was reduced by half after the 1948 war, and began to grow only at the end of the 1960s, increasing fivefold between 1960 and 1967.

East Jerusalem was designed by the British architect Kandel, who submitted a master plan for the entire city during the mandate. In 1965, he presented another master plan specifically relating to East Jerusalem. Most of the new building took place in the open spaces in the north of the city, mainly along the Jerusalem–Ramallah road, in the area that came under the jurisdiction of Shu'afat and Beit Hanina, in which Oriental-style villas were erected by affluent persons. The nearby villages of Eizariyya and Abu Dis also developed and became suburbs of the city.

In the economic area, Christian and Muslim tourism expanded, and many hotels were opened in East Jerusalem. One of the most impressive was the Intercontinental Hotel on the Mount of Olives. No industry of consequence developed, except for the cigarette factory in Eizariyya. A commercial center began to flourish in Salah ed-Din Street and in the surrounding streets. The former commercial center at the Damascus Gate and its vicinity deteriorated because of its proximity to the border area. In the vicinity of Salah ed-Din Street, the law courts, the Jordanian governor's residence and the main post office were built. The most impressive buildings constructed during this period were the YMCA on Nablus Road, the governor's residence and two hospitals in Sheikh Jarrah.

Ruined and abandoned houses along the length of the border between the two sectors of the city constituted an eyesore in the municipal landscape. During the 1960s, a modern highway was built connecting Jerusalem to the Abdallah Bridge, and another road through Wadi el-Joz connecting the city entrance from Ramallah to the Rockefeller Museum area. A narrow winding mountain road ran along the Kidron Valley and through Beit Sahur, connecting Bethlehem and Hebron with Jerusalem and Nablus. A few years later an additional road was built through Sur Bahir and Government House which reduced the distance between Jerusalem and Bethlehem. Military positions were erected to guard this road near Government House and Sur Bahir. An electricity plant was built near Shu'afat to provide electricity

for the city, and a water supply system which derived its water from Ein Fara and Solomon's Pools.

Public Buildings

The Jewish city quickly recovered from the War of Independence and life soon returned to normal. Government offices were housed in temporary quarters throughout the city. The prime minister's office took up residence in a wing of the Jewish Agency compound. The Knesset was housed in the Froumine building in King George Street, and the Ministry for Foreign Affairs in wooden huts in Romema. The Hebrew University and the Hadassah Hospital, whose buildings on Mount Scopus were no longer accessible, were spread out among a number of locations: the Department of Biochemistry was set up in a building in Mamilla, the Department of Genetics in the former military court building in Talbieh, and the Department of Zoology in Bible House near the Russian Compound.

During the 1950s, a plot of land between Rehavia and Beit Hakerem, on a ridge called Giv'at Ram—beginning at Sheikh Badr in the north (now the Hilton Hotel) and ending in the Rehavia valley in the south—was selected for the construction of a number of public buildings. Here were built the government offices, the Knesset, the Hebrew University and the Israel Museum. In the west of the city, above the village of Ein Kerem, the Hadassah Medical Center was erected. The Hebrew University campus at Giv'at Ram and the Hadassah Hospital at Ein Kerem were opened at the beginning of the 1960s, and the new Knesset building was inaugurated in 1968. A large convention center, Binyanei Ha'ooma, was built at Sheikh Badr. Hakirya (the government offices complex) was erected between Giv'at Ram and the Sha'arei Hessed quarter, and the Israel Museum, at the southern end of the area, was completed in 1967. In the center of the city, Hekhal Shlomo was built to house the office of the Chief Rabbinate and, opposite, a large high-rise apartment building was erected with a supermarket on its ground floor. In Strauss Street, the multistoreyed Histadrut building went up, from whose roof Mount Scopus and the Mount of Olives could be seen. In 1949, the remains of Theodor Herzl were reinterred on a mountain named for him in the west of the city, and this area became the burial place of leading national figures. A military cemetery was placed on the slopes of this hill.

Economy

The city's economy was based mainly on the provision of services. The majority of the city's breadwinners were employed by government offices, the Hebrew University, the national institutions, the Hadassah Hospital and other public institutions. In an effort to balance the income of the city's population, certain areas were selected as industrial centers in Romema, Giv'at Sha'ul, and Talpiot. Here light industries were set up in the fields of electronics, printing, pharmaceuticals and metalwork. A large flour mill was also erected. Even so, industry still accounted for a small sector of Jerusalem's economy. Only 17 percent of all employees in Jerusalem were engaged by industrial concerns, while the public services employed 44.3 percent. In 1965, about one-quarter of Jerusalem's employees worked for factories with over 100 workers.

Municipal Administration

During the course of the War of Independence, civil life was administered by the Jerusalem Committee, headed by Dov Joseph, who was appointed military governor of the city. On January 17, 1949, the Minister of the Interior appointed a temporary city council, consisting of representatives of Jerusalem residents, and in 1950, the first elections were held for the city council. During the 1950s, the city was faced by major political, administrative, economic and social problems, and in 1955 the city council was disbanded and a special committee appointed to run its affairs. Since then, the city has been administered by a mayor and city council elected every four years.

United Jerusalem
Since 1967

The area of **Jaffa Gate** underwent a radical change after the unification of the city in 1967. Ruins of buildings and mounds of garbage were cleared away from outside the city wall, and a promenade has been built from Tzahal Square to Jaffa Gate. The roads running parallel to the walls have been repaired and adapted to the requirements of the heavy traffic using them. This is the section west of the point of contact between the Old City and the "New City," and both sides of it are the main commercial areas of the two sectors of the city. This fact was the reason for the immediate development of the area after the city's unification, to enable easy access by pedestrians and vehicles between the two parts of the city.

The Six-Day War

On June 5, 1967, the Six-Day War broke out, in the course of which the Israel Defense Forces conquered the Sinai desert, Judea and Samaria, and the Golan Heights. The climax of this war from the Israeli viewpoint was the liberation of East Jerusalem from Jordanian rule on June 6, 1967.

The war opened on the Egyptian front on June 5. Despite a number of messages sent by the Israeli government to King Hussein stressing that Israel had no intention of attacking Jordan, the king declared war. In the morning the Jordanians opened fire with light weapons along the municipal boundary, and this soon developed into a mass bombardment of most of Jewish Jerusalem's neighborhoods. At 1:30 p.m., the Jordanian Legion took control of the Government House area, which was in no-man's land. This act on the part of Jordan caused army headquarters to send forces of the Central Command to attack Government House, and to join up with the forces on Mount Scopus, which was in danger of falling to the Jordanians.

At 3 p.m. the forces of the 16th Brigade (the Jerusalem Brigade) began its attack on Government House, and during the night captured the Jordanian posts ("Naknik" and "Pa'amon") east of Talpiot and Arnona. At the same time, the 10th Armored Brigade was concentrated in the area of the Castel and the 55th Parachute Brigade were also brought up.

The 10th Brigade was sent into action immediately, and broke through the Jordanian defenses in the Radar Hill and Sheikh Abd el-Aziz areas in the early evening. Anti-tank barricades presented some problems, and passage was only finally made at 2 a.m. At dawn an advance party succeeded in reaching Tell es-Sahira, after having bypassed Nabi Samwil and blocked off the Jerusalem–Ramallah road.

The 55th Parachute Brigade organized in Beit Hakerem, and at night took up positions along the municipal boundary.

The attack began at 2:15 a.m. on two fronts. The 66th Parachute Regiment broke through at site of the Police School and captured it. A company then moved in the direction of Ammunition Hill and came under a strong Jordanian barrage. After a long and courageous battle, the parachutists succeeded in routing the Jordanians and the hill was taken by 6 a.m. On the second front, the 28th Regiment broke through the Jordanian line in the vicinity of Nahalat Shimon, and made its way along Nablus Road with the aim of reaching Salah ed-Din Street. However, the advance party lost its bearings, and failing to recognize the turn into the street, continued along Nablus Road. Thus its advance was held up by the encounters with the enemy positions along the municipal boundary to the west of Nablus Road. Heavy fighting was encountered in the vicinity of the Sa'ad Vesa'id Mosque. The regiment then moved forward, crossed es-Sahira cemetery and completed its mission by 8 a.m. The 71st Regiment, which had crossed the boundary in the wake of the 28th, turned westward and completed the operation in the American Colony, Herod's Gate and Wadi el-Joz, and during the course of the morning took the Rockefeller Museum.

In the early morning, the 10th Brigade fought a tank battle in the Tell el-Ful area. At 8:30 a.m. the brigade moved on to the next phase. While fighting constantly it moved southward and by 12:30 had taken the positions at Tell el-Ful, Shu'afat, Giv'at Hamivtar and French Hill. The end of this phase of the battle opened up the road to Mount Scopus, and thus the entire northern sector of Jerusalem and the ridge to the north was in the hands of the Israel Defense Forces. In the afternoon, a regiment of the 16th Brigade set out to capture Abu Tor. The battle for the positions along the Jordanian municipal boundary was particularly difficult and ended only in the evening. Throughout the day the Israel Air Force strafed Jordanian troops at Ma'aleh Adumim and along the approach roads to Jerusalem.

The Minister of Defense issued orders to encircle the Old City, but not to break into it, and during the course of the evening a reconnaissance patrol of the 80th Brigade and a tank force began the attack on the Mount of Olives ridge. However, as a consequence of an error in navigation, the attacking forces were trapped on the bridge across the Kidron Valley near Gethsemane, and the attack was called off. The Jordanian forces began to retreat to the east, and the rumbling of the tanks raised a false alarm and preparations were made to stave off an attack by tanks, which by morning proved to have been unnecessary. The battle with the advance guard continued throughout the night.

On the morning of June 6, after heavy bombing from the air, the Mount of Olives ridge was in Israeli hands by 9:30 a.m. Troops of the 55th Brigade entered the Old City through the Lions' Gate, and took the city with little resistance. Two companies of the 16th Brigade entered the city through the Dung Gate and liberated the Jewish Quarter. At 11 a.m., the Jordanian military commander, Anwar el-Hattib, surrendered. Because of the difficult situation of fighting in

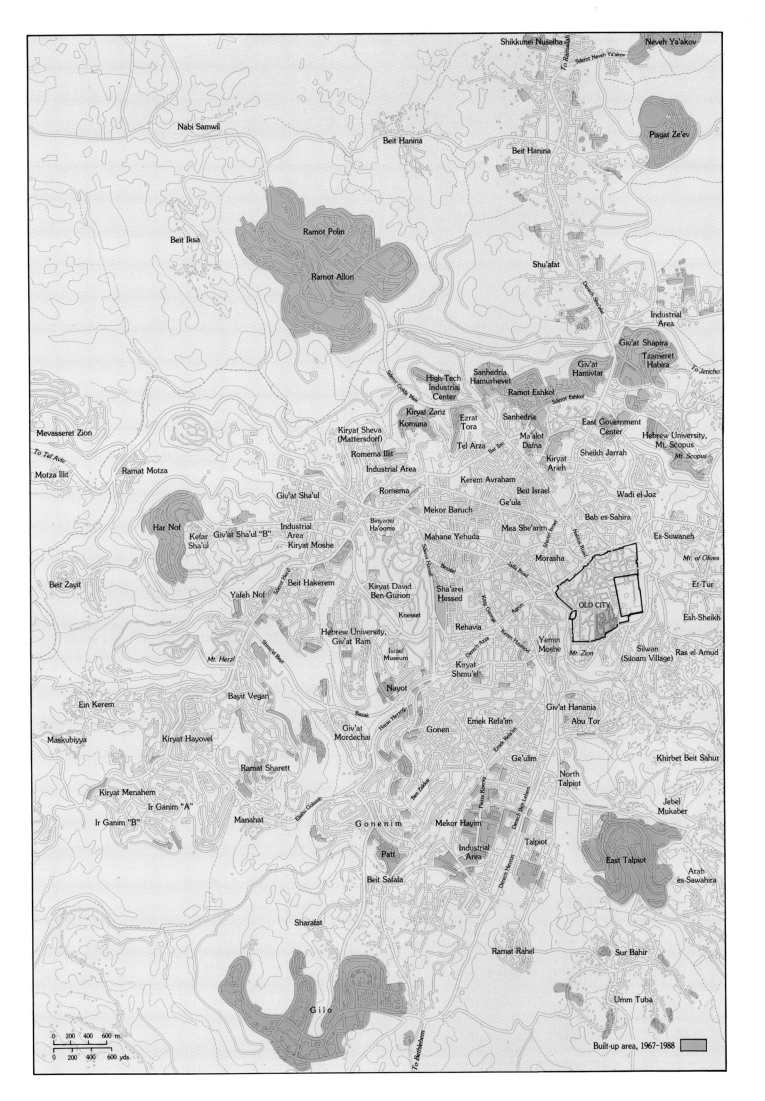

Nabi Samwil

Shikkunei Nuseiba

Neveh Ya'akov

Beit Hanina

Beit Hanina

Sderot Neveh Ya'akov

To Ramallah

Pisgat Ze'ev

Beit Iksa

Ramot Polin

Ramot Allon

Shu'afat

Derech Shu'afat

Industrial
Area

Giv'at Shapira
Tzameret
Habira

High-Tech
Industrial
Center

Sanhedria
Hamurhevet

Giv'at
Hamivtar

Ramot Eshkol

To Jericho

Sderot Golda Meir

Mevasseret Zion

Kiryat Zanz
Komuna

Kiryat Sheva
(Mattersdorf)

Ezrat
Tora

Sanhedria

Sderot Eshkol

East Government
Center

To Tel Aviv

Motza Illit

Ramat Motza

Romema Illit

Tel Arza

Ma'alot
Dafna

Kiryat
Arieh

Sheikh Jarrah

Hebrew University,
Mt. Scopus

Mt. Scopus

Industrial Area

Kerem Avraham

Ben Itai

Giv'at Sha'ul

Romema

Beit Israel

Ge'ula

Wadi el-Joz

Har Nof

Kefar
Sha'ul

Giv'at Sha'ul "B"

Industrial
Area
Kiryat Moshe

Binyanei
Ha'ooma

Mekor Baruch

Mahane Yehuda

Mea She'arim

Shmuel Hanavi

Nablus Road

Bab es-Sahira

Es-Suwaneh

Morasha

Mt. of Olives

Beit Zayit

Yafeh Nof

Beit Hakerem

Kiryat David
Ben-Gurion

Bezalel

Sha'arei
Hessed

Jaffa Road

OLD CITY

Et-Tur

Sderot Herzl

Sderot Hanasi

Knesset

King George

Aaron

Esh-Sheikh

Mt. Herzl

Shmuel Bayit

Hebrew University,
Giv'at Ram

Israel
Museum

Rehavia

Kerem Hafeseh

Yemin
Moshe

Silwan
(Siloam Village)

Ras el-Amud

Mt. Zion

Kiryat
Shmu'el

Derech Azza

Bayit Vegan

Bazak

Nayot

Giv'at Hanania

Abu Tor

Ein Kerem

Harav Herzog

Giv'at
Mordechai

Gonen

Emek Refa'im

Maskubiyya

Kiryat Hayovel

Khirbet Beit Sahur

Ge'ulim

North
Talpiot

Jebel
Mukaber

Kiryat Menahem

Ramat Sharett

Elahu Golomb

Emek Refa'im

Ir Ganim "A"

Manahat

G o n e n i m

Ben Zakkai

Mekor Hayim

Pierre Koenig

Talpiot

Ir Ganim "B"

Patt

Industrial
Area

Derech Beit Lehem

East Talpiot

Arab
es-Sawahira

Beit Safafa

Derech Hevron

Sharafat

Ramat Rahel

Sur Bahir

G i l o

Umm Tuba

To Bethlehem

0   200 400   600 m.

0   200 400   600 yds.

Built-up area, 1967–1988

a built-up area, Israel suffered heavy casualties during the battle for Jerusalem. One hundred and eighty-three soldiers of the Israel Defense Forces were killed in this battle.

Development of the Built-Up Area

The unification of Jerusalem led to an unprecedented spate of building in the city. As soon as the fighting ceased, the barrier walls were torn down, the military positions demolished, minefields detonated, and the ruins along the old border cleared away. Old streets were rebuilt, and new roads laid to provide easy access between both parts of the city. Soon after the war, Jerusalem extended the area under its jurisdiction from 9,400 acres to 26,800 acres. The city's boundaries were determined by both military and political considerations, and were aimed at consolidating the unity of the city and guaranteeing Jewish presence throughout the entire city of Jerusalem. The city now included strategic positions around its boundaries, with a limited number of Arabs. To the north, the boundary was set to include the Atarot airfield. These principles, together with political development, also determined the location of the new neighborhoods. About 5,200 acres were requisitioned in the new areas annexed to the city for the purpose of building new residential districts.

In the first phase (1968–1970), the area between Mount Scopus and Shmu'el Hanavi Street was built up so as to ensure a physical link between them. In this area the neighborhoods of Sanhedria Hamurhevet, Ramot Eshkol, Ma'alot Dafna, Giv'at Hamivtar and Giv'at Shapira (French Hill) were established. This area, on which 5,500 housing units were built, encompassed the Sheikh Jarrah quarter, and created a direct link with the institutions rebuilt on Mount Scopus. Within the Old City, the Jewish Quarter, which had lain in ruins since the War of Independence, was now being rebuilt completely, with the addition of some 600 housing units, the restoration of synagogues and the construction of new ones.

In the second phase (1970–1980), four huge neighborhoods were established in the north and south of the city. Neveh Ya'akov, Ramot Allon, East Talpiot and Gilo comprised a total of 27,000 housing units. When these housing projects are finally completed, they will accommodate approximately one-quarter of Jerusalem's entire population.

The plans for the construction of these new neighborhoods sparked off a public controversy at the end of the 1970s, in

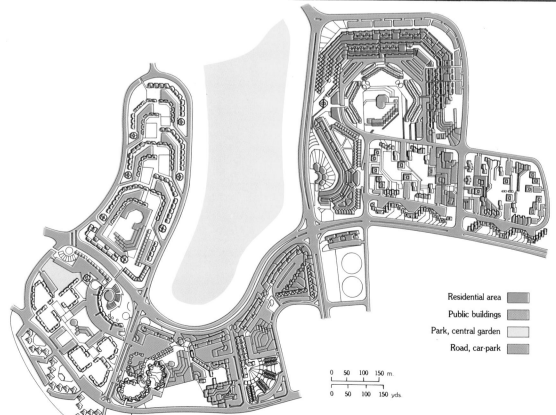

(above) House in the **Gilo** neighborhood with an entrance gate. Built in the 1970s, the new neighborhoods were particularly impressive because of their architectural diversity, which is well expressed in Gilo. The building in this photograph has many of the elements commonly found in the neighborhoods established at the end of the nineteenth century, such as the wall, the entrance gate and the courtyard. Some people believe that the basic principle behind these buildings, both the preservation and innovation of typical Jerusalem elements, failed, mainly because it was not possible to transfer all those factors which gave rise to the use of the original elements.

(left) **The Gilo neighborhood** is part of the "wall" surrounding Jerusalem from the north by the ridges of Mount Scopus, French Hill (Giv'at Shapira) and Ramot. This "wall" was a conspicuous character of the massive construction of residential quarters after the unification of Jerusalem in 1967. The map depicts the first four phases in the construction of the neighborhood. It was designed mainly as a residential quarter, and thus no areas were allocated for industry or workshops.

Residential area
Public buildings
Park, central garden
Road, car-park

0 50 100 150 m.
0 50 100 150 yds.

(opposite above) **The Golem**, or as it is commonly known, "The Monster," was erected in 1971/72 in the Rabinowitz Park at Kiryat Hayovel. This is an example of modern art sculpture in public places, reflecting the introduction of modern art to the Jerusalem population after the reunification of the city.

(below) The battle for Jerusalem during the **Six-Day War, June 5–7, 1967**.

fear that hasty planning and rapid building could change Jerusalem's unique character. However, these fears proved unfounded to a great extent. Leading architects were given a free hand and their designs have enriched the neighborhoods with architectural diversity. The principle of facing all buildings with Jerusalem stone was meticulously maintained, and in most cases the buildings were integrated as far as possible with the mountain terrain. Considerable attention was paid to physical and social planning—the network of streets and infrastructure, public institutions and parks.

In the third phase, which began at the beginning of the 1980s, the gap between Neveh Ya'akov and Giv'at Shapira

was closed through the building of the Pisgat Ze'ev neighborhood, planned to contain 12,000 housing units. A new road was built to link these neighborhoods with Giv'at Shapira. In the west, the Har Nof neighborhood was established, the majority of whose residents are Orthodox.

At the same time, building continued in the veteran quarters, some of which were built at the end of the nineteenth century, and in some of them the number of apartments was doubled. Old houses were renovated and adapted to the needs of prosperous residents. Apartment houses were erected at Ramat Denia and nearby Ramat Sharett, at Giv'at Haveradim and San Simon, Beit Hakerem, Bayit Vegan, Talpiot, Arnona, Giv'at Mordechai and on the edge of Sha'arei Hessed (Kiryat Wolfsohn), Bak'a and Romema. Eight Jerusalem neighborhoods were included in the country-wide Project Renewal for the major renovation of immigrant housing erected during the early years of the state in the time of mass immigration.

In the majority of neighborhoods the buildings comprised several score apartments of various sizes. The new quarters were designed for a more prosperous class of resident, with many of the units built in the style of cottages. In Gilo and Ramot Allon, special areas have been allocated for "build your own house" projects.

In the process of building and development, a number of public buildings have been erected in the eastern sector of the city. The government office complex was built at the foot of Mount Scopus and next to it the national headquarters of the Israel Police Force. The southern district headquarters of the Israel Police Force was erected at Ras el-Amud. The campus of the Hebrew University and the Hadassah Hospital on Mount Scopus were renovated and greatly expanded. At Atarot a huge industrial area was set up and nearby are the headquarters of the army's Central Command. At Har Hahotzavim and Sanhedria, areas were devoted specifically for high-tech industries. The industrial areas at Giv'at Sha'ul and Talpiot have been extended considerably. A number of veteran institutions have moved from the city center to the outskirts. The central bus station was moved to the entrance to the city in 1968. The Sha'arei Tzedek hospital moved from Jaffa Road to beneath the Bayit Vegan quarter. The Ezrat Nashim hospital moved to Giv'at Sha'ul, and Misgav Ladach moved to new premises on the edge of Katamon. The Bank of Israel was erected in the government complex at Kiryat David Ben-Gurion.

During this period the city's commercial center also developed. A number of high-rise office buildings were erected such as Clal, Eilon, Rassco and others. Additional commercial centers were set up in the new neighborhoods as well as in the industrial centers. Special emphasis was placed on improving the city's external appearance and the development of centers of art and culture. Parks were opened—the Liberty Bell, Sacher, San Simon, the Haas Promenade and others; landscape gardens were planted. Sports grounds and recreation centers were opened, and sculptures and works of art were placed at various points throughout the city. Cultural centers were built, such as the Center for the Performing Arts in Talbieh, the Jerusalem Khan, the Cinematheque and the music center at Mishkenot Sha'ananim. Archaeological sites have been excavated, marked out and opened up to the public. These include the archaeological excavations at the southwest of the Temple Mount, the Broad Wall, the Burnt House, the Palatial Mansion, the Néa Church and the Cardo in the Jewish Quarter; David's City, the Citadel, and the Roman ruins at Damascus Gate. A national park has been planted around the perimeter of the Old City wall, and inside basic improvements have been made to the drainage, telephone and electricity networks. Existing houses have been repaired and renovated, streets repaved and the walk along the ramparts opened to the public.

Building for the Arab inhabitants has been concentrated mainly to the north of the city, along the road to Ramallah (Shu'afat, Beit Hanina, er-Ram), and in the villages of Sur Bahir, Beit Safafa, Ras el-Amud and et-Tur. These buildings

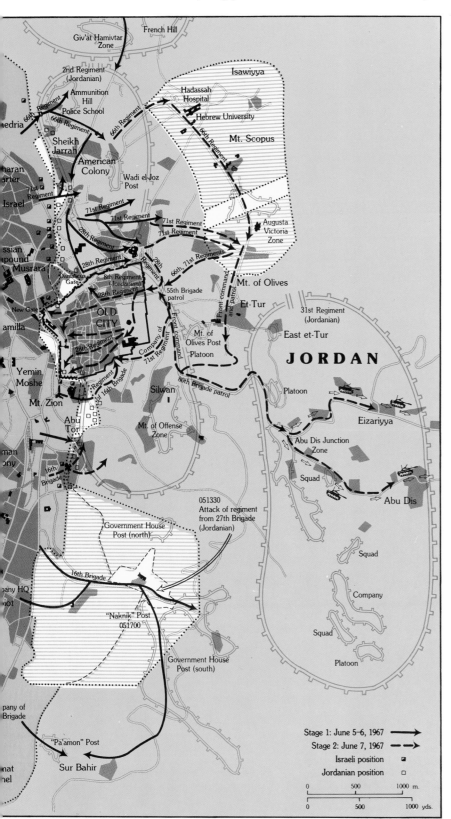

Stage 1: June 5–6, 1967 ⟶
Stage 2: June 7, 1967 ⇢
Israeli position ■
Jordanian position □

0 ... 500 ... 1000 m.
0 ... 500 ... 1000 yds.

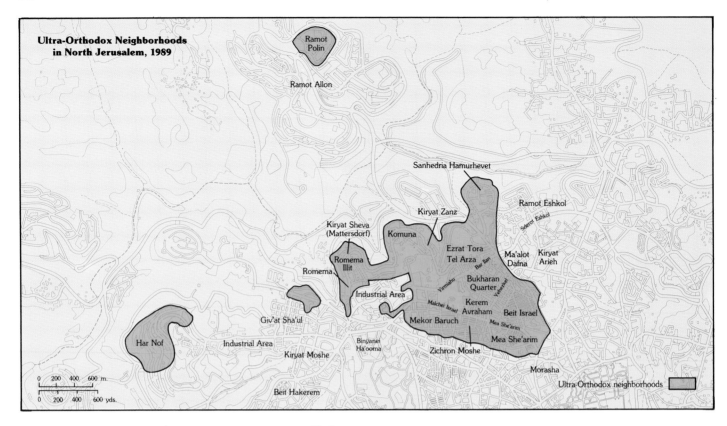

Ultra-Orthodox Neighborhoods in North Jerusalem, 1989

Ramot Polin

Ramot Allon

Sanhedria Hamurhevet

Kiryat Zanz

Ramot Eshkol

Kiryat Sheva (Mattersdorf)

Komuna

Sderot Eshkol

Ezrat Tora Tel Arza

Ma'alot Dafna

Kiryat Arieh

Romema Illit

Romema

Bar Ilan

Bukharan Quarter

Yehezkel

Industrial Area

Yirmiahu

Kerem Avraham

Beit Israel

Giv'at Sha'ul

Malchei Israel

Mekor Baruch

Mea She'arim

Mea She'arim

Har Nof

Industrial Area

Binyanei Ha'ooma

Zichron Moshe

Kiryat Moshe

Morasha

Ultra-Orthodox neighborhoods

0 200 400 600 m.

0 200 400 600 yds.

Beit Hakerem

are mainly private projects, but the Ministry of Housing has constructed apartment houses for Arab residents in Beit Hanina, Wadi el-Joz and Eizariyya.

The city's expansion has been accompanied by the building of a network of modern roads leading to Jerusalem and within it. A highway has been built from Tel Aviv and an additional road runs to the north of the city from Ben Shemen. A road now runs from the entrance to the city directly to Ramot Allon and Giv'at Shapira. This road also joins up with the new road that goes down to the Jordan Valley. At the eastern approaches to the city a road links the Jericho Road with Giv'at Shapira. The new neighborhoods have been connected to the city by wide roads, and many of the roads carrying heavy traffic within the city have been broadened and repaved, as for example Sderot Herzl, Sderot Herzog, Sderot Eliahu Golomb and Sderot Eshkol.

On the outskirts of Jerusalem, three urban settlements have been established: Giv'at Ze'ev to the north, Ma'aleh Adumim to the east and Efrata to the south. A number of smaller settlements have been established whose members depend on Jerusalem for employment and for the supply of services—the Etzion bloc, Beit El and the settlements in the Jordan Valley.

Jerusalem's Population

When Jerusalem was united it had 267,000 residents. Since 1967 the population has grown by about 80 percent, and it has become the largest city in Israel, both by number and in area. In 1988 the population of Jerusalem was 488,100, of whom 350,000 were Jews (71.7 percent of the city's total population), 123,600 Muslims (25.3 percent) and 14,400 Christians (3 percent). However, despite these impressive figures, the city's Jewish population growth rate is declining as a result of migration of its residents to other cities (predominantly young couples) and as a consequence of a slowdown in natural increase and cessation of immigration. The growth rate of the Arab population is higher than that of the Jewish population, and proportionately it is increasing. The Arab population of the city is relatively young (the median age is 17.7) as compared with the Jewish population (the median age is 25.1). The proportion of elderly (above 65) is highest among the Christians (10.4 percent); among the Jews it is 8.5 percent and is the lowest among the

Muslims—3.3 percent.

The city's demographic structure has undergone a transformation as a result of the developments in building. Many middle-class families, young couples, new immigrants and former inhabitants of distress areas have moved to the new neighborhoods (the average number of persons per family is 3.8). Residents are vacating the city center (the average number of persons per family—2.3) and the percentage of aged in this area is increasing. The Arab population has increased, especially in the neighborhoods along the Jerusalem–Ramallah road and in the districts to the east of the Old City. In the Jewish Orthodox quarters on the edge of the city (Bayit Vegan, Kiryat Zanz, Har Nof) there is also a major increase. This is the result of the rise in prices of apartments in the center of the city, which are competing with commercial areas, and the desire for a high standard of living and the social principles of the population groupings.

Jewish-Arab Relations

Even though the physical and political borders have been removed between the Jewish and Arab residents of Jerusalem, and despite the fact that Jewish neighborhoods have been established in the eastern sector of the city, complete segregation exists between the two communities. There are no mixed neighborhoods, and the few attempts by Jewish families to settle in Arab districts did not meet with success.

Many separate municipal networks continued to exist, even after the city was united. The reason for this is partly in consideration of the needs of the Arab community, partly for political reasons, and also through habit. There are two separate bus services and two central bus stations, two wholesale markets and two separate electricity companies (even though the company in the eastern sector of the city received a large quantity of its electricity from the Jewish company). Gas for cooking and heating is supplied separately, and a special banking network exists in the eastern sector of the city alongside the Israeli banks. Most of the trade unions and economic associations in the city, such as chambers of commerce, medical practitioners' organizations, travel agents, and so on, have not joined forces.

However, there are many areas of contact between the residents of the eastern and western sectors of the city. The majority of Arab workers are employed by Jews.

(above) **The ultra-Orthodox belt** in the north of the city, from Mea She'arim and Beit Israel in the east up to Har Nof in the west, is bisected by the industrial centers (Romema, Giv'at Sha'ul) and by the intersection at the city entrance. Additional neighborhoods into which the ultra-Orthodox have expanded, by the provision of accommodation and educational and religious institutions, are Neveh Ya'akov (Kamenitz), Ramot (Ramot Polin), Kiryat Moshe, Bayit Vegan and Giv'at Mordechai.

(opposite below) **The Bank of Israel** was the last of the government buildings erected in Kiryat David Ben-Gurion prior to the unification of the city, and the first of a series of buildings which were to be constructed to the north. The building was constructed in the form of an inverted pyramid, and is an example of the monumental type of building erected in the city and being integrated into the Jerusalem landscape.

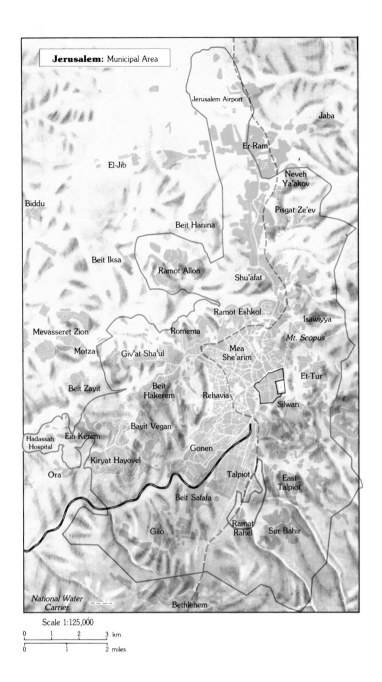

Jerusalem: Municipal Area

Scale 1:125,000

Arabs use the services of Jewish professionals, such as lawyers, architects, economists to represent them before the authorities. Arab hospitals are given professional assistance by Jewish specialists. Many of the Arab businesses are no longer linked with Amman, as for example airline companies, travel agents and banks, and their substitutes are found in the western sector of the city. The Jewish population uses the lower-priced services and goods found in the eastern sector of the city.

In imposing the Israeli law, many compromises have been reached in the areas of education, employment and taxation. Even though many organizations and members of the professions do not recognize the unification of the city de jure, daily life has prevailed over politics, and the unification has been to the advantage of the residents.

In the area of security, Jewish-Arab relations have fluctuated. In general, after any terrorist activity tension increases, which is often expressed in attacks on Arab passersby in attempts of revenge.

Since the *intifada* (uprising) began in December 1987, confrontations between young Palestinians and police increasingly led to violence in the eastern part of the city. As cars were stoned and even torched, tension between Arabs and Jews grew. This and frequent strikes by the Arab merchants have reduced the usually steady flow of visitors to the Old City of Jerusalem.

Relations Between Religious and Secular Jews

A source of tension in the city is the relations between the religious (especially ultra-Orthodox) and nonreligious Jewish residents of Jerusalem. In recent years there has been an increasing tendency to extremism among the ultra-Orthodox communities. This community constitutes about 27 percent of the Jewish population of Jerusalem, and its rapid growth has increased its relative significance in the municipal configuration. In many areas in the north of the city, in the belt extending from Beit Israel and Mea She'arim up to Har Nof in the west of the city, the ultra-Orthodox community has attained an absolute majority. Furthermore, there is a constant process of expansion as the consequence of the high rate of natural increase and the advent of new immigrants. This expansion into nearby quarters causes friction between the ultra-Orthodox and nonreligious communities which are the cause of many unpleasant incidents. These relate to travel by car on the Sabbath to Ramot and setting fire to bus shelters. It must be pointed out that these acts of violence are limited to a small segment of the ultra-Orthodox, but they signify a tendency which threatens to lead to a rift between the two groups.

Economy

The public sector has always been the main source of employment in Jerusalem. This is followed by the various branches of industry, commerce and finance. The main branches of industry in Jerusalem are printing, food, wood and metal products. Since 1979, high-tech industries have developed in Jerusalem through the connections with the staff of the Hebrew University and other scientific institutions in the city. The number of non-Jews employed in industry is relatively high, but on the other hand nearly all the employees in high-tech industries are Jews. The Arab industrial sector is limited mainly to workshops and small factories.

Businesses have increased in the city, especially offices and services of various kinds. Although the city center has developed considerably, other business centers have gone up in the new neighborhoods and in the industrial centers in Giv'at Sha'ul and Talpiot. In the Arab sector, the commercial centers have moved out of the municipal boundaries to Shu'afat and on the Jericho road, in the Eizariyya area.

United Jerusalem has attracted tourism. The number of visitors has increased considerably, new hotels have been built (mainly along King George and Keren Hayesod Streets and Sderot Herzl), the number of employees in the branch has grown and the income has increased.

Bibliography

Amiran, D. H. K., A. Shachar, and I. Kimhi (eds.), *Atlas of Jerusalem*. Berlin and New York, 1973.

Amiran, D. H. K., "A Revised Earthquake Catalogue of Palestine." *Israel Exploration Journal* 2 (1952).

Amiran, R., and A. Eitan, "Excavations in the Courtyard of the Citadel, Jerusalem, 1968–1969. Preliminary Report." *Israel Exploration Journal* 20 (1970): 9–17.

Avigad, N., *Ancient Monuments in the Kidron Valley*. Jerusalem, 1954.

Avigad, N., "A Building Inscription of the Emperor Justinian and the Nea in Jerusalem." *Israel Exploration Journal* 27 (1977): 145–151.

Avigad, N., *Discovering Jerusalem*. New York, 1983.

Avi-Yonah, M., *The Madaba Mosaic Map*. Jerusalem, 1954.

Avi-Yonah, M. (ed.), *Sefer Yerushalayim* I. Jerusalem and Tel Aviv, 1956.

Avi-Yonah, M., "The Walls of Nehemiah—A Minimalist View." *Israel Exploration Journal* 4 (1954): 239.

Ben-Arieh, Y., *A City Reflected in Its Time*. 2 vols. Jerusalem, 1984, 1986.

Ben-Dov, M., "The Omayyad Structures Near the Temple Mount." In B. Mazar, *Excavations in the Old City of Jerusalem Near the Temple Mount. Preliminary Report of the Second and Third Seasons, 1969–1970*. Jerusalem, 1971.

Benvenisti, M., *Jerusalem, the Torn City*. Minneapolis, 1976.

Berchem, M. van, *Matériaux pour un Corpus Inscriptionum Arabicarum*. Syrie de Sud. Jerusalem "Ville," 1922, Jerusalem "Haram," 1927.

Bliss, F. J., and A. C. Dickie, *Excavations at Jerusalem, 1894–1897*. London, 1898.

Burgoyne, M. H., *Mamluk Jerusalem*. n.p., 1987.

Burgoyne, M. H., and A. Abul-Hajj, "Twenty-four Mediaeval Arabic Inscriptions from Jerusalem." *Levant* XI (1979).

Clermont-Ganneau, C., *Archaeological Researches in Palestine 1873–1874*. 2 vols. London, 1896, 1899.

Collins, L., and D. LaPierre, *O Jerusalem!* New York, 1972.

Conder, C. R., *The City of Jerusalem*. London, 1909.

Creswell, K. A. C., *Early Muslim Architecture*. Oxford, 1969.

Fergusson, J., *The Temples of the Jews and Other Buildings in the Haram Area at Jerusalem*. London, 1878.

Hamilton, R. W., "Excavations Against the North Wall of Jerusalem." *Quarterly of the Department of Antiquities in Palestine* 10 (1940): 1–54.

Hamilton, R. W., *The Structural History of the Aqsa Mosque*. London, 1949.

Hollis, F. J., *The Archaeology of Herod's Temple*. London, 1934.

Hyman, B., I. Kimhi, and J. Savitzky, *Jerusalem in Transition. Urban Growth and Change 1970's–1980's*. Jerusalem, 1985.

Johns, C. N., "The Citadel, Jerusalem. A Summary of Work Since 1934." *Quarterly of the Department of Antiquities in Palestine* 14 (1950): 121–190.

Johns, C. N., "Recent Excavations at the Citadel." *Palestine Exploration Quarterly* (1940): 36–58.

Kendall, H., *Jerusalem, the City Plan: Preservation and Development During the British Mandate, 1918–1948*. London, 1948.

Kenyon, K. M., *Digging Up Jerusalem*. London, 1974.

Kenyon, K. M., *Jerusalem. Excavating 3000 Years of History*. London, 1967.

Kroyanker, D., *Jerusalem Architecture—Periods and Styles: Arab Buildings Outside the Old City Walls* (in Hebrew). Jerusalem, 1985.

Kroyanker, D., *Jerusalem Architecture—Periods and Styles: European–Christian Buildings Outside the Old City Walls* (in Hebrew). Jerusalem, 1987.

Kroyanker, D., *Jerusalem Architecture—Periods and Styles: Neighborhoods and Jewish Public Buildings Outside the Old City Walls, 1860–1914* (in Hebrew). Jerusalem, 1983.

Kroyanker, D., *Jerusalem Architecture—Periods and Styles: The British Mandate Period, 1918–1948* (in Hebrew). Jerusalem, 1989.

Kuemmel, A., *Materialien zur Topographie des alten Jerusalem*. Begleittext zu der "Karte der Materialien zur Topographie des alten Jerusalem" (1904). Halle a. S., 1906.

Kutcher, A., *The New Jerusalem: Planning and Politics*. Cambridge, Mass., 1975.

Le Strange, G., *Palestine Under the Moslems*. London, 1890. Reprinted Beirut, 1965.

Little, D. P., *A Catalogue of the Islamic Documents in al-Haram ash-Sharif in Jerusalem*. Beirut, 1984.

Lutfi, H., *Al-Quds al-Mamlukiyya*. Berlin, 1985.

Lux, U., "Vorläufiger Bericht über die Ausgrabung unter der Erlöserkirche in Muristan in der Altstadt von Jerusalem in den Jahren 1970 und 1971." *Zeitschrift des Deutschen Palästina-Vereins* 88 (1972): 185–201.

Macalister, R. A. S., and J. G. Duncan, *Excavations on the Hill of Ophel, Jerusalem, 1923–1925*. London, 1926.

Marmadji, A. S., *Textes Geographiques Arabes sur la Palestine*. Paris, 1915.

Mazar, B., *The Excavations in the Old City of Jerusalem Near the Temple Mount. Preliminary Report of the First Season, 1968*. Jerusalem, 1969.

Mazar, B., *The Excavations in the Old City of Jerusalem Near the Temple Mount. Preliminary Report of the Second and Third Seasons, 1969–1970*. Jerusalem, 1971.

Mazar, B., "Herodian Jerusalem in the Light of the Excavations South and South-West of the Temple Mount." *Israel Exploration Journal* 28 (1978): 230–237.

Mazar, B., and E. Mazar, *Excavations in the South of the Temple Mount*. Jerusalem, 1989.

Milik, J. T., "La Topographia de Jérusalem vers la fins de l'époque byzantine." *Mélanges de l'Université Saint Joseph* (Beirut) 37 (1960–1961): 127–189.

Narkiss, U., *The Liberation of Jerusalem: The Battle of 1967*. Totowa, N.J., and London, 1983.

Palestine Pilgrims Texts Society. Vols. I–XIII. London, 1892–1898.

Peters, F. E., *Jerusalem: The Holy City in the Eyes of Chroniclers, Visitors, Pilgrims, and Prophets from the Days of Abraham to the Beginning of Time*. Princeton, 1985.

Pierotti, E., *Jerusalem Explored, Being a Description of the Ancient and Modern City*. 2 vols. London, 1864.

Rabinovich, A., *The Battle for Jerusalem, June 5–7, 1967*. Philadelphia, 1972.

Richmond, E. T., *The Dome of the Rock*. Oxford, 1924.

Robinson, E., *Biblical Researches in Palestine and the Adjacent Countries. Later Biblical Researches, etc.* 3 vols. London, 1867.

Rosen-Ayalon, M., *The Early Islamic Monuments of al-Haram ash-Sharif*. QEDEM 28. Jerusalem, 1989.

Sauvaire, H., *Histoire de Jérusalem et d'Hébron depuis Abraham jusqu'à la fin du XVe siècle de J.C.* Paris, 1876.

Schmelz, U. O., *Modern Jerusalem's Demographic Evolution*. Jerusalem, 1988.

Sharon, A., *Planning Jerusalem: The Old City and Its Environs*. Jerusalem and London, 1973.

Shiloh, Y., *Excavations at the City of David*. QEDEM 19. Jerusalem, 1984.

Simons, J., *Jerusalem in the Old Testament*. Leiden, 1952.

Sivan, E., *L'Islam et la Croisade: Idéologie et Propagande dans les Réactions musulmanes aux Croisades*. Paris, 1968.

Sukenik, E. L., and L. A. Mayer, *The Third Wall of Jerusalem. An Account of Excavations*. Jerusalem, 1930.

Tobler, T., *Zwei Bücher Topographie von Jerusalem und seine Umgebungen*. 2 vols. Berlin, 1853, 1854.

Tsafrir, Y., *Zion—The South-Western Hill of Jerusalem and Its Place in the Urban Development of the City in the Byzantine Period*. Jerusalem, 1975.

Tushingham, A. D., *Excavations in Jerusalem, 1965–1967*. Vol. I. Toronto, 1985.

Tushingham, A. D., "The Western Hill Under the Monarchy." *Zeitschrift der Deutschen Palästina-Vereins* 95 (1979): 39–55.

Vincent, L. H., and F. M. Abel, *Jérusalem nouvelle*. Vols. I–III. Paris, 1914–1926.

Vincent, L. H., and M. A. Steve, *Jérusalem de l'ancien Testament*. Vols. I–III. Paris, 1954–1956.

Vogüé, M. de, *Le temple de Jérusalem. Monographie du Haram ech-Chérif, suivie d'un essai sur la topographie de la Ville Sainte*. Paris, 1864–1865.

Warren, C., *Notes on the Survey and on Some of the Most Remarkable Localities and Buildings in and About Jerusalem*. London, 1865.

Warren, C., *Plans, Elevations, Sections, etc., Showing the Results of the Excavations at Jerusalem, 1867–1870*. London, 1884.

Warren, C., *Underground Jerusalem. An Account of the Principal Difficulties Encountered in Its Exploration and the Results Obtained*. London, 1876.

Warren, C., and C. R. Conder, *The Survey of Western Palestine, Jerusalem*. London, 1889.

Weill, R., *La Cité de David, Compte rendu des fouilles exécutées à Jérusalem, sur le site de la ville primitive, Campagne de 1913–1914*. Paris, 1920.

Weill, R., *La Cité de David, Compte rendu des fouilles exécutées à Jérusalem, sur le site de la ville primitive, Campagne de 1923–1924*. Paris, 1947.

Williams, G., *The Holy City of Historical and Topographical Notices of Jerusalem, with some account of its antiquities and of its present condition*. London, 1845.

Wilson, C. W., *Ordnance Survey of Jerusalem, 1864–5*. London, 1865.

Wilson, C. W., and C. Warren, *The Recovery of Jerusalem. A Narrative of Exploration and Discovery in the City and the Holy Land*. London, 1871.

Yadin, Y. (ed.), *Jerusalem Revealed. Archaeology in the Holy City, 1968–1974*. Jerusalem and New Haven, 1976.

Index

Page numbers in italics refer to maps and illustrations or their captions.
The Arabic definite articles (el-, en-, et-, etc.) are disregarded in the
alphabetical listing.